By bringing together and examining a diverse body of literature from the Arab and Persian worlds of the eighth to the thirteenth centuries, Louise Marlow explores the tension that existed between the traditional egalitarian ideas of early Islam and the hierarchical impulses of the classical period. The literature demonstrates that while Islam's initial orientation was markedly egalitarian in both religious and social terms, the social aspect of this egalitarianism was soon undermined in the aftermath of Islam's political success, and as hierarchical social ideas from older cultures in the Middle East were incorporated into the new polity. Although the memory of its early promise never entirely receded and remnants of the ideal survive in many parts of the tradition, social egalitarianism quickly came to be associated with political subversion and various attempts were made to dilute its influence. On account of its originality and chronological scope, Louise Marlow's book will be of use to a wide and interested readership, not only of Islamic and medieval historians, but also of scholars assessing the impact of the recent Islamic revival.

Cambridge Studies in Islamic Civilization

Editorial board
DAVID MORGAN (general editor)
MICHAEL COOK JOSEF VAN ESS BARBARA FLEMMING
TARIF KHALIDI METIN KUNT W. F. MADELUNG
ROY MOTTAHEDEH BASIM MUSALLAM

Titles in the series

STEFAN SPERL. *Mannerism in Arabic poetry: a structural analysis of selected texts, 3rd century AH/9th century AD–5th century AH/11th century AD*
BEATRICE FORBES MANZ. *The rise and rule of Tamerlane*
AMNON COHEN. *Economic life in Ottoman Jerusalem*
PAUL E. WALKER. *Early philosophical Shiism: the Ismaili Neoplatonism of Abū Ya'qūb al-Sijistānī*
BOAZ SHOSHAN. *Popular culture in medieval Cairo*
STEPHEN FREDERIC DALE. *Indian merchants and Eurasian trade, 1600–1750*
AMY SINGER. *Palestinian peasants and Ottoman officials: rural administration around sixteenth-century Jerusalem*
MICHAEL CHAMBERLAIN. *Knowledge and social practice in medieval Damascus, 1190–1350*
TARIF KHALIDI. *Arabic historical thought in the classical period*
REUVEN AMITAI-PREISS. *Mongols and Mamluks: the Mamluk–Īlkhānid war, 1260–1281*
JANE HATHAWAY. *The politics of households in Ottoman Egypt: the rise of the Qazdağlis*

Cambridge Studies in Islamic Civilization

Hierarchy and egalitarianism in Islamic thought

Hierarchy and egalitarianism in Islamic thought

LOUISE MARLOW
Wellesley College

CAMBRIDGE
UNIVERSITY PRESS

PUBLISHED BY THE PRESS SYNDICATE OF THE UNIVERSITY OF CAMBRIDGE
The Pitt Building, Trumpington Street, Cambridge, United Kingdom

CAMBRIDGE UNIVERSITY PRESS
The Edinburgh Building, Cambridge CB2 2RU, UK
40 West 20th Street, New York NY 10011–4211, USA
477 Williamstown Road, Port Melbourne, VIC 3207, Australia
Ruiz de Alarcón 13, 28014 Madrid, Spain
Dock House, The Waterfront, Cape Town 8001, South Africa

http://www.cambridge.org

First published 1997
First paperback edition 2002

A catalogue record for this book is available from the British Library

Library of Congress Cataloguing in Publication data
Marlow, Louise.
Hierarchy and egalitarianism in Islamic thought / Louise Marlow.
p. cm. – (Cambridge studies in Islamic civilization)
Includes bibliographical references (p.).
ISBN 0 521 56430 1
1. Equality – Islamic countries – History. 2. Equality – Religious aspects – Islam. 3. Social justice – Islamic countries – History. 4. Social structure – Islamic countries – History. 5. Occupational prestige – Islamic countries – History. I. Title. II. Series.
HN768.Z9S66 1997
305′.0917′671–dc20 96-15400 CIP

ISBN 0 521 56430 1 hardback
ISBN 0 521 89428 X paperback

For my parents

Contents

Preface — *page* xi
Note on transliteration — xiv
List of abbreviations — xv

Introduction — 1

Part I Sources for Islamic social ideals

1 Egalitarianism and the growth of a pious opposition — 13
2 The Muslim reception of Greek ideas — 42
3 The Muslim reception of Iranian models — 66

Part II The taming of Islamic egalitarianism

4 The dissociation of egalitarianism and opposition — 93
5 The didactic literature of the courts — 117
6 Rationalisations of inequalities — 143
7 Hierarchies of occupations — 156

Conclusion — 174

Bibliography — 178
Index to Qurʾānic verses — 195
General index — 196

Preface

Islam is probably the most uncompromising of the world's religions in its insistence on the equality of all believers before God. In God's eyes, differences of rank and affluence are irrelevant, and all Muslims, regardless of their positions in this world, are equally capable of salvation in the next. At least in theory, this egalitarianism is extended in large part to the social plane as well. The religious and social aspects of Islamic egalitarianism are sometimes closely linked; for example, Muslims do not require the intermediacy of a priesthood in order to gain access to the divine. In other cases, the tradition draws a clear distinction between religious and social equality; thus women and slaves are regarded as the religious but not the social equals of free male believers. But among these last, Islam's egalitarianism can be said to have a social as well as a religious application. The resistance of the Islamic religious tradition to infringements of this egalitarian ideal, in its religious and social dimensions, is surely one of Islam's strongest and most universal attractions. It has probably never been more appealing to Muslims across the world than it is today, when, as many Muslims become newly conscious of their religious identity, and as immigrants (and increasingly converts) create a Muslim presence in traditionally non-Muslim areas, the insignificance attached to status, wealth and social background provides an inspiring sense of community.[1]

This book sets out to explore the tension between this powerful egalitarian ideal and the forms of social differentiation that inevitably characterised Muslim societies in the classical and early medieval periods of Islamic history (I use these terms loosely to refer to the period covered roughly by the second/eighth to seventh/thirteenth centuries). In particular it examines

[1] The modern emphasis on Islamic egalitarianism is evident in the works of several modern Muslim thinkers (see for example S. Abul Aʿla Maududi, *Political Theory of Islam* (Lahore, 1980), pp. 35–8; *idem*, *Witnesses unto Mankind. The Purpose and Duty of the Muslim Umma* (Leicester, 1986), pp. 32–3). The distinction between theory and practice naturally remains; in the United States, in areas where the Muslim population is relatively large, socio-economic status is likely to be a factor in the process of internal stratification (cf. Y.Y. Haddad and A.T. Lummis, *Islamic Values in the United States. A Comparative Study* (New York and Oxford, 1987), pp. 43–44).

Muslims' varied imaginings of an ideal society, a topic to which I was first drawn as a graduate student at Princeton University and which I began to explore in my doctoral dissertation (completed at Princeton in 1987). What follows is thus a study in an aspect of Islamic utopian thought and not, I wish to emphasise, in the sociology of any particular Muslim community during the period under discussion. The social ideals that form the focus of my study are drawn from a wide range of literary materials generated over a relatively long period and over an extensive cultural–geographical area. My purpose in considering such widely differing sources is not, as may perhaps have been the case in some earlier studies of Islamic social thought, to uncover a generic sociology that might be applied to all medieval Muslim societies.[2] It is rather to demonstrate that the diverse social visualisations attested in classical and early medieval sources constitute several traditions of utopian thought based on a variety of historical and cultural experiences, and that these traditions intersect with each other, and again to some extent with historical realities, in ways that are intrinsically interesting. While I have drawn my materials from many parts of the classical Islamic (primarily Arabic and Persian) literary corpus, it is abundantly clear that no work of this kind can be fully comprehensive; indeed, the number of potentially relevant sources for such a project is daunting to contemplate. But I have sought to include enough materials to render the topic cohesive and, I hope, to convey to the reader some of the excitement that I have found in exploring it.

I should like to acknowledge here the assistance and encouragement that I have received from several individuals in the course of my work. My principal debt is to Keith Lewinstein, who has read this material in countless incarnations over the past eight years, has discussed its larger and smaller points with me, and has offered thoughtful suggestions at every stage; his interest and involvement have sustained me throughout my studies of Islamic thought. I should also like to express my gratitude to Michael Cook, who initially encouraged me to write this book and read an early draft of the entire manuscript; I have benefited immeasurably from his generous sharing of his insights and knowledge, and from his criticisms and suggestions. I am also indebted to Roy Mottahedeh, whose own work first stimulated my interest in the subject matter of this book and whose sensitivity to the complexities of the relationship between historical realities and literary texts I have found consistently instructive; I am grateful for his sharing of my enthusiasm for my work both during and after my years as a graduate student, and for his helpful comments on several versions of the manuscript. In addition I am extremely grateful to Patricia Crone and Wadad al-Qadi, both of whom read the manuscript with the utmost care; it has been inestimably improved as a result of their thought-

[2] The works to which I refer are R. Levy, *The Sociology of Islam* (London, 1931–3; 2nd edition *The Social Structure of Islam* (Cambridge, 1957)) and G. von Grunebaum, *Medieval Islam, A Study in Cultural Orientation* (Chicago, 1946).

ful criticisms and advice. For assistance of various kinds I am also indebted to Hossein Modarressi, Cornell Fleischer, Jere Bacharach, and the late Martin Dickson and Martin Hinds. I should also like to acknowledge the practical and moral support that I have received from my colleagues in the Department of Religion at Wellesley College, especially Edward Hobbs, who has assisted me with numerous computer-related problems; in addition I am very grateful to Karen Jensen and the long-suffering staff of the Interlibrary Loan department of the Wellesley College Library. Finally I should like to thank Marigold Acland of Cambridge University Press for her unfailing attentiveness and her kindness.

The initial research for this study was supported by the American Research Institute in Turkey, the British Institute of Persian Studies, the American Institute of Iranian Studies and the Giles Whiting Foundation. I should also like to express my gratitude to the National Endowment for the Humanities, the American Philosophical Society and Wellesley College for their support of my work in its later stages.

Note on transliteration

In my transliteration of Arabic words and names, I have followed the system adopted in the *Encyclopaedia of Islam*, second edition, with the modifications that *q* replaces *ḳ* and *j* replaces *dj*. My transliteration from Persian generally reflects the consonants as in Arabic, although I have substituted *v* for *w*; this modification has also been adopted in cases where Arabic terms appear in a Persian context. I have made some attempt to preserve Persian vowel sounds, such as *o* and *e*.

Abbreviations

AEIO	*Annales de l'Institut d'Etudes Orientales*
BEO	*Bulletin d'études orientales*
BSOAS	*Bulletin of the School of Oriental and African Studies*
*EI*1	*Encyclopaedia of Islam*, First Edition, Leiden 1913–1938
*EI*2	*Encyclopaedia of Islam*, Second Edition, Leiden, 1954–
GAL	C. Brockelmann, *Geschichte der arabischen Literatur*, 3 vols. and 2 supplements, Leiden 1937–1942
GAS	F. Sezgin, *Geschichte des arabischen Schrifttums*, 9 vols., Leiden 1967–
IC	*Islamic Culture*
IJMES	*International Journal of Middle East Studies*
IQ	*Islamic Quarterly*
JA	*Journal Asiatique*
JAAS	*Journal of Asian and African Studies*
JAOS	*Journal of the American Oriental Society*
JESHO	*Journal of the Economic and Social History of the Orient*
JNES	*Journal of Near Eastern Studies*
JRAS	*Journal of the Royal Asiatic Society*
JSAI	*Jerusalem Studies in Arabic and Islam*
JSS	*Journal of Semitic Studies*
REI	*Revue des études islamiques*
RSO	*Rivista degli studi orientali*
SI	*Studia Islamica*
WZKM	*Wiener Zeitschrift für die Kunde des Morgenlandes*
ZDMG	*Zeitschrift der deutschen morgenländischen Gesellschaft*

Introduction

The problematic conjunction of social privilege and a demand for equal justice constitutes a central theme in the history of the Middle East, and one that long precedes the rise of Islam in the region.[1] But it assumes a particular urgency in the period under discussion here because Islam, unlike Christianity, enjoyed spectacular political success from the very beginning. On the one hand, the fruits of this early success contributed to the inevitable emergence of stratification within the early Muslim community; and on the other, the political power gained by the early Muslims meant that their religious egalitarianism could not fail to have strong social implications.

That Muslim societies between the second/eighth and seventh/thirteenth centuries were stratified despite the egalitarian orientation of the Islamic religious ethos requires no demonstration. It is necessary, however, to consider the kind of egalitarianism that may be said to characterise the Islamic tradition, and to indicate briefly that Islamic cultures were also in possession of a full repertoire of hierarchical ideas. In the section that follows I shall examine accordingly the evidence of the Qur'ān and consider the ways in which Islam's emphasis on equality may have been generated or reinforced by early Muslim experience. I shall then turn to a single instance of hierarchical consciousness from the period under study. Out of a vast number of possible examples, several of which will be discussed in the chapters of this book, I shall focus here on what is probably the most notable of all social models produced in a medieval Islamic environment, that of the seventh/thirteenth-century scientist and philosopher Naṣīr al-Dīn Ṭūsī (597–672/1201–1274).

Egalitarian consciousness

In certain respects, the Islamic tradition of classical times may be said to be strikingly egalitarian. By the end of the formative period, neither a church nor a priesthood had developed, and classical Islamic law, with the significant

[1] The importance of this dilemma in Middle Eastern history has been particularly stressed by M.G.S. Hodgson; see *The Venture of Islam* (Chicago and London, 1974), vol. 1, pp. 105ff, 128ff.

exception of marriage equality,[2] overwhelmingly assumed the equality of free male believers.[3] Whether this egalitarian spirit was present in the Arab monotheism that generated the conquests of the seventh century is more difficult to establish. This difficulty lies partly in the problematic nature of the sources for the early period, a point to which I shall return in the first chapter. But there are, I believe, reasonable grounds for assuming that the Arab monotheism that later developed into Islam was egalitarian in nature. This supposition is based firstly on the fact that in some respects Middle Eastern monotheism in general has tended to have a certain egalitarian element, and secondly on the egalitarian aspects of the tribalism with which the Arab monotheism was fused. I shall discuss these two elements in turn.

There may be a logical connexion of sorts between an affirmation of the oneness of God and the upholding of the principle of equality among the human beings created by him; in principle, at least, the monotheistic religions treat their adherents as brothers, regardless of the difference in their origins.[4] Such an outlook, however, need not go beyond the conviction that human beings are equal in the sight of God. This kind of religious or moral egalitarianism is reflected in the Qur'ān as it is in the Gospels, while neither scripture is overtly concerned with the subject of social stratification. The Qur'ān, like earlier scriptures, has a good deal to say about the moral standing of human beings, but it is left to human beings to apply these sentiments to the question of worldly status.[5]

In the minds of later commentators, the most important Qur'ānic verse in this context was 49:13: 'O men! We have created you from male and female, and have made you into peoples and tribes that you may know one another. The most noble among you in the sight of God is the most pious ('yā ayyuhā 'l-nās innā khalaqnākum min dhakarin wa unthā wa ja'alnākum shu'ūban wa qabā'ila li-ta'ārafū inna akramakum 'inda'llāhi atqākum')'. On the face of it, this verse appears to be concerned with tribal or ethnic rather than with social differentiation; its main point is that the various 'peoples and tribes' into which God has divided humanity have no bearing on the personal merit of the individual. Nevertheless, 49:13 proved remarkably flexible and in it Muslims have found sanction for egalitarianism of many kinds. Some have taken it as a reference to inter-Arab tribal differences; some have seen in it a reference to

2 On which see ch. 1.

3 See P. Crone, 'The Tribe and the State', in *States in History*, ed. J.A. Hall (Oxford, 1986), pp. 73–77.

4 Hodgson, *Venture*, vol. 1, pp. 103ff; see also I.M. Lapidus, 'The Arab Conquests and the Formation of Islamic Society', in *Studies on the First Century of Islamic Society*, ed. G.H.A. Juynboll (Carbondale and Edwardsville, 1982), p. 52.

5 For a comprehensive view of the Qur'ānic understanding of human society and its reflection in the career of the Prophet, see R. al-Sayyid, 'Min al-shu'ūb wa'l-qabā'il ilā'l-umma. Dirāsa fī takawwun mafhūm al-umma fī'l-Islām', in *al-Umma wa'l-jamā'a wa'l-salṭa* (Beirut, 1404/1984), pp. 17–87; *idem*, 'Jadaliyyāt al-'aql wa'l-naql wa'l-tajriba al-ta'rīkhiyya lil-umma fī'l-fikr al-siyāsī al-'arabī al-islāmī' in *al-Umma wa'l-jamā'a*, pp. 152ff.

the distinction between Arabs and non-Arab converts; some have seen in it an implied moral objection to a hierarchy of degrees.[6]

Similar in tone are the several places in which the Qur'ān makes plain that sons and wealth, while they may be marks of precedence in this world, will be of no assistance in attaining salvation in the next. Such passages include 26:88–89, 'The day when neither wealth nor sons shall profit except for him who comes to God with a pure heart ('yawma lā yanfa'u mālun wa lā banūna / illā man atā 'llāha bi-qalbin salīm')';[7] 18:47, 'Wealth and sons are the adornment of the present world ('al-mālu wa'l-banūna zīnatu'l-ḥayāti 'l-dunyā')', which, according to a common interpretation, reminds men that these fleeting goods are of lesser importance in God's sight than good works;[8] and 2:247, where Saul's people object that he is not wealthy enough to be their king.[9] The effect of these verses, as of 49:13, is not to deny the significance of such marks of rank in this world, but to declare them useless in terms of individual salvation.

Still other verses make no mention of worldly status, but emphasise inequalities based on religious virtue. These include 16:75, 'God has struck a similitude: a servant possessed by his master, having no power over anything, and whom we have provided of ourselves with a fair provision, and he expends of it secretly and openly; are they equal? ('ḍaraba 'llāhu mathalan 'abdan mamlūkan lā yaqdiru 'alā shay'in wa man razaqnāhu minnā rizqan ḥasanan fa-huwa yunfiqu minhu sirran wa jahran hal yastawūna')'[10] 32:18, 'Is he who has been a believer like unto him who has been ungodly? They are not equal ('a-fa-man kāna mu'minan ka-man kāna fāsiqan lā yastawūna')';[11] 4:95, 'Such of the believers as sit at home – unless they have an injury – are not the equals of those who struggle in the path of God with their possessions and their selves ('lā yastawī 'l-qā'idūna min al-mu'minīna ghayru ūlī

[6] For the exegetical history of 49:13, see R.P. Mottahedeh, 'The Shu'ûbîyah Controversy and the Social History of Early Islamic Iran', *IJMES* 7 (1976), pp. 161–182; R. al-Sayyid, 'Min al-shu'ūb wa'l-qabā'il ilā'l-umma', expecially pp. 26–31; and ch. 4.

[7] Cf. al-Bayḍāwī, *Anwār al-tanzīl wa asrār al-ta'wīl*, ed. H.O. Fleischer (Leipzig), vol. 2 (1848), p. 54.

[8] Cf. Maḥmūd b. 'Umar al-Zamakhsharī, *al-Kashshāf 'an ḥaqā'iq al-tanzīl wa 'uyūn al-aqāwīl* (Cairo, 1385/1966), vol. 2, p. 486; al-Bayḍāwī, *Anwār al-tanzīl*, vol. 1, p. 564.

[9] It is interesting to note that according to the commentators, the Israelites' real objection to Saul's right to authority had less to do with his poverty than with the lack of kingship or prophethood in his family history, and with his lowly occupation (he is variously said to have been a water-carrier, tanner, or shepherd); see Abū Ja'far al-Ṭabarī, *Jāmi' al-bayān 'an ta'wīl al-Qur'ān*, eds. M.M. Shākir and A.M. Shākir (Cairo, 1373/1954–), vol. 5, pp. 306–312; al-Zamakhsharī, *al-Kashshāf*, vol. 1, p. 379; al-Bayḍāwī, *Anwār al-tanzīl*, vol. 1, pp. 127–128; Ibn Kathīr, *Tafsīr al-Qur'ān al-'aẓīm* (Beirut, 1966), vol. 1, p. 534.

Other passages on the ultimate irrelevance of wealth and progeny occur in verses 63:9, 64:15, 34:37, 23:55–56, 8:28 and 68:14–15.

[10] Cf. al-Ṭabarī, *Jāmi' al-bayān*, vol. 14, pp. 148–149, where the analogy is taken to refer to infidels, who fail to use their wealth in the path of God, and to believers, who spend their money in ways pleasing to God; al-Zamakhsharī, *al-Kashshāf*, vol. 2, pp. 420–421; Fakhr al-Dīn al-Rāzī, *al-Tafsīr al-kabīr* (Cairo), vol. 20 (1357/1938), pp. 83–84; al-Bayḍāwī, *Anwār al-tanzīl*, vol. 1, p. 522; Ibn Kathīr, *Tafsīr*, vol. 4, p. 211.

[11] Al-Bayḍāwī, *Anwār al-tanzīl*, vol. 2, p. 120.

'l-ḍarari wa'l-mujāhidūna fī sabīli 'llāhi bi-amwālihim wa anfusihim').'[12] This last verse established an important distinction for some Khārijites, who at an early date came to regard inactive support as less meritorious than activism.[13]

It appears, then, that while the Qur'ān frequently points out the meaninglessness of differences in rank in terms of the afterlife, it certainly does not attempt to abolish them in the present world. On the contrary, it might be observed that the Qur'ān endorses several forms of worldly inequality: in addition to its acceptance of slavery and the social superiority of men over women, it notes that 'were it not for God's restraint of the people, some by means of others, the world would surely have been corrupted (2:251, 'wa law lā daf'u'llāhi 'l-nāsa ba'ḍahum bi-ba'ḍin la-fasadat al-arḍ')',[14] and that God has 'raised some over others in terms of rank, so that some may take others in servitude (43:32, 'rafa'nā ba'ḍahum fawqa ba'ḍin darajātin li-yattakhidha ba'ḍuhum ba'ḍan sukhriyyan').'[15] It also proclaims, 'Behold how we favoured some of them over others, and the next world will be greater in degrees and greater in favour (17:21, 'unẓur kayfa faḍḍalnā ba'ḍahum 'alā ba'ḍin wa lal-ākhiratu akbaru darajātin wa akbaru tafḍīlan')'.[16] Its central point thus appears to be that such inequalities have no bearing on an individual's moral worth and ultimate fate in the next world.

The religious egalitarianism of Arab monotheism was accentuated, however, by its conjunction with a second force, that of Arab tribalism. Arab tribal society, like its counterparts in some other pastoral settings, appears to have been in certain important respects strongly egalitarian. At least in the northern parts of the peninsula, insufficient local resources were available for a highly refined system of stratification to develop, and consequently Arab tribalism lacked the forms of social differentiation that characterised Central

[12] Cf. al-Ṭabarī, *Jāmi' al-bayān*, vol. 9, pp. 85–96; al-Zamakhsharī, *al-Kashshāf*, vol. 1, p. 555; al-Bayḍāwī, *Anwār al-tanzīl*, vol. 1, pp. 225–226; Ibn Kathīr, *Tafsīr*, vol. 2, pp. 365–368.

[13] E.A. Salem, *Political Theory and Institutions of the Khawārij* (Baltimore, 1956), pp. 87–88.

[14] Cf. al-Bayḍāwī, *Anwār al-tanzīl*, vol. 1, pp. 129–130, where the principal reference is to God granting assistance to the Muslims against the infidels, rather than to degrees of authority among Muslims.

[15] For al-Bayḍāwī, God allots people different kinds of sustenance and other unspecified goods, 'so that they may make use of one another for their needs, and thereby foster harmony and association such that the order of the world is upheld' (*Anwār al-tanzīl*, vol. 2, p. 238; on this kind of argument see also ch. 6). For Ibn Kathīr, God grants people different degrees of wealth, sustenance, intellect, understanding and other gifts, both external and internal (*Tafsīr*, vol. 6, p. 225).

[16] According to al-Bayḍāwī, this verse refers to the differences in sustenance created by God, and to the greater differences among people in the afterlife, where people are consigned to the various levels of paradise and hell (*Anwār al-tanzīl*, vol. 1, p. 536). For Fakhr al-Dīn al-Rāzī, it refers to unspecified worldly goods which are bestowed on or withheld from believers and polytheists impartially in this world, although the different stations of the two categories will be clearly apparent in the next life (*al-Tafsīr al-kabīr*, vol. 20, p. 181). Ibn Kathīr interprets the verse as a reference to worldly differences of wealth and poverty, good looks and ugliness, early death and a long life, and so on (*Tafsīr*, vol. 4, p. 297). For the use of these and other Qur'ānic proof-texts in justification of hierarchy, see ch. 6.

Asia, let alone the agrarian regions of the Middle East.[17] One of the most obvious indications of this lies in the nature of authority among the Arab tribes. Tribal leaders exercised only a limited kind of authority, based more on their ability to persuade than on their right to command; they also remained accessible to the generality of the tribesmen.[18]

The relative absence of stratification should not be taken to imply an absence of rivalry for status, power and such resources as were available. On the contrary, tribal society was fiercely competitive. In a society that lacked hierarchy, genealogy was an essential organising principle; it was especially important in matters of leadership, and in determining alliances and antagonisms.[19] Both individuals and descent groups as a whole vied for prestige, and in their rivalry frequently invoked the principles of genealogy (*nasab*) and inherited merit (*ḥasab*).[20] The lack of ascribed ranks and stations may in fact have led to a particularly high degree of competitiveness.[21] Rank was not regarded as an inherent attribute, and the lack of formal stratification entitled all individuals to seek prestige on their own account.[22] Thus within the framework of lineage, each man sought to attain honour and respect. In this regard the system was one of strong individualism, but it was also one in which a man's own honour was linked with that of his kinsmen.[23]

In both the pre-Islamic and Islamic periods, an egalitarian ideology coexisted with observable inequalities in the actual distribution of power, wealth and social esteem. (These inequalities were, of course, on a much larger scale after the conquests.) But whereas in the pre-Islamic Arab context anyone wishing to challenge this unequal distribution could attempt to do so (at least in theory), in the Islamic context this became increasingly difficult as the realities of state authority and a hierarchical social structure became established. The resulting tension was rendered all the more acute since sanction for such

[17] P. Crone, *Slaves on Horses. The Evolution of the Islamic Polity* (Cambridge, 1980), pp. 18ff; C. Lindholm, 'Kinship Structure and Political Authority: The Middle East and Central Asia', *Comparative Studies in Society and History* 28 (1986), pp. 334–355 (I owe this reference to Patricia Crone). On the contrasting social structure of Central Asian nomads, see L. Krader, *Peoples of Central Asia* (The Hague, 1971), pp. 152–153; *idem*, *Social Organization of the Mongol-Turkic Pastoral Nomads* (The Hague, 1963), especially pp. 318–326. (The situation was quite different in South Arabia; see n. 27.)

[18] Cf. Crone, *Slaves*, p. 23; Lapidus, 'The Arab Conquests and the Formation of Islamic Society', p. 55. [19] Lindholm, 'Kinship Structure and Political Authority', p. 341.

[20] '*Ḥasab wa-nasab*', *EI2*; see also R.P. Mottahedeh, *Loyalty and Leadership in an Early Islamic Society* (Princeton, 1980), pp. 98–104. On *ḥasab* (often understood as a store of merit inherited by a man as a result of the deeds of his forefathers, but one which he could either increase or decrease by his own actions), see Ibn Manẓūr, *Lisān al-ʿarab* (Beirut), vol. 1 (1374/1955), pp. 310ff, and I. Goldziher, *Muslim Studies*, ed. and tr. C.R. Barber and S.M. Stern (London and Chicago), vol. 1 (1967), pp. 45ff.

[21] Cf. C. Lindholm, 'Quandaries of Command in Egalitarian Societies: Examples from Swat and Morocco', in *Comparing Muslim Societies. Knowledge and the State in a World Civilization*, ed. J.R. Cole (Ann Arbor, 1992), p. 65.

[22] Lindholm, 'Kinship Structure and Political Authority', pp. 345–346, 349–350.

[23] Lindholm, 'Kinship Structure and Political Authority', p. 345.

a challenge could now be found not only in the attitudes and practice of tribalism but also in the egalitarian potential of Muḥammad's message. It was also intensified, and most significantly so, by the Muslims' early political success. The upheaval occasioned by the conquests created an environment in which the Arab monotheists, even those of lowly origins, became to a substantial degree equal members of a new polity.[24] The dissociation between Christianity and the state in the early centuries of that religion's history meant that the social aspects of the equality taught by Christians could remain relatively unexplored. By contrast, the immediate political success of the Muslims meant that their religious egalitarianism was bound to have strong social implications.

Hierarchical consciousness

Despite the notion of equality that lies at the heart of the Islamic tradition, the members of sedentary pre-modern Muslim societies, like those of other complex pre-industrial societies, perceived themselves and those around them as occupying positions in a hierarchy.[25] It is true that, despite the existence in the pre-Islamic period of orders or classes in many of the regions that came to comprise the Islamic world, the hierarchies of the Islamic period were often rather looser, and the religious ethos no doubt played a role in this partial softening of social boundaries. But few Muslims (or at least, few of those whose opinions have been recorded) were prepared to go very far in extending the religious ideal to the social sphere, and widely acknowledged, if informal, conceptions of social hierarchy were part of common experience in pre-modern Islamic communities as elsewhere.[26] Some such conceptions were limited to local settings;[27] others came to form part of a broadly shared Islamic culture.

[24] P. Crone, *Roman, Provincial and Islamic Law* (Cambridge, 1987), p. 88.

[25] Cf. P. Crone, *Pre-Industrial Societies* (Oxford, 1989), pp. 99f.

[26] Among the small number of communities that actively experimented with the implementation of egalitarian ideals, the example of the Qarmaṭīs of Baḥrayn is best known. On the taxation practices of the Qarmaṭīs and the social services enjoyed by them in Baḥrayn, see Abū'l-Qāsim Ibn Ḥawqal, *Kitāb ṣūrat al-arḍ* (ed. J.H. Kramers) (Leiden, 1967), pp. 25–27, and especially Nāṣir-i Khusraw, *Safarnāmeh*, ed. M. Dabīr Siyāqī (Tehran, 1354), pp. 148–149; tr. C. Schefer, *Sefernameh. Relation du voyage de Nassiri Khosrau* (Amsterdam, 1970), pp. 227–228. Both passages are discussed in B. Lewis, *The Origins of Ismā'īlism* (Cambridge, 1940), pp. 99–100. Such utopian experiments seem to have been short-lived, however, and they were not rooted in Ismā'īlī ideology (cf. W. Madelung, 'Ḳarmaṭī', *EI2*; P. Crone, 'Kavād's Heresy and Mazdak's Revolt', *Iran* 29 (1991), p. 29).

[27] Among the most striking examples are the ideas underlying the distinctive social arrangements that evolved in several South Asian Muslim communities (see, for instance, F. Barth 'The System of Social Stratification in Swat, North Pakistan', in *Aspects of Caste in South India, Ceylon and North-West Pakistan*, ed. E.R. Leach (Cambridge, 1969), pp. 113–46; I. Ahmad, 'Caste and Kinship in a Muslim Village of Eastern Uttar Pradesh', in *Family, Kinship and Marriage among Muslims in India*, ed. I. Ahmad (New Delhi, 1976), pp. 319–45, esp. n. 2; and R. Ahmed, *The Bengal Muslims 1871–1906. A Quest for Identity* (Delhi and Oxford, 1988), pp. 1–38), and in south Arabia (see P. Dresch, *Tribes, Government, and History in Yemen* (Oxford, 1989), pp. 117ff; R.B. Serjeant, 'South Arabia', in *Commoners, Climbers and Notables. A*

Particularly remarkable among conceptions of the latter type is the quadripartite social model articulated in the seventh/thirteenth century by Naṣīr al-Dīn Ṭūsī:

The first condition for justice is that he [the ruler] should keep the categories (*aṣnāf*) of mankind in correspondence with each other (*mutakāfī*), for just as balanced temperaments result from the correspondence of the four elements, so balanced societies are formed by the correspondence of the four categories.

The first [category] consists of the men of the pen, such as the masters of the sciences and the branches of knowledge (*arbāb-i ʿulūm va maʿārif*), the jurists, judges, secretaries, accountants, geometers, astronomers, physicians and poets, on whose existence depends the stability of this world and the next; among the natural elements these correspond to water. The second [category] are the men of the sword; soldiers, warriors, volunteers, skirmishers, frontier-guards, men of strength and courage, guardians of the realm and protectors of the state, by whose intermediacy the order of the world is effected; among the natural elements these correspond to fire. The third [category] are the men of transactions, merchants who carry goods from one region to another, tradesmen, masters of crafts and professions, and tax-collectors, without whose co-operation the livelihood of the species would be prevented; among the natural elements, they are like air. The fourth [category] consists of the men of agriculture, such as sowers, farmers, ploughmen and cultivators, who organise the feeding of all the communities, and without whose help the survival of individuals would be impossible; among the natural elements, they have the same rank as earth.[28]

As its immediate context indicates, Ṭūsī's model is both descriptive and prescriptive: Ṭūsī provides an account of his own society as he saw it, but at the same time his didactic tone suggests that his perceptions were shaped by a certain utopian vision. (This blurring of the distinction between description and imagination, or the real and the ideal, will be observed more than once in the course of what follows.) Ṭūsī's model is especially noteworthy in two respects. Firstly, as Lambton has pointed out, it is in several ways reminiscent of pre-Islamic Iranian social ideals.[29] With these it shares its quadripartite structure, the broad composition of its constituent categories, its emphasis on the importance of agriculture, its vision of all four social groups as interdependent, and its stress on the need for harmony among them. In its incarnation in Ṭūsī's *Akhlāq-i Nāṣirī*, however, the Sasanian framework for this visualisation of society has undergone significant modifications. Most

Sampler of Studies on Social Ranking in the Middle East, ed. C.A.O. van Nieuwenhuijze (Leiden, 1977), pp. 226–247; and T. Gerholm, *Market, Mosque and Mafraj. Social Inequality in a Yemeni Town* (Stockholm, 1977), especially pp. 102–158).

28 Naṣīr al-Dīn Ṭūsī, *Akhlāq-i Nāṣirī*, ed. M. Minovi (Tehran, 1356/1978), p. 305; tr. G.M. Wickens, *The Nasirean Ethics* (London, 1964), p. 230.

29 A.K.S. Lambton, *Islamic Society in Persia* (London, 1954), p. 3–4; *idem*, 'Justice in the Medieval Persian Theory of Kingship', *SI* 17 (1962), p. 97. Ṭūsī's theory has also sometimes been linked to Platonic ideas (E.I.J. Rosenthal, *Political Thought in Medieval Islam* (Cambridge, 1962), p. 221 (in the context of Davvānī's ninth/fifteenth-century version of the model); K. Karpat, 'Some Historical and Methodological Considerations Concerning Social Stratification in the Middle East', in *Commoners, Climbers and Notables*, pp. 86–87).

obviously, whereas Sasanian models customarily placed the various priestly occupations and those associated with the court and administration in the first and third categories respectively, here these groups have been amalgamated; secretaries and other figures attached to the court (physicians, poets and astrologers) have been grouped together with religious functionaries in the single composite category labelled 'men of the pen'.[30] The vacancy created in the third rank is now filled by the merchants, who are thus elevated to a respectable and independent position whereas in Sasanian models, when acknowledged at all, they appear as a despised appendage to the fourth group.[31]

Secondly, Ṭūsī's description became immensely popular, especially in the Perso-, Turko- and Indo-Islamic cultural areas, where it was rapidly established as a standard, indeed a normative, model for the conceptualisation of society.[32] No earlier social model had achieved such a dominant position in Islamic political culture.[33] The present study deals largely with the social imaginings that preceded Ṭūsī's model and contributed to its intellectual context.

It should be emphasised that this study is concerned with social ideals and their place in the intellectual and cultural life of Muslim communities in the classical and early medieval periods, rather than with the actual social organ-

[30] In his treatise on finance, Ṭūsī lists four similar groups under the heading 'men of the pen': (1) the men of religion, (2) masters of subtle sciences such as philosophy, astronomy and medicine, (3) the men of great affairs, such as viziers and *yārghūchī*s ('investigators') and (4) accountants (M. Minovi and V. Minorsky, 'Naṣīr al-Dīn Ṭūsī on Finance', *BSOAS* 10 (1940), pp. 758, 771).

[31] On the social models of pre-Islamic Iran, see ch. 3.

[32] What follows is a brief and far from comprehensive list of some important later passages of social description that are informed by Ṭūsī's model. Shams al-Dīn Ibrāhīm Abarqūhī, who acknowledges his debt to Ṭūsī's *Akhlāq* in his *Majmaʿ al-baḥrayn* (711–714/1311–1314) (ed. N.M. Haravī (Tehran, 1364/1406), p. 82), introduces minor modifications in his reproduction of this passage (*Majmaʿ al-baḥrayn*, p. 92; I owe this reference to Hossein Modarressi). Ḥusayn b. Muḥammad Āvī, in his 'translation' (c. 729/1329) of ʿAlī's letter to Mālik al-Ashtar, reduces the original five social categories of the *Nahj al-balāgha* to three in a fashion that suggests his familiarity with Ṭūsī's model (*Farmān-i Mālik-i Ashtar*, ed. M.T. Dānishpazhūh (Tehran, 1359/1400), p. 89). An almost exact copy of Ṭūsī's model appears in an early Ottoman source, the *Mir'ât ül-mülûk* of Ahmed b. Hüsamüddin al-Amâsî, composed for Mehmed I (d. 824/1421) (ms. Esed Ef. 1890, ff. 56a–b; I owe this reference to Cornell Fleischer). A similar, although differently arranged, quadripartite model appears in the letters spuriously ascribed to the vizier Rashīd al-Dīn (*Mukātabāt-i Rashīd al-Dīn Faḍl Allāh*, ed. M. Shafīʿ (Lahore, 1376/1947), p. 12). Very similar models also appear in the two well-known adaptations of the *Akhlāq-i Nāṣirī* by Jalāl al-Dīn Davvānī (830–907/1427–1501) (*Lavāmiʿ al-ishrāq fī makārim al-akhlāq=Akhlāq-i Jalālī* (Lucknow, 1377/1957), pp. 270–271; tr. W.F. Thompson, *Practical Philosophy of the Muhammadan People* (London, 1839), pp. 388–389) and Ḥusayn Vāʿiẓ Kāshifī (d. 910/1504–1505) (*Akhlāq-i Muḥsinī* (Hertford, 1850), pp. 57–58). For the place of Ṭūsī's model in the thought of later Ottoman writers, see C. Fleischer, 'Royal Authority, Dynastic Cyclism, and "Ibn Khaldûnism" in Sixteenth-Century Ottoman Letters', *JAAS* 18 (1983), pp. 198–220. In India, a rearranged version of Ṭūsī's model (soldiers, artisans and merchants, men of the pen (among whom, as in the *Akhlāq-i Muḥsinī*, the *ʿulamāʾ* do not appear) and cultivators) is found in the *Āʾīn-i Akbarī* of Abū'l-Faẓl (ed. H. Blochmann (Calcutta, 1872), vol. 1, pp. 3–4).

[33] See further H. Inalcik, *The Ottoman Empire. The Classical Age 1300–1600* (New York and Washington, 1973), pp. 65–69, and N. Itzkowitz, *Ottoman Empire and Islamic Tradition* (New York, 1972), pp. 58ff.

isation of any particular pre-modern Muslim society. Such ideals probably never corresponded very closely to the social organisations of the communities in which they were produced; in so far as they corresponded to real conditions at all, it was to different extents in different places at different times.[34] Nevertheless it is worth noting the constancy of certain ideas, since this suggests that some form of ranking was widely regarded not only as a legitimate, but also as a necessary, characteristic of social organisation in settings that were distant from each other in time and space. The distinction between the upper and lower strata of society, the *khāṣṣa* and the *ʿāmma*, for example, is attested as early as Ibn al-Muqaffaʿ (d. c. 139/756) and endures throughout the pre-modern period. The term *khāṣṣa* (pl. *khawāṣṣ*) generally refers to the holders of political, bureaucratic, military and sometimes religious offices, and to the literate, urban groups, who might include educated merchants and landowners. Such persons could be differentiated in terms of their culture and affluence from the *ʿāmma* (pl. *ʿawāmm*), the illiterate or semiliterate mass of the population.[35] It might be said that such a general distinction as 'upper' and 'lower' (or 'special' and 'general') is an insufficient basis on which to argue for a widespread sensitivity to social differences. There are also, however, indications in the classical literature of a more defined and complex awareness of social stratification. These include the references to *ṭabaqāt al-nās*, literally 'the strata of society' and *aṣnāf al-nās*, 'the categories of society'. The latter term need not imply a scale of social value, although it was frequently used in discussions of rank; the former, however, gives graphic expression to a vertically layered structure.[36] The phrase *ṭabaqāt al-nās* was sometimes used, especially in the second/eighth and third/ninth centuries, specifically to refer to the various ranks of attendants at court, differentiated according to an elaborate system of protocol reminiscent of that of Sasanian Iran.[37] Later it came to be used in a general sense, to describe a hierarchical vision of society as a whole.

[34] See for example the comments of C. Fleischer, *Bureaucrat and Intellectual in the Ottoman Empire. The Historian Mustafa Âli (1541–1600)* (Princeton, 1986), pp. 5–7.

[35] Cf. M.A.J. Beg, 'al-Khāṣṣa wa'l-ʿāmma', *EI2*; I. Lapidus, *Muslim Cities in the Later Middle Ages* (Cambridge, Massachusetts, 1967), pp. 80ff; B. Lewis, *The Political Language of Islam* (Chicago and London, 1988), pp. 67–68; A.K.S. Lambton, *Continuity and Change in Medieval Persia* (Albany, New York, 1988), p. 224.

[36] Cf. M. Rodinson, 'Histoire économique et histoire des classes sociales dans le monde musulman', in *Studies in the Economic History of the Middle East*, ed. M.A. Cook (Oxford, 1970), pp. 142–148, where other terms that imply a consciousness of stratification are also discussed; R. al-Sayyid, *Mafāhīm al-jamāʿāt fīʾl-Islām* (Beirut, 1984), pp. 84ff (on '*ṣinf*'); Mottahedeh, *Loyalty and Leadership*, pp. 105ff. Following Mottahedeh, I have in general adopted neutral terms such as 'category' and 'group' rather than such commonly used terms as 'estate', 'caste' and 'class'. Since there seems to be little consensus regarding the precise definitions of 'estate' and 'caste', the use of these terms might make for less clarity rather than more; and since the term 'class', whether in its Marxian or Weberian sense, connotes the primacy of economic relations, it is not entirely appropriate for the forms of social stratification under discussion here. On the application of common sociological terminology to Middle Eastern history, cf. K. Karpat, 'Some Historical and Methodological Considerations', pp. 83–101.

[37] See for example pseudo-Jaḥiẓ, *K. al-taj fī akhlāq al-mulūk*, ed. Aḥmad Zakī Pāshā (Cairo, 1332/1914), p. 25.

On its own the term *ṭabaqa* is frequently employed to denote a particular functional group,[38] and the phrase *ʿalā qadri ṭabaqātihim* is used to convey differences in social and economic status.[39] Such expressions do not refer to any formal system of estates or 'orders', but they do suggest that the concept of a graded form of social organisation was taken for granted among the inhabitants of pre-modern Muslim societies just as it was among their neighbours in the more formally structured societies of China, India and Europe.

Whatever the relationship of such terms and concepts may have been to any particular set of historical circumstances, it seems clear that for many people the Islamic insistence on the ultimate irrelevance of worldly differences coexisted not only with hierarchical social structures on the ground but also with an array of more or less appealing ideas that sought to justify such structures. It is the interplay between various manifestations of egalitarian and hierarchical consciousness that forms the subject of the ensuing chapters. Many of the attitudes, sentiments and prejudices that the reader will encounter in what follows were common to other pre-modern societies. But in an Islamic context they take on somewhat different forms, partly, it is argued, because of the circumstances of early Islamic history and partly because the Islamic religious tradition could not be used easily to support the principle of hierarchy. As a result the élites who benefited from hierarchical forms of social organisation in the Islamic world found themselves in moral difficulties that their counterparts in other civilisations did not always share, or at least not to the same degree or in the same way. Much of this book is devoted to the ways in which such people responded to the complexities of this state of affairs.

[38] See for example Ḥasan al-Khūʾī, *Ghunyat al-kātib wa munyat al-ṭālib*, ed. A.S. Erzi (Ankara, 1963).

[39] Thus al-Shayzarī, in his instructions to the *muḥtasib* on the exaction of the *jizya* from the *ahl al-dhimma* (*Nihāyat al-rutba fī ṭalab al-ḥisba*, ed. al-ʿArīnī (Cairo, 1365/1946), p. 107).

PART I

Sources for Islamic social ideals

CHAPTER 1

Egalitarianism and the growth of a pious opposition

The main emphasis of this chapter is on the assorted dicta that, according to authors of the classical period, represent the literary remains of the first century or so. It should be stated at the outset that although most of the aphorisms and anecdotes presented here purport to represent the opinions of prominent Muslims of the early period, they are in many cases more likely to have taken form in the first half of the second century (that is, in the late Umayyad and early ʿAbbāsid periods) and to have been ascribed at that time or subsequently to figures of the first century. They are probably not, in other words, authentic utterances of the pre-classical period. Instead, they are indicative of the ideas that later generations of Muslims, as they formulated their own views on social organisation, came to associate with the earliest period of Islam.

What these sayings and maxims reveal is that a number of different social ideals were in competition in the early second century, and that the exponents of each were eager to claim the authority of the past. Many examples, naturally enough, reflect the struggles of various groups to assert their own sense of superiority. Some are expressions of egalitarianism or responses to it and are compatible with the interpretation that the Islamic egalitarian ethos might have been understood in the early period to have had both religious and social significance. But the classical sources also allow us to glimpse a gradual whittling away of the social aspect of Islamic egalitarianism, as well as a certain resistance to this process of erosion.

In what follows I shall attempt to establish the viewpoints represented in the literary fragments and to suggest a context in which they may have emerged. My analysis of these materials will be preceded by a brief summary of some historical developments which may have conditioned the emergence of early Muslim social imaginings. I shall suggest that the ideal of social, as well as religious, equality may have been present in Islamic thought from an early date, and I shall seek to demonstrate that concerted efforts were made to undermine this ideal, chiefly because of the political opposition it quickly came to imply. (A detailed account of the process of taming will follow in the second half of this book.)

Stratification and the appeal of egalitarianism in the early Islamic period

The initial phase of the conquests was accompanied by radical social change among the Arabs, but the opportunity for social equalising came to an end within decades.[1] In the aftermath of the conquests, differences of status among the Arabs rapidly became far greater than they had been in the past.[2] Not everyone shared in the power that came from the administration of the new empire, and the Arabs did not benefit equally from the enormous resources now at their disposal. The tension generated by the appearance of increased inequalities became particularly clear in the early Umayyad period, when kinship was established as the main criterion for appointments,[3] and the tribal leaders (*ashrāf al-qabā'il*) acted as the intermediaries in the official power structure. These tribal leaders were supposed to support, and were in turn supported by, the government.[4] Some authors claim that this tribal system represented a departure from attempts by earlier caliphs to establish a different kind of social order, and those who opposed the tribal order, notably the Khārijites and the Shīʿa, looked back wistfully to the days of ʿUmar and ʿAlī respectively. ʿUmar is said to have sought to establish Islamic priority (*sābiqa*) as the main criterion of worth, with the result that under him the Prophet's Companions (the *ṣaḥāba*, Anṣār and others) had enjoyed prominence; ʿAlī is associated with egalitarian fiscal measures, which had attracted the support of Kūfan newcomers in particular.[5] The opposition between those who supported Muʿāwiya's tribal system and those who advocated more 'Islamic' arrangements was not simply one between early-comers and newcomers (that is, those possessed of *sābiqa* and those who lacked it), but also within the ranks of the

[1] Crone, *Roman, Provincial and Islamic Law*, p. 89.

[2] For a discussion of the processes involved in this development, see Lapidus, 'The Arab Conquests and the Formation of Islamic Society', pp. 49–72.

[3] Crone, *Slaves*, p. 32. Kinship continued to be important in the Marwānid period, as is evident from ʿAbd al-Ḥamīd's letter on behalf of Marwān to the governor Ibn Hubayra (I. ʿAbbās, *ʿAbd al-Ḥamīd ibn Yaḥyā al-Kātib wa mā tabaqqā min rasā'ilihi wa rasā'il Sālim Abī'l-ʿAlā'* (Amman, 1988), pp. 191–192) and Sālim's letter on behalf of Hishām to Khālid al-Qasrī (ʿAbbās, *ʿAbd al-Ḥamīd ibn Yaḥyā al-Kātib*, pp. 305–306; I owe this reference to Wadād al-Qāḍī). On the authenticity of the correspondence ascribed to ʿAbd al-Ḥamīd, see W. al-Qāḍī, 'Early Islamic State Letters: The Question of Authenticity', in *The Byzantine and Early Islamic Near East*, vol. 1, *Problems in the Literary Source Material*, eds. Averil Cameron and L.I. Conrad (Princeton, 1992), pp. 215–275.

[4] This system became firmly established in Iraq under Muʿāwiya (41–60/661–680) and Ziyād (d. c. 54/673), and lasted there until the time of al-Ḥajjāj (governor of the east, 74–96/694–714); M. Hinds, 'Kūfan Political Alignments and their Background in the Mid-Seventh Century A.D.', *IJMES* 2 (1971), pp. 346–347; Crone, *Slaves*, pp. 31–32.

[5] Hinds, 'Kūfan Political Alignments', pp. 348–349, 363, 366. For some examples of the egalitarianism associated with ʿUmar, see al-Jāḥiẓ, *al-Bayān wa'l-tabyīn*, ed. ʿAbd al-Salām Muḥammad Hārūn (Cairo), vol. 2 (1405/1985), pp. 46–50; and for some examples associated with ʿAlī, see below. It should be noted that the Khārijites did not possess *sharaf* according to traditional tribal criteria, but claimed an 'Islamic' *sharaf* and the attendant privileges accorded to Iraqi early-comers in the time of ʿUmar (Hinds, 'Kūfan Political Alignments', p. 347).

early-comers themselves. This may have begun after the battle of Nihāvand (21/642), when the principle of priority was modified in such a way that the stipends of newcomers who had 'shown valour' were raised. More important, however, seems to have been the status of the early-comers within their clans; those who were both early-comers and clan leaders of some importance seem generally to have favoured the tribal organisation supported by Muʿāwiya, whereas those early-comers who were not clan leaders opposed it, since their sole claim to status rested on their *sābiqa*.[6]

ʿUmar and ʿAlī, then, were portrayed by opponents of the tribal order as social egalitarians who sought to promote a new society in which 'Islamic' credentials were of greater significance than traditional ones. It is important to note, however, that these expressions of egalitarianism were limited to Arabs, and may in fact have coincided with a strong resistance to assimilation.[7] In Iraq, the dissatisfaction of many Muslim Arabs with the growing disparities of wealth and influence often seems to have been accompanied by a distaste for the prevailing (Persian) aristocratic culture. Both ʿUmar and to a lesser extent ʿAlī are said to have forbidden or disapproved of Persian upper-class habits.[8]

Tribal identity remained an important source of prestige long after Arab civilians had ceased to live tribally.[9] This was partly due to the institution of clientage, which perpetuated tribal distinctions.[10] The continuing importance of genealogy (*nasab*) is reflected in its uninterrupted transmission from the conquests throughout the Umayyad period and even under the ʿAbbāsids. Initially, knowledge of genealogy was a necessary element in the administration of the state, and in the affiliation of new converts with tribal groups. It was also of considerable significance in maintaining the differentiation between the conquerors and the conquered population, since it provided for an Arab sense of identity in contradistinction to the *mawālī*, who only later responded with works on their own genealogies.[11]

[6] Hinds, 'Kūfan Political Alignments', pp. 352–356.

[7] Most telling here is the well-known advice attributed to ʿUmar, according to which he exhorts the Arabs to learn their genealogies, and not to become like the settled peoples who thought of their origins in terms of place (Ibn ʿAbd al-Barr, *al-Inbāh ʿalā qabāʾil al-ruwāh* (Cairo, 1350/1931), p. 43; Ibn ʿAbd Rabbihi, *al-ʿIqd al-farīd*, ed. K. al-Bustānī (Beirut), vol. 12 (1952), p. 5).

[8] Cf. Hinds, 'Kūfan Political Alignments', pp. 347ff. On ʿUmar, see al-Jāḥiẓ, *Rasāʾil al-Jāḥiẓ*, ed. ʿAbd al-Salām Muḥammad Hārūn (Cairo, 1399/1979), vol. 2, *K. al-ḥijāb*, p. 31; Levy, *Social Structure*, p. 56, n. 1; M. Morony, *Iraq after the Muslim Conquest* (Princeton, 1984), p. 262. On ʿAlī, see Morony, *Iraq*, p. 262, and below. See also R. al-Sayyid, 'Naẓarāt fī jadaliyyāt al-ʿilāqa bayn al-namūdhajayn al-siyāsiyyayn al-taʾrīkhiyyayn al-īrānī al-qadīm waʾl-islāmī al-wasīṭ', in *al-Umma waʾl-jamāʿa*, p. 117.

[9] See Crone, *Slaves*, pp. 42–43, and also F. Donner, 'Tribal Settlement in Basra during the First Century A.H.', in *Land Tenure and Social Transformation in the Middle East*, ed. T. Khalidi (Beirut, 1984), pp. 97–109.

[10] Crone, *Slaves*, esp. pp. 39–40; *idem*, *Roman, Provincial and Islamic Law*, p. 90.

[11] M.J. Kister and M. Plessner, 'Notes on Caskel's Ǧamharat an-nasab', *Oriens* 25–26 (1976–7), pp. 50–1, 54ff.

In the materials under consideration in this chapter, the topic of rank may be approached from a number of different perspectives. It may be discussed, firstly, in moral and religious terms; secondly, in terms of the relative standing of the Arab tribes; thirdly, in terms of the relative status of Arabs and *mawālī*; and fourthly, in terms of the social hierarchies in which many Muslims came to live. It is important to note the distinction between these various facets of the issue, and to realise that some of them are more relevant to certain stages of Islamic history than to others. In the period in which the Islamic tradition was in its formative phase, ethnicity was often of great significance in the assessment of social status, and consequently ethnic and social stratification are extremely closely connected in the materials that survive from this time. Egalitarian arguments may have been used initially in an inner-Arab context, rather than to press for full social recognition of non-Arab converts.[12] But as the numbers and influence of such converts increased, they began to avail themselves of the egalitarian tradition in their efforts to gain access to the élites. In the course of the first and early second centuries, then, the question of the status of non-Arab Muslims emerged alongside the question of the relative standing of the Arab tribes, and new attention was devoted to the ethnic and social implications of the Qur'ān's emphasis on the moral equality of the believers. The linking of ethnic and social stratification endured long after the issue of Islam's universalism had been solved, and it was only in the course of the late second/eighth and especially the third/ninth centuries that discussions of hierarchy and equality began to lose their ethnic overtones.[13]

Sources for the study of early social thought

The materials on which the following study is based are of a fragmentary nature. They consist of short sayings and anecdotes that purport to record the actions, utterances and sentiments of Muslims of the first and early second centuries. They include assorted axioms (proverbs, Prophetic *ḥadīth* and sayings attributed to ʿAlī b. Abī Ṭālib); materials pertaining to the issues of marriage equality and the holding of audiences; and brief descriptions of the groups that, according to some visualisations, ought to constitute the new society.

Before examining this mixed body of aphoristic and anecdotal material, some discussion of the problems it presents is necessary. Firstly, although in many cases they claim to date from the early decades of the Islamic period, most of these dicta were probably generated in the first half of the second

[12] It should be remembered that the correspondences between the categories of conquerors and conquered, rulers and subjects, Arabs and non-Arabs, and Muslims and non-Muslims were not absolute. For the case of Iran, see M. Morony, 'Conquerors and Conquered: Iran', in *Studies on the First Century of Islamic Society*, ed. G.H.A. Juynboll (Carbondale and Edwardsville, 1982), pp. 74ff.

[13] The possible role of egalitarian ideas in the revolts of the second/eighth and early third/ninth centuries will be discussed in ch. 4.

century or, in some cases, later still. One indication of the relatively late date at which several of these literary fragments seem to have been shaped is that they appear to reflect later political and cultural developments such as the *shuʿūbiyya* controversy.[14] Most of the contents of the oldest extant written collection of proverbs, the *Kitāb al-amthāl* of Abū ʿUbayd (d. 224/838), date from the Umayyad or early ʿAbbāsid period.[15] The contents of the famous third/ninth- and fourth/tenth-century literary anthologies, such as the *ʿUyūn al-akhbār* of Ibn Qutayba (213–276/828–889) and *al-ʿIqd al-farīd* Ibn ʿAbd Rabbihi (246–328/860–940), as well as those of the *maḥāsin* literature, are of a similar or even later vintage.[16] All of these collections reflect what had come to be regarded as the necessary cultural knowledge of the learned élite by the time of their composition. It follows that the anecdotes and *bons mots* reproduced in them must have been in circulation long enough to have acquired the status of received wisdom. Moreover, the several slightly different forms in which many of these axioms and anecdotes have come down to us suggest that they continued to circulate orally for some time after they had attained this status.

A further problem with the aphorisms and anecdotes preserved in the classical sources is that they are usually presented with little or no context. The removal of a *bon mot* from its historical context and its collection together with other *bons mots* is part of the process whereby it takes on a universal significance and becomes part of received wisdom; it also makes it all the more difficult to retrieve its historical meaning.[17] There is, however, some reason to

[14] Some literary fragments that seem to reflect *shuʿūbī* concerns are discussed in the present chapter; the *shuʿūbī* controversy as a whole, and the extended prose works it generated, are discussed in ch. 4.

[15] Some of Abū ʿUbayd's proverbs may have taken shape in the pre-Islamic Arabian context, but, despite the author's statement that the materials he had collected constituted 'the wisdom of the Arabs in the Jāhiliyya and in Islam', the majority are likely to belong to the period after the conquests (R. Sellheim, *Die klassisch-arabischen Sprichwörtersammlungen insbesondere die des Abū ʿUbaid* (The Hague, 1954), p. 24). It should not, of course, be assumed that Abū ʿUbayd's sources were written, since proverbs continued to be transmitted orally until well into the fourth/tenth century (R. Sellheim, 'Abū ʿAlī al-Qālī. Zum Problem mündlicher und schriftlicher Überlieferung am Beispiel von Sprichwörtersammlungen', *Studien zur Geschichte und Kultur des Vorderen Orients. Festschrift für Bertold Spuler zum 70sten Geburtstag*, eds. H.R. Roemer and A. Noth (Leiden, 1981), pp. 362–374).

[16] On the sources for the *ʿUyūn al-akhbār*, see G. Lecomte, *Ibn Qutayba (mort en 276/889). L'homme, son oeuvre, ses idées* (Damascus, 1965), pp. 179–211; and on those for *al-ʿIqd al-farīd*, see W. Werkmeister, *Quellenuntersuchungen zum Kitāb al-ʿIqd al-farīd des Andalusiers Ibn ʿAbdrabbih (246/860–328/940)* (Berlin, 1983). On the *maḥāsin* literature, the two chief extant examples of which are the *Kitāb al-maḥāsin wa'l-masāwī* of Ibrāhīm b. Muḥammad al-Bayhaqī and the *Kitāb al-maḥāsin wa'l-aḍdād* attributed to al-Jāḥiẓ, see I. Gériès, *Un genre littéraire arabe, al-Maḥāsin wa-l-masāwī* (Paris, 1977).

[17] The classical grammarians and literati frequently comment on the interpretation of the maxims they record in their collections, but we cannot be sure that they understood these materials in the same ways that they had been understood in the contexts in which they were generated. And although the philologists sometimes provide an account of the incident which prompted the initial coining of a proverb, this is likely to represent a secondary interpretation (Sellheim, *Die klassisch-arabischen Sprichwörtersammlungen*, p. 28). The process is familiar from the development of *ḥadīth*.

suppose that a good deal of the material under discussion in this chapter is of Iraqi origin: where a dictum is attributed to an individual, this is usually a figure associated with Baṣra, Kūfa or Baghdad; furthermore, the classical authors who record these aphorisms generally spent all or most of their lives in Iraq.[18]

Proverbs

The first group of materials I should like to consider consists of Arabic proverbs on the subject of human characteristics. Some of these maxims were well enough known in the early second/eighth century to appear in contemporary poetry, and most are included in Abū ʿUbayd's collection. Presumably all of them were in circulation in Baṣra and Kūfa by the beginning of the third/ninth century.

What is striking about these proverbs is that they could be interpreted in either an ethical or a social sense. They might refer to the likeness or unlikeness of human beings in terms of their moral worth, or to questions of tribal, ethnic or social equality or inequality. The use of the same vocabulary to refer to both moral standing and social position is consistent with the explicit correlation of moral baseness with low social station in certain literary works, notably those of al-Jāḥiẓ, produced in the cities of Islamic Iraq in classical times.[19]

Of chief importance among the proverbs dealing with similarity and equality are the maxim 'equals like the teeth of a comb (*sawāʾ ka-asnān al-mushṭ*)' and its variants. Unlike its derisive companion proverb, 'equals like the teeth of a donkey (*sawāsiya ka-asnān al-ḥimār*)', the comb saying seems to have had only positive connotations, and it was eventually considered by some to be a Prophetic *ḥadīth*. It is not known as such by Abū ʿUbayd,[20] but it is included by Abū'l-Shaykh al-Iṣfahānī (d. 369/979) in his collection of Prophetic proverbs and comes to be widely regarded as a Prophetic utterance in the form 'al-nās ka-asnān al-mushṭ wa innamā yatafāḍalūna bi'l-ʿāfiya' ('men are equals like the teeth of a comb; one has precedence over another only in well-being').[21] Al-ʿAskarī (d. after 400/1010) suggests that it has principally a moral relevance in that, unlike its counterpart, it refers to human uniformity in good-

[18] Ibn ʿAbd Rabbihi is a notable exception to this pattern, but his *Kitāb al-ʿiqd al-farīd* contains much material that may be linked, if only indirectly, to the works of Iraqi writers. On the relationship between Ibn ʿAbd Rabbihi's work and the works of Iraqi men of letters, see Werkmeister, *Quellenuntersuchungen*, especially pp. 463ff.

[19] See chs. 4 and 7.

[20] Abū ʿUbayd al-Qāsim b. al-Sallām, *Kitāb al-amthāl*, ed. ʿAbd al-Majīd Qaṭāmish (Damascus, 1400/1980), p. 132. Ibn ʿAbd Rabbihi (*al-ʿIqd al-farīd*, vol. 9, p. 65) and al-Maydānī (*Majmaʿ al-amthāl* (Beirut), vol. 2 (1962), p. 389) are also silent on the Prophetic connexions of this proverb.

[21] Abū'l-Shaykh al-Iṣfāhanī, *K. al-amthāl fī'l-ḥadīth al-nabawī*, ed. ʿAbd al-ʿAlī ʿAbd al-Ḥamīd (Bombay, 1402/1982), pp. 99–100 (with one variant); Abū Hilāl al-ʿAskarī, *Jamharat al-amthāl*, eds. M. Abū'l-Faḍl Ibrāhīm and ʿAbd al-Majīd Qaṭāmish (Cairo, 1384/1964), vol. 1, pp. 522–23; al-Bakrī, *Faṣl al-maqāl fī sharḥ kitāb al-amthāl*, eds. I. ʿAbbās and ʿAbd al-Majīd ʿĀbidīn (Beirut, 1403/1983), p. 197; cf. M. al-Gharawī, *al-Amthāl al-nabawiyya* (Beirut, 1401/1980), vol. 2, p. 303.

ness and badness alike.[22] Only al-Maydānī (d. 518/1124) is explicit in giving the aphorism an ethnic and possibly a social dimension; for him, it connotes the equality of men in terms of lineage (*nasab*), since all men are the descendants of Adam.[23]

Whatever its original force, the comb proverb was certainly interpreted and employed by classical and later writers as a proof-text for ethnic and social equality. The Qur'anic interpreter Abū'l-Futūḥ al-Rāzī (d. 538/1144) adduced it, possibly for egalitarian purposes, in his commentary on the verse 3:195 ('And their Lord has hearkened to them, [saying], "I will not allow the [pious] work performed by anyone among you, whether male or female, to be lost. The one of you is of the other (*ba'ḍukum min ba'ḍin*)"'). On the basis of the comb proverb, which he too considered a Prophetic *ḥadīth*, al-Rāzī paraphrased the Qur'ānic verse as 'All men are one in my sight in respect of their inborn characteristics (*khilqat*).'[24] It is also used with unambiguous ethnic significance by al-Sarakhsī (d. 483/1090), who, in his discussion of marriage equality (*kafā'a*), cites it in a form that reflects *shu'ūbī* concerns: 'People are equal like the teeth of a comb, the Arab has no superiority over the non-Arab, and superiority is only in piety.'[25]

The companion proverb, 'equals like the teeth of a donkey (*sawāsiya ka-asnān al-ḥimār*)', is considered by the classical authors to be an example of extreme satire (*hijā'*).[26] According to al-'Askarī, it connotes equivalence only in what is wrong and reprehensible,[27] a view obviously shared by the early fifth/eleventh-century philosopher al-Rāghib al-Iṣfahānī,[28] who included it in a section devoted to 'people who are equals in baseness'.[29] Its appearance in the poetry of Kuthayyir (d. 105/723)[30] and al-Farazdaq (d. 110 or 112/728 or

22 Al-'Askarī, *Jamharat al-amthāl*, vol. 1, p. 522.

23 Al-Maydānī, *Majma' al-amthāl*, vol. 2, p. 389; cf. the commentaries on Q. 49:13 (see ch. 4).

24 *Rawḥ al-jinān* (Tehran), vol. 3 (1398), p. 291; quoted in Mottahedeh, 'The Shu'ûbîyah Controversy', p. 165, n. 10. (In his subsequent comments on this verse, al-Rāzī emphasises the religious equality of men and women rather than that of men of different stations; *Rawḥ al-jinān*, vol. 3, p. 292.)

25 *Al-Mabsūṭ* (Cairo), vol. 5 (1324), p. 23. Cf. F.J. Ziadeh, 'Equality (*kafā'a*) in the Muslim Law of Marriage', *American Journal of Comparative Law* 6 (1957), p. 508, and n. 25.

26 Abū 'Ubayd, *K. al-amthāl*, p. 132; al-Bakrī, *Faṣl al-maqāl*, pp. 196–97; al-Maydānī, *Majma' al-amthāl*, vol. 1, p. 463; Ibn 'Abd Rabbihi, *al-'Iqd al-farīd*, vol. 9, p. 65; vol. 12, p. 182; and see G.W. Freytag, *Arabum Proverbia*, vol. 1 (Bonn, 1838), p. 602.

27 *Jamharat al-amthāl*, vol. 1, p. 522.

28 On the dates of al-Rāghib's literary activity, see W. Madelung, 'Ar-Rāġib al-Iṣfahānī und die Ethik al-Ġazālīs', *Islamwissenschaftliche Abhandlungen*, ed. R. Gramlich (Wiesbaden, 1974), pp. 156–157.

29 Al-Rāghib al-Iṣfahānī, *Muḥāḍarāt al-udabā' wa muḥāwarāt al-shu'arā' wa'l-bulaghā'* (Beirut, 1961), vol. 1, p. 339.

30 *Sawāsiyatun ka-asnān al-ḥimār fa-lā tarā / li-dhī kabratin minhum 'alā nāshi'in faḍlan* ('equals like the teeth of a donkey, and you will not see / any preference given to the elderly among them over the young'), *Sharḥ dīwān Kuthayyir 'Azza*, ed. H. Pérès (Paris-Algiers, 1930), vol. 2, p. 18; variants in *Lisān al-'arab*, vol. 14, p. 409; al-Maydānī, *Majma' al-amthāl*, vol. 1, p. 463; al-Rāghib al-Iṣfahānī, *Muḥāḍarāt al-udabā'*, vol. 1, p. 339; Ibn Qutayba, *'Uyūn al-akhbār* (Cairo, 1925–30), vol. 2, *K. al-ṭabā'i'*, p. 2 (without attribution).

730)[31] suggests that it was already in circulation by the beginning of the second/eighth century. In both these cases, it is associated with a failure to recognise the preference due to age and seniority and thus it seems likely that, unlike its positive counterpart, it was used not by advocates of egalitarianism but in the context of tribal boasting contests.

Another proverbial saying cited in connexion with the moral and social aspects of the human condition, *al-nās akhyāf* ('men are of various conditions'),[32] explicitly draws attention to the differences and inequalities among men. It is sometimes found in the versified form 'al-nāsu akhyāfun wa shattā fī'l-shiyam / fa kulluhum yajma'uhum baytu'l-adam' ('men are of various sorts and unlike in nature, but the house of skin unites them all').[33] This proverb appears in the writings of 'Abd al-Ḥamīd and must therefore have been in circulation by the later Umayyad period.[34] All the commentators agree that the proverb refers to people's moral characteristics (*aklāq*);[35] for al-'Askarī, it also refers to their inherited merit (*aḥsāb*), and thus suggests the social esteem in which they are held as well.[36] In association with this axiom, several authors adduce the saying 'lā yazāl al-nās bi-khayr mā tabāyanū fa-idhā 'stawaw halakū' ('men will not cease to prosper as long as they differ; if they become alike, they will perish').[37] Here the prosperity in question is again conceived of in both moral and social terms. Some authors explain that, since wickedness is what predominates in people, if everyone were alike, all men would be wicked.[38] Other writers concentrate on the proverb's social implications: Ibn Qutayba paraphrases it by writing that 'men will not cease to prosper as long as there are men of nobility and excellence (*ashrāf wa akhyār*) among them';[39] al-Zamakhsharī (467–538/1075–1144) records a variant

[31] *Shabābuhum wa shaybuhum sawā'un / wa hum fī'l-lu'm asnān al-ḥimār* ('Their young and old are equal, / and they are [like] a donkey's teeth in baseness'), al-'Askarī, *Jamharat al-amthāl*, vol. 1, p. 523. Ibn Manẓūr also records another verse in which al-Farazdaq uses the donkey proverb (*Lisan al-'arab*, vol. 14, p. 409).

[32] Abū 'Ubayd, *K. al-amthāl*, p. 133; Ibn 'Abd Rabbihi *al-'Iqd al-farīd*, vol. 9, p. 65; al-'Askarī, *Jamharat al-amthāl*, vol. 2, p. 302; al-Maydānī, *Majma' al-amthāl*, vol. 2, p. 397; al-Zamakhsharī, *al-Mustaqṣā fī amthāl al-'arab* (Hyderabad), vol. 1 (1381/1962), p. 351. The metaphor is derived from *akhyaf*, the term for a horse with one blue eye and one black one.

[33] Al-'Askarī, *Jamharat al-amthāl*, vol. 2, p. 303; Ibn Manẓūr *Lisān al-'arab*, vol. 12, p. 13, where *Ādam* and *al-arḍ* are listed as alternatives for *adam*. Variants appear in Abū 'Ubayd, *K. al-amthāl*, p. 132; al-Maydānī, *Majma' al-amthāl*, vol. 2, p. 382 (first *miṣrā'* only); Ibn Qutayba, *'Uyūn al-akhbār*, vol. 2, *Kitāb al-ṭabā'i'*, p. 2; Ibn 'Abd Rabbihi, *al-'Iqd al-farīd*, vol. 9, p. 65 (first *miṣrā'* only).

[34] I. 'Abbās, *'Abd al-Ḥamīd ibn Yaḥyā al-Kātib*, p. 279.

[35] Abū 'Ubayd, *K. al-amthāl*, p. 133; al-Maydānī *Majma' al-mathāl*, vol. 2, p. 397; Ibn 'Abd Rabbihi, *al-'Iqd al-farīd*, vol. 9, p. 65.

[36] *Jamharat al-amthāl*, vol. 2, p. 302. The proverb was also adduced with explicit reference to social differences; see the observation attributed to Ṣa'ṣa'a b. Ṣūḥān below.

[37] Abū 'Ubayd, *K. al-amthāl*, p. 132; Ibn Qutayba, *'Uyūn al-akhbār*, vol. 2, *Kitāb al-ṭabā'i'*, p. 2; Ibn 'Abd Rabbihi, *al-'Iqd al-farīd*, vol. 9, pp. 64–65; al-Maydānī, *Majma' al-amthāl*, vol. 2, p. 390; al-Jāḥiẓ, *Kitāb al-nisā'*, *Rasā'il*, vol. 3, p. 149 (variant).

[38] Abū 'Ubayd, *K. al-amthāl*, p. 132; al-'Askarī, *Jamharat al-amthāl*, vol. 2, p. 302; Ibn Manẓūr, *Lisān al-'arab*, vol. 14, p. 409.

[39] Quoted in Ibn 'Abd Rabbihi, *al-'Iqd al-farīd*, vol. 12, p. 182.

according to which men will prosper as long as they differ in station (*rutab*);[40] for al-Maydānī, the aphorism refers to the existence of leaders and those who follow them (*ra'īs* and *mar'ūs*);[41] and al-Rāghib al-Iṣfahānī uses it to justify social inequalities in religious terms.[42]

Two further proverbs, widely regarded as 'Prophetic', echo the cynical view of human moral propensities evident in some of the commentary noted above. The first, 'All of you are the sons of Adam, like the surface of a full bucket (*kullukum banū ādam ṭaff al-ṣāʿ*)', is sometimes considered part of Muḥammad's speech on the occasion of his farewell pilgrimage, and is associated primarily with ethnic egalitarianism.[43] The second, 'People are like a hundred camels among which there is no she-camel fit to be saddled (*al-nās ka-ibilin mi'atin lā tajidu fīhā rāḥila*)', is widely attested in the standard collections of *ḥadīth*.[44] These aphorisms are generally interpreted by the classical writers to mean that although human beings are beyond number, human frailty is such that very few people can be considered good.[45] Al-Yaʿqūbī (d. 284/897), Abū'l-Shaykh al-Iṣfahānī (d. 369/979) and al-ʿAskarī combine one or both of these sayings with the *ḥadīth*, 'none of you has any excellence over another, except in piety', and thus emphasise the equality of all men before God. Al-ʿAskarī understands both sayings in the context of the tribal group feeling (*ʿaṣabiyya*) prevalent at the time of the Prophet's mission when, he notes, human lives were not valued equally, since blood-money was exacted according to the standing of the family; in these *ḥadīth*, the Prophet taught his followers that no individual possessed any superiority over others in terms of religious regulations. Al-ʿAskarī also notes that if they were taken literally, these *ḥadīth* would annul the concept of superiority in worldly matters, such that there would be no distinction between the noble and the less noble (*sharīf* and *mashrūf*), nor between a leader and a follower (*sayyid* and *masūd*); thus

40 *Al-Mustaqṣā*, vol. 1, p. 351. 41 *Majmaʿ al-amthāl*, vol. 2, p. 390.

42 *Tafṣīl al-nash'atayn wa taḥṣīl al-saʿādatayn*, ed. ʿAbd al-Majīd al-Najjār (Beirut, 1408/1988), p. 114, and *K. al-dharīʿa ilā makārim al-sharīʿa* (Beirut, 1400/1980), p. 264. For a discussion of the passages in which al-Rāghib invokes this saying, see ch. 6.

43 According to al-Yaʿqūbī, the Prophet said, 'People are equal in Islam; people are equal like the surface of a full bucket in terms of their common descent from Adam and Eve; the Arab has no superiority over the non-Arab, nor the non-Arab over the Arab, except in piety to God' (*Ta'rīkh al-Yaʿqūbī* (Beirut, n.d.), vol. 2, p. 110; and see Goldziher, *Muslim Studies*, vol. 1, p. 72, n. 4). See also Ibn Ḥanbal, *Musnad* (Beirut, n.d.), vol. 4, pp. 145, 158; al-ʿAskarī, *Jamharat al-amthāl*, vol. 1, p. 523; Abū'l-Shaykh al-Iṣfahānī, *Kitāb al-amthāl*, pp. 81–82, 96; Ibn al-Athīr, *al-Nihāya fī gharīb al-ḥadīth* (Cairo, n.d.), vol. 3, p. 44.

44 Al-Bukhārī, *al-Jāmiʿ al-ṣaḥīḥ* (Cairo, n.d.), vol. 8, *riqāq*, p. 130; Muslim, *al-Jāmiʿ al-ṣaḥīḥ* (Beirut, n.d.), vol. 6, *faḍā'il al-ṣaḥāba*, p. 192; Ibn Ḥanbal, *Musnad*, vol. 2, pp. 7, 44, 70, 88, 109, 121–3, 139; Ibn Māja, *Sunan*, ed. M. Fu'ād ʿAbd al-Bāqī (Cairo), vol. 2 (1373/1954), *fitan*, ch. 16, p. 1321, no. 3990; al-Maydānī, *Majmaʿ al-amthāl*, vol. 2, p. 390 (for *wāḥila* read *rāḥila*); alʿAskarī, *Jamharat al-amthāl*, vol. 1, p. 523; Abū'l-Shaykh al-Iṣfahānī, *Kitāb al-amthāl*, pp. 81–82, 96; al-Gharawī, *al-Amthāl al-nabawiyya*, vol. 2, p. 302.

45 A similar view of human nature is implied in the following verse: 'You see people as equals when they are sitting together; / But there are bad persons among them, just as there are bad dirhams', (Ibn Manẓūr, *Lisān al-ʿarab*, vol. 14, p. 14 (attributed to al-Liḥyānī); Ibn Qutayba, *ʿUyūn al-akhbār*, vol. 2, *Kitāb al-ṭabāʾiʿ*, p. 3 (unattributed)).

he assumes that they should not be taken in this sense, since they would then contradict other well-known Prophetic *ḥadīth* in which these differing degrees of social status are taken for granted.[46] Al-ʿAskarī, then, was aware of the egalitarian possibilities of these texts. So was al-Sarakhsī who, unlike al-ʿAskarī, was quite happy to take the two *ḥadīth* in their literal sense, and to see in them an indication of ethnic equality (*musāwāt*), for he writes, 'superiority is in deeds; he who is slow in his actions will not be made faster by his lineage'.[47]

The testimony of the classical writers thus points towards primarily a moral, and secondarily an ethnic and social understanding of these Arabic aphorisms. Probably the most powerfully egalitarian of these examples is the phrase *sawā' ka-asnān al-mushṭ*, the force of which was preserved and intensified by its later placement in the Prophet's mouth. The satirical *sawāsiya ka-asnān al-ḥimār* was used only for purposes of ridicule and never to express an egalitarian ideal. *Al-nās akhyāf*, which clearly accentuates human diversity, seems from its uses in the classical literature to have carried both a moral and an ethnic and social significance. The maxims *kullukum banū ādam ṭaff al-ṣāʿ* and *al-nās ka-ibilin mi'atin lā tajidu fīhā rāḥila* imply a cynical view of men's moral worth, but they are invested with piety through their frequent attribution to the Prophet, and they thus become possible proof-texts for an egalitarian social ideal. Any of these proverbial sayings could be combined or versified in ways that altered their meanings. *Al-nās akhyāf*, for example, when combined in a line of poetry with the saying *fa-kulluhum yajmaʿuhum bayt al-adam*, conveys the sense that although people are of many kinds, they are all essentially alike, since all share the same origin and the same fate.

Prophetic *ḥadīth*

In the examples cited in the previous section, when a proverb was attributed to the Prophet it tended to become explicitly egalitarian, in an ethnic or a social sense or both. If one looks at the larger corpus of *ḥadīth* literature, however, egalitarian assertions are scarcely more in evidence than acknowledgements of differences among people. This suggests, not surprisingly, that the Prophet came to be regarded as a desirable authority for holders of egalitarian and hierarchical ideals alike. All four of the areas of concern mentioned earlier in this chapter – religious, tribal, ethnic and social – are represented in the reports.

Some anthologists, in discussions of the good and bad aspects of genealogical rivalry, have the Prophet and his relatives both exhibiting tribal pride and deploring it.[48] Certain *ḥadīth* insist, in tribal terms, on the Prophet's high

46 Al-ʿAskarī, *Jamharat al-amthāl*, vol. 1, pp. 523–24. 47 *Al-Mabsūṭ*, vol. 5, p. 23.
48 Ibrāhīm b. Muḥammad al-Bayhaqī, *al-Maḥāsin wa'l-masāwī* (Beirut, 1380/1960), pp. 75ff; pseudo-Jāḥiẓ, *al-Maḥāsin wa'l-aḍdād* (Beirut, n.d.), pp. 106ff.

status (*anā sayyid walad Ādam wa lā fakhr* ('I am the lord of Adam's offspring, but this is no reason to boast');[49] *khayr al-bashar Ādam wa khayr al-ʿarab Muḥammad* ('Adam is the best of men, Muḥammad is the best of the Arabs . . .')),[50] and even though the continuation of these examples makes it clear that it is ostensibly spiritual status that is meant, they are invoked by some authors as evidence of the excellence of genealogical rivalry.[51] Another tradition sometimes adduced in this connexion is one in which the Prophet displays pride in his own ancestry as well as sensitivity to tribal slights. According to this *ḥadīth*, which reflects ʿAbbāsid interests, the Prophet's uncle al-ʿAbbās overheard certain members of Quraysh comparing the Prophet's position among his people to that of a date-palm growing in a pile of rubbish. Al-ʿAbbās passed this on to the Prophet, who was infuriated, sought the offenders out and asked them, 'Who am I?' 'The Messenger of God.' 'I am Muḥammad, the son of ʿAbd Allāh, the son of ʿAbd al-Muṭṭalib. God brought the created world into being and made me the best of his creatures. Then he divided his creatures (of whom I am one) into two sections (*jaʿala al-khalq . . . firqatayn*), and he placed me in the better of the two sections. Then he made them into peoples (*jaʿalahum shuʿūban*), and he placed me among the best people in his creation. Then he made them into families (*jaʿalahum buyūtan*), and he placed me in the best family among them. So I am the best of you in family and ancestry.' Then he asked al-ʿAbbās to stand to his right and Saʿd to his left, and challenged any one of his detractors to present such a pair of paternal and maternal uncles.[52] This *ḥadīth* is followed in some anthologies by lengthy accounts of contests among various Umayyads and Hāshimites over their respective claims to nobility; despite their differences, those on both sides are said to conceive of nobility in terms of the qualities

[49] Ibn Ḥanbal, *Musnad*, vol. 1, pp. 5, 281, 295; vol. 3, pp. 2, 144; vol. 5, pp. 137, 138, 293; M. b. ʿĪsā al-Tirmidhī, *al-Jāmiʿ al-ṣaḥīḥ*, ed. ʿAbd al-Raḥmān Muḥammad ʿUthmān (Medina, n.d.), vol. 4, *tafsīr al-Qurʾān*, p. 370, no. 5156; vol. 5, *manāqib*, p. 345, no. 3689; Ibn Māja, *Sunan*, vol. 2, *zuhd*, ch. 37, p. 1440, no. 4308.

[50] Several other *ḥadīth* present the Prophet as God's final choice in a progressively selective list (e.g. the Arabs, Muḍar, Quraysh, Hāshim, Muḥammad); al-Tirmidhī, *Ṣaḥīḥ*, vol. 5, *manāqib*, p. 343, no. 3684; p. 345, no, 3687; ʿAlī b. ʿAbd al-Malik al-Muttaqī al-Hindī, *Kanz al-ʿummāl fī sunan al-aqwāl wa'l-afʿāl* (Aleppo 1969–78), vol. 12, p. 43, no. 33918; p. 45, no. 33926; pp. 45–46, no. 33927. See also the examples pointing to the excellence of Quraysh cited in R. al-Sayyid, 'al-Khilāfa wa'l-mulk: Dirāsa fī'l-ru'ya al-umawiyya lil-salṭa', in *Proceedings of the Fourth International Conference on the History of Bilād al-Shām during the Umayyad Period*, ed. M.ʿA. al-Bakhīt (Amman, 1989), pp. 99–100.

[51] Al-Bayhaqī, *al-Maḥāsin wa'l-masāwī*, p. 75; al-Jāḥiẓ, *al-Maḥāsin wa'l-aḍdād*, p. 106.

[52] Al-Bayhaqī, *al-Maḥāsin wa'l-masāwī*, p. 76; al-Jāḥiẓ, *al-Maḥāsin wa'l-aḍdād*, pp. 106–107; see also al-Tirmidhī, *Ṣaḥīḥ*, vol. 5, *manāqib*, pp. 243–244, nos. 3685, 3686; Ibn Ḥanbal, *Musnad*, vol. 4, pp. 165–166, where the reference to al-ʿAbbās does not occur, and Ibn Manẓūr, *Lisān al-ʿarab*, vol. 15, p. 213; cf. Ibn ʿAbd Rabbihi, *al-ʿIqd al-farīd*, vol. 12, p. 13, for a shorter version of the assertion, without the involvement of any uncles. This *ḥadīth* is reminiscent of other (non-Prophetic) tribal claims (see Goldziher, *Muslim Studies*, vol. 1, p. 15). Other *ḥadīth* in which the Prophet discusses genealogies and often elevates Quraysh over other tribes appear in the *K. amthāl al-ḥadīth* of al-Ḥasan b. ʿAbd al-Raḥmān al-Rāmhurmuzī (d. 360/971), ed. Amatulkarim Qureshi (Hyderabad, 1388/1968), pp. 148ff.

and achievements of their fathers and relatives.[53] Needless to say, these contests are invariably won by the Hāshimite party, sometimes thanks to divine intervention.[54]

Furthermore, it is clear that the existence of the egalitarian Qur'ānic verse 49:13 generated a large number of *ḥadīth*, and that these *ḥadīth* reflect differences of opinion on the verse's interpretation. Few writers concerned with the issues of similarity and difference, equality and inequality felt they could afford to ignore this verse, and they availed themselves of *ḥadīth* that restated the Qur'ānic text, reinforced its egalitarian message, applied it to the interests of particular social groups, qualified it, or contradicted it. A large number of traditions use the nobility–piety equation to deny explicitly the significance of old tribal values (for example, 'A man's nobility is his piety, his manliness (*muruwwa*) is his intellect, his inherited merit (*ḥasab*) his character'),[55] and especially to deny the importance of genealogy. According to one *ḥadīth*, God will have it proclaimed at the Day of Judgement that he had established a genealogy (*nasab*) based on piety, but that human beings had insisted on claiming that one lineage was superior to another; on that day God will abolish tribal lineage once and for all, and will establish his own *nasab*.[56] These examples appear to have primarily a tribal or ethnic relevance. They may

[53] Al-Bayhaqī, *al-Maḥāsin wa'l-masāwī*, pp. 78ff; al-Jāḥiẓ, *al-Mahāṣin wa'l-aḍdād*, pp. 108ff. On these competitions, said to have been held at the courts of various 'Abbāsid caliphs, see Goldziher, *Muslim Studies*, vol. 1, pp. 58–59, 85, and C.E. Bosworth, *Al-Maqrīzī's "Book of Contention and Strife Concerning the Relations between the Banū Umayya and the Banū Hāshim"* (Manchester, 1980), pp. 12ff.

[54] For instance, when 'Abd al-Malik was singing the praises of the Banū Umayya to 'Alī b. 'Abd Allāh b. 'Abbās, he was reportedly interrupted by the *adhān* (al-Bayhaqī, *al-Maḥāsin wa'l-masāwī*, pp. 98–99; al-Jāḥiẓ, *al-Maḥāsin wa'l-aḍdād*, p. 124).

[55] *Musnad*, vol. 2, p. 365; *Kanz al-'ummāl*, vol. 3, p. 94, no. 5648; *Lisān al-'arab*, vol. 1, p. 311. The many comparable *ḥadīth* include 'There is no intellect like forethought (*tadbīr*), no piety (*wara'*) like abstinence, and no *ḥasab* like good character' (Ibn Māja, *Sunan*, vol. 2, ch. 24, *zuhd*, p. 1410, no. 4218; M. b. 'Alī Ibn Bābawayh, *Man lā yaḥḍuruhu al-faqīh*, ed. al-Sayyid Ḥasan al-Mūsawī (Najaf 1377–8/1957), vol. 4, p. 270; Aḥmad b. Muḥammad al-Barqī, *Kitāb al-maḥāsin* (Najaf, 1384/1964) p. 13 [said to have been addressed to 'Alī]); 'A man's nobility is his religion, his manliness (*muruwwa*) is his intellect, and his inherited merit his actions' (M. b. al-Ḥasan Ibn Ḥamdūn, *al-Tadhkira al-Ḥamdūniyya*, ed. I. 'Abbās (Beirut), vol. 2 (1984), p. 172, no. 383); 'The believer's nobility is his piety, his inherited merit is his religion, his manliness is his good character', attributed to 'Umar (Mālik, *al-Muwaṭṭa'*, ed. M.F. 'Abd al-Bāqī (Cairo, 1370/1951), vol. 2, *jihād*, p. 463, no. 35; Goldziher, *Muslim Studies*, vol. 1, p. 71, n. 4); al-Bukhārī, *Ṣaḥīḥ*, vol. 6, *tafsīr sūrat Yūsuf*, p. 95. Cf. 'Umar's remarks to a boastful man: 'If you have religion, you have high birth; if you have intellect, you have *muruwwa*; if you have knowledge, you have nobility; otherwise, you are but an ass' (*Muḥāḍarāt al-udabā'*, vol. 1, p. 340; see also a similar remark in the *K. al-aghānī*, cited in Goldziher, *Muslim Studies*, vol. 1, p. 61).

[56] Al-Ṭabarānī, *al-Mu'jam al-ṣaghīr*, ed. 'Abd al-Raḥmān Muḥammad 'Uthmān (Cairo, 1388/1968), vol. 1, p. 230; cited in Kister and Plessner, 'Notes on Caskel's Ǧamharat an-nasab', p. 53. Other traditions in which the importance of genealogy is denied appear in Sulaymān b. al-Ash'ath al-Sijistānī, Abū Dā'ūd, *Sunan*, ed. M. Muḥyī'l-Dīn 'Abd al-Ḥamīd (Cairo, 1935), vol. 4, *adab*, p. 331, no. 5116; Ibn Ḥanbal, *Musnad*, vol. 1, p. 301; al-Muttaqī al-Hindī, *Kanz al-'ummāl*, vol. 3, p. 93, nos. 5643, 5644, 5645; p. 94, no. 5651; p. 96, nos. 5657, 5659; p. 97, nos. 5661, 5662; al-Bayhaqī, *al-Maḥāsin wa'l-masāwī*, pp. 100–101; al-Jāḥiẓ, *al-Maḥāsin wa'l-aḍdād*, pp. 125–26.

reflect inter-Arab disagreements or *shuʿūbī* concerns, and could perhaps have been generated in the ethnically mixed conditions of the early second/eighth-century Iraqi cities, where they might have expressed the social and political grievances of both Arabs and non-Arabs in an increasingly stratified environment. Other traditions, also egalitarian in nature and sometimes linked to Muḥammad's words on the occasion of his farewell pilgrimage, specifically address the interests of clients and converts by announcing the equality of Arabs and non-Arabs.[57]

A significant quantity of *ḥadīth* draw on the Qur'ānic nobility–piety equation to argue for the precedence of particular social groups. Some use it to emphasise the excellence of the *ʿulamā'*, and date perhaps from the period in which the latter's influence and prestige were not yet fully established.[58] A rather large number appear to reflect the aspirations of affluent, but not particularly high-born, Muslims who felt entitled to social recognition on the grounds of their wealth.[59] *Ḥadīth* of this type add various new equations to the Qur'ānic association of *karam* and *taqwā*. Among the most common examples are the several variants of the well-known *ḥadīth* which runs *al-ḥasab al-māl wa'l-karam al-taqwā* ('merit is in wealth, and nobility is in piety'),[60] including 'High birth is in piety, nobility is in modesty, and certainty is in wealth';[61] 'The nobility of this world is in riches, the nobility of the next world is in piety; you are male and female, your nobility is your riches, your high birth your piety, your inherited merit (*aḥsāb*) your moral characteristics (*akhlāq*), your genealogies your deeds';[62] 'God loves the man who is pious, rich and discrete (*khafī*).'[63] All of these examples reject the significance of noble birth and associate wealth with piety. They may reflect the social aspirations of those well-to-do commercial groups who were in part responsible for the elaboration of the law in the Iraqi towns, and who may have been particularly associated with the

57 See n. 43; al-Muttaqī al-Hindī, *Kanz al-ʿummāl*, vol. 3, p. 95, nos. 5652, 5655.

58 *Kanz al-ʿummāl*, vol. 3, p. 95, nos. 5653, 5654.

59 Some traditions of this kind refer to wealth attained through the acquisition of land (M.J. Kister, 'Land Property and *jihād*', *JESHO* 34 (1991), pp. 270–311); many refer to wealth acquired through trade. Although *ḥadīth* in favour of many occupations can be found, those that elevate commerce are often particularly extravagant in their praise (al-Muttaqī al-Hindī, *Kanz al-ʿummāl*, vol. 4, p. 7, nos. 9216, 9217, 9218; p. 8, no. 9219; p. 11, nos. 9244, 9245, 9246; p. 30, nos. 9340, 9341; al-Ghazālī, *Iḥyā' ʿulūm al-dīn* (Cairo), vol. 2, pp. 63f; cf. H. Ritter 'Ein arabisches Handbuch der Handelswissenschaft', *Der Islam* 7 (1917), pp. 28–29; R. Brunschvig, 'Métiers vils en Islam', *Études d'islamologie* (Paris, 1976), vol. 1, p. 149).

60 Al-Tirmidhī, *Ṣaḥīḥ*, vol. 5, *tafsīr sūrat al-ḥujarāt*, p. 65, no. 3325; Ibn Māja, *Sunan*, vol. 2, *zuhd*, ch. 14, p. 1410, no. 4219; *Musnad*, vol. 5, p. 10; al-Muttaqī al-Hindī, *Kanz al-ʿummāl*, vol. 3, p. 92, no. 5634; p. 94, no. 5649; p. 241, no. 6342; Ibn Manẓūr, *Lisān al-ʿarab*, vol. 1, p. 310; cf. the tradition attributed to ʿAbd Allāh b. ʿAbbās, in *al-ʿIqd al-farīd*, vol. 8, p. 145. On the use of the tradition *al-ḥasab al-māl wa'l-karam al-taqwā* in discussions of *kafā'a*, see Ibn Ḥajar, *Fatḥ al-bārī bi-sharḥ al-Bukhārī* (Cairo, 1378/1959), vol. 11, p. 37.

61 Al-Muttaqī al-Hindī, *Kanz al-ʿummāl*, vol. 3, p. 92, no. 5637.

62 *Kanz al-ʿummāl*, vol. 3, p. 94, no. 5650.

63 *Kanz al-ʿummāl*, vol. 3, p. 91, no. 5630; p. 96, no. 5656. See also the reports attributed to the Prophet and ʿUmar in *al-ʿIqd al-farīd*, vol. 8, p. 144.

strength of the populist and egalitarian strands of the Islamic tradition. Such *ḥadīth* may have been generated in order to counter reports of an ascetic orientation, in which wealth in general and commerce in particular were discouraged or despised: 'O people! Make piety your trade, and your sustenance will come to you without goods or commerce';[64] 'riches derive not from an abundance of possessions; [true] riches are the riches of the soul';[65] 'merchants are wicked (*al-tājir fājir*)'.[66] Eventually, although the world-affirming strain of the former group of traditions would in many contexts predominate over the ascetic strain of the latter, both would find a place in mainstream Islamic culture, and this is reflected in the fact that anthologists frequently included one section devoted to the praiseworthy aspects of wealth, and another to its faults.[67]

While most of the examples given above take the Qur'ānic piety clause as the base for an egalitarian, or at least an open social ideal, others blatantly attach to it a reassertion of the value of tribal nobility.[68] Several *ḥadīth* assert that the best of men in the Jāhiliyya are also the best in Islam ('al-nās maʿādin khiyāruhum fī'l-jāhiliyya khiyāruhum fī'l-islām' ('Men are sources [to be mined for their qualities]; the best of them in the Jāhiliyya are the best of them in Islam')), to which they usually (although not invariably) add the qualifying phrase 'if they possess religious understanding (*idhā faquhū*)'.[69] A similar recognition of differences in worldly status, also expressed in largely tribal terms and coupled with an assertion of the greater ultimate importance of piety and faith, appears in a remark attributed to Ibn ʿAbbās (d. c. 68/687–688): '[Men] differ in excellence in this world with respect to their nobility (*sharaf*), families (*buyūtāt*),

[64] Al-Muttaqī al-Hindī, *Kanz al-ʿummāl*, vol. 3, p. 98, no. 5666; Abū'l-Shaykh al-Iṣfahānī, *K. al-amthāl*, p. 36.

[65] Ibn Ḥajar al-ʿAsqalānī, *Fatḥ al-bārī*, vol. 14, pp. 49–50; Ibn Māja, *Sunan*, vol. 2, *zuhd*, ch. 9, p. 1386, no. 4137; Ibn Ḥanbal, *Musnad*, vol. 2, p. 438.

[66] Al-Gharawī, *al-Amthāl al-nabawiyya*, vol. 1, pp. 305–306; cf. Ritter, 'Handbuch', p. 28. For variants of this *ḥadīth*, together with others that portray wealth and piety as incompatible, see L. Kinberg, 'Compromise of Commerce. A Study of Early Traditions Concerning Poverty and Wealth', *Der Islam* 66 (1989), pp. 193–212, especially p. 201. It is interesting to note that Salmān, echoing a traditional Persian prejudice, is reported to have encouraged people to seek a virtuous death in pilgrimage, war or the mosque, rather than as merchants and deceivers (al-Ghazālī, *Iḥyā'*, vol. 2, p. 65; Ritter, 'Handbuch', p. 32). See also Kister, 'Land Property', pp. 280–281, for the tradition according to which the Prophet describes merchants and tillers of the soil as the worst of people, and claims to have been sent as a messenger of mercy and war.

[67] Like social egalitarianism, however, the ascetic strain underwent a certain taming as it was adopted into the mainstream; see ch. 4.

[68] See for example al-Muttaqī al-Hindī, *Kanz al-ʿummāl*, vol. 3, p. 92, nos. 5633, 5636.

[69] Ibn Ḥanbal always cites the *ḥadīth* with the qualifying final clause (*Musnad*, vol. 2, pp. 257, 260, 391, 438, 485, 498, 525, 539; vol. 3, p. 367); al-Bukhārī includes it in *Ṣaḥīḥ*, vol. 4, *manāqib*, p. 217, and in vol. 6, *tafsīr sūrat Yūsuf*, p. 95, but it does not appear in vol. 4, *manāqib*, p. 238; it appears in Muslim, *Ṣaḥīḥ*, vol. 6, *faḍā'il al-ṣaḥāba*, p. 181; al-Wāqidī adds the phrase *idhā faquhū fī'l-dīn* (*Kitāb al-maghāzī*, ed. M. Jones (London), vol. 2 (1966), p. 547); Abū'l-Shaykh al-Iṣfahānī lists the *ḥadīth* in three versions, only one of which adds the qualifier *idhā faquhū* (*K. al-amthāl*, p. 106). The *ḥadīth* sometimes includes the clause *ka-maʿādin al-dhahab wa'l-fiḍḍa*, 'like deposits of gold and silver' (Ibn Ḥanbal, *Musnad*, vol. 2, p. 539), a phrase which is interpreted by Abū'l-Futūḥ al-Rāzī to refer to human differences (*Rawḥ al-jinān*, vol. 3, p. 292).

ranks of authority (*imārāt*), wealth,[70] attractiveness, stature (*hay'a*) and eloquence. In terms of the world to come, they differ in excellence with regard to their piety and their religious conviction. For the most pious of them is the most convinced, the purest in his actions, and the highest in rank (*daraja*).'[71]

Another cluster of *ḥadīth* acknowledges worldly criteria for social status and ignores the piety verse altogether. According to one very widely quoted example, which is explicitly concerned with social rather than tribal or ethnic differences, the Prophet recommended that 'When the noble member of a group comes to you, honour him (*idhā atākum karīmu qawmin fa-'akrimūhu*).'[72] This *ḥadīth* is said to have been uttered by the Prophet to Qays b. 'Āṣim (d. 47/667) when he came to Medina with the Tamīmī delegation.[73] It certainly lent itself to ethnic struggles, and was accordingly employed by Ibn Qutayba in his refutation of the *shu'ūbiyya*.[74] But al-'Āmirī adduces the same report in his discussion of the relativity of social rank, where he points out that there is always someone more noble, or more base, than oneself.[75] The *ḥadīth* is also cited in 584/1188–1189 by Afḍal al-Dīn Kirmānī as an authority for his recommendation that men of nobility, great families and knowledge be granted the social position and deference due to them, lest they become disaffected.[76] In an example that might have ethnic and social significance, the Prophet is said to have paid his respects to a Zoroastrian; when his Companions informed him of the identity of the man whom he had greeted, he announced that Gabriel himself had instructed him to honour the noble among every people.[77] In the classical period, then, it seems clear that this *ḥadīth* was understood to imply respect for social hierarchy. A similar sentiment, also associated with Aristotle and the Iranian monarch Parvīz, appears in the form of a Prophetic proverb as early as Abū 'Ubayd: 'Overlook the offences of men of good qualities (*aqīlū dhawī'l-hay'āt 'atharātihim*).'[78] Again,

70 Following Ps.-Jāḥiẓ, *ghinan*, *al-Maḥāsin wa'-aḍdād*, p. 125.

71 Al-Jāḥiẓ, *al-Maḥāsin wa'l-aḍdād*, p. 125; al-Bayhaqī, *al-Maḥāsin wa'l-masāwī*, p. 102.

72 Ibn Māja, *Sunan*, vol. 2, *adab*, ch. 19, p. 1223, no. 3712; Ibn Ḥanbal, *Musnad*, vol. 3, p. 500; vol. 5, p. 224; Abū'l-Shaykh al-Iṣfahānī, *K. al-amthāl*, pp. 85–86; al-Gharawī, *al-Amthāl al-nabawiyya*, vol. 1, p. 61; al-Kulīnī, *al-Kāfī* (Tehran), vol. 2 (1381/1961), p. 659; cf. al-Dārimī, *Sunan*, ed. al-Sayyid 'Abd Allāh Hāshim Yamānī al-Madanī (Medina, 1386/1966), vol. 1, *muqaddima*, ch. 14, p. 39, no. 82.

73 The Prophet's recognition of Qays' special status is also reflected in his alleged reference to him as *sayyid ahl al-wabar* ('chief of the nomad people'); Ibn 'Abd Rabbihi, *al-'Iqd al-farīd*, vol. 12, p. 182; M.J. Kister, 'Ḳays b. 'Āṣim', *EI*2.

74 As cited in Ibn 'Abd Rabbihi, *al-'Iqd al-farīd*, vol. 12, p. 182. On Ibn Qutayba's refutation, see ch. 4.

75 *Kitāb al-i'lām bi-manāqib al-Islām*, ed. A. Ghorab (Cairo, 1387/1967), p. 165.

76 *'Iqd al-'ulā lil-mawqif al-a'lā* (Tehran, 1311), p. 58.

77 Al-Rāghib al-Iṣfahānī, *Muḥāḍarāt al-udabā'*, vol. 1, p. 349. On the etiquette of greeting non-Muslims, see M.J. Kister, '"Do not assimilate yourselves . . ." *Lā tashabbahū*', *JSAI* 12 (1989), pp. 325ff.

78 Al-Bukhārī, *Ṣaḥīḥ*, vol. 1, *adab*, p. 552; Abū Dā'ūd, *Sunan*, vol. 4, *ḥudūd*, p. 133, no. 4375 (*aqīlū dhawī al-hay'āt 'atharātihim illā al-ḥudūd*); Ibn Ḥanbal, *Musnad*, vol. 6, p. 181; 'Alī b. al-Ḥusayn al-Mas'ūdī, *Murūj al-dhahab* (Beirut, 1404/1984), vol. 2, p. 296 (*aqīlū 'atharāt al-kirām*); Abū 'Ubayd, *K. al-amthāl*, p. 52; Abū'l-Shaykh al-Iṣfahānī, *K. al-amthāl*, pp. 76–77; al-Maydānī, *Majma' al-amthāl*, vol. 2, p. 123; cf. al-Gharawī, *al-Amthāl al-nabawiyya*, vol. 1,

Ibn Qutayba adduces this *ḥadīth* as proof of divine sanction for ethnic inequalities,[79] but al-Ṭurṭūshī clearly sees in this maxim an endorsement of social hierarchy as he goes on to add, 'Those who transgress should be requited according to the degree of their ranks and the gravity of their crimes.'[80] Recognition of social distinctions is also implied in the report according to which 'Ā'isha, when she encountered a beggar, gave him a small piece of bread, while when she encountered a man of obvious wealth and status, she invited him to sit and eat. When questioned about her behaviour, she reported that the Prophet had said, 'Treat people according to their stations (*anzilū'l-nās manāzilahum*).'[81] A similar acceptance of differences in social status is apparent in the *ḥadīth*, 'Look to those below you, not to those above you, because it is fitting that you should not belittle the bounty of God.'[82]

The *ḥadīth* literature pertaining to difference and equality, then, reflects the great variety of points of view among those who sought the Prophet's authority. In many cases, a *ḥadīth* is built on the most relevant Qur'ānic verse, 49:13, the levelling import of which provided an opportunity for all persons not of high status (whether in a tribal, ethnic or more broadly social context) to lay claim to personal dignity and social esteem. Such *ḥadīth* may be consistent with the Qur'ānic view, or may modify it by adding other principles to the nobility–piety equation; they were used to support arguments for an open society in which mobility was possible, and also to assert the claims to social precedence of the scholarly and commercial groups. Other *ḥadīth*, either by qualifying the egalitarian message of the Qur'ānic verse or without taking it into account, confirm pre-Islamic tribal values, and particularly the importance of noble genealogy. Some of these examples may have been generated in the course of the *shu'ūbī* controversy, but they were also employed to rationalise social hierarchies based on broader principles.

Sayings attributed to 'Alī

A large number of aphorisms attributed to 'Alī b. Abī Ṭālib illustrate a wider use of the opposition between hereditary and meritocratic conceptions of

pp. 154–55. Note also a similar *ḥadīth* which runs, 'Avoid punishing a man of *muruwwa* as long as a *ḥadd* has not been violated' (M. b. Manṣūr Ibn al-Ḥaddād, *al-Jawhar al-nafīs fī siyāsat al-ra'īs*, ed. R. al-Sayyid (Beirut, 1983), p. 117). The variant attributed to Aristotle appears in the *Kitāb al-sa'āda wa'l-is'ād* of al-'Āmirī (ed. M. Minovi (Wiesbaden, 1957), p. 378), and in Kirmānī, *'Iqd al-'ulā*, p. 58. Ibn Qutayba and Ibn 'Abd Rabbihi, citing the *Kitāb al-tāj*, quote Parvīz (Abrawīz) as admonishing his son to be properly solicitous of nobles wronged or down on their luck (*'Uyūn al-akhbār*, vol. 1, p. 15; *al-'Iqd al-farīd*, vol. 1, p. 42); see also a well-known saying ascribed to Anūshīrvān (Ibn al-Ḥaddād, *al-Jawhar al-nafīs*, pp. 74–76). The caliph al-Manṣūr is said to have uttered a similar thought: 'Three kinds of people are deserving of pity: a rich man who has fallen into poverty, a man who was great among his people and has now fallen low, and a learned man made fun of by the ignorant' (al-Ya'qūbī, *Ta'rīkh*, vol. 2, p. 381).

79 *Al'-Iqd al-farīd*, vol. 12, p. 182.

80 Ibn Abī Randaqa al-Ṭurṭūshī, *Sirāj al-mulūk* (Cairo, 1354/1935), p. 153. Cf. Aḥmad b. Maḥmūd al-Jīlī, *Minhāj al-vuzarā' fī'l-naṣīḥa*, ms. AS 2907, f.101b.

81 Abū Dā'ūd, *Sunan*, vol. 4, *adab*, p. 261, no. 4842.

82 Ibn Māja, *Sunan*, vol. 2, *zuhd*, p. 1387, no. 4142.

status. If the Prophetic *ḥadīth* discussed above variously reflect the interests of established élites, the aspirations of the recently successful, and the grievances of those who had neither hereditary claims to social precedence nor new-found wealth, the numerous maxims placed in the mouth of ʿAlī have a distinctly populist flavour. Overwhelmingly, they emphasise the egalitarian ethic and give preference to personal qualities over hereditary ones. They are worded so generally that the context in which they emerged cannot be recovered. Among the many statements of this sort ascribed to ʿAlī are: 'He who boasts of wealth and descent [is mistaken], for only knowledge and personal merit are worthy of pride'; 'He who is without knowledge (*adab*) is without merit (*ḥasab*)';[83] 'There is no merit (*ḥasab*) more effective than knowledge (*adab*)';[84] 'There is no nobility higher than Islam';[85] 'There is no nobility higher than piety';[86] 'The value of each man is that in which he is proficient';[87] 'Men are the sons of that in which they are proficient'; 'Nobility is in learning and culture, and not in origin and lineage';[88] 'The degrees of knowledge are the highest degrees';[89] 'He who is lowly in poverty is great in God's sight';[90] 'The quest for *adab* is better than the quest for gold';[91] 'A man's pride in his excellence is better than his pride in his origins';[92] 'A man's worth lies in his aspiration';[93] 'A man without excellence has no riches';[94] 'Love of wealth and nobility nurtures hypocrisy, just as water nurtures plants';[95] 'With sincerity, a man can reach the stations of the great.'[96] Some of these maxims were already contained in the first extant collection of ʿAlī's purported sayings, the *Mi'at kalima* attributed to al-Jāḥiẓ;[97] several appear in the *khuṭbat al-wasīla* ascribed

83 Al-Kulīnī, *al-Kāfī*, vol. 8, p. 22. 84 Ibn Bābawayh, *Man lā yaḥḍuruhu al-faqīh*, vol. 4, p. 291.

85 Al-Kulīnī, *al-Kāfī*, vol. 8, p. 19; Ibn Bābawayh, *Man lā yaḥḍuruhu al-faqīh*, vol. 4, pp. 276, 290; Rashīd al-Dīn Vaṭvāṭ, *Maṭlūb kull ṭālib min kalām ʿAlī b. Abī Ṭālib*, ed. M.H.L. Fleischer, *Ali's hundert Sprüche* (Leipzig, 1837), p. 19, no. 27.

86 Al-Kulīnī, *al-Kāfī*, vol. 8, p. 19; Vaṭvāṭ, *Maṭlūb kull ṭālib*, p. 19, no. 26.

87 Ibn Bābawayh, *Man lā yaḥḍuruhu al-faqīh*, vol. 4, p. 278, where the maxim appears in ʿAlī's testament to Ibn al-Ḥanafiyya. It also appears, attributed to ʿAlī, in several works by al-Jāḥiẓ, who praises it lavishly for its concision, aptness, eloquence and effectiveness in putting the feeble-minded in their place (*K. fī'l-muʿallimīn* in *Rasā'il*, vol. 3, p. 29; *al-Bayān wa'l-tabyīn*, vol. 2, p. 77); cf. Vaṭvāṭ, *Maṭlūb kull ṭālib*, p. 7, no. 5; p. 120; *al-Tuḥfa al-bahiyya wa'l-ṭurfa al-shahriyya* (Constantinople, 1302), p. 112; and *Jamharat rasā'il al-ʿarab fī ʿuṣūr al-ʿarabiyya al-zāhira*, ed. A. Zakī Ṣafwat (Cairo, 1356/1937), vol. 1, p. 608, with further references.

88 Vaṭvāṭ, *Maṭlūb kull ṭālib*, p. 51, no. 79. 89 *Al-Tuḥfa al-bahiyya*, p. 109.

90 *Al-Tuḥfa al-bahiyya*, p. 109.

91 *Al-Tuḥfa al-bahiyya*, p. 111; cf. Vaṭvāṭ, *Maṭlūb kull ṭālib*, p. 13, no. 17; p. 53, no. 81.

92 *Al-Tuḥfa al-bahiyya*, p. 112. 93 *Al-Tuḥfa al-bahiyya*, p. 113.

94 *Al-Tuḥfa al-bahiyya*, p. 114. See also the similar utterance attributed to the Prophet, n. 65.

95 Naṣīr al-Dīn Ṭūsī, *Akhlāq-i Muḥtashamī* (Tehran, 1339), p. 177.

96 *Al-Tuḥfa al-bahiyya*, p. 114. Similar pious sentiments, also frequently expressed in rhyming prose, are ascribed to the Prophet by Ibn Bābawayh (*Man lā yaḥḍuruhu al-faqīh*, vol. 4, pp. 281–282).

97 Later expanded by al-Āmidī (d. c. 550/1155) into the collection *Ghurar al-ḥikam*, and further augmented after him (cf. E. Kohlberg, 'Āmedī, Abu'l-Fatḥ Nāṣeḥ al-Dīn', *Encyclopaedia Iranica*). On the attribution to al-Jāḥiẓ, see C. Pellat, 'Nouvel essai d'inventaire de l'oeuvre ǧāḥiẓienne', *Arabica* 31 (1984), p. 131. Several of the aphorisms contained in the *Mi'at kalima* appear without attribution in the *K. al-ādāb* of Ibn al-Muʿtazz (247–296/861–908), although by the time al-Ābī wrote in the early fifth/eleventh century, they were regarded as statements of ʿAlī's (I. Kratchkovsky, 'Le *kitāb al-ādāb* d'Ibn al-Muʿtazz', *Le monde oriental* 16 (1924), pp. 62–63).

to ʿAlī as well. When and in what context they first came to be associated with ʿAlī, however, is unknown.[98] The maxims were extremly popular in classical and later *belles-lettres*, and formed the subject of many elaborate commentaries.[99]

It may also be appropriate to include here an anecdote which asserts the equality of Arabs and non-Arabs and which may perhaps have originated in proto-Shīʿī circles in Iraq. It concerns Wāṣil b. ʿAṭāʾ (80–131/700–748), whose pro-ʿAlid sympathies were well known,[100] and the Umayyad governor of Iraq, Khālid al-Qasrī (d. 120/738). The latter asked Wāṣil (a *mawlā*) about his lineage, and Wāṣil replied: 'My lineage is Islam. Whoever neglects Islam forfeits his lineage, whereas whoever upholds it retains his lineage.' Khālid commented '[You have] the face of a slave, but [have spoken] the words of a free [i.e. noble] man.'[101] Here Wāṣil echoes Salmān's reputed reply to ʿUmar, when the latter asked him about his lineage; Salmān described himself as 'Salmān son of Islam'.[102] The same idea occurs in certain examples of Khārijite poetry.[103] Although the original context for the material related to ʿAlī cannot be established with certainty, such aphorisms indicate that ʿAlī, like ʿUmar, came to be regarded in some quarters as a champion of egalitarian and meritocratic values.

Equality in marriage

If the traditions discussed in the preceding sections have lost their context and taken on a general meaning, other reports have retained a specific application. Such reports include, most notably, those that pertain to the issue of marriage equality, or *kafāʾa*. Although all schools consider lack of marriage equality

[98] The strong egalitarian and meritocratic emphasis of these axioms contrasts with the views of society expressed in the letter to Mālik al-Ashtar attributed to ʿAlī in the *Nahj al-balāgha* (see ch. 5). The circumstances in which the two forms of expression arose must therefore have been different, the letter to Mālik almost certainly having been composed later than the maxims, possibly in North Africa (see W. al-Qāḍī, 'An Early Fāṭimid Political Document', *SI* 48 (1978), pp. 95ff). [99] See ch. 5.

[100] S. Stroumsa, 'The Beginnings of the Muʿtazila Reconsidered', *JSAI* 13 (1990), pp. 265–293.

[101] Ibn Ḥamdūn, *al-Tadhkira al-Ḥamdūniyya*, vol. 2, p. 96, no. 192. It is unclear to which tribe Wāṣil was affiliated; see Stroumsa, 'Beginnings of the Muʿtazila', p. 266, n. 4. Opponents of Wāṣil (also *mawālī*) attempted to discredit him by suggesting that he was a weaver by profession; see J. van Ess, *Theologie und Gesellschaft* (Berlin, 1991), vol. 2, pp. 237ff.

[102] Al-Sarakhsī, *Kitāb al-Mahsūṭ*, (Cairo) vol. 5 (1324), p. 23.

[103] For instance, to the Khārijite poet ʿĪsā b. Fātik al-Khaṭṭī are attributed the following verses: 'abī ʾl-islāmu lā aba siwāhu / idhā fakharū bi-Bakrin aw Tamīm / wa mā ḥasabun wa law karumat ʿurūqun / wa lākinna ʾl-taqī huwa ʾl-karīm' ('My father is Islam; I have no other, however others may boast of Bakr or Tamīm; / Nobility of descent does not constitute *ḥasab*; it is the man of piety who is noble') (I. ʿAbbās, *Dīwān shiʿr al-Khawārij* (Beirut, 1402/1982), p. 72, no. 45; I owe this reference to Annie Higgins). See also Goldziher, *Muslim Studies*, vol. 1, p. 130. Elsewhere, the same literary formula is used to rather less pious effect, as in Shihāb al-Dīn M. b. A. al-Ibshīhī, *al-Mustaṭraf fī kull fann mustaẓraf* (Beirut, 1406/1986), vol. 1, p. 56, where a man is said to have made a favourable impression on al-Maʾmūn by identifying himself as 'the son of culture (*adab*)'.

to be grounds for a woman to refuse marriage to a man,[104] both the scope and the application of the requirement for equal status were topics of considerable disagreement. The issue is usually treated in connexion with the question of marriage guardianship (*wilāya*), and it is the role of the guardian or *walī* on which the differences among the jurists seem to depend.[105] Thus the Ḥanafīs, who allow a woman past puberty to contract her own marriage without the assistance of a guardian, have the most stringent requirements for marriage equality,[106] whereas Mālik (93–179/712–795), Aḥmad b. Ḥanbal (164–241/780–855) and al-Shāfiʿī (d. 204/820), who insist on the necessity of a guardian, attach fewer conditions for equality between spouses. The authority extended to the woman to act on her own behalf in the Ḥanafī school is accordingly limited by the rules of marriage equality: she is permitted to contract a marriage that may or may not fulfil these requirements, but in the latter case, her guardians have the right to separate the couple.[107] For al-Shāfiʿī, it is the clear responsibility of a woman's guardians to ensure that she is married according to the requirements for marriage equality. She may be married by any one of those persons eligible to act as her guardian, regardless of whether the others approve of the match, but in the case of a marriage concluded with the woman's consent to a social unequal, it is necessary that all the guardians agree.[108]

On the qualities by which marriage equality is ascertained, all agree on the importance of equality in religion, and a virgin is entitled to refuse marriage to a man who offends against religion. Other factors recognised by some scholars include descent, free status, wealth, absence of physical defects and profession. For Mālik, religion is the only criterion, and a woman who is no longer a virgin (*thayyib*), whose father or guardian refuses to marry her to a man equal to her in religion but of lesser merit (*ḥasab*) and nobility, should be married to him by the authorities.[109] Al-Shāfiʿī assesses equality on the basis of five factors: religion, lineage, profession, free status and lack of defects. Abū Yūsuf (d. 182/798) and al-Shaybānī (d. 189/805) take equality of religion for granted except in cases of extreme indiscretion, such as public drunkenness.[110] Ibn Abī Laylā (74–148/693–765) is said to have recognised the criteria of

104 M. b. A. Ibn Rushd, *Bidāyat al-mujtahid wa nihāyat al-muqtaṣid* (Cairo, 1386/1966), vol. 2, p. 17. 105 Y. Linant de Bellefonds, 'Kafā'a', *EI2*.

106 Ziadeh, 'Equality (*kafā'a*)', pp. 509, 510–514; Goldziher, *Mulim Studies*, vol. 1, pp. 123–125.

107 Al-Sarakhsī, *al-Mabsūṭ*, vol. 5, pp. 25–26; 'Alī b. Aḥmad Ibn Ḥazm, *al-Muḥallā*, ed. A.M. Shākir (Beirut 1969), vol. 9, pp. 455–456; Ibn Rushd, *Bidāyat al-mujtahid*, vol. 2, p. 9; 'Abd al-Wahhāb b. A. al-Shaʿrānī, *al-Mīzān al-kubrā* (Cairo 1940), vol. 2, p. 109. Abū Yūsuf considers a marriage valid if it satisfies *kafā'a* and is approved of subsequently by the *walī* or the *qāḍī*; al-Shaybānī, on the other hand, insists on the *walī*'s approval (Ibn Ḥazm, *al-Muḥallā*, vol. 9, pp. 455–456). 108 Al-Shāfiʿī, *Kitāb al-umm* (Cairo, 1381/1961), vol. 5, p. 15.

109 Saḥnūn b. Saʿīd al-Tanūkhī, *al-Mudawwana al-kubrā* (Cairo), vol. 4 (1323), p. 13; cf. p. 20, where Mālik judges that if a woman's guardian has once given his approval for an unequal marriage that subsequently ends in divorce, he cannot later refuse permission if the woman wishes to be remarried to the man.

110 Al-Sarakhsī, *al-Mabsūṭ*, vol. 5, p. 25; al-Shaʿrānī, *al-Mīzān*, p. 110.

religion, lineage and wealth. For Aḥmad, two teachings are recorded, one of which lists the categories of religion and profession, while the other lists religion, livelihood and wealth.[111] These various opinions are substantiated by different interpretations of the *ḥadīth* 'Marry a woman for her religion, beauty, wealth and merit (*ḥasab*).'[112]

One of the crucial issues at stake in the early phases of the formulation of the law was the question of intermarriage between Arab women and *mawālī*. Mālik, on the basis of 49:13, allowed such marriages;[113] Sufyān al-Thawrī (d. 161/778) is said to have rejected lineage as a criterion for marriage equality, and is considered by some to have regarded Arabs and non-Arabs as equal;[114] and Abū Ḥanīfa (d. 150/767) is said to have insisted that Qurashī women marry Qurashī men, Arab women, Arab men.[115] The idea that Sufyān, an Arab, should have allowed intermarriage while Abū Ḥanīfa, a *mawlā*, did not obviously puzzled al-Sarakhsī, who attributed the strange situation to the exceptional humility of both men.[116]

Mālik, despite his minimal definition of marriage equality and his provision for intermarriage between Arab women and *mawālī*, was not as blind to social differences as he might seem. Again in the context of marriage guardianship, he distinguishes between the woman of social standing and the 'lowly' woman (*danī'a*), a category in which he includes black women, female converts, poor women, *nabaṭī* women and client women. A 'lowly' woman may be married by a neighbour or some other person who is not her guardian, whereas a woman of position (*al-mar'a allatī lahā al-mawḍi'*) who is married by someone other than her guardian should be separated from her husband, unless the marriage is allowed to stand by her guardian or by the authorities.[117] It therefore appears that even a scholar such as Mālik, who was surrounded by a far less diverse population than his contemporaries in Iraq and in some respects sought to put the early Islamic egalitarian ideal into effect in the sphere of marriage, took differences in social standing for granted.

As far as the issue of marriage equality is concerned, there does not appear to be a clear or consistent correlation between political opposition and social egalitarianism. Most notably, the Khārijites do not appear to have extended the

111 Al-Sha'rānī, *al-Mīzān*, pp. 110–111.

112 Ibn Māja, *Sunan*, vol. 1, *nikāḥ*, p. 597, no. 1858; cf. a *ḥadīth* in which only religion is mentioned (al-Kulīnī, *al-Kāfī*, vol. 5, p. 332) and one in which marriage for the sake of wealth and beauty is discouraged (al-Kulīnī, *al-Kāfī*, vol. 5, p. 333; Ibn Bābawayh, *Man lā yaḥḍuruhu al-faqīh*, vol. 3, p. 248). On the importance of this *ḥadīth* (as cited here) for rulings on *kafā'a*, see Ibn Rushd, *Bidāyat al-mujtahid*, vol. 2, pp. 17–18; Ibn Ḥajar, *Fatḥ al-bārī*, vol. 11, pp. 36f.

113 Saḥnūn, *al-Mudawwana*, vol. 4, pp. 13–14.

114 Al-Sarakhsī, *al-Mabsūṭ*, vol. 5, p. 22; Ziadeh, 'Equality (*kafā'a*)', p. 507. This conflicts with Ibn Rushd's assertion that Sufyān did not accept intermarriage between Arab women and *mawālī* (*Bidāyat al-mujtahid*, p. 17).

115 Al-Sarakhsį, *al-Mabsūṭ*, vol. 5, pp. 22–23; cf. Goldziher, *Muslim Studies*, vol. 1, p. 124.

116 Al-Sarakhsī, *al-Mabsūṭ*, vol. 5, pp. 22–23.

117 Saḥnūn, *al-Mudawwana*, p. 14; Ibn Ḥazm, *al-Muḥallā*, vol. 9, p. 455 (cf. Ibn Ḥazm's criticism on p. 456); al-Sha'rānī, *al-Mīzān*, vol. 2, p. 109.

ethnic egalitarianism of their political views to the social sphere.[118] In Shīʿite sources, by contrast, there is some evidence that may indicate a more egalitarian attitude. Such an attitude is certainly discernible in Kūfan law, and is reflected in the uncompromising insistence on the equality of Arab and non-Arab Muslims in marriage and other matters in the *Majmūʿ al-fiqh* ascribed to Zayd b. ʿAlī.[119] Also instructive are certain *ḥadīth* recorded by al-Kulīnī and Ibn Bābawayh on the subject of marriage: the Prophet marries a poor and ugly black man to a woman of the Anṣār, on the grounds that 'By Islam, God has brought low those who were noble in the *Jāhiliyya* and ennobled those who previously were low'; the believing man is declared to be the equal of the believing woman;[120] decay and sedition are said to be the inevitable outcome if people refuse to marry pleasing persons of suitable religion, regardless of their social station;[121] the requirement of marriage equality is said to be satisfied as long as the man is chaste and possesses adequate means (*ʿafīfan wa ʿindahu yasār*).[122] Certainly, there are also Shīʿite traditions that suggest the opposite social outlook,[123] and at the same time, even Ḥanafī scholars accept some egalitarian *ḥadīth*, and they are thus forced to justify their extensive list of criteria for marriage equality by arguing that the precedence of piety applies only to the afterlife.[124] Some of these egalitarian *ḥadīth* also appear in early Ibāḍī sources, although here too an emphasis is placed on hierarchical ideas of suitability for marriage: Abū Ghānim cites with approval the *ḥadīth* 'Marry your equals (*ankiḥū'l-akfāʾ*)';[125] the statement ascribed to ʿUmar according to which he forbids the marriage of a woman of rank (*dhāt al-aḥsāb*) to a man other than her equal; the legal opinion of al-Rabīʿ (b. Ḥabīb al-Farāhīdī, d. c. 170/786), according to which free members of the *ahl al-tawḥīd* were equals, with the exception of the client, the cupper, the weaver and the grocer;[126] and the *ḥadīth* 'The Arabs are equal one to another except for the weaver and the cupper.'[127]

118 On Khārijite attitudes towards intermarriage between Arab women and *mawālī*, see R. al-Sayyid, *Mafāhīm al-jamāʿāt fī'l-Islām*, p. 59.

119 E. Griffini (ed.), *"Corpus Iuris" di Zaid ibn ʿAlī* (Milan, 1919), pp. 199–201.

120 Al-Kulīnī, *al-Kāfī*, vol. 5, pp. 337, 340ff; Ibn Bābawayh, *Man lā yaḥḍuruhu al-faqīh*, vol. 3, p. 249. See also the account concerning ʿAlī b. al-Ḥusayn and ʿAbd al-Malik: the former frees a slave girl and marries her; the caliph writes to rebuke ʿAlī for this transgression of the rules of *kafāʾa*, whereupon the latter replies that through Islam God has elevated the lowly (*al-Kāfī*, vol. 5, pp. 344–345).

121 Al-Kulīnī, *al-Kāfī*, vol. 5, p. 347; Ibn Bābawayh, *Man lā yaḥḍuruhu al-faqīh*, vol. 3, pp. 248–249. This *ḥadīth* also appears in Ibn Māja, *Sunan*, vol. 1, pp. 632–633, no. 1967; al-Sarakhsī, *al-Mabsūṭ*, p. 23; Abū Ghānim Bishr b. Ghānim al-Khurāsānī al-Ibāḍī, *al-Mudawwana al-kubrā*, ed. M. b. Yūsuf Aṭfayyish (Beirut, 1394/1974), p. 10.

122 Al-Kulīnī, *al-Kāfī*, vol. 5, p. 347; Ibn Bābawayh, *Man lā yaḥḍuruhu al-faqīh*, vol. 3, p. 249.

123 Al-Kulīnī records *ḥadīth* that discourage marriage with blacks, Kurds and others (*al-Kāfī*, vol. 5, p. 352).

124 Al-Sarakhsī, *al-Mabsūṭ*, vol. 5, p. 23.

125 Abū Ghānim, *al-Mudawwana al-kubrā*, p. 10. This *ḥadith* also appears in Ibn Māja, *Sunan*, vol. 1, p. 633, no. 1968.

126 Abū Ghānim, *al-Mudawwana al-kubrā*, p. 10; also given as a *ḥadīth* in the twelfth-century collection attributed to al-Rabīʿ b. Ḥabīb al-Farāhīdī (*al-Jāmiʿ al-ṣaḥīḥ* (Cairo, 1970), vol. 2, p. 30, no. 513; cf. J.C. Wilkinson, 'Ibāḍī Ḥadīth: An Essay on Normalization', *Der Islam* 62 (1985), pp. 231–259).

127 Abū Ghānim, *al-Mudawwana al-kubrā*, p. 10.

The various *ḥadīth* generated by the issue of marriage equality suggest the prevalence in most legal circles of a strong sense of social differences. The range of criteria for marriage equality, and the difference of opinion even among scholars of the same school regarding their relative importance, suggest a diversity and perhaps a degree of informality in actual social practice, but this lack of uniformity does not negate the impression given by the sources of a profound consciousness of social rank among scholars in many environments. The attention given to descent, wealth and profession among the criteria for marriage equality in a legal tradition that largely emphasises the equality of free Muslim males should not necessarily surprise us; even the most convinced egalitarian might baulk at the prospect of his womenfolk marrying in a socially random fashion. More striking is the sizable number of traditions that seek to eliminate all criteria other than religion, the great social equaliser. Such traditions certainly seem to suggest that Muslims in some quarters, perhaps encouraged by memories of the earliest experience of the new community, at least aspired to transform the societies in which they lived by drawing attention to the logical social concomitants of the egalitarianism of the Islamic religious ethos. Such hopes may possibly have been particularly characteristic of pro-ʿAlid circles in Kūfa, where an inclination towards social egalitarianism was combined with a pious opposition to the political authorities. But it is also evident that egalitarian tendencies regarding marriage equality did not necessarily accompany political opposition, since there seems to be nothing to suggest that such an attitude was prevalent among Khārijites.

The holding of audiences

Another specific context for early debates over social status involved the question of admission to the ruler's or governor's presence. That the holding of audiences, like the issue of marriage equality, generated a good deal of strong feeling is evident in the inclusion of sections on the chamberlain's office in anthologies, as well as the composition of epistles exclusively devoted to it.[128] The subject is frequently used as a vehicle for a kind of political commentary. Like the Sasanians, the Muslims in Iraq and elsewhere found themselves faced with the tension between the ideal of general access to the ruler's presence, which was necessary to fulfil the demands of justice, and the reality of selective admission, which reinforced and indeed created social differences.[129] ʿUmar is said to have advised Abū Mūsā, his governor at Baṣra, to

[128] Ibn Qutayba, *ʿUyūn al-akhbār*, vol. 1, *K. al-sulṭān*, pp. 82ff; Ibn ʿAbd Rabbihi, *al-ʿIqd al-farīd*, vol. 1, pp. 107ff; al-Rāghib al-Iṣfahānī, *Muḥāḍarāt al-udabāʾ*, vol. 1, pp. 205ff; al-Jāḥiẓ, *K. al-ḥijāb*, *Rasāʾil*, vol. 2, pp. 25ff. See also Abū Manṣūr al-Thaʿālibī, *Laṭāʾif al-maʿārif*, eds. Ibrāhīm al-Ibyārī and Ḥasan Kāmil al-Ṣayrafī (Cairo, 1379/1960), p. 19 (tr. C.E. Bosworth, *The Book of Curious and Entertaining Information* (Edinburgh, 1968), p. 48), for some general observations on Umayyad practices of reception.

[129] See Morony, *Iraq*, pp. 81, 96. The ideal is suggested in a passage recorded by Ibn ʿAbd Rabbihi: 'The ruler should not invite people to approach on the basis of the proximity of their fathers,

give precedence to those of honourable status (*ahl al-sharaf*), reciters of the Qur'ān (*ahl al-Qur'ān*) and men of piety and religion (*al-taqwā wa'l-dīn*), and only to admit the common people after these groups had taken their seats.[130] This account reflects the common association of 'Umar with an 'Islamic' social policy and may have been invoked to suggest the injustice of later arrangements. By contrast, 'Ajlān, Ziyād's chamberlain, is said to have admitted people according to their families (*buyūtāt*), their genealogies (*ansāb*) and finally their education and culture (*ādāb*).[131] This report is likely to reflect an egalitarian undercurrent of opposition to the Umayyads, and its historicity is questionable, although the criteria for precedence associated with 'Ajlān in this example are in fact consistent with our understanding of the influential role played by the tribal leaders in the system established by Mu'āwiya. Those who were not privileged with prompt access were obliged to wait, unless they had connexions with those who enjoyed the ruler's favour.

The resentment aroused by the practice of selective admission is still more obvious in the following anecdote. The caliph 'Umar is said to have heard the sound of voices outside his door. He asked someone to see who was there and to admit any of the Muhājirūn. This was done, whereupon Salmān al-Fārisī, Bilāl and Ṣuhayb b. Sinān entered. Meanwhile, Abū Sufyān b. Ḥarb and Suhayl b. 'Amr waited outside with a group of Qurashīs. Abū Sufyān said, 'O people of Quraysh! You, who are the chiefs (*ṣanādīd*) of the Arabs, the noble leaders (*ashrāf*) and horsemen among them, wait at the door, while an Abyssinian, a Persian and a Greek are allowed to enter!' Suhayl answered, 'Abū Sufyān, you [Qurashīs] should blame yourselves, not the Commander of the Faithful. [These] people were called [to Islam], and they responded, while you, who were also invited, rejected the summons. On the Day of Resurrection, they [will be] of greater degrees and more favour.'[132] Abū Sufyān declared, 'There is no good in a place where Bilāl is [considered] noble (*sharīf*).'[133]

This anecdote, which clearly expresses hostility to the Umayyads, illustrates the pious ideal. The formerly powerful tribal leaders have been supplanted by

nor keep them at a distance because their fathers were distant; he should look at the qualities of each man among them, and invite a distant person to approach on the basis of his usefulness, and keep a close person distant because of the damage he may cause. A rat, even though he is as close as the house next door, is rejected because he is harmful, while a falcon, who is wild, is sought after and purchased for his usefulness' (*al-'Iqd al-farīd*, vol. 1, pp. 110–111). This piece of political wisdom is attributed to an Indian source, and is indeed reminiscent of a passage in *Kalīla wa Dimna* (see ch. 3, n. 60).

130 R.B. Serjeant, 'The Caliph 'Umar's Letters to Abū Mūsā al-Ash'arī and Mu'āwiya', *JSS* 29 (1984), pp. 68–69.

131 Ibn 'Abd Rabbihi, *al-'Iqd al-farīd*, vol. 20, p. 20; vol. 1, p. 107 substitutes 'age' (*asnān*) for *ansāb*. The passage is cited in Morony, *Iraq*, p. 82. Note also the speech supposedly uttered by Ziyād, in which he emphasises the respect due to men of nobility, learning and seniority (*dhaw[ū] 'l-sharaf, ahl al-'ilm, dhaw[ū] 'l-asnān*); Ibn al-Ḥaddād, *al-Jawhar al-nafīs*, pp. 71–72.

132 Cf. Q. 17:21.

133 Al-Bayhaqī, *al-Maḥāsin wa'l-masāwī*, p. 102; al-Jāḥiẓ, *al-Maḥāsin wa'l-aḍdād*, pp. 126–27.

men of the lowest possible social origin on account of their impeccable Islamic credentials. The account shows both the resentment of the tribal leaders at being kept waiting and the egalitarian principle of general access without regard to social differences – differentiation on moral and religious grounds is regarded as perfectly proper. It also demonstrates the overlap between ethnic and social egalitarianism. The anecdote could have been shaped by *shuʿūbī* concerns; at the very least its ethnic dimension adds emphasis to the point that extreme social baseness, when accompanied by piety, should be given precedence over noble genealogy without piety.[134] It seems more likely that the report reflects a general anti-Umayyad nostalgia for ʿUmar's day, when status is said to have depended chiefly on Islamic priority.[135]

In these anecdotes concerning the holding of audiences, it seems clear that a leaning towards pious egalitarianism almost invariably connoted a certain resistance to the political authorities. Since many of these examples involve members of the Umayyad clan, it seems likely that they took shape in the first half of the second/eighth century, when dissatisfaction with the current order was expressed by ascribing a desired practice to a revered figure from the past and by associating a deviation from this practice with the current holders of power or their forebears. The obvious political overtones of such stories suggest the subversive nature of early social egalitarianism.

Early descriptions of society

The last group of materials that I should like to consider in this chapter is a cluster of rudimentary descriptions of society associated with figures of the pre-classical and early classical periods. One of the most striking features of these examples is their thoroughly urban character. They reflect no concern for the agrarian base of the local (Iraqi) economy and culture, and certainly no hankering for a pastoral way of life. What these early social models do seem to reflect is the competition among various groups for social precedence in the Iraqi towns during the later Umayyad and early ʿAbbāsid periods.

It seems likely that these examples originated in a spontaneous form of oral

134 On the theme of the religious superiority of the *mawālī* to the Arabs, see also the dialogue between ʿAbd al-Malik and al-Zuhrī in Abū Ḥayyān al-Tawḥīdī, *al-Baṣāʾir waʾl-dhakhāʾir*, ed. W. al-Qāḍī (Beirut, 1408/1988), vol. 8, p. 85, no. 288.

135 Elsewhere, ʿUmar is said to have condescended to welcome Abū Sufyān by offering him a cushion, and to have explained his unexpected action by quoting the Prophetic *ḥadīth* that runs *idhā atākum karīmu qawmin fa-ʾakrimūhu* (Ibn ʿAbd Rabbihi, *al-ʿIqd al-farīd*, vol. 1, p. 28). The offer of a cushion was a mark of honour and respect (S. Shaked, 'From Iran to Islam: On Some Symbols of Royalty', *JSAI* 7 (1986), pp. 77f). ʿAlī is said to have offered two men cushions; one accepted, the other declined, and this incident prompted ʿAlī to coin the proverb, 'Only a donkey refuses a mark of honour (*lā yaʾbā al-karāma illā al-ḥimār*)' (al-Kulīnī, *al-Kāfī*, vol. 2, p. 659; vol. (1379), p. 513; al-Gharawī, *al-Amthāl al-nabawiyya*, vol. 1, p. 240 [with variants]). Another anecdote concerning Abū Sufyān's reception (this time by ʿUthmān) appears in al-Jāḥiẓ, *K. al-ḥijāb*, *Rasāʾil*, vol. 2, p. 83, and al-Rāghib al-Iṣfahānī, *Muḥāḍarāt al-udabāʾ*, vol. 1, p. 208.

literature which gradually acquired a number of formal characteristics. They possess a common structure in that they pick out and elevate certain social groups (usually four, occasionally three or five) over the mass of society, and conclude with formulaic expressions of contempt for all persons who do not belong to the élites enumerated. A significant number involve a caliph who asks to be enlightened on the nature of society and receives a list of its respectable constituent groups in reply; this may suggest that this literary form may also have emerged in the context of political opposition.

Among these models is one attributed to Ṣaʿṣaʿa b. Ṣūḥān (d. 60/680). This example appears in several versions, and is presented as Ṣaʿṣaʿa's reponse to an enquiry addressed to him by Muʿāwiya. According to one version, Ṣaʿṣaʿa says, 'Men are created of various conditions (*akhyāfan*): a group (*ṭāʾifa*) for worship, a group for commerce, a group of preachers, and a group for courage and valour. The remaining rabble merely muddy the waters, cause prices to rise, and make the way narrow.'[136] According to a second account, Ṣaʿṣaʿa declares, 'God created men in levels (*aṭwāran*):[137] a group for worship, a group for government, a group for religious understanding (*fiqh*) and practice (*sunna*), a group for bravery and valour, and a group for crafts and professions. All the rest merely muddy the waters and cause prices to rise.'[138]

Ṣaʿṣaʿa's models may be regarded as 'Islamic' versions of the literary formula adopted for social description. Ṣaʿṣaʿa himself was among the early-comers to Kūfa and his status seems to have been more 'Islamic' than tribal; he was an active opponent of ʿUthmān and Muʿāwiya.[139] The models attributed to him may thus reflect an anti-Umayyad political orientation.

A similar model is attributed to Khālid b. Ṣafwān (d. c. 135/752), who is said to have described society as consisting of three strata: scholars, preachers and men of culture; the remaining rabble merely 'cause prices to rise, constrict the markets, and muddy the waters'.[140] Khālid, who was famous for his eloquence,

[136] Abū ʿAlī Al-Qālī, *Kitāb al-Amālī* (Cairo, 1344/1926), vol. 1, p. 257. [137] Cf. Q. 71:14.

[138] Al-Tawḥīdī, *al-Baṣāʾir waʾl-dhakhāʾir*, vol. 1, p. 45, no. 110. The last group does not always appear; variants are listed in n. 110 of al-Qāḍī's edition. The version recorded in al-Rāghib al-Iṣfahānī, *Muḥāḍarāt al-udabāʾ*, vol. 1, p. 306, lists only three groups: 'a group for leadership and authority, a group for religious understanding and practice, and a group for bravery and valour'.

[139] Ṣaʿṣaʿa was among the most prominent of the dissidents expelled from Kūfa in 33/653–654 by Saʿīd b. al-ʿĀṣ; see al-Ṭabarī, *Taʾrīkh al-rusul waʾl-mulūk*, ed. M. Abūʾl-Faḍl Ibrāhīm (Cairo, 1977), vol. 4, pp. 317ff. See especially p. 319, where Muʿāwiya tells Ṣaʿṣaʿa and those expelled from Kūfa with him that they have 'attained nobility through Islam, conquered the nations and appropriated their ranks and estates'. This account is discussed by R. al-Sayyid, 'al-Khilāfa waʾl-mulk', pp. 96ff; see also Hinds, 'Kūfan Political Alignments', p. 357, and I. ʿAbbās, *Taʾrīkh bilād al-Shām min mā qabl al-Islām ḥattā bidāyat al-ʿaṣr al-umawī* (Amman, 1410/1990), p. 402. On Ṣaʿṣaʿa, see also al-Ṣafadī, *al-Wāfī biʾl-wafayāt* (Wiesbaden), vol. 16, ed. W. al-Qāḍī (1402/1982), p. 309; Ibn Ḥajar, *Tahdhīb al-tahdhīb* (Hyderabad), vol. 4 (1325), p. 422; Ibn Saʿd, *alṬabaqāt al-kubrā* (Beirut), vol. 6 (1377/1957), p. 221; Ibn Qutayba, *al-Maʿārif*, ed. Tharwat ʿUkāsha (Cairo, 1388/1969), pp. 402, 624; al-Najāshī, *Kitāb al-rijāl* (Tehran, n.d.), p. 153; M. b. ʿUmar al-Kashshī, *Rijāl al-Kashshī*, ed. S.A. al-Ḥusaynī (Karbalāʾ, n.d.), pp. 64–65; J. Wellhausen, *Die religiös-politischen Oppositionsparteien im alten Islam* (Berlin, 1901), p. 21. [140] *Al-ʿIqd al-farīd*, vol. 6, p. 155.

associated with the governor Khālid al-Qasrī and the caliphs ʿUmar b. ʿAbd al-ʿAzīz (99–101/717–720) and Hishām b. ʿAbd al-Malik (105–125/724–743), and there is thus no reason to regard the statement attributed to him as an expression of political resistance; he is also said to have been one of the richest – if most miserly – inhabitants of Baṣra.[141] The social model ascribed to him is again an 'Islamic' version of the formula. It is noteworthy that soldiers have dropped out of the model, which is geared towards incipient civilian élites.

Ibn al-Faqīh opens his *Kitāb al-buldān*, the geographical work composed in (or shortly after) 289/902–903, with two versions of a social model attributed to different individuals:

Al-Faḍl b. Yaḥyā [al-Barmakī, d. 193/808] said: 'Men consist of four strata: rulers, whose pre-eminence derives from their right to rule (*istiḥqāq*);[142] viziers, who owe their status to their astuteness (*fiṭna*) and judgement; the wealthy who are elevated by their affluence; and the middling people, linked with them by their education (*ta'addub*). The remainder of mankind are vanishing scum,[143] floating refuse, despicable men and women bound to baseness, their single concern being for food and sleep.'[144]

Muʿāwiya once said to al-Aḥnaf [b. Qays], 'Describe society to me'. The latter replied, '[It consists of] heads, elevated by fortune (*ḥazz*); shoulders exalted by [their] administrative ability (*tadbīr*); rumps, who owe their fame to their wealth; and the men of culture (*udabā'*), who owe their rank to their education. The rest of the people are similar to beasts – if they are hungry, they demand; if they are replete, they sleep.'[145]

The social models presented in these two passages are almost identical. Both are quadripartite, and they single out substantially the same social élites, while exhibiting a particularly striking contempt for the common people.

These models seem less markedly 'Islamic' than those associated with Ṣaʿṣaʿa and Khālid. The association of one of them with the Barmakids, notorious for their fondness for Persian culture, may be meant to alert the reader to a certain Persianising element. The attribution of the second to al-Aḥnaf b. Qays causes it to follow the well-established anecdotal pattern in which the alleged conversations between the leader of Tamīm at Baṣra and the caliph Muʿāwiya are recorded.[146]

Although not a social model as such, an interesting observation attributed by

[141] On Khālid, see Ibn Khallikān, *Wafayāt al-aʿyān*, ed. I. ʿAbbās (Beirut, 1397/1977), vol. 3, pp. 11–12; al-Ṣafadī, *al-Wāfī bi'l-wafayāt*, vol. 13, ed. M. al-Ḥujayrī (1404/1984), pp. 254–55; Yāqūt, *Muʿjam al-udabā'* (Cairo, n.d.), vol. 11, pp. 24–35; Ibn Qutayba, *al-Maʿārif*, p. 403. Khālid also appears in the writings of al-Jāḥiẓ (*K. al-bukhalā'* (Beirut, 1399/1979), pp. 210, 214–215, 216, and *al-Bayān wa'l-tabyīn*, vol. 1, pp. 339–340).

[142] *Irth* and *istiḥqāq*, 'heredity and merit', were claimed by many rulers as sources of legitimation (R.P. Mottahedeh, 'Attitudes Towards Absolutism', *Israel Oriental Studies* 10 (1980), p. 89 (Seljuks); H. Inalcik, 'Comments on "Sultanism". Max Weber's Typification of the Ottoman Polity', *Princeton Papers* 1 (1992), p. 59 (Ottomans)).

[143] Cf. Q. 13:18.

[144] Based on the translation in B. Lewis, *Islam from the Prophet Muhammad to the Capture of Constantinople* (New York and Oxford, 1987), vol. 2, p. 198.

[145] Ibn al-Faqīh, *Kitāb al-buldān*, ed. M.J. de Goeje (Leiden, 1967), p. 1.

[146] Cf. C. Pellat, 'al-Aḥnaf b. Ḳays', *EI*2.

Ibn Ḥamdūn to Hishām b. ʿAbd al-Malik is also relevant here: a family (*bayt*) could be deemed well established (*qā'im*) on account of 'inherited nobility (*sālifa*), acquired nobility (*lāḥiqa*), the means to support its condition (*ʿimādu ḥālin*), and a firm handle on fortune (*misāku dahrin*)'. According to Ibn Ḥamdūn's interpretation of these terms, 'By *sālifa*, he [Hishām] meant the nobility possessed by a man's ancestors, a nobility that had preceded him; by *lāḥiqa*, he meant that which accrued to him through the nobility of his sons; by *ʿimād al-ḥāl*, he meant wealth; and by *misāk al-dahr*, he meant stature in the eyes of the authorities'.[147] Hishām, then, is said to have acknowledged first the importance of the Arab principles of *nasab* and *ḥasab*, but also to have added to them the acquisition of wealth and the attainment of a high-ranking post in the ruler's confidence. This set of criteria for social precedence is not inconsistent with what we know of the development of Islamic political culture under Hishām. That the culture of the state secretarial staff in his reign was characterised by an awareness of social stratification is evident from ʿAbd al-Ḥamīd's correspondence, including his somewhat Sasanian-sounding assumption that God, after he has chosen his messengers and kings, divides the rest of mankind into commoners (*suwaqan*) and designates a particular craft and livelihood for each.[148]

Part of the significance of these examples of early indigenous social description is that they seek to identify the occupations and activities suitable for Muslims in an urban environment. It is noteworthy that the soldiery are absent in almost all of these examples, a feature that may suggest the emergence of civilian élites and an increasing alienation of the urban population from the state.

Perhaps the single most striking feature of these accounts is the extremely low opinion in which the common people are held. It is unclear whether the phrase 'the rest' refers only to the common townspeople or to the peasantry as well. Disparagement of the (urban) *ʿāmma* is a common theme in classical Arabic *adab* literature, especially in the writings of al-Jāḥiẓ, whose contempt was possibly intensified by his Muʿtazilite leanings.[149] Such hostility towards

[147] *Al-Tadhkira al-Ḥamdūniyya*, vol. 2, p. 28, no. 36.

[148] *Risāla ilā'l-kuttāb*, in I. ʿAbbās, *ʿAbd al-Ḥamīd ibn Yaḥyā al-Kātib*, p. 281. It is interesting to note that ʿAbd al-Ḥamīd's letter appears to have been Islamised in later versions, according to which the 'commoners' become 'categories' (*aṣnāfan*) which are said to be 'in reality of equal status' (ʿAbbās, p. 281, n. 3; see also W. al-Qāḍī, 'Early Islamic State Letters', p. 255). See also ch. 5, where ʿAbd al-Ḥamīd's letter on behalf of the caliph Marwān to the latter's son is discussed.

[149] See, for instance, al-Jāḥiẓ's *Risāla fī wasf al-ʿawāmm* (O. Rescher, *Excerpte und Übersetzungen aus den Schriften des Philologen und Dogmatikers Ǧâḥiẓ aus Baçra (150–250 H.)*, Erster Teil (Stuttgart, 1931), pp. 550–552), and his *K. dhamm akhlāq al-kuttāb* (*Rasā'il*, vol. 2, pp. 196–97). In al-Jāḥiẓ's circle, the common people appear to have been regarded as incapable of independent judgement and easily swayed. There was always a danger that their gullibility could be exploited by self-interested parties who would lead them into rebellions, making it necessary that they be continually suppressed; cf. the story of the *muḥtasib* who, in league with Muḥammad al-Nafs al-Zakiyya and his brother Ibrāhīm, 'led the lower classes (*al-sifla*) astray' and prompted al-Manṣūr to move the markets outside the city of Baghdad (al-Ṭabarī, *Ta'rīkh*, vol. 7, p. 653).

and suspicion of commoners is also evident, naturally, in the attitudes of the Byzantine and Iranian aristocracies.[150]

A few general remarks may now be made on the basis of the various literary fragments that have come down to us from the early second/eighth century and later. These literary fragments are in many cases consistent with the interpretation that a strongly egalitarian orientation was forming in the first century and a half, and that its formation, rooted in the memory of the social levelling among the Arabs that had accompanied the early conquests, was very much in opposition to the various inequalities that inevitably emerged and intensified subsequently. Many examples appear to articulate the disappointments and resentments of Arab and, increasingly, non-Arab Muslims who felt excluded from the wealth and power won by the conquests. In these conditions, the religious egalitarianism of the Qur'ān, reinforced by the newly forming Islamic tradition, seemed to suggest divine criticism of the established tribal order and its leaders. Those who sought to support and justify their status sometimes did so through the traditional tribal methods of rivalry, but increasingly felt obliged to respond to the view that religious equality ought to have social implications as well. Islamic egalitarianism may have gathered strength in the context of opposition to the tribal order established by Muʿāwiya and those who supported it; it was certainly taken up to express resistance to the order that gave precedence to Arab over non-Arab Muslims. There is much to suggest that expressions of egalitarianism were frequently also expressions of political discontent, and that they were unavoidably subversive in the eyes of the authorities and those groups whose claims to precedence and privileges rested on their place in the power of structure.

The history of social egalitarianism in the Islamic world may be somewhat analogous to that of political activism. It was quietism that was endorsed by mainstream Sunnī and Imāmī political thinkers, but the latter still felt obliged to defend their quietism, since it was activism that had been suggested most strongly by early Muslim experience.[151] The same thinkers also wrote in

[150] On the Byzantines, see for example Averil Cameron, *Procopius and the Sixth Century* (Berkeley, 1985), pp. 227–228. On the Iranians, see the views ascribed to Ardashīr in Firdawsī's *Shāhnāmeh*: 'Do not seek truthfulness in the hearts of commoners (*ʿāmmīyān*); the more you seek, the less you will find. If a bad report [concerning someone] reaches you from them, pay no heed to it and do not be disturbed; they are devoted neither to the king nor to God, and if you wish to seize one of them by the foot, you will find his head in your hands. Such is the measure (of the worth) of the common people' (*Shāhnāmeh*, ed. and tr. J. Mohl, *Le livre des rois* (Paris, 1976), vol. 5, pp. 382–383; quoted in M. Shaki, 'Class System', iii, *Encyclopaedia Iranica*). But Ardashīr is frequently said to have adopted a more pragmatic attitude towards peasants; more typical of his utterances concerning the latter is 'Wherever lies the treasure of the cultivator (*dihqān*), there lies his [the king's] treasure; and whatever effort and trouble it costs him, the king must be the guardian of the subject's treasure, and ensure that his travail bears fruit' (*Shāhnāmeh*, vol. 5, pp. 380–381).

[151] M.A. Cook, 'Activism and Quietism in Islam: The Case of the Early Murji'a', in *Islam and Power*, eds. A. Cudsi and A. Dessouki (Baltimore, 1981), pp. 21–22; I am grateful to K. Lewinstein for suggesting the analogy to me.

support of social stratification, but again felt constrained to justify their views, perhaps because of the awareness of the brief period in which Islam brought a substantial degree of equality to the Arab conquerors.[152] As will be seen further in the following chapters, the realities of power and status meant that in time the social significance of this egalitarian spirit was diluted. It was not, however, eliminated; and as a result, the distressed voices whose echoes are faintly perceptible in early Islamic aphorisms and *ḥadīth* were not only remembered but in many cases came to be regarded as expressions of particular wisdom.

[152] See further, especially ch. 6.

CHAPTER 2

The Muslim reception of Greek ideas

In the previous chapter, it was suggested that the ideology of the early Muslims had a marked egalitarian orientation, and that this egalitarianism inevitably collided with the expectations and ambitions of groups who laid claim to high status in the course of the century following the conquests. The remainder of the first section of this book is devoted to the Muslim reception of inegalitarian social ideals, a complex set of processes occasioned by the Arab conquest of areas in which hierarchical social structures and ideologies that supported such arrangements had long been characteristic. The present chapter, which is concerned with the Greek tradition, emphasises the transmission of ideas through a body of translated literature, since it is through these literary channels that Greek social thought most obviously came to shape Muslim social ideals. This discussion will be preceded, however, by a brief account of the living traditions encountered by the early Muslims in Syria and Egypt, and a consideration of the impact these encounters may have had on the emergence of social conceptions among the Muslims who first settled in these regions.

Social structure in the eastern Mediterranean world in Late Antiquity

On the eve of their conquest by the Arabs, Syria and Egypt were provinces of the Byzantine empire. In the past their societies had been integrated accordingly into an elaborately hierarchical system in which those who held official ranks, whether in the military or civil administration, were entitled to substantial legal and financial privileges.[1] Each post was associated with specific functions, competences and duties, and brought its holder a fixed degree of authority and status. A notable feature of this system in the period preceding the conquests was the tendency for ranks to derive less from hereditary birthright than from the emperor's favour, a situation that found support in the traditional imperial ideology according to which the emperor was the paterfamilias of his subjects. Also striking is the fact that social formations in

[1] See A.H.M. Jones, *The Later Roman Empire, 284–602* (Oxford, 1973), vol. 1, pp. 523ff; J.F. Haldon, *Byzantium in the Seventh Century* (Cambridge, 1990), pp. 9–40.

the sixth century and before seem to have been characterised by a certain openness and looseness. Social and economic status depended on a variety of attributes, including birth and family name; occupation of an imperial position and possession of a title; origin, and position in the local community; wealth; and possession of the appropriate cultural credentials. There were thus multiple ways of acquiring status and, although these criteria sometimes went together, they did not invariably coincide.[2]

Underlying the highly classified order of official ranks were several different societies that evolved in various ways under Byzantine rule. Some widespread and far-reaching changes in the composition of both the ruling élite and the rural population may be indicated for the late sixth and early seventh centuries,[3] but it is clear that the Byzantine hierarchy interacted with local social structures in different ways from time to time and from region to region. It seems, for example, that there was often considerably greater social mobility in the eastern Mediterranean than in the west;[4] and, perhaps in addition to *coloni* tied in various ways to the estates on which they worked, there were also significant numbers of free peasants in Syria, Egypt and elsewhere.[5] The political and social structures of Syria and Egypt had also been affected by a complex of specific factors in the period preceding the Arab conquests. Significant social and economic dislocation accompanied the recurrent outbreaks of bubonic plague in the eastern provinces during the sixth and seventh centuries, which struck rich and poor indiscriminately and affected the relationship between settled and nomadic populations.[6] Moreover, both Syria and Egypt had been restored to Byzantine rule in about 630 after some fifteen years of Sasanian occupation, and the Persian invasions, followed by the Byzantine reconquest, may have contributed to the weakening of some sections of the official hierarchy, if not of the bureaucratic mentality.[7] Furthermore, the deep divisions within the Christian church may have

[2] Haldon, *Byzantium*, pp. 388–389; cf. F. Winkelmann, *Quellenstudien zur herrschenden Klasse von Byzanz im 8. und 9. Jahrhundert* (Berlin, 1987), pp. 14–17.

[3] On developments within the élite, see Haldon, *Byzantium*, pp. 125–132, 160–172, 387–402; Winkelmann, *Quellenstudien*; *idem*, 'Zum byzantinischen Staat', in *Byzanz im 7. Jahrhundert. Untersuchungen zur Herausbildung des Feudalismus*, eds. F. Winkelmann, H. Köpstein, H. Ditten and I. Rochow (Berlin, 1978), pp. 180–190. For a discussion of the rural population and the colonate, see Averil Cameron, *The Mediterranean World in Late Antiquity, A.D. 395–600* (London and New York, 1993), pp. 86–87.

[4] Jones, *Later Roman Empire*, p. 551; Cameron, *Mediterranean World*, pp. 90–91.

[5] Haldon, *Byzantium*, pp. 27–28; 125ff; H. Köpstein, 'Das 7. Jahrhundert (565–711) im Prozess der Herausbildung des Feudalismus in Byzanz', in *Byzanz im 7. Jahrhundert*, p. 289. For Syria, see I. ʿAbbās, *Taʾrīkh bilād al-Shām*, pp. 163ff; for Egypt, see R.S. Bagnall, *Egypt in Late Antiquity* (Princeton, 1993), pp. 114–119, 225–229.

[6] L.I. Conrad, 'The Plague in Bilād al-Shām in Pre-Islamic Times', in *Proceedings of the Symposium on Bilād al-Shām during the Byzantine Period*, eds. M.ʿA. Bakhīt and M. ʿAṣfūr (Amman, 1986), vol. 2, pp. 143–163; *idem*, 'The Plague in the Early Medieval Near East', unpublished Ph.D. dissertation (Princeton, 1981), especially pp. 448–489.

[7] See further W.E. Kaegi, 'New Perspectives on the Last Decades of the Byzantine Era', in *Proceedings of the Symposium on Bilād al-Shām during the Byzantine Period*, eds. M.ʿA. Bakhīt and M. ʿAṣfūr (Amman, 1986), vol. 2, pp. 76–87.

contributed to a sense of confusion among some of the local people as to their social and cultural identities as well as to their religious beliefs.[8]

Christianisation itself had had some important effects on social organisation in the Byzantine provinces. By the seventh century the Christian church had developed a profoundly hierarchical structure of its own; and yet at the same time, Christianisation had to some extent undermined the hierarchies that revolved round the Byzantine state, if only because it offered an alternative to them. Partially as a reflection of these changes, towns in the late sixth century had increasingly come to be administered and represented by the local ecclesiastical authorities.[9] In addition, both the Christian church and imperial legislation in this period tended to give greater prominence to individuals and families than to larger social groups.[10] One of the concomitants of these changes was the tendency for individuals to be identified by their membership of religious communities rather than as subjects of the state. As Christianisation encompassed ever-greater areas of public life, religious leaders also became the custodians of culture, with the result that the distinction between religious and secular culture gradually receded. This development is of great importance here, since the established secular culture, with its emphasis on the classics, had been aristocratic in nature, and its gradual disappearance brought with it a blurring of the distinction between aristocratic and popular culture.[11]

In order to assess the ways in which this 'simplification of culture' may have affected Syrian and Egyptian social ideals,[12] it is necessary to consider the role of Hellenism in the eastern Mediterranean and its interaction with local cultures, particularly given the widespread Christianisation of these regions in the course of the sixth century. By the seventh century, in both Syria and Egypt, many of the ingredients of Hellenism had been assimilated into Christian thought, and the chief bearers of Hellenic culture, in the broadest sense, in the eastern Mediterranean were Christians, regardless of the language in which their thought found expression.[13] It is also important to note that Hellenism was not limited to urban environments, but adapted to local traditions in rural

[8] Cameron, 'The Eastern Provinces in the Seventh Century A.D. Hellenism and the Emergence of Islam', in *Hellenismos. Quelques jalons pour une histoire de l'identité grecque*, ed. S. Saïd (Leiden and New York, 1991), pp. 287–313 (see especially pp. 288–289); *idem*, 'New Themes and Styles in Greek Literature: Seventh–Eighth Centuries', in *The Byzantine and Early Islamic Near East*, vol. 1, *Problems in the Literary Source Material*, (eds.) Averil Cameron and L.I. Conrad (Princeton, 1992) p. 86.

[9] P. Brown, *The World of Late Antiquity, A.D. 150–750* (London, 1971), pp. 185–186; J. Herrin, *The Formation of Christendom* (Princeton, 1987), pp. 58, 72ff; Haldon, *Byzantium*, pp. 292–293.

[10] Haldon, *Byzantium*, pp. 376ff.

[11] Brown, *Late Antiquity*, pp. 172–187; Cameron, *Mediterranean World*, pp. 128–151; idem, 'New Themes and Styles', pp. 85–86.

[12] The phrase is Brown's; from *Late Antiquity*, p. 174.

[13] See G. Bowersock, *Hellenism in Late Antiquity* (Ann Arbor, 1990), pp. 40, 55–69; Bagnall, *Egypt*, pp. 99–105, 230–260; Cameron, 'Hellenism and the Emergence of Islam'; S. Brock, 'From Antagonism to Assimilation: Syriac Attitudes to Greek Learning', in *East of Byzantium: Syria and Armenia in the Formative Period*, eds. N.G. Garsoïan, T.F. Mathews and R.W. Thomson (Washington, 1982), pp. 17–34.

areas as well. In other words, Hellenism was not necessarily something that was imposed on Syria and Egypt (and indeed elsewhere) from above and outside; it was in many cases something that had developed indigenous roots as a result of its own capacity for adaptation.[14] Despite the decreased cultivation of classical philosophy in the coastal cities of the eastern Mediterranean, Syriac scholars preserved much of the classical tradition, as well as the intensely hierarchical thought of the Neoplatonists.[15] The assimilation of Hellenism into the cultures of the eastern Mediterranean in the course of the sixth and seventh centuries foreshadowed the permeation of Islamic thought by classical Greek and Neoplatonic social ideas.

It thus appears that the rise of Christianity had stimulated developments that in some ways anticipated the collision between hierarchical and egalitarian sentiments that would accompany the rise of Islam. Like Islam, Christianity placed an emphasis on religious equality. Whereas classical culture was essentially geared to élites, Christianity sought to reach all levels of society, including slaves and women; Christianisation also coincided with a new attention to the poor and other groups considered beneath contempt in the pagan Roman world.[16] Such populist and egalitarian elements were appealing to some among the urban poor.[17] Furthermore, although those involved in its formation probably never set out to eliminate hierarchical forms of social organisation, Christianity certainly provided alternative ways of life that might potentially undermine the status and privileges of the traditional élites. Among the clearest examples of this potential subversiveness were celibacy, which provided an alternative social norm even for women, and the renunciation of wealth.[18] But Christians found, as Muslims would also find, that their religious egalitarianism need not imply a rejection of the existing social order. Although some members of the élite chose a path of renunciation, it seems probable that many of the wealthy and privileged men and women who converted to Christianity retained an inegalitarian outlook, possibly without any sense that it might be inconsistent with their religious views,

[14] Bowersock, *Hellenism*, esp. pp. 29–40. Also suggestive is I. Shahîd, 'Ghassānid and Umayyad Structures: A Case of *Byzance après Byzance*', in *La Syrie de Byzance à l'Islam VIIe–VIIIe siècles,* eds. P. Canivet and J.-P. Rey-Coquais (Damascus, 1992), pp. 299–307.

[15] Cf. Cameron, 'Byzantium and the Past in the Seventh Century: The Search for Redefinition', in *Le septième siècle. Changements et continuités*, eds. J. Fontaine and J.N. Hillgarth (London, 1992), pp. 250–271; J.F. Haldon, 'Ideology and Social Change in the Seventh Century: Military Discontent as a Barometer', *Klio* 68 (1986), pp. 171–172; Bowersock, *Hellenism*, p. 72. On the translation into Syriac of the works of pseudo-Dionysios the Areopagite and other Neoplatonists, see J.-M. Hornus, 'Le corpus dionysien en syriaque', *Parole de l'Orient* 1 (1970), pp. 69–93, and Brock, 'From Antagonism to Assimilation'. On changes in urban life and culture, see also H. Kennedy, 'The Last Century of Byzantine Syria: A Reinterpretation', in *Byzantinische Forschungen* 10 (1985), pp. 141–183.

[16] E. Patlagean, *Pauvreté économique et pauvreté sociale à Byzance, 4e–7e siècles* (Paris, 1977), pp. 11–35; Cameron, *Mediterranean World*, pp. 86–87, 138–139; Herrin, *The Formation of Christendom*, p. 57.

[17] Herrin, *The Formation of Christendom*, p. 58.

[18] Cameron, *Mediterranean World*, pp. 144–146; P. Brown, *The Body and Society. Men, Women and Sexual Renunciation in Early Christianity* (New York, 1988), pp. 366–386.

just as Justinian (527–565) saw himself both as the upholder of Roman tradition and as a crusader for the faith.[19]

Finally, it should be noted that after the conquests of Syria and Egypt, the former administration continued to function and Greek-speaking officials continued to run it to a considerable extent. Although some Greek-speaking Syrians fled from the cities at the time of the conquests, it is clear that enough remained or returned to man the Umayyad bureaucracy. It is perhaps significant that in Syria, in contrast to the situation in Egypt or Iraq, the Arab immigrants settled not in specially constructed garrison towns but in established cities such as Damascus, Homs and Aleppo, as well as in the surrounding countryside.[20] Since the Arabs in Syria tended to settle among the native inhabitants rather than in deliberate isolation from them, and since considerable numbers of Arabs had migrated to Syria in the period before the conquests, they came into contact with the Syrian population more quickly than was the case elsewhere.[21] The unself-consciously Hellenistic style of Quṣayr ʿAmra may even suggest that the earlier migrations had prepared the way for the Arabs, like other eastern Mediterranean peoples, to create an indigenous Hellenistic sub-culture.[22] But there seems to be little reason to suppose that the first Arab Muslims in Syria were much more sympathetic to local hierarchical ideals than they were in Iraq. Here too, ʿUmar is made the spokesman for a number of hostile comments on local customs, particularly those that smacked of luxury and ostentation.[23] When, in the late Umayyad and early ʿAbbāsid periods, the transmission of Greek ideals to the Muslims began in earnest, it was not through contact with the living remnants of the Byzantine provincial communities but through the translation of Greek texts.

The translations into Arabic

Owing to their conquest of Egypt, the Muslims inherited the Alexandrine tradition of Aristotelianism, which was underpinned by a deep layer of Neoplatonic metaphysics. But, although the Alexandrine school survived into the early eighth century, and although some translations into Arabic were prepared in Damascus in the late Umayyad period, it was not in the eastern Mediterranean that the Muslim involvement in philosophy became firmly established. The impulse to reclaim the classical tradition grew stronger after the centre of gravity in the Islamic Middle East had moved from Syria to Iraq,

[19] Cameron, *Christianity and the Rhetoric of Empire. The Development of Christian Discourse* (Berkeley, 1991), p. 194.

[20] F. M. Donner, *The Early Islamic Conquests* (Princeton, 1981), pp. 245–249; ʿAbbās, *Ta'rīkh bilād al-Shām*, pp. 321–336.

[21] On the contacts between the Arabs and the Syrians, see ʿAbbās, *Ta'rīkh bilād al-Shām*, pp. 387ff.

[22] Bowersock, *Hellenism*, pp. 71–82. See also G. Fowden, *Empire to Commonwealth. Consequences of Monotheism in Late Antiquity* (Princeton, 1993), pp. 138–152.

[23] ʿAbbās, *Ta'rīkh bilād al-Shām*, pp. 389–390.

where Muslims had access to Greek culture through the learning of the Hellenised Syrian Christian communities of Mesopotamia, as well as that of the non-Christian Hellenised community of Ḥarrān. The Islamic reworkings of the classical tradition began with the translation of several works into Arabic, usually through the intermediary language of Syriac.[24]

By the seventh and eighth centuries, as has been noted, Greek high culture had suffered from long-standing neglect in the eastern Mediterranean world, and Muslims had some difficulty unearthing the classical literature. This problem is one of the factors involved in the proliferation of pseudepigraphy, which resulted in the area of political philosophy in the popular purported correspondence between Alexander and Aristotle.[25]

One of the most intensely hierarchical parts of the Islamic intellectual tradition is its esoteric branch, and this was informed to a considerable degree by the Hermetic tradition. It is noteworthy that some sources associate the origin of stratification itself with 'the first Hermes', who comes to be identified with Enoch and the prophet Idrīs.[26] Muslim sources describe Idrīs in terms that combine standard prophetic motifs with the foundation of civilisation. Thus Idrīs calls people to monotheism, and imposes prayers, fasts and sacrifices.[27] He also introduces the use of the pen and the making of clothing,[28] and,

[24] F.E. Peters, *Aristotle and the Arabs, The Aristotelian Tradition in Islam* (New York, 1968), pp. 10, 58–59; Brown, *Late Antiquity*, p. 202.

[25] Cf. F. Zimmermann, 'The Origins of the So-Called *Theology of Aristotle*', in *Pseudo-Aristotle in the Middle Ages*, eds. J. Kraye, W.F. Ryan and C.B. Schmitt (London, 1986), pp. 111–112. (I owe this reference to P. Crone.) There are two principal sources that purport to preserve the supposed correspondence between Aristotle and Alexander. The first is known as *al-Siyāsa al-ʿāmmiyya*; see M. Steinschneider, *Die hebräischen Übersetzungen des Mittelalters* (Graz, 1956), p. 270, para. 145.8; M. Grignaschi, 'La «*Siyāsatu-l-ʿāmmiyya*» et l'influence iranienne sur la pensée politique islamique', *Acta Iranica*, 2e série, *Hommages et opera minora* 3, 1975, pp. 33–287; *idem*, 'Les «Rasā'il 'Arisṭāṭālīsa 'ilā-l-Iskandar» de Sālim Abū-l-'Alā' et l'activité culturelle à l'époque Omayyade', *BEO* 19 (1965–6), pp. 7–83; *idem*, 'Le roman épistolaire classique conservé dans la version arabe de Sâlim Abû-l-'Alâ'', *Muséon* 80 (1967), pp. 211–264. The second is the *Sirr al-asrār*, known to medieval Europe as the *Secretum Secretorum* and sometimes identified as Aristotle's *Politics*; see Steinschneider, *Die hebräischen Übersetzungen des Mittelalters*, pp. 245–249, paras. 131–132; *idem*, 'Über die arabischen Übersetzungen aus dem Griechischen', Erster Abschnitt, *Zentralblatt für Bibliothekswesen*, Beiheft 12 (1893), pp. 117–120; ʿAbd al-Raḥmān Badawī, *al-Uṣūl al-yūnāniyya lil-naẓariyyāt al-siyāsiyya fī'l-Islām* (Cairo, 1954), pp. 3–4.

[26] The identification of Hermes with Idrīs was already established by the time of al-Jāḥiẓ (*K. al-tarbīʿ wa'l-tadwīr*, ed. C. Pellat (Damascus, 1955), p. 26), and appeared in the roughly contemporary *Kitāb al-ulūf* of Abū Maʿshar; cf. D. Pingree, *The Thousands of Abū Maʿshar* (London, 1968), pp. 10–11, 14–15.

[27] Al-Mubashshir b. Fātik, *Mukhtār al-ḥikam wa maḥāsin al-kalim*, ed. ʿAbd al-Raḥmān Badawī (Madrid, 1377/1958) pp. 8–10; ʿAlī b. Yūsuf Ibn al-Qifṭī, *Ta'rīkh al-ḥukamā'*, ed. J. Lippert (Leipzig, 1903), p. 4. Among the other prophetic motifs associated with Idrīs are the exhortation to perform *jihād* and *zakāt*; the observance of ritual purity; the prohibition of donkey- and dog-meat, and, according to al-Mubashshir, camel-meat and pork; the prohibition of drunkenness; and the prediction of future prophets.

[28] Al-Ṭabarī, *Ta'rīkh*, vol. 1, p. 170; Balʿamī, *Tārīkh-i Balʿami*, ed. M.T. Bahār (Tehran, 1353/1974), vol. 1, p. 111; al-Masʿūdī, *Murūj al-dhahab*, vol. 1, p. 50; Ibn Qutayba, *ʿUyūn al-akhbār*, vol. 1, p. 43; al-Yaʿqūbī, *Ta'rīkh*, vol. 1, p. 11; al-Maqdisī, *al-Bad' wa'l-ta'rīkh* (Beirut), vol. 3, pp. 11–13; Ibn Juljul, *Ṭabaqāt al-aṭibbā' wa'l-ḥukamā'*, ed. F. Sayyid (Cairo, 1955), p. 6

according to some accounts, he teaches men to found and govern cities, gains the obedience of kings, establishes laws appropriate for each clime, summons people to religion, and classifies them into three categories: priests (*kahana*), rulers and subjects, ranked in order of their proximity to God.[29] One of the functions associated with the figure of Hermes/Thoth was the foundation and upholding of the social order in a general sense, and it is possible that the Muslim authors who transmit this myth may have stumbled on a product of the singular interaction of Greek culture with an Egyptian environment.[30] It is also striking that the depiction of Idrīs as the bringer of civilisation bears a strong resemblance to the accounts of certain primordial Iranian kings, especially Jamshīd. Abū Maʿshar seems to have identified Hermes/Idrīs with the monarch Hūshang, and the projection of Iranian legends on to the figure of Idrīs also appears in several other instances.[31]

Nevertheless, Muslim philosophers and men of letters also had access to social concepts of classical Greek provenance, especially those expressed in the writings of Plato, as interpreted by middle Platonic thinkers, and, perhaps to a lesser extent, Aristotle, as understood by the Greek commentators of Late Antiquity. They were thus heirs to the classical Greek idea that social hierarchy reflected the organisation of the city, a view which had gradually been supplanted in Byzantine thought by conceptions based on economic categories.[32] From Plato they became acquainted with philosophical arguments for the importance of hierarchy and the role of heredity in determining its structure, and also with the tripartite division of the ideal polity into philosopher-rulers,

(here acknowledging a source other than Abū Maʿshar); al-Thaʿlabī, *ʿArāʾis al-majālis* (Cairo, 1929), p. 42; Ibn al-Qifṭī, *Taʾrīkh al-ḥukamāʾ*, p. 7 (where Idrīs is reported to have introduced the manufacture of clothing, but his use of the pen is not mentioned); Ibn Abī Uṣaybiʿa, *ʿUyūn al-anbāʾ fī ṭabaqāt al-aṭibbāʾ*, ed. A. Müller (Göttingen, 1884), p. 17.

[29] Al-Mubashshir, *Mukhtār al-ḥikam*, p. 9; Ibn al-Qifṭī, *Taʾrīkh al-ḥukamāʾ*, pp. 3–4. Although Ibn al-Qifṭī copies substantially from Ibn Juljul, the latter does not record this part of Idrīs's story. Since Ibn Juljul, Ṣāʿid al-Andalusī and Ibn Abī Uṣaybiʿa all cite Abū Maʿshar, there is no evidence to suggest that Hermes/Idrīs was associated with the initiation of stratification in the *Kitāb al-ulūf*. It also seems unlikely that al-Mubashshir's book was Ibn al-Qifṭī's immediate source (cf. F. Rosenthal, 'Al-Mubashshir b. Fātik: Prolegomena to an Abortive Edition', *Oriens* 13 (1961), p. 145).

[30] On the association of Hermes/Thoth with the invention of writing, cf. A.-J. Festugière, *La révélation d'Hermès Trismégiste*, vol. 1 (Paris, 1950), pp. 67ff. Thoth is generally regarded as the founder and upholder of the social order (M.-T. Derchain-Urtel, *Thot à travers ses épithètes dans les scènes d'offrandes des temples d'époque gréco-romaine* (Brussels, 1981), p. 100; P. Boylan, *Thoth the Hermes of Egypt. A Study of some Aspects of Theological Thought in Ancient Egypt* (London and Bombay, 1922), pp. 88–91). On the origins of various other activities associated with the first Hermes in Arabic sources, see M. Plessner, 'Hermes Trismegistus and Arab Science', *SI* 2 (1954), pp. 53ff.

[31] On Abū Maʿshar's identification of Hermes with Hūshang, see Pingree, *Thousands*, p. 15, n. 3. Ṣāʿid al-Andalusī's account of Idrīs assimilates elements associated elsewhere with Ṭahmūrath (R. Blachère, *Kitâb Ṭabaḳât al-Umam (Livre des Catégories des Nations)* (Paris, 1935), p. 85, n. 1). Al-Ṭabarī includes the manufacture of clothing among the accomplishments of Jamshīd (see ch. 3) as well as Idrīs, while Balʿamī has Gayūmarth learn the art of sewing from Idrīs (Balʿamī, *Tārīkh*, vol. 1, p. 128). On the role of Jamshīd in the foundation of civilisation in Iranian sources, see ch. 3.

[32] Patlagean, *Pauvreté économique et pauvreté sociale*, pp. 9–35.

guardians (soldiers) and the productive categories (artisans and cultivators), each of which corresponded to a faculty of the individual soul.[33] Many Muslim writers appear to have been relatively well acquainted with the contents of Plato's *Republic* and *Laws*. Arabic translations existed of both texts, or at least of summaries of and commentaries on them; according to the *Fihrist*, Ḥunayn b. Isḥāq (c. 194–260/809–873) wrote a commentary on the *Republic*, and both he and Yaḥyā b. ʿAdī (c. 280–363/893–974) made translations of the *Laws*.[34] Although these translations were probably not complete, the explicated summary of the *Laws* by al-Fārābī (*Talkhīṣ Nawāmīs Aflāṭūn*) and that of the *Republic* by Ibn Rushd (extant only in a fourteenth-century Hebrew translation), as well as the accurate quotations found in some other Islamic texts, indicate that the general contents of both works were well known.[35]

It seems likely that an Arabic translation of the *Politics*, or at least an abridgement of a part of it, was available to al-Fārābī, and perhaps to some other Muslim philosophers too.[36] The contents of the *Nichomachean Ethics* were probably rather better known. An incomplete version of that work, under the title of *Kitāb al-akhlāq*, existed in Arabic,[37] but probably more important was a translation of a commentary written on the text by Porphyry and translated into Arabic by Isḥāq b. Ḥunayn.[38] Paraphrases of the text were written by al-Fārābī and Ibn Rushd.[39] The *Nichomachean Ethics* contributed to Muslim understandings of human nature and the nature of man's life in a community, and thus provided a wider philosophical context for the discussion of social stratification.

Social stratification in the works of the *falāsifa*

The writings of the Muslim philosophers reflect a tendency to conceptualise in terms of hierarchies; a rational cosmos is one in which categories, including social ones, are clearly ordered and ranked.[40] Like Plato, the *falāsifa* discuss social stratification in the context of various hypothetical types of polity, the 'city' (*madīna* = *polis*) being the smallest communal unit in which human perfection is possible. For them, differences in social function are reflections of people's various intellectual capacities and moral qualities. The

33 *Republic*, IV, 412ff., 440E–441A; cf. G. Dumézil, *L'Idéologie tripartie des Indo-Européens* (Brussels, 1958), p. 16.

34 Ibn al-Nadīm, *Kitāb al-fihrist*, ed. G. Flügel (Beirut, 1966), p. 246.

35 See A.J. Arberry, 'Some Plato in an Arabic Epitome', *IQ* 2 (1955), pp. 86–99; F. Rosenthal, 'On the Knowledge of Plato's Philosophy in the Islamic World', *IC* 14 (1940), pp. 395–397.

36 S. Pines, 'Aristotle's *Politics* in Arabic Philosophy', *Israel Oriental Studies* 5 (1975), pp. 150–160.

37 A.J. Arberry, 'The Nichomachean Ethics in Arabic', *BSOAS* 17 (1955), pp. 1–9.

38 Ibn al-Nadīm, *Fihrist*, p. 252; according to Ibn al-Qifṭī (*Ta'rīkh al-ḥukamā'*, p. 42), it was translated by Ḥunayn b. Isḥāq.

39 Steinschneider, 'Über die arabischen Übersetzungen aus dem Griechischen', pp. 69–71; *idem*, *Die hebräischen Übersetzungen des Mittelalters*, pp. 215–216, para. 112.

40 On the philosophers' understandings of society, see also R. al-Sayyid, 'Dirāsa muqārina li-mafāhīm al-ijtimāʿ al-basharī wa'l-ʿaql wa'l-tadbīr ʿind al-falāsifa wa'l-fuqahā'', in *al-Umma wa'l-jamāʿa wa'l-salṭa*, pp. 179–200.

philosophers frequently envisage an abstract hierarchy of intellects affiliated to a scale of spiritual and political authority, since the proper qualifications for the exercise of political power are knowledge and wisdom; those possessed of a lower degree of intellectual aptitude have commensurately less authority, down to the level of the 'ultimate servants'. This kind of hierarchy is evident not only throughout human society as a whole, but also within each profession, as those who are masters of a craft are superior to and exercise authority over those who are less adept. Professions are similarly ranked in a hierarchy of excellence, and men should be assigned to a 'higher' or a 'lower' occupation depending on their innate capacities.

The earliest extant philosophical treatments of social organisation are found in the works of al-Fārābī (d. 339/950), whose ideas dominate the political thought of many later Muslim philosophers.[41] Al-Fārābī wrote several political treatises in which he addressed issues related to the topic of hierarchy; his treatments of these subjects are sometimes almost identical but sometimes quite different – and even inconsistent. This variation in the content of his writings, and the lack of scholarly consensus on the order in which al-Fārābī wrote his works, render the task of interpretation particularly difficult.[42] The main works under consideration here are his *Mabādi' ārā' ahl al-madīna al-fāḍila*, the *Fuṣūl muntaza'a* (*Fuṣūl al-madanī*), the *Kitāb taḥṣīl al-sa'āda* and the *Kitāb al-siyāsa al-madaniyya*.

Although much of what al-Fārābī has to say about social organisation derives from Platonic sources, there are a number of instances in which his writings reflect at least an acquaintance with Aristotelian thought.[43] In the tradition of Platonists and Aristotelians alike, al-Fārābī considers it 'natural' for men to live in association with others.[44] On the one hand, he maintains that man is compelled by necessity to live in a society because alone he would be unable to provide for all of his complex needs. He has neither the time nor the skill necessary to supply his own food, clothing and shelter, for all these three basic requirements demand a variety of lengthy processes; he is therefore obliged to seek the co-operation of his fellows.[45] In addition, however, al-

[41] It is possible that al-Kindī (d. after 256/870) and his student Aḥmad b. al-Ṭayyib al-Sarakhsī (d. 286/899) also wrote works that dealt with political matters, and that these may have included some discussion of the composition of society; see Ibn al-Nadīm, *Fihrist*, pp. 260, 262, and F. Rosenthal, 'From Arabic Books and Manuscripts, XVI: As-Sarakhsī (?) on the Appropriate Behavior for Kings', *JAOS* 115 (1995), pp. 105–109.

[42] M. Galston, *Politics and Excellence. The Political Philosophy of Alfarabi* (Princeton, 1990), pp. 3–5, and n. 1; cf. pp. 200ff.

[43] See Pines, 'Aristotle's *Politics*', pp. 150–160. On the prevailing view that al-Fārābī's political philosophy is Platonic whereas his theoretical philosophy is Aristotelian or Neoplatonic, see Galston, *Politics and Excellence*, p. 11, n. 35.

[44] Cf. *Mabādi' ārā' ahl al-madīna al-fāḍila*, ed. and tr. R. Walzer, *Al-Fārābī on the Perfect State* (Oxford, 1985), p. 429.

[45] *Ārā'*, ed. Walzer, pp. 228–229. Cf. a similar passage ascribed to Aristotle (*ṣāḥib al-manṭiq*) by Abū'l-Ḥasan al-'Āmirī – apparently a paraphrase of a section from the *Politics* (*al-Sa'āda wa'l-is'ād*, p. 150; see further Pines, 'Aristotle's *Politics*', p. 151).

Fārābī belives that human nature itself disposes men to live in communities, since man is, in Aristotle's phrase, a 'political animal' (rendered in Arabic as *ḥayawān insī, ḥayawān madanī*).[46] These two points form the foundation for later Muslim philosophical treatments of social stratification; the first, moreover, is widely adopted by the literate élite in general, including its moralising elements.

The majority of Muslim philosophers also follow al-Fārābī in his Greek-inspired views on the significance of human life. Al-Fārābī maintains that man's basic purpose as a living being is to strive for happiness (*sa'āda*), which he sometimes describes as having two stages: lesser happiness (*al-sa'āda al-dunyā*) and ultimate happiness (*al-sa'āda al-quswā*).[47] It is this aim that provides the context for al-Fārābī's discussion of human society, for he holds that this two-fold happiness can only be achieved by living in a community. Communities (*ijtimā'āt*), he states, vary in size and type, and are either perfect and complete (*kāmila*) or incomplete; the smallest communal unit with the potential for perfection is the city.[48] In order for an individual to attain happiness, al-Fārābī maintains, it is preferable (although not absolutely necessary) that he live in Plato's excellent city (*al-madīna al-fāḍila*).[49] He defines such a polity as one whose inhabitants, under the guidance of learned and excellent men, co-operate towards the attainment of ultimate happiness, so that this common aim determines each man's place in the social structure.[50]

In general, the writings of the Muslim philosophers give the impression that their authors' interest in social organisation arises less from any particular concern for social relations than from a desire to demonstrate a consistent and rational pattern by which the whole universe is governed. Accordingly, the *falāsifa* perceive a parallel between the precise hierarchical order which prevails in the natural world, from the First Cause to primordial matter and the elements, and the order in human society, by which men are suited, both by their individual natures (*fiṭar*) and by their voluntarily acquired talents (*malakāt*), to belong to certain ranks. Similarly, just as the First Cause, whose

[46] Al-Fārābī, *Kitāb taḥṣīl al-sa'āda*, in *Rasā'il al-Fārābī* (Hyderabad, 1345/1946), p. 14; cf. Galston, *Politics and Excellence*, pp. 147ff. Cf. al-'Āmirī, *al-Sa'āda wa'l-is'ād*, pp. 218–220, where the relevant passages from Plato and Aristotle are supplemented by quotations from al-Jāḥiẓ. Elsewhere, al-Fārābī records the 'ignorant' view that mutual affection and attachment do not exist, and that people should live in mutual hostility except when they are obliged to come together by necessity (al-Fārābī, *Ārā'*, pp. 290ff).

[47] Al-Fārābī, *Taḥṣīl al-sa'āda*, p. 2; *al-Siyāsa al-madaniyya* (Beirut, 1964), pp. 74, 78; tr. F. Dieterici, *Die Staatsleitung* (Leiden, 1904), p. 60; cf. al-Fārābī, *Ārā'*, pp. 204ff. On the various representations of happiness in al-Fārābī's writings, see Galston, *Politics and Excellence*, pp. 59–68.

[48] *Ārā'*, pp. 228–231; *Siyāsa*, pp. 69–70, tr. 50–51; *Talkhīṣ Nawāmīs Aflāṭūn*, ed. F. Gabrieli (London, 1952), p. 5; cf. Walzer, p. 430, on the various 'associations' envisaged by al-Fārābī.

[49] Al-Fārābī considered it possible to achieve happiness in other types of polity: Galston, *Politics and Excellence*, pp. 175–179.

[50] *Ārā'*, pp. 230–231; *Siyāsa*, p. 80; *Fuṣūl al-madanī*, ed. and tr. D.M. Dunlop, *Aphorisms of the Statesman* (Cambridge, 1961), pp. 120–121, tr. 39–40.

existence is the point of origin for all contingent beings, has arranged the natural world in its ranks, so it is the task of the ruler of the city to appoint men to their due positions in society.[51] The need for government to take a firm hand in the arrangement of society is also expressed by Ibn Sīnā (370–428/980–1037) who, it is interesting to note, was himself (unlike al-Fārābī) involved in administration and served several times as a vizier.[52] Ibn Sīnā observes that the essential sharing of necessities among men can only be effected through social transaction (*muʿāmala*), which in turn requires a law (*sunna*) and justice (*ʿadl*); these must be enforced by a legislator (*sānn*) and preserver of justice (*muʿaddil*).[53] This idea is also taken up by the Andalusian Ibn Bājja (d. 533/1138), who holds that it is the responsibility of the ruler to assign tasks to the inhabitants of the city, and to ensure that each man undertakes the most excellent task of which he is capable.[54] By and large, however, the philosophers in the eastern parts of the Islamic world seem to have had a greater interest in social organisation than those in the west. Naṣīr al-Dīn Ṭūsī, who explicitly acknowledges his debt to al-Fārābī,[55] argues that although it is the diversity among people that renders co-operation between them possible, this co-operation still cannot be realised without firm administration (*tadbīr*), because, if men were left to their own natures, they would be intent on mutual destruction. Government (*siyāsat*) is necessary to ensure that each man is content with the station that is appropriate for him, that he receives what is due to him, and that others do not infringe on his rights.[56] The philosophers thus emphasise the notion that social harmony can only be achieved through the legitimate and conscientious use of absolute power.

Al-Fārābī, like Aristotle, describes the various social categories which make up a polity not as 'strata' (*ṭabaqāt*) but as 'parts' (*ajzāʾ*). Despite his use of such a neutral term, it is clear that the 'parts' of al-Fārābī's excellent polity are strictly ranked, and each acts in accordance with the designs of the 'part' ranked directly above it. Ultimately, therefore, all the parts follow the purpose of their first leader (*al-raʾīs al-awwal*).[57] To convey this pattern, al-Fārābī uses

51 *Ārāʾ*, pp. 234–237; Walzer, p. 436; *Siyāsa*, pp. 83–84.

52 A.-M. Goichon, 'Ibn Sīnā, *EI2*. Ibn Sīnā made explicit use of philosophical categorisations of 'cities' to describe the conditions of his own time; see al-Sayyid, 'Ibn Sīnā al-mufakkir al-siyāsī wa'l-ijtimāʿī, in *al-Umma wa'l-jamāʿa wa'l-salṭa*, p. 203.

53 *Al-Najāt* (Beirut, 1405/1985), pp. 338–339; cf. *al-Ilāhiyyāt* (Cairo, 1380/1960), p. 447. See also al-Sayyid, 'Ibn Sīnā', pp. 207–208.

54 Ibn Bājja, *Risālat al-wadāʿ*, ed. M. Asín Palacios, *Andalus* 8 (1943), pp. 30, 37; *idem*, *Tadbīr al-mutawaḥḥid*, ed. M. Asín Palacios (Madrid-Granada, 1946), p. 9.

55 *Akhlāq*, p. 248; tr. Wickens, *Nasirean Ethics*, p. 187. It is clear that Ṭūsī used al-Fārābī's *al-Siyāsa al-madaniyya*, his *Fuṣūl al-madanī*, and his admonitions quoted in Miskawayh's *al-Ḥikma al-khālida*; whether he used the *Ārāʾ ahl al-madīna al-fāḍila* is not yet established (W. Madelung, 'Naṣīr ad-Dīn Ṭūsī's Ethics between Philosophy, Shiʿism and Sufism', in *Ethics in Islam*, ed. R.G. Hovannisian (Malibu, 1985), p. 86).

56 *Akhlāq*, pp. 249–252; tr. Wickens, *Nasirean Ethics*, pp. 189–191; cf. *Akhlāq*, pp. 63–64, 205, 280; tr. pp. 47, 153, 211.

57 *Ārāʾ*, pp. 234ff. Cf. Naṣīr al-Dīn Ṭūsī, *Akhlāq*, pp. 287–288, p. 256; tr. Wickens, *Nasirean Ethics*, pp. 217, 193–194.

the common metaphor of the human body. He likens the role of the heart in the body to that of the ruler in society. In a perfect, healthy body, all the limbs, under the direction of the heart and according to their status, co-operate to achieve and preserve the perfection of the animal, just as the parts of the excellent polity, governed by the ruler and according to their positions in the social hierarchy, co-operate to ensure the wellbeing of their community:

Just as the limbs of the body differ, some being by their nature and powers superior to others, and as they include one leading member, namely the heart, after which come other limbs whose ranks are close to that leader; and as each of these other limbs is endowed by nature with a power through which it willingly performs its function, according to that which is by nature the purpose of that leading limb; as other limbs, likewise endowed with powers, perform their functions according to the purposes of these last, which are separated from the leader by no intermediary, and which are therefore on the second level; as other limbs perform functions according to the purposes of those on the second level, and so on until the [level] is reached of those who serve and do not rule at all; so is the city. Its parts vary in nature, and some are superior to others in disposition. One man in it is the ruler (*raʾīs*). Others exist in ranks close to the ruler, and each rank is characterised by a disposition and a faculty through which it performs a function according to the intention of the ruler. These are the members of the first ranks (*ūlū'l-marātib al-uwal*). Below them are a group of people who perform actions according to their purposes; they are on the second level. Below these, also, are those who act in accordance with their intents. The parts of the city are thus ranked (*yatarattab*) down to those who perform their tasks only according to the designs of others; they are those who serve and are not served, the lowest of the ranks and the most base.[58]

Al-Fārābī qualifies his analogy between the human body and the polity, however, by stating that, while the limbs of the body are naturally disposed to execute their tasks, the parts of the city act voluntarily.[59] Since all parts of the excellent city are involved in an unceasing and unified endeavour towards the fulfilment of the ruler's purpose, namely the happiness of his community, all rulers of excellent polities throughout the world are like one single ruler, and each part, despite the constant change in its individual members, is essentially as it was in earlier times.[60] Undisturbed by the succession of new generations, all the parts of the city are linked together into a harmonious whole by their concerted efforts.[61] This harmonious co-operation is presented in sharp contrast to the disparate and often antagonistic groups that characterise imperfect polities.[62]

For the Muslim philosophers, like their Greek predecessors, the primary determinant of rank in the hierarchical order of being is knowledge; and an individual's degree of knowledge is inseparable from his occupation. Naṣīr

[58] *Ārā'*, pp. 230–233; cf. Walzer, p. 434. On the possibly Aristotelian source for the idea of people who are 'slaves by nature', see Pines, 'Aristotle's *Politics*', pp. 151–155. See also al-Fārābī's discussion of the relative ranks of the faculties of the soul and the limbs and organs of the body, *Ārā'*, pp. 164ff, 174ff; cf. Lewis, *Political Language*, p. 128, n. 1.

[59] *Ārā'*, pp. 232–235; cf. *Fuṣūl*, pp. 22, 117–118.

[60] *Ārā'*, pp. 258–261; *Siyāsa*, p. 82.

[61] *Siyāsa*, pp. 83–84, tr. pp. 66–67; cf. *Talkhīṣ*, pp. 29–30.

[62] *Siyāsa*, p. 99.

al-Dīn Ṭūsī situates humanity in a 'middle rank' between the realm of the angels and the animal world. Within the middle rank, the highest position is occupied by persons who, by means of revelation and inspiration, possess knowledge of divine realities and laws; this category includes prophets and saints, and borders on the realm of the angels. Beneath this group are those who, by means of intellectual application, reflection and meditation, pursue the sciences, the branches of knowledge and the acquisition of virtues. The third category of humanity comprises those who, by the use of their intellects and intuition, practise noble crafts and professions, and produce instruments.[63]

At its highest levels, then, knowledge is not accessible to all men. Instead, it is the preserve of a small élite, and should be forcibly withheld from those who do not belong to this initiated circle.[64] Al-Fārābī distinguishes between the élite (*khāṣṣa*) and the commoners (*'āmma*), the former being composed of those who possess superior knowledge and understanding and are thus capable of ultimate happiness, while the latter do not possess such gifts and are capable only of a lower degree of happiness.[65] All men must belong to one or other of these two general categories. While all the inhabitants of the excellent polity have a certain measure of knowledge in common, they differ in the depth of their understanding. The élite know the true nature of things by virtue of rational proofs and their own insight; the rest of society can understand only by analogy and comparison, and then with varying degrees of accuracy.[66] Like Aristotle, al-Fārābī also envisages a hierarchy of excellence among the various occupations and sciences and their subdivisions.[67]

The same distinction between the élite and the common people appears in the *Rasā'il* of the Ikhwān al-Ṣafā': the élite consist of those gifted with spiritual enlightenment and innate knowledge of the esoteric dimension of things (the *bāṭin*), while the commoners are those limited in their spirituality to mere acceptance of the exoteric (the *ẓāhir*).[68] Between these two poles, the authors envisage a countless number of strata through which men can progress in proportion to their spiritual growth. But these various degrees can be divided into three more basic categories: the *'āmma*, composed of women, children and the ignorant; the *khāṣṣa*, or scholars of religious and secular learning, who are

[63] *Akhlāq*, pp. 62–63; tr. Wickens, *Nasirean Ethics*, pp. 46–47; cf. a similar discussion of man's situation between the animals and the angels, also ascribed to Ṭūsī, in the *Rawḍat al-taslīm*, ed. W. Ivanow (Leiden, 1950), pp. 43, 57–58. See also al-Fārābī, *Ārā'*, pp. 222ff.

[64] *Talkhīṣ*, p. 2. [65] *Taḥṣīl al-sa'āda*, p. 16.

[66] *Ārā'*, pp. 260–261, 278–281; cf. *Taḥṣīl al-sa'āda*, pp. 36–37; *Siyāsa*, pp. 85–86, tr. pp. 68–70. See also Ibn Sīnā, *al-Najāt*, pp. 500ff. Cf. *Republic*, 376E–412B, 521C–541B, 471C–480, 484A–487A.

[67] *Siyāsa*, p. 77, tr. pp. 58–60; cf. *Ārā'*, pp. 266–267; *Talkhīṣ*, pp. 7, 20–21. Cf. *Nichomachean Ethics*, I, 1.

[68] *Rasā'il Ikhwān al-Ṣafā'* (Beirut, 1957), vol. 3, p. 511. The strongly hierarchical tendency in the world-view of the Ikhwān al-Ṣafā' is reminiscent of the thought of Pseudo-Dionysios (cf. R. Roques, *L'Univers dionysien: structure hiérarchique du monde selon le Pseudo-Denys* (Paris, 1983), especially pp. 101–111).

advanced and well-founded in their knowledge; and the middling people, who fall between these two extremes.[69] Along similar lines, Ṭūsī enumerates five ranks among the inhabitants of the excellent polity: the best philosophers (*afāḍil al-ḥukamā*), the men of faith (*ahl-i īmān*), the men of assent (*ahl-i taslīm*), the weak-minded (*mustaḍʿafān*), and the image-worshippers (*ṣūrat-parastān*).[70]

One of the central characteristics of the philosophical understanding of social rank is the idea that men's intellectual and spiritual aptitudes qualify them for different degrees of political and spiritual authority within the community. In al-Fārābī's writings, the terms *raʾīs* and *malik* (and occasionally *imām*), which connote political leadership, are used to refer to people of the highest intellectual level; the terms *marʾūs* and *khadam* refer to the commoners.[71] The man who emerges as the elect of the elect (*akhaṣṣ al-khawāṣṣ*), he writes, has nothing to learn from anyone and is therefore the only person suitable to assume the responsibilities of the supreme leader (*al-raʾīs al-awwal*).[72] At the other extreme, some men are so lacking in understanding that they are incapable of passing on knowledge to anyone else and are fit only for service.[73] Most people are situated between these two extremes: they learn from, and are governed by, those above them, while they in turn instruct, and govern, those below themselves.[74] As a result, there are several degrees between the highest ruler and the lowest ranks of the ruled; this graded arrangement of society as a whole is duplicated on a smaller scale within specific functions, such as agriculture, commerce and medicine.[75]

The Platonic tripartite social model

Although Plato's celebrated tripartite model was probably well known to the *falāsifa* and to other literate men, it was not commonly reproduced, even in the works of the philosophers themselves. Al-Fārābī implicitly adopts it when he discusses the particular qualities of the three 'parts' (the governing, military and financial functions) of the city,[76] but in most of his political writings his main concern is with the ruler himself.[77] The three categories are also discussed by al-ʿĀmirī in his *Kitāb al-saʿāda waʾl-isʿād*.[78] The fullest discussion, however, is that

[69] *Rasāʾil*, vol. 3, pp. 511–512. [70] *Akhlāq*, pp. 281–285; tr. Wickens, pp. 212–215.

[71] *Siyāsa*, pp. 78–89, tr. pp. 60–61; p. 84, tr. p. 67; *Taḥṣīl al-saʿāda*, pp. 29, 36–37; *Talkhīṣ*, pp. 19–20. On al-Fārābī's use of these terms, cf. Walzer, p. 436.

[72] *Taḥṣīl al-saʿāda*, p. 37; *Siyāsa*, pp. 85–86, tr. pp. 68–70; *Talkhīṣ*, p. 13. Cf. al-Sayyid, 'al-ʿAql waʾl-dawla fīʾl-Islām. Dirāsa muqārina li-mafāhīm al-ijtimāʿ al-basharī', *al-Umma waʾl-jamāʿa waʾl-salṭa*, pp. 186ff.

[73] *Ārāʾ*, pp. 232–233. Cf. F. Rosenthal, *The Muslim Concept of Freedom* (Leiden, 1960), p. 91, n. 285; Pines, 'Aristotle's *Politics*', pp. 151ff. [74] *Siyāsa*, p. 83, tr. p. 66.

[75] *Siyāsa*, pp. 78–79, tr. pp. 60–61. Cf. *Rasāʾil Ikhwān al-Ṣafāʾ*, vol. 3, pp. 511, 428–429.

[76] *Taḥṣīl al-saʿāda*, pp. 22ff.

[77] *Ārāʾ*, pp. 238ff; cf. Walzer, pp. 436, 439ff; Galston, *Politics and Excellence*, esp. pp. 95–145.

[78] *Kitāb al-saʿāda waʾl-isʿād*, *passim*.

of Ibn Sīnā, who reproduces the model faithfully in his treatment of the rulers or administrators (*mudabbirūn*), the artisans (*ṣunnā'*), and the guardians (*ḥafaẓa*). Ibn Sīnā considers it the first purpose of the legislator to arrange the inhabitants of the city into these three parts, which should themselves be organised internally as hierarchies. He regards it as necessary that the legislator should establish in each 'species' (*jins*) a leader (*ra'īs*), who should in turn appoint lesser leaders, beneath whom should be leaders of still less authority, down to the level of the least of men. According to Ibn Sīnā, the polity should not contain any man without a task and a defined position (*maḥall maḥdūd*). Everyone should provide a benefit for the city; idleness should be forbidden, and no one should be able to satisfy his needs by dint of someone else's efforts. Wealth in the city should be derived from a variety of sources and spent in several different ways. One of the most important items of expenditure was the maintenance of the guardians, who, as in the *Republic*, were forbidden to practise a craft.[79]

Abū'l-Faḍl Bayhaqī (385–470/995–1077), the secretary and historian of the Ghaznavids, adopted the Platonic tripartite functional model and applied it explicitly to the polity in which he himself participated. In his *Tārīkh-i Mas'ūdī*, Bayhaqī not only lists the three Platonic categories, but also follows Plato in envisaging them as manifestations on the communal plane of the three faculties of the individual soul:

> You must realise very clearly that the rational soul (*nafs-i gūyandeh*) corresponds to the ruler – commanding, masterful and overbearing. He must administer justice and punishment as whole-heartedly and firmly as possible, and not in an ineffective manner; and when he shows kindness, it must not be so as to leave an impression of weakness. Furthermore, anger (*khashm*) corresponds to the army of the ruler, by means of which he uncovers [the enemy's] weak points, makes secure [his own] vital points, frustrates the enemy and protects the subjects. The army must be fully prepared; when it is thus ready, it is able to carry out the ruler's command. The appetitive soul (*nafs-i arzū*) corresponds to the subject population of this ruler; it is vital that they should be in complete fear and trembling of the ruler and the army, and give [them] obedience.[80]

Like Ibn Sīnā, Bayhaqī explicitly applies philosophical categories to a concrete situation. He also adapts the abstract language of the philosophical tradition to accommodate the edifying, didactic tone that characterises his history; he addresses his audience in a directly instructive voice and substitutes the terms *lashkar* and *ra'iyyat*, which were becoming standard elements in the vocabulary of didactic works on statecraft, for the technical terms used by Ibn Sīnā.[81]

Elsewhere, al-Fārābī describes another model, in which he enumerates five

[79] *Al-Ilāhiyyāt*, p. 447; cf. *Republic*, II, 374B–E. See further R. al-Sayyid, 'Ibn Sīnā', p. 211.

[80] Abū'l-Faḍl Bayhaqī, *Tārīkh-i Mas'ūdī*, ed. Q. Ghanī and A.A. Fayyāḍ (Tehran, 1324/1945), pp. 101–102; the passage is also cited in C.E. Bosworth, *The Ghaznavids. Their Empire in Afghanistan and Eastern Iran, 994–1040* (Edinburgh, 1963), p. 50. Cf. *Republic*, IV, 428, 429, 431E, 433; cf. 435Bff.

[81] On the didactic nature of Bayhaqī's history, see M.R. Waldman, *Toward a Theory of Historical Narrative: A Case Study in Perso-Islamicate Historiography* (Columbus, Ohio, 1980), pp. 9–10.

functional categories rather than three: firstly, the most excellent persons (*afāḍil*), who are the philosophers (*ḥukamā'*), men of practical knowledge (*muta'aqqilūn*) and those with opinions on great affairs; secondly, 'masters of the spoken word and the upholders of religion': the preachers (*khuṭabā'*), masters of rhetoric (*bulaghā'*), poets, musicians and secretaries; thirdly, the 'assessors' (*muqaddirūn*): accountants, geometers, physicians and astrologers; fourthly, the fighting men: soldiers and guardians; and fifthly, those who deal with financial matters (*māliyyūn*) and those who procure the wealth in the city: the agriculturalists, herdsmen and merchants.[82] It seems that this model was developed by later Platonists.[83] The fourth and fifth categories coincide with Plato's tripartite schema, and Dunlop has suggested that the third may derive from the 'art of measurement' described by Plato in his *Statesman*.[84] Plato's single ruling class of philosophers, however, has been augmented to include two further groups, which probably also appeared in late Greek elaborations of Plato's scheme. Particularly striking in this five-fold schema are the association of religious functionaries with secretaries and other persons of secular culture, and the wide gulf between the rulers and the guardians.

Heredity in occupations

Most Muslim philosophers share Plato's trust in the workings of heredity and consequent social conservatism. Like him, they regard each man as endowed with an innate disposition to perform a certain function, and they assume that in most cases, this will be the occupation indicated by the category into which he is born.[85] Al-Fārābī maintains that each man is naturally disposed towards a certain occupation, and that men consequently differ in excellence (*yatafāḍalūna*); an individual's exact rank depends on his aptitude (*isti'dād*) for his particular occupation or branch of knowledge, his education (*ta'addub*) in it, and his achievements (*istinbāṭ*). Those sufficiently gifted to teach are of higher status than those they instruct.[86] In his epitome of Plato's *Laws*, al-Fārābī advocates that deviation from an occupation should be prevented and punished, for 'transfer from one occupation to another without pretext is a major cause of disturbances and decay of the social order'.[87]

[82] *Fuṣūl*, pp. 136–137. Ṭūsī and Davvānī follow al-Fārābī in quoting this model; Ṭūsī, *Akhlāq-i Nāṣirī*, pp. 285–286, tr. Wickens, *Nasirean Ethics*, pp. 215–216; Davvānī, *Akhlāq-i Jalālī*, pp. 258–260, tr. Thompson, *Practical Philosophy*, pp. 372–373.

[83] Al-Fārābī, *Ārā'*, p. 437.

[84] Although there is no record of an Arabic translation of this work, there are other indications that al-Fārābī was familiar with its general contents; al-Fārābī, *Fuṣūl al-madanī*, introduction, pp. 17–18.

[85] *Republic*, II, 369B–372C.

[86] *Siyāsa*, p. 77, tr. pp. 58–60.

[87] *Talkhīṣ*, pp. 39–40. Al-Fārābī may occasionally hold out the possibility of an individual increasing the level of understanding suggested by his descent. See for instance the views expressed in a *Risāla fī'l-akhlāq* ascribed to him: 'In the case of those above him, let him attain their level; as for his peers, let him surpass them; and as for those who are base, let him not sink to their level' (*Risāla fī'l-akhlāq*, ms. Aya Sofya 1957, f. 135; I owe this reference to L. Miller). See also *Ārā'*, pp. 280–283; *Siyāsa*, p. 105, tr. pp. 89–90; Ṭūsī, *Akhlāq*, p. 334, tr. Wickens, *Nasirean Ethics*, p. 253.

Abū'l-Ḥasan al-ʿĀmirī (d. 381/992), in his philosophical anthology *Kitāb al-saʿāda wa'l-isʿād*, similarly cites Plato for the view that men are not equally skilled at all crafts, and that each man should therefore undertake the task to which he is naturally disposed and avoid those for which his nature is not suited.[88] Since he cannot master a craft unless he perseveres at it from his youth onwards and devotes himself to it exclusively, the law (*sunna*) stipulates that each man should undertake only one task, and that he should not deviate from it.[89] For Plato, if a man is at one moment a philosopher, at another a politician, at another a soldier, at another a man of business, as well as a participant in a number of leisurely activities, this will result in injustice and the lawlessness characteristic of democratic polities.[90] Al-ʿĀmirī records the opinion that since for the most part children's natures are determined by those of their parents, they should take up the activities of their parents. But he also adopts the Platonic metaphor of different metals to convey these different types of human nature. According to Plato, some men are fashioned with an intermixture of gold in their souls; such men are fit for leadership. Others are born with an intermixture of silver and are fit to fulfil the role of guardians. Still others are born with iron or brass in their souls, and are fitted to become farmers and craftsmen. Although these types almost always breed according to their kinds, it is the ruler's first duty to observe men intently in order to ascertain their proper status.[91] Al-ʿĀmirī follows Plato in allowing that on rare occasions a 'copper' son might be born to a 'golden' father, or vice versa.[92]

Ṭūsī also discusses the virtue of being content with one's lot, and sees each person as being fitted for a particular discipline or craft in which he finds happiness.[93] For him, justice (*ʿadālat*) requires that each man pursue one occupation only, since people's natures have their own particularities, which render some men unsuited to certain activities. Moreover, since a man masters the rules of a craft only after lengthy study and endeavour, if he divides his attention between several different occupations, he will reach a lower level of

[88] I follow here the identification by Minovi of the Abū'l-Ḥasan b. Abī Dharr named in the text with Abū'l-Ḥasan al-ʿĀmirī (M. Minovi, 'Az khazā'in-i Turkīyeh', *Majalleh-yi Dānishkadeh-yi Adabīyāt* 4 (1335/1957), p. 79; *Kitāb al-saʿāda wa'l-isʿād*, introduction, p. 4), although al-ʿĀmirī does not refer to this book in the list of his works compiled in his *K. al-amad ʿalā'l-abad*, written only six years before his death (E.K. Rowson, 'al-ʿĀmirī', *EI2* (Suppl.); see also Rowson's discussion of the authorship of the *Kitāb al-saʿāda wa'l-isʿād* in his *A Muslim Philosopher on the Soul and its Fate* (New Haven, 1988), pp. 15–17).

[89] *Al-saʿāda wa'l-isʿād*, pp. 396–397; cf. *Republic*, II, 374; III, 397E, 415A; IV, 421, 433A, 434, 441E, 443; V, 453; VIII, 552A, and *Laws*, VIII, 846E. See also Ibn Khaldūn, tr. F. Rosenthal, *The Muqaddimah, An Introduction to History* (Princeton, 1967), vol. 2, pp. 354–355.

[90] *Republic*, IV, 433A, 434B–C; VIII, 544C, 555B–562, 561C–D.

[91] *Republic*, IV, 415A–C; 423D–E. The practicability of the Platonic notion of transfer is criticised by Aristotle, *Politics*, II, 4 and 5.

[92] *Al-saʿāda wa'l-isʿād*, p. 398.

[93] Ṭūsī, *Akhlāq*, p. 197; tr. Wickens, *Nasirean Ethics*, p. 145. Ṭūsī cites the Qur'ānic *kullu ḥizbin bi-mā ladayhim fariḥūn* ('Each party rejoices in what is theirs', Q.23:53, 30:31), a phrase generally interpreted as a reference to the religious certainty enjoyed by separate religious groups (M. b. al-Ḥasan Shaykh al-Ṭā'ifa al-Ṭūsī, *Tafsīr al-tibyān*, ed. A.Ḥ.Q. al-ʿĀmilī (Najaf), vol. 7 (1381/1962), p. 375; al-Bayḍāwī, *Anwār al-tanzīl*, vol. 2, pp. 8, 107).

accomplishment in each of them. When each man pursues the one task for which he is best suited, co-operation is achieved, benefits are increased, and harms decreased.[94]

According to the Ikhwān al-Ṣafā', the Greeks used to determine the profession for which a child should be trained through the practice of astrology.[95] It was the position of the stars at the time of his birth that determined a man's capacity for learning, and consequently his social rank too. Unlike Plato and the Muslim philosophers who follow him, the Ikhwān do not specify that an individual can master only one activity: some men, in their view, are capable of learning only one occupation, while others can manage several; still others are incapable of mastering any occupation at all. In the last group the Ikhwān include four categories of men: the offspring of rulers, whose pride prevents them from learning a profession; prophets and their followers, who are satisfied with little and inclined towards the other world; beggars, who are lazy and slothful; and women and effeminate men, who are base and lacking in understanding.[96]

The author of the pseudo-Aristotelian *Sirr al-asrār* also attributes an individual's rank to astrological factors which, he asserts, can even contravene heredity: if it were so determined, the son of a weaver might become a learned and cultured minister, while the son of one of the kings of India, unable to withstand the dictates of his nature, inevitably became a blacksmith.[97]

Despite this acceptance of the principle of heredity, Muslim philosophers sometimes associate meritocratic tendencies, as well as despotic ones, with Plato. According to al-ʿĀmirī, Plato asserted that men should be honoured not according to their wealth, but according to the use they made of their wealth; not according to their power, but according to their use of power; not according to their knowledge, but according to their use of knowledge; and not for their fine appearance, but for their virtue. Al-ʿĀmirī himself adds that whoever believes that a man should be exalted for his speech, beauty or appearance is greatly mistaken; a man should be exalted for his fine deeds and character, his observance and temperance.[98] He also attributes to Plato the idea that it is the ruler's duty to arrange men in ranks according to their excellence, and not according to wealth or privilege. Each man should be treated

[94] *Akhlāq*, p. 288; tr. pp. 217–218. [95] *Rasā'il*, vol. 1, pp. 290–292.

[96] *Rasā'il*, vol. 1, pp. 290–292. On the view that beggars adopt their means of subsistence on account of an innate propensity to laziness, see C.E. Bosworth, *The Mediaeval Islamic Underworld. The Banū Sāsān in Arabic Society and Literature* (Leiden), vol. 1 (1976), pp. 4ff. (The idea is not, of course, peculiar to Islamic societies; for an example taken from seventeenth-century France, see R. Mousnier, *Social Hierarchies, 1450 to the Present* (New York, 1973), tr. P. Evans, p. 69.)

[97] Badawī, *al-Uṣūl al-yūnāniyya*, pp. 134–135. On this text, see *al-Uṣūl al-yūnāniyya*, pp. 38–41; Grignaschi, 'Le roman épistolaire classique', p. 212; S. Shaked, 'From Iran to Islam: Notes on Some Themes in Transmission', *JSAI* 4, 1984, pp. 41ff.

[98] *Al-saʿāda wa'l-isʿād*, p. 151. These quotations from Plato follow a similarly meritocratic statement attributed to Aristotle.

with the respect and honour proper to the rank in which the ruler has placed him; opposition to the ruler's arrangement of society, by the undue advancement of an unworthy person, is not to be tolerated.[99] Al-ʿĀmirī then adds a quotation attributed to Aristotle, in which the philosopher advocates the protection of men of manly virtues and beneficence (*ahl al-muruwwāt wa man lahu qidam fī'l-khayr*) even when their fortunes have declined, for 'injury to men's social positions (*marātib*) is more serious than injury to their bodies or possessions, because men squander their wealth and risk their bodies in order to avoid injury to their manly honour (*muruwwāt*)'.[100]

Al-ʿĀmirī also includes quotations from Iranian and Islamic sources in his anthology. As further support for the necessity of social distinctions, he cites the well-known speech ascribed to Ziyād (b. Abī Sufyān) in which the latter announces that if any noble person should come into his presence in the company of a base man, thus failing to appreciate the value of his nobility, or any elderly man should enter with a youth, failing to appreciate the value of his seniority, or any learned man with an ignorant man, failing to recognise the worth of his learning, he would punish him and publicise his punishment.[101] Al-ʿĀmirī then quotes the well-known verse by al-Afwah al-Awdī:

> The people will not prosper if there is no distinction between them and no head over them;
> And they will have no head as long as their ignorant ones prevail.[102]

Finally on this subject, al-ʿĀmirī quotes from the testament of an unidentified ruler (probably Ardashīr): 'Make it your duty to uphold the social strata according to their limits and ranks, so that those worthy of esteem (*ḥurma*) may be distinguished from those unworthy of it, and the tested (*dhū'l-balā'*) from the untested (*man lā balā' lahu*). For nothing is more destructive to the subjects and more indicative of bad government than to combine the beneficent (*muḥsin*) and the iniquitous (*musī'*) in one station.'[103]

Social organisation in 'ignorant' polities

Excellent polities, in the view of the philosophers, were emphatically hierarchical, and movement from one social category to another was exceedingly difficult in them. The various errant polities diverged from this standard either by taking an egalitarian view of social existence or by placing people in high rank for the wrong reasons. In some cases, men refused to recognise any ranks (*marātib*), any established order (*niẓām*) or any position of merit (*isti'hāl*) by

[99] *Al-saʿāda wa'l-isʿād*, pp. 377–378. [100] *Al-saʿāda wa'l-isʿād*, p. 378. [101] See ch. 1.

[102] Al-ʿĀmirī, *al-saʿāda wa'l-isʿād*, p. 378. The same verse is quoted for similar purposes by Ibn al-Muqaffaʿ, *Risāla fī'l-ṣaḥāba*, in *Āthār Ibn al-Muqaffaʿ*, ed. ʿUmar Abū'l-Naṣr (Beirut, 1966), p. 357, and al-Māwardī, *al-Aḥkām al-sulṭāniyya* (Cairo, 1960), p. 5.

[103] *Al-saʿāda wa'l-isʿād*, p. 379. On the dangers of placing the *muḥsin* and the *musī'* on an equal level, cf. ʿIzz al-Din Ibn Abī'l-Ḥadīd, *Sharḥ nahj al-balāgha*, ed. M. Abū'l-Faḍl Ibrāhīm (Cairo), vol. 17 (1963), p. 44.

which some individuals might be placed before others; such an attitude caused each man to cling to such goods as he possessed and to seek to gain the goods of other people by force.[104]

The 'communal polity' (*al-madīna al-jamā'iyya*, also known as *ijtimā' al-ḥurriyya*, or *madīnat al-aḥrār*) lacked virtue because its inhabitants were wholly free, left to do as they pleased and all were equal (*mutasāwūn*). No person was regarded as superior to any other in any respect whatsoever; no inhabitant had any authority over any other inhabitant, lest the freedom of the latter be diminished. Such communities consisted of countless groups (*ṭawā'if*), each of which decided on its own criteria for leadership. The authority of each leader depended on the will of those whom he led (*mar'ūsūn*), so that, properly considered, there was no real *ra'īs* (leader) or *mar'ūs* (led) among them. In the opinion of the inhabitants of the communal polity, praise and honour were due to those who brought them to freedom, facilitated the attainment of their hopes and desires, safeguarded their liberty, and protected the various interests of each group, both from other groups within the community and from external enemies. Such men were considered honourable, superior, fit to be obeyed and excellent. If, however, a genuinely excellent man, who would place limits on their freedom of action and guide them towards happiness, were to appear among the inhabitants of such a polity, they would not make him their leader; and if he nevertheless became such, he would be speedily deposed or killed.[105]

Other types of polity were imperfect because they were founded on false criteria, and these were reflected in their social organisation. In the 'necessary polity' (*al-madīna al-ḍarūriyya*), whose inhabitants co-operated merely to procure the necessary food and clothing, whoever could best contrive to acquire such necessities or, alternatively, whoever distributed such things to the community, was deemed the most excellent among them and became their leader.[106] The inhabitants of the 'servile polity' (*madīnat al-nadhāla*), on the other hand, co-operated in order to obtain wealth and affluence in excess of their needs; in their estimation, the wealthiest person and the person most skilled in attaining wealth were the most excellent; their leader was the person best able to direct them in the earning and preservation of wealth.[107] In the 'base polity' (*madīnat al-khissa*), whose inhabitants co-operated for the sake of sensual pleasures and frivolity, the person with the greatest capacity for such pleasures was considered the most excellent.[108]

The inhabitants of the 'polity of nobility' (*madīnat al-karāma*) were superior to those of the previously mentioned states; they co-operated in order to

104 Al-Fārābī, *Ārā'*, pp. 290–291.

105 Al-Fārābī, *Siyāsa*, pp. 95, 99–101; al-Fārābī, *Ārā'*, pp. 256–257; cf. Walzer, *Al-Fārābī on the Perfect State*, p. 454. Cf. Rosenthal, *Freedom*, pp. 100–101.

106 Al-Fārābī, *Siyāsa*, p. 88; *idem*, *Ārā'*, pp. 254–255; cf. pp. 452–453.

107 *Idem*, *Siyāsa*, pp. 88–89; *idem*, *Ārā'*, pp. 254–255; cf. p. 453.

108 *Idem*, *Siyāsa*, p. 89; *idem*, *Ārā'*, pp. 254–255; cf. p. 453.

win honour by word and deed. In their opinion, wealth, the attainment of the means of pleasure, the attainment of basic necessities in excess of the required amount, and the benefiting of others in these three respects were considered honourable, but virtue was not.[109] Another means of winning honour, in the opinions of the inhabitants of ignorant polities, was domination (*ghalaba*); still another was inherited merit (*ḥasab*), which a man was considered to possess if his forefathers and ancestors had been wealthy, or had disposed of the means of pleasure, or had dominated several things, or had benefited others in these matters, or if they had been characterised by fine appearance, strength, or contempt for death, all of which were the instruments of domination. In the polity of nobility, the man considered most worthy among the inhabitants became their leader, so that, if *ḥasab* were deemed the major mark of worthiness, then he whose *ḥasab* was greatest would be their leader; if wealth, then the wealthiest; and so on.[110] The leader of the 'polity of domination' (*madīnat al-taghallub*), whose inhabitants co-operated in order to gain domination, was the person most skilled in employing them to dominate others, the most cunning and prudent in ensuring that they were always regarded as dominators, and in protecting them from the domination of others.[111]

Social conflict

For al-Fārābī and those philosophers who follow him, social harmony is an ideal that is realised in the excellent polity, whose inhabitants, under the guidance of their wise and despotic ruler, are brought to perfect co-operation. But most Muslim philosophers also perceive a natural state of conflict between the élite and the commoners. This idea is genuinely Platonic; in his *Laws*, Plato upholds a fundamental distinction between the rulers and the ruled, and envisages a natural and permanent state of tension between them. He regards it as the responsibility of the legislator to control this conflict, and advocates that extremes of wealth and poverty, which may incite hostility among men, be avoided.[112] Al-ʿĀmirī cites Plato and Aristotle to suggest that the gulf between the rich and the poor is inevitable and unbridgeable,[113] and agrees with Plato that 'it is not the way of the ruler to allocate all good things to every single inhabitant of the city or to every category of them, because that is simply impossible; but it is imperative that he allocate a number of good things to a

[109] *Idem, Ārā'*, pp. 256–257; cf. p. 453.
[110] *Idem, Siyāsa*, pp. 89–94; *idem, Ārā'*, pp. 256–257; cf. *Fuṣūl al-madanī*, pp. 122–123, tr. pp. 40–41.
[111] Al-Fārābī, *Siyāsa*, p. 95; Walzer, *Al-Fārābī on the Perfect State* p. 453. This description of systems in which one social function is elevated above all others and constitutes the basis for a hierarchical social order anticipates a similar discussion in modern sociology (Mousnier, *Social Hierarchies*, p. 11).
[112] *Laws*, III, 689–691. Cf. Aristotle, *Pols.*, IV, 3 and 4; VII, 8, 9 and 10.
[113] *Al-saʿāda wa'l-isʿād*, p. 90.

number of the people of the city, so that they do not want for good things. Then it is necessary that he give to each one of the inhabitants that which his kind deserves to be given . . . and the way of order and wellbeing is that he should give to each category in the city that which is fitting for its kind. Then it will not happen that a man abandons his state, seeks what is not his, and is not content with what is his'.[114]

The same notion of social conflict appears in the pseudo-philosophical literature, and is discussed at length in the *Kitāb al-ʿuhūd al-yūnāniyya*, or 'Book of Greek Testaments (derived from the symbols in Plato's *Republic* and what was added to it)', of Aḥmad b. Yūsuf b. al-Dāya (d. c. 331/942–3). This work consists of three testaments, which the author presents as a corrective to the view that the Greek contribution to the theory of statecraft had been negligible and vastly inferior to that of the Persians.[115] Despite the claims of its title, the work contains no direct quotations from the *Republic* or from any other known Greek text, but presents materials of varied provenance in the didactic fashion characteristic of testaments.[116] The first testament, which purports to be that of the emperor Hadrian to his son, recognises the dangers of social conflict: 'Know that there is a war between the poor and the rich, the weak and the strong, the vengeance of which does not sleep as long as each of the two continues to be bound by it.'[117] The text goes on to explain that the poor man covets any bounty withheld from him and enjoyed by the rich and yet, in the unlikely event that he succeeds in attaining it, he is soon disappointed, and consequently yearns for even greater bounties. He is never satisfied with what he has, so that his change of status does him no good at all, and his acquisitiveness becomes a sickness. A state of conflict between the élite and the commoners is therefore inevitable. This applies not only to the rich and poor, but also to the government appointee (*wālī*) and the dismissed official (*maʿzūl*), and to the prominent man of high rank (*dhūʾl-jāh*) and the undistinguished man (*khāmil*).[118]

A state of envious conflict between the rich and poor is similarly depicted in the *Mukhtār al-ḥikam wa maḥāsin al-kalim* (440/1048–1049) of al-Mubashshir b. Fātik. Again, the poor man is portrayed as being constantly desirous of what the rich man possesses, a condition that results in hostility. The author attributes to Plato a speech in which he recognises only the most

[114] *Al-saʿāda waʾl-isʿād*, p. 402.

[115] ʿAbd al-Raḥmān Badawī, *al-Uṣūl al-yūnāniyya*, pp. 3–4, 26. Badawī regards this collection of testaments, together with the *Sirr al-asrār*, as expressions of opposition to the influence of Iranian traditions in ʿAbbāsid social and political organisation. [116] See ch. 5.

[117] Badawī, *al-Uṣūl al-yūnāniyya*, p. 16.

[118] Badawī, *al-Uṣūl al-yūnāniyya*, p. 17. The author also alludes to the enmity between the élite and the common people in the following passage: 'Know that, in the opinion of the subjects, justice means that their state should be made equal with that of the members of the highest station, while in the opinion of the latter, it means that the common people should be driven by humiliation into agreement with the leaders; both of these two paths are unjust' (*al-Uṣūl al-yūnāniyya*, p. 22).

basic level of equality among people, and admonishes his listeners not to covet anything beyond their natural lot:

> Know that Almighty God made his creatures equal in the bestowing of [certain] bounties . . . [For example], good health is not acquired by rank, nor do the weak lose it because of their weakness. So this bounty exceeds all those on which the rich pride themselves. The senses, too, are given to everyone. God's gifts to you and the afflictions which he averts from you make gratitude to him incumbent upon you night and day. So avert your minds from coveting that which you do not need. Know that what is inherent in [your] nature (*fiṭra*) is the natural law, and it brings benefits and riches to you. Nature has prepared for you that whereby your affairs will prosper in this world and the next. What incites you to labour and toil for something that breeds hatred and hostility among you? I tell you truly: if you knew what was involved in that for which you struggle, perhaps you would abstain from the object of your desire.[119]

In conclusion, it may be said that when the Arabs conquered Syria and Egypt they came to settle in regions with long hierarchical traditions, although the institutional aspects of these traditions had probably loosened somewhat in the decades immediately preceding the Arabs' arrival. The cultivation of classical philosophy, which assumed and justified gross social inequalities, had lapsed in the century or so before the conquests. The Syrian and Egyptian élites no doubt continued to hold many of the general ideas that had characterised Greek political literature: respect for the importance of heredity, a strong tendency to social conservatism, the conflation of intellectual and moral stature in the classifications of professions, and the ideal of social harmony based on a division of labour. They may not, however, have retained more distinctively Greek visualisations of the ideal society. The social ideas of the Muslim philosophers have a somewhat similar fate in mainstream Islamic culture: although the general assumptions that underlie them reappear, variously modified, in many areas of the Islamic tradition, their specific social models, with very few exceptions, do not. In the cases of both late antique Christianity and classical Islam, the generalities are, of course, retained because they resonate with the general outlook of élites. And in both cases, it is often unclear whether those who adopt classical arguments for their élitist ideas do so consciously or unwittingly.

In the case of the Muslim reception of classical Greek thought, it may be noted that many Muslims seem to have regarded the Greeks as theorists rather than as exemplars of a practical, living social system. Al-Jāḥiẓ gives expression to this perception in a discussion of the characteristics and aptitudes of different peoples: 'Consider the fact that the Greeks, who speculated on the causes of things, were not merchants or artisans, nor did they take up agriculture, farming, building or cultivation, nor did they concern themselves with collecting, hoarding or hard work. Their rulers released them from these

[119] *Mukhtār al-ḥikam*, p. 129.

responsibilities by supplying their needs for them . . . They were thinkers, not doers.'[120] This attitude is in striking contrast to Muslims' perceptions of Iran, and it is instructive to consider the context for this contrast. In the case of Iran, the Arabs rapidly conquered the entire region of the former Sasanian empire, and Iranians converted to Islam early and in large numbers. As a result, in Iran (and Iraq) the Arabs came into contact with a living tradition which had large numbers of spokesmen to ensure that it was perpetuated. In the case of the Greek tradition, on the other hand, the Arabs succeeded in conquering only Syria and Egypt, and their contact with the Byzantine tradition was thus limited to what they saw among the Syrians and Copts, some of whom were themselves ambivalent towards Hellenistic culture. The Syrians and Copts, moreover, were slower to convert than the Iranians, and were thus less able to participate effectively in the struggles over the cultural orientation of Islamic civilisation which are discernible in much of what follows.

[120] *Manāqib al-turk*, in *Rasā'il al-Jāḥiẓ*, vol. 3, pp. 214–215; cf. F. Gabrieli, 'La «*Risāla*» di al-Ǵāḥiẓ sui Turchi', *RSO* 32 (1957), p. 481.

CHAPTER 3

The Muslim reception of Iranian models

[From the Persian kings] we adopted the rules for kingship and the kingdom (*qawānīn al-mulk wa'l-mamlaka*), the ranking of the élite and the commoners (*tartīb al-khāṣṣa wa'l-'āmma*), the government of the subjects, the compelling of each category to its lot and the restriction of it to its own kind.[1]

This is how the author of the mid-third/ninth-century book known as the *Kitāb al-tāj* describes the contribution of Iranian models to Islamic practices of social stratification. The contrast between this passage and al-Jāḥiẓ's account of the Greek tradition, cited towards the end of the preceding chapter, is striking. The Iranian author's remarks should, of course, be taken with considerable caution. He is conspicuously aware of his Persian heritage and inclined to exaggerate the debt of Islamic governmental practices to Sasanian administrative norms;[2] indeed, in this passage he seems to imply that Sasanian models were at the root of a kind of social regimentation that did not exist in the classical Islamic period. It is nevertheless clear, especially from the fourth/tenth century onwards, that certain hierarchical aspects of Islamic political culture were indeed linked to Persian models of kingship;[3] and at the very least it may be said that the author of the *Kitāb al-tāj* attests to the appeal of Iranian social ideals and practices for some influential members of the Iranian Muslim population in his period. He thus observes one stage in the lengthy process whereby such ideals were adapted to accommodate new con-

[1] *K. al-tāj*, p. 23; tr. C. Pellat, *Le livre de la couronne* (Paris, 1944), p. 51. The author of this work has been identified as Muḥammad b. al-Ḥārith al-Taghlibī (or al-Tha'labī), and the correct title is *Kitāb akhlāq al-mulūk* (G. Schoeler, 'Verfasser und Titel des dem Ǧāḥiẓ zugeschriebenen sog. *Kitāb at-Tāǧ*', *ZDMG* 130 (1980), pp. 217–225). Aḥmad Zakī Pāshā, who edited the text, gives *ā'īn* as a variant for *qawānīn* in this passage (*K. al-tāj*, p. 23, n. 1); on this basis, Richter has suggested that the materials dealing with social ranks may derive from the *Āyīnnāmaj* said to have been translated from Pahlavī into Arabic by Ibn al-Muqaffa' (G. Richter, *Studien zur Geschichte der älteren arabischen Fürstenspiegel* (Leipzig, 1932), p. 45); the variant has also been noted by Rosenthal, 'As-Sarakhsī (?) on the Appropriate Behavior for Kings', p. 108.

[2] See further Morony, *Iraq*, p. 27.

[3] See D. Sourdel, 'Questions de cérémonial 'abbaside', *REI* 28 (1960), pp. 121–148.

ditions, and would ultimately become, to a greater extent than alternative models, a standard form of social description in many medieval Muslim communities.

This chapter sets out firstly to provide a brief account of the social structures of Sasanian Iraq and Iran on the eve of the Arab conquests, followed by a discussion of pre-Islamic Iranian social conceptions; and secondly to discuss the processes of literary transmission by which Iranian social ideas found their way into Arabic and New Persian compositions, and to analyse the ways in which they are understood there.

Sasanian social structure

Compared with earlier periods of Iranian history, the Sasanian era (226–651) offers an abundance of sources in which considerable attention is devoted to social arrangements. The accounts contained in these sources derive, however, in large part from the official self-presentation of the Sasanian administration itself, and thus they probably reflect the state's ideology more than any actual forms of social organisation. The well-known quadripartite system of stratification,[4] which features prominently in much of this literature, is portrayed as both rigid and static, and probably never corresponded very closely to the societies underneath the bureaucratic apparatus of the government.

It is nevertheless clear that the societies of Iraq and Iran in Sasanian times were indeed strongly hierarchical, and that, although some social mobility was possible, the status of individuals was to a very large extent a matter of heredity. There is considerable evidence to suggest that the principal social distinction was that between nobles and the common people, so that the main forms of stratification reflect a binary rather than a quadripartite structure.[5] The concentration of political, social and economic matters in the hands of the landed nobility created an enormous barrier between the aristocracy, including the higher members of the religious establishment, and peasants, artisans and merchants.[6] Nobles were exempt from the poll-tax, which thus fell exclusively on the shoulders of those in the productive, wage-earning categories. At least in some periods and places, nobles seem also to have been visibly distinguished from commoners by their clothing and other symbols, and intermarriage between the two groups was prohibited.

Despite its emphasis on hierarchy, the Iranian tradition also had its egalitarian undercurrents. Chief among these are the heretical movements associated with the teachings of the third-century figure Zarādusht of Fasā,

[4] See further below.

[5] See for example the *Tansarnāmeh*, ed. M. Minovi (Tehran, 1932), p. 19; tr. M. Boyce, *The Letter of Tansar* (Rome, 1968), p. 44.

[6] Shaki, 'Class System'; R.N. Frye, 'Feudalism in Sasanian and Early Islamic Iran', *JSAI* 9 (1987), pp. 13–17. For the situation in Khurāsān, see also E. Daniel, *The Political and Social History of Khurasan under Abbasid Rule 747–820* (Minneapolis and Chicago, 1979), pp. 16–17.

including, in the first half of the sixth century, the rebellion of Mazdak. Zarādusht is said to have introduced the idea that the sins of concupiscence, lust, envy and infamy could be averted if women and property were held in common.[7] The view that no one should have exclusive rights of possession to any assets or to women underlay the popular revolt of Mazdak's followers in Iraq (and perhaps parts of Iran), a revolt possibly stimulated by fiscal reforms initiated by the monarch Kavād (488–496, 498–531); and Kavād himself called for communal ownership of women.[8] Whether women, property or both were at issue, such communist principles sought to undermine the social hierarchy which was based, in theory and to a considerable extent in practice, on descent: if women were equally available to all men, an individual's paternal lineage could not be determined, and the rights and privileges associated with noble birth would be called into question; and if exclusive rights to ownership of property were denied, noble families could not retain their status. The recurrence of such ideas and movements is perhaps itself indicative of the intensity with which the customary social distinctions were felt.

It appears that Sasanian social organisation reached its most highly developed form in the latter half of the sixth century, when, in the aftermath of the Mazdakite revolt, the central administration attempted to assert a higher degree of social control than ever before.[9] In theory, each of the four estates was organised internally as a hierarchy of groups; each estate was bound by a separate code and its members were obliged to display their status in their dress and other visual signs; individuals were to be prevented from changing occupation except in the most extraordinary circumstances; and special instructors were to be appointed to train the members of each group.[10] Later Arabic authors associate Khusraw Parvīz in particular with authoritarian control and hierarchic centralisation, and ascribe to him the maxim, 'He who does not obey his superior is not obeyed by his subordinates.'[11] In any event the division into nobles and commoners, together with discrepancies in taxation, was intact in Sasanian Iraq on the eve of the Arab conquests.[12]

Iranian social ideals

The official social model of the Sasanian era, as has been noted, was quadripartite. This model may have had relatively little observable impact on the social systems of Iraq and Iran, but it certainly played an important role in

[7] Shaki, 'The Social Doctrine of Mazdak in the Light of Middle Persian Evidence', *Archiv Orientální* 46 (1978), pp. 289–306.
[8] Crone, 'Kavād's Heresy and Mazdek's Revolt', pp. 21–42.
[9] See R. C. Zaehner, *The Dawn and Twilight of Zoroastrianism* (London, 1961), pp. 188–189.
[10] Minovi (ed.), *Tansarnāmeh*, pp. 38–41; al-Jāḥiẓ, *K. al-tāj*, pp. 25ff; M. b. ʿAbdūs al-Jahshiyārī, *Kitāb al-wuzarāʾ waʾl-kuttāb*, ed. ʿAbd Allāh al-Ṣāwī (Cairo, 1357/1938), p. 3; cf. A. Christensen, *L'Iran sous les Sassanides*, 2nd edition (Copenhagen, 1944), p. 99.
[11] Al-Thaʿālibī, *Ghurar akhbār mulūk al-Furs wa siyarihim*, ed. H. Zotenberg (Paris, 1900), p. 690.
[12] Morony, *Iraq*, pp. 108ff, pp. 185ff.

royal ideology. Here, as in the Indian tradition, the figure four was associated with universality.[13] It seems likely that the establishment of Zoroastrianism as the official religion of the state intensified the ideological connexion between good government and the protection of the social order, and this is reflected in Sasanian court literature.[14]

Yet social ideals had been part of Iranian culture long before the appearance of the Sasanians, and seem in fact to have derived from the distant Indo-Iranian past. The Avesta itself contains the earliest Iranian social models, which are, in every case except one, not quadripartite but tripartite, consisting of priests (*āthrauuan-*), warriors (*rathaēštar-*) and cattle breeders (*vāstriia-*, *fšuiiant-*).[15] Like the Ṛg-Veda, the Avesta gives sacred authority to the concept of a functionally differentiated society. The institution of functional stratification is sometimes associated with the figure of Zoroaster himself, or with his sons;[16] and implicit references to the social categories appear elsewhere in the Zoroastrian texts.[17] In a single, younger Avestan passage (Yasna 19:17), a

13 The quadripartite system of estates, the four quarters of the realm, the four-fold administrative bureaux, the marking of the quadrants of late Sasanian coins by stars and crescents, and the four-legged throne of Hurmuzd IV (579–590) all symbolised the cosmic significance of the Sasanian empire; Morony, *Iraq*, p. 29.

14 The institution of the three great fires, emblems of the three higher (Avestan) social categories, probably dates from Sasanian times; M. Molé, *Culte, mythe et cosmologie dans l'Iran ancien. Le problème zoroastrien et la tradition mazdéenne* (Paris, 1963), pp. 452ff; see also Frye, *The Heritage of Persia* (Cleveland, 1963), p. 228, where an Arsacid origin for this ritual is postulated.

15 The terms used for these categories vary according to the age of the passage in question. On the references to social categories in the Gathas, see Boyce, 'The Bipartite Society of the Ancient Iranians', in *Societies and Languages of the Ancient Near East*, ed. M.A. Dandamayev (Warminster, 1982), pp. 33–37; cf. *idem*, *A History of Zoroastrianism* (Leiden), vol. 1 (1989), pp. 5f. The practical significance of the tripartite schema for the peoples who produced the Avestan texts is unknown; see O. Bucci, 'Caste e classi sociali nell'antico diritto iranico', *Apollinaris* 45 (1972), pp. 741–760; Frye, *Heritage*, pp. 50–51.

16 In *Farvardīn Yasht* (13:89) and also in the ninth-century *Zādsparam* (18:2–3), Zoroaster appears as the embodiment of all three social categories. In addition, it is probably correct to see an indirect reference to Zoroaster's triple ordination in the ninth-century *Dēnkard*, where three elements, which may be interpreted as emblems of the priesthood, warriors and herdsmen respectively, are said to have combined at Zoroaster's conception to fashion the perfect man: his *khwarr* (Avestan *xvarənah*), or 'heaven-sent glory'; his *fravahr*, or 'guarding and informing spirit'; and his *tan-gōhr*, or 'physical body' (Boyce, *History of Zoroastrianism*, vol. 1, pp. 277–278). In the *Bundahishn* (32:5), Zoroaster's three sons are described as the founders of the three groups; see Boyce, *History of Zoroastrianism*, vol. 1, p. 281; E. Benveniste, 'Les classes sociales dans la tradition avestique', *JA* 221 (1932), pp. 118–119; Molé, *Culte, mythe et cosmologie*, pp. 463ff.

17 Great distress, for example, is sometimes conveyed by the mention of three calamities: invasion, famine and impiety; these three afflictions, as Benveniste has perceived, affect the warriors, herdsmen and priests respectively. Benveniste has also noted a reference to these three misfortunes in one of the inscriptions of Darius I (521–486 BC) at Persepolis: 'May Ahura Mazdā protect this country from a [hostile] army, from famine, from the Lie! Upon this country may there not come an army, nor famine, nor the Lie' (R.G. Kent, *Old Persian* (New Haven, 1953), p. 136; Benveniste, 'Traditions indo-iraniennes sur les classes sociales', *JA* 230 (1938), pp. 537–543; *idem*, *Le vocabulaire des institutions indo-européennes* (Paris, 1969), 20ff). This possible invocation of the tripartite division in the official proclamations of the early Achaemenids may suggest that it played a role in the legitimation of their dynasty, as it would in later Iranian history.

fourth category, that of the artisans (*hūiti-*, 'those who exert themselves'), is added to the customary three.[18] The causes of the transformation of the Iranian social ideal from tripartite to quadripartite are unknown, but the close resemblance of the quadripartite Avestan model to that of the Ṛg-Veda is striking.[19] It is this four-fold conception of society that becomes the characteristic social model in the ninth-century Pahlavī Zoroastrian texts, which, despite the late date at which they were committed to writing, are assumed to consist largely of materials current in the Sasanian period.[20]

Like its Brahmanic and Hindu counterparts, Zoroastrian literature is concerned with the inauguration of a divine order in the cosmos, and it is in this context that the origins of the social strata are presented. In several parts of the Zoroastrian tradition (and in many later Islamic sources), the initial division of mankind into four categories is attributed to Jima (New Persian Jamshīd).[21] Jima's classification of men into four groups (priests, warriors, cultivators and artisans) is often described as one of his services to Ahura Mazdā.[22] According to one tradition, the *xvarənah* split into three parts after Jima's death, and the (three) social groups similarly became separate; they were only reunited in the person of Zoroaster who, like Jima, combined in his own person the essences of all three functions.[23] As Jima's role developed from that of first man to ideal ruler, his representation of the divinely ordained social strata became a central and enduring element in the Iranian conception of perfect kingship.[24]

[18] See Benveniste, 'Les classes sociales', pp. 117–134; M. Schwartz, 'The Old Eastern Iranian World View According to the Avesta', *Cambridge History of Iran* (Cambridge), vol. 2 (1985), ed. I. Gershevitch, pp. 650–652; Bucci, 'Caste e classi sociali', pp. 747–748. Bucci also notes in this passage the first appearance of the term *pištra* to designate a social grouping; earlier references to social distinctions had mentioned 'soldiers, priests, cultivators' rather than 'the category of soldiers, the category of priests' and so on.

[19] Compare *RV* 10:90:11–14; tr. W. Doniger, *The Rig Veda* (Harmondsworth, 1981), p. 31. In this passage, the four primal social categories result from the dismemberment of Puruṣa, the primordial man. For similar comparisons of the four social groups with parts of the human body in Zoroastrian literature, see Molé, *Culte, mythe et cosmologie*, pp. 423–424.

[20] Bucci, 'Caste e classi sociali', p. 748. There is, however, one exception. The *Kārnāmag ī Ardashīr ī Pāpagān*, written in Pahlavī and possibly of Islamic rather than late Sasanian origin, preserves the tripartite division of the Avesta, which it associates with the founder of the Sasanian dynasty, Ardashīr (c. AD 226–240). In this work, Ardashīr's father Pāpak is said to have had a series of dreams which, when interpreted, foretold his son's rule over the priests, warriors and cultivators (*The Kârnâmê î Artakhshîr î Pâpakân*, ed. and tr. D.D.P. Sanjana (Bombay, 1896), p. 4; cf. Th. Nöldeke, 'Geschichte des Artachšîr i Pâpakân', *Beiträge zur Kunde der indo-germanischen Sprachen* 4 (1878), pp. 37–38). It is also of interest that Pāpak himself was a priest, and his family thus straddled the two uppermost groups.

[21] See Christensen, *Les types du premier homme et du premier roi dans l'histoire légendaire des Iraniens* (Leiden, 1934), vol. 1, and Dumézil, *Mythe et épopée*, vol. 2, *Types épiques indo-européens: un héros, un sorcier, un roi* (Paris, 1971), pp. 243ff.

[22] *Dēnkard*, 7:1:20–24; tr. E.W. West, *Pahlavi Texts*, Part V (Oxford, 1897), p. 9.

[23] Molé, *Culte, mythe et cosmologie*, pp. 462f. On the parallels and differences between Jamshīd and Zoroaster, see further Molé, *Culte, mythe et cosmologie*, pp. 36ff.

[24] Cf. G. Widengren, 'The Sacral Kingship of Iran', *Studies in the History of Religions*, Supplements to *Numen*, vol. 4, *The Sacral Kingship, la regalità sacra* (Leiden 1959), p. 249.

In general, Iranian social ideals placed a good deal of emphasis on the excellence of each task and its necessity for the health and continuity of the cosmic order as a whole. In both social and religious terms, each man had a set place in the cosmic system, and his contribution to the attainment of salvation was defined according to his historical and social situation.[25] All social functions were equally necessary and, according to the *Dēnkard*, every activity was meritorious as long as it conformed with justice, and every occupation had religious value if it was performed with piety. But of the four occupations listed – those of the priesthood, military, cultivators and artisans – the priesthood was supreme and thus set apart.[26] The remaining three functions were all ranked above commerce, the most base occupation of all; nevertheless, if a man could not earn his living in any of the preferred ways, even commerce was permissible, as long as it was conducted legally.[27]

If the first and second categories in the Iranian tradition appear to be relatively stable, the third and fourth vary considerably. This reflects on the one hand the enduring power of the first two groups, whose competition occasionally resulted in the reversal of the order in which they appeared at the apex of society, but whose dominant position was consistently protected; and on the other, the relative powerlessness of the third and fourth groups, who could thus be made to share their status as it became necessary to include others in the paradigm.[28]

The instability of the third category also reflects changes in the social composition of the Iranian élite. Sasanian sources emanating from court circles recognise a second quadripartite model, in which the third category consists of scribes and bureaucrats, while artisans and peasants are grouped together in the fourth estate. Thus the *Tansarnāmeh* refers to the clergy; the military; scribes and administrators, together with physicians, poets and astronomers;

[25] *Dēnkard*, 45:15–19, 12–19; cf. *Bhagavad Gītā*, 4:13; Molé, *Culte, mythe et cosmologie*, pp. 41–42, 423.

[26] The justification for the superiority of the priests over soldiers and farmers is particularly emphasised; Molé, *Culte, mythe et cosmologie*, pp. 423–24. Cf. *Laws of Manu*, 1:92–110.

[27] *Dēnkard*, 59:11–61:7; Molé, *Culte, mythe et cosmologie*, pp. 424–25.

[28] In the case of the fourth group, it is interesting to consider the similarities and differences between the Zoroastrian category of artisans and the *śūdra*s of the Indian system. Although in times of duress some authorities allow *śūdra*s to engage in various economic activities including agriculture, trade and crafts, their primary task remains (theoretically) the performance of services for the three higher castes (R.P. Kangle, *The Kauṭilīya Arthaśāstra* (Bombay, 1963), vol. 2, 1:3:1, p. 8). More commonly, if it is impossible for a man to practise the occupation prescribed by his caste status, he is permitted to engage in one of the professions open to the castes below him until his circumstances improve; but he may not take up an activity that is the prerogative of a higher caste (*Laws of Manu*, 10:80–100). In the Zoroastrian models, the duty of service is sometimes noted, but it is usually subordinated to the practice of crafts (in an interesting passage, the *Zādsparam* lists the four classes as priests who teach, soldiers who fight, peasants who provide nourishment, and artisans *who serve*; Molé, *Culte, mythe et cosmologie*, p. 460). In Arabic accounts, the confusion as to whether the fourth group are servants or artisans is exacerbated by the dual meanings of the root *m-h-n* (Ibn Manẓūr, *Lisān al-ʿarab*, vol. 13, pp. 424–425; cf. al-Jāḥiẓ, *K. al-tāj*, p. 25, n. 4).

and artisans, peasants, traders, cattle breeders and others who had to earn their living.[29] The recognition of a scribal class or bureaucracy as a separate estate may perhaps have begun under the Achaemenids, and the division was very well established in Sasanian times, when administrative secretaryship constituted a virtually hereditary profession.

Translations from Pahlavī

The first phase in the transmission and reception of Iranian social conceptions in classical Islamic culture is represented, as in the case of Greek philosophy, by the translation of a number of relevant texts into Arabic.[30] Although it is impossible to distinguish precisely between 'religious' and secular heroic (or, in Christensen's term, 'national') literature in the Sasanian period,[31] the two quadripartite social models discussed above do seem to a large extent to have characterised different types of writing. The earlier model (priests, soldiers, cultivators, artisans) survived chiefly in the sacred Zoroastrian tradition embodied in the Avesta and the supplementary and explanatory texts inspired by it. As a result of its associations with explicitly Zoroastrian literature, this form of social ideal was less familiar to Muslim writers than the later, 'bureaucratic' model (priests, soldiers, secretaries, artisans and cultivators), which came to dominate the political ethos of the Sasanian court and administration and was thus recorded in Sasanian historiography and other overtly didactic works, some of which were translated into Arabic.[32]

Of principal importance in the literary transmission of Iranian social ideals are the historiographical *Khwadāynāmag*, or 'Book of Kings', and two ethico-political texts, known in the Islamic period as the *'Ahd Ardashīr* and the *Tansarnāmeh*. The versions of the *Khwadāynāmag* to which Muslim authors had access appear to have narrated the history of Iran down to the reign of Khusraw Parvīz (590–628), and probably date from the reign of the last Sasanian monarch, Yazdagird III (632–651).[33] The *Khwadāynāmag* was apparently translated from Pahlavī into Arabic more than once, and also into

[29] Minovi (ed.), *Tansarnāmeh*, pp. 12–13; tr. Boyce, *Letter of Tansar*, pp. 37–38.

[30] On the Arab reception of Iranian quadripartite social models, see also al-Sayyid, 'Naẓarāt fī jadaliyyāt al-'ilāqa bayn al-namūdhajayn', in *al-Umma wa'l-jamā'a wa'l-salṭa*, pp. 92–96.

[31] Christensen, *Les gestes des rois dans les traditions de l'Iran antique* (Paris, 1936), pp. 33ff; *idem*, *Les Kayanides* (Copenhagen, 1931), pp. 35ff; see also E. Yarshater, 'Iranian National History', *Cambridge History of Iran*, vol. 3 (1), ed. E. Yarshater (Cambridge 1983), pp. 393ff, and Ẓabīḥ Allāh Ṣafā, *Hamāseh-sarā'ī dar Īrān* (Tehran, 1363), especially pp. 21–137.

[32] Of course, Sasanian historiography itself incorporated much of the sacred history of the Zoroastrian tradition, as well as the 'epic' or 'heroic' tradition of eastern Iran, which narrated not only the legendary history of the early Iranian kings but also that of families of heroic warriors (*pahlavānān*), whom it portrayed as guardians of the Iranian throne. The priesthood similarly made use of the heroic tradition where it found it helpful to do so, and the scribes (*dabīrān*) who recorded the *Khwadāynāmag* shared the outlook of the priests by virtue of their training (Yarshater, 'Iranian National History', p. 394).

[33] Grignaschi, 'La *Nihāyatu-l-'arab fī aḫbāri-l-Furs wa-l-'Arab* et les *Siyaru mulūki-l-'Ağam* du Ps. Ibn-al-Muqaffa'', *BEO* 26 (1973), pp. 83–148.

New Persian.[34] Although none of the Pahlavī originals nor any of these translations is extant, it seems from Ḥamza al-Iṣfahānī's introduction to his *Ta'rīkh sinī mulūk al-arḍ wa'l-anbiyā'* that several Arabic versions were available to him when he composed his history in 350/961.[35] Some version of the text is probably at the base of virtually all Muslim narratives of pre-Islamic Iranian history, including those of al-Ṭabarī, al-Tha'ālibī and Firdawsī; the differences in the accounts of Iranian history given by Muslim authors are perhaps in part due to the different Pahlavī versions at the base of the various translations. The *'Ahd Ardashīr* and the *Tansarnāmeh* purportedly date from the reign of the first Sasanian monarch Ardashīr (c. 226–240), although some scholars regard both texts as dating substantially from late Sasanian times.[36] They were translated more than once into Arabic, probably initially in the late Umayyad period, and appear to have enjoyed a considerable circulation.[37] According to Ibn al-Nadīm, several other works of *andarz*, or 'advice', appear to have been translated from Pahlavī into Arabic as well.[38]

The *'Ahd Ardashīr* apparently represents Ardashīr's testament to his successors or (according to later versions), to his son Shāpūr.[39] Many Arabic histories quote from this text; parts of it are also cited by Firdawsī.[40] In its complete form, it survives in the anonymous *Kitāb al-ghurar* (probably composed in the second decade of the fourth century), in Miskawayh's *Tajārib al-umam* and in Abū Sa'd al-Ābī's *Nathr al-durar*.[41] All versions of the *'Ahd* include an account of four social categories: the soldiery (*asāwira*); the priests (*'ubbād*), ascetics and guardians of the fire-temples; the secretaries, astronomers and physicians; and the cultivators, artisans (*muhhān*) and merchants.[42] Some manuscripts of the *'Ahd* contain an interpolation in which a further set of four social divisions (*aqsām*) appears: the men of religion (*aṣḥāb al-dīn*), the men of war ([*aṣḥāb*] *al-ḥarb*), the men of administration ([*aṣḥāb*] *al-tadbīr*) and the men of service ([*aṣḥāb*] *al-khidma*).[43]

In the *'Ahd Ardashīr*, it is the wellbeing of the realm that is emphasised most in discussions of social stratification. The text is replete with admonitions to

[34] Ibn al-Nadīm, *Fihrist*, pp. 118, 244–245, 305; V. Minorsky, 'The Older Preface to the *Shāh-nāma*', *Studi orientalistici in onore di G. Levi della Vida* (1956), vol. 2, pp. 161, 166.

[35] Ḥamza al-Iṣfahānī, *Ta'rīkh sinī mulūk al-arḍ wa'l-anbiyā'* (Beirut, 1961), pp. 13–14.

[36] Christensen, *L'Iran*, pp. 63–66, suggests that the works were composed in the reign of Khusraw; Boyce, *Letter of Tansar*, pp. 11–12, posits an original third-century version of the *Tansarnāmeh* to which interpolations were added at a later date. Shaked, on the other hand, sees nothing in either text to indicate conclusively that it was not composed in early Sasanian times ('From Iran to Islam. Notes on Some Themes in Transmission', p. 55, n. 22).

[37] On the translation of the *'Ahd Ardashīr*, see 'Abbās's introduction to his edition of the text (Beirut, 1387/1967), pp. 33ff.

[38] *Fihrist*, pp. 315–316; cf. J.P. de Menasce, 'Andarz Literature', *Cambridge History of Iran*, vol. 3 (2), pp. 1180–1186; Richter, *Studien*, pp. 63ff.

[39] Grignaschi, 'Quelques spécimens de la littérature sassanide conservés dans les bibliothèques d'Istanbul', *JA* 254 (1966), p. 11, n. 9.

[40] Cf. Christensen, *Les gestes*, pp. 91ff; 'Abbās, *'Ahd Ardashīr*, introduction, pp. 33–38.

[41] See 'Abbās, *'Ahd Ardashīr*, introduction, pp. 35, 39–45.

[42] 'Abbās, *'Ahd Ardashīr*, p. 63.

[43] *Idem*, *'Ahd Ardashīr*, p. 63.

the monarch's successors that they should enforce strict social distinctions and with warnings of the chaos that would otherwise ensue, both for the ruler and for his subjects. The means of enforcing these distinctions is discipline or control (*siyāsa*); only by strict control (*iṣābat al-siyāsa*) would Ardashīr's successors acquire honour.[44] They should therefore not be more concerned about the loss of their own powers than about the transfer of an individual from his category to one unsuitable for his rank. If such social mobility were tolerated, the individual would become covetous of yet higher rank, and it would only be a matter of time before the ruler himself was forced to relinquish his powers, whether by deposition or assassination.[45]

The second didactic text which appears to have been widely known among early Muslim writers is the *Tansarnāmeh*. This is ostensibly a letter from Ardashīr's chief *hērbad* Tansar (or Tōsar) to Gushnāsp, the ruler of Parishvār and Ṭabaristān, who, in a previous letter, had expounded the reasons for his reluctance to submit to Ardashīr.[46] Tansar's response is a systematic attempt to justify Ardashīr's conduct. One of the ways in which the letter seeks to demonstrate the legitimacy of Ardashīr's government is by emphasising the latter's strict observation of the distinctions between social groups. Short passages from the *Tansarnāmeh* are cited by al-Masʿūdī and al-Bīrūnī,[47] while more extensive versions survive in New Persian. As late as the seventh/thirteenth century, Ibn Isfandiyār claims to have come across an Arabic translation of the text by Ibn al-Muqaffaʿ, and to have incorporated his own Persian translation of this work into his *Tārīkh-i Ṭabaristān* (c. 613/1216–1217).[48] The fullest form in which the *Tansarnāmeh* survives, then, is a considerably modified version of the Pahlavī original.[49]

Like the *ʿAhd Ardashīr*, the *Tansarnāmeh* emphasises the ruler's relationship to the social strata. The king is portrayed as above and outside all social groups, and as responsible for achieving a harmony among them:

> Know that men, according to [our] religion, are of four estates ['limbs'], and in many places in the books of religion, it is written and made clear beyond dispute, interpretation, disagreement or speculation that they are said to fall into four estates, and that at the head of these estates is the ruler. The first estate consists of the men of religion. This estate in turn is composed of categories: judges, priests, ascetics, temple guardians and teachers. The second estate is that of the military, that is, the fighting men. They are of two divisions, cavalry and infantry, and furthermore they differ in rank (*marātib*) and

[44] *Idem*, *ʿAhd Ardashīr*, pp. 58, 60. [45] *Idem*, *ʿAhd Ardashīr*, p. 63.

[46] Boyce, *Letter of Tansar*, pp. 3, 7.

[47] See Christensen, 'Abarsām et Tansar', *Acta Orientalia* 10 (1932), p. 46.

[48] It is possible that Ibn al-Muqaffaʿ may have translated the *Tansarnāmeh* into Arabic, but Ibn al-Nadīm does not mention the work among the books translated by Ibn al-Muqaffaʿ; see also Gabrieli, 'L'Opera di Ibn al-Muqaffaʿ', *RSO* 13/3 (1932), pp. 217–218.

[49] It has been embellished by quotations from the Qur'ān and the Bible, as well as by several verses of poetry. Somewhat less obvious are the accretions that may have resulted from Ibn Isfandiyār's notorious loquacity; see Christensen's comparison of the versions found in the *Fārsnāmeh* and the *Tārīkh-i Ṭabaristān* ('Abarsām et Tansar', pp. 50–55; cf. p. 46, n. 9).

function (*a'māl*). The third estate is composed of the secretaries. They too are of various strata and types: secretaries for correspondence, accounts, legal judgments, registrations and covenants, and recorders of chronicles; physicians, poets and astrologers are [also] among their ranks. The fourth estate is called that of the artisans (*mahaneh*). They are the cultivators, herdsmen, merchants and other craftsmen (*muḥtarifeh*). It is through these estates that humanity will prosper as long as it endures.[50]

The *Tansarnāmeh*, then, expresses the Sasanian 'bureaucratic' ideal, in which the four categories are clearly differentiated and internally subdivided. The typically dismissive reference to merchants is followed in a later passage by an explicit expression of contempt for commerce: 'Ignoble offspring appear; they adopt the habits of boors (*ajlāf*) and abandon the ways of nobility; their dignity is lost in the sight of the common people. Like tradesmen, they occupy themselves with the acquisition of money, and they omit to cultivate praiseworthy attributes.'[51]

In addition, there is much in the *Tansarnāmeh* that appears to have been written in defence of Ardashīr's reported intransigence in enforcing social distinctions. Even before the main body of the text begins, in a passage said to have been appended to the text by Ibn al-Muqaffaʿ, Aristotle is reported to have advised Alexander not to kill the Iranian nobility after his conquest of Fārs, for 'when the noblemen (*buzurgān*) have disappeared, you will be compelled without choice to promote base persons (*furūmāyagān*) to the stations and ranks of the noble. Know truly that there is no evil, misfortune, sedition or plague in the world which causes as much corruption as a base person who rises to the rank of the noble.'[52] Ardashīr's establishment of the four-fold scheme is portrayed as a healthful restoration, in accordance with the divine plan, after a period of sickness:

The veil of restraint and discipline was lifted, and there appeared a people adorned neither by the nobility of skill or achievement, nor by [the possession of] inherited estates; caring neither for inherited merit and lineage (*ḥasab va nasab*), nor for craft (*ḥirfat*) and profession (*ṣan'at*); empty of all concern, and lacking any occupation (*pīsheh*); prepared [only] for spying and iniquity . . . [Ardashīr] caused these four estates, which had collapsed, to be restored, and brought back each to its own place and its own particular position. He kept each in its own rank, and prevented any of them from occupying itself with a profession other than that for which God . . . had created it. By his hand, God's decree has opened for the denizens of the world a door that was inconceivable to men in ancient times.[53]

The author goes on to justify, and even praise, the severe punishments said to have been instituted by Ardashīr in order to enforce the separation of the estates.[54]

50 Minovi (ed.), *Tansarnāmeh*, pp. 12–13; tr. Boyce, *Letter of Tansar*, pp. 37–38.
51 *Idem*, *Tansarnāmeh*, p. 19; tr. Boyce, *Letter of Tansar*, p. 44.
52 *Idem*, *Tansarnāmeh*, p. 2; tr. Boyce, *Letter of Tansar*, p. 27.
53 *Idem*, *Tansarnāmeh*, pp. 13–14; tr. Boyce, *Letter of Tansar*, p. 39.
54 *Idem*, *Tansarnāmeh*, p. 15; tr. Boyce, *Letter of Tansar*, pp. 40–41.

The author's deepest anxiety seems to be that the more general distinction between nobles and commoners might be lost. He expresses repugnance for those who marry beneath their own station and thereby beget heirs of low birth and low character – a phenomenon which he describes as 'decadence of rank (*tahjīn-i marātib*)'.[55] He thoroughly approves of Ardashīr's insistence on 'an obvious and general distinction between men of high rank (*ahl-i darajāt*) and common people (*'āmma*) with regard to horses, clothes, houses and gardens, women and servants . . .' and general comportment.[56]

Ibn al-Muqaffa''s most popular contribution to the transmission of Persian social and political ideals to an Arab-Muslim context was his 'translation' of the collection, originally composed in Sanskrit, known as *Kalīla wa Dimna*.[57] The fables contained in this work illustrate the Indo-Iranian ideals of social harmony and political stability through royal absolutism and a strict social hierarchy. Each man is born into the social rank to which he is inherently suited, and both the health of the realm and the contentment of the individual depend on his sticking to it, however lowly. These ideals are expressed in the voice of Kalīla, who maintains that, 'Each person has his station (*manzila*) and [social] worth (*qadr*), and if he sticks to the station in which he finds himself, then he is likely to be content . . . As a man's station has been determined for him since the beginning of time, he has no alternative but to be satisfied with it, whatever it is.'[58] Dimna, however, is ambitious, and says, 'There are some people who lack manliness (*muruwwa*); they are the ones who are satisfied with little and pleased with an inferior position, just as a dog, on finding a dry bone, is delighted with it. But men of excellence (*faḍl*) and manliness are not content with little, nor satisfied with it, until their souls have lifted them up to the position to which they are entitled and which is also worthy of them. In the same way, the lion tears apart a rabbit, but when he sees an onager, he drops the rabbit and pursues the onager . . . Stations are contested, and shared out according to the degree of manliness [which men possess]. A man can be raised by his manliness from the lowest station to the highest, while he who

[55] The term *hajīn* denotes a person born of a union between a man and a woman of different and unequal backgrounds; cf. *Lisān al-'arab*, vol. 13, p. 431.

[56] Minovi (ed.), *Tansarnāmeh*, pp. 19–20, and pp. 23–24; Boyce tr., *Letter of Tansar*, pp. 44–45, and pp. 48–49. The threat to hereditary ranking posed by Mazdak's revolt is described with similar alarm (Crone, 'Kavād's Heresy and Mazdak's Revolt', p. 25). See also the *Ā'īn-i Ardashīr* (Grignaschi, 'Quelques spécimens', pp. 94, 113–114); al-Jāḥiẓ, *Kitāb al-tāj*, pp. 46ff, tr. Pellat, *Le livre de la couronne*, pp. 74ff; al-Jahshiyārī, *Kitāb al-wuzarā' wa'l-kuttāb*, p. 2. Many of the ideas expressed in the *Tansarnāmeh* have counterparts in other pre-modern cultures; they are remarkably similar to those found in the writings of the seventeenth-century French magistrate Loyseau and his contemporary, Montchrestien (Mousnier, *Social Hierarchies*, pp. 67–89).

[57] Properly an adaptation as the text from which Ibn al-Muqaffa' worked had already absorbed many currents of Middle Eastern wisdom literature (Richter, *Studien*, pp. 28f). Ibn al-Muqaffa''s work itself survives only in later, heavily rewritten versions, so that it is impossible to recognise the 'original' (C. Brockelmann, 'Kalīla wa-Dimna', *EI2*).

[58] *Kalīla wa Dimna*, in Ibn al-Muqaffa', *Āthār Ibn al-Muqaffa'*, p. 101. In what follows, all references to Ibn al-Muqaffa''s works are to the same edition.

lacks manliness lowers himself from the highest position to the lowest.'[59] Against Kalīla's advice, Dimna approaches the lion, and encourages him not to neglect true merit in whomsoever he finds it: 'You, O ruler, are not such as to despise the manliness you discern in a man of mean station; for sometimes, the little man becomes great, just as a tendon taken from a corpse, once made into a bow, becomes honourable; rulers take it up and stand in need of it in battle and in play . . . The ruler should not bring people close on account of the proximity enjoyed by their fathers; neither should he keep them at a distance. Instead, he should look for the true qualities of each man.'[60] But, although Dimna is elevated to a high position in the ruler's entourage for a period of time, ultimately the sagacity of Kalīla's caution is proven, as Dimna suffers a cruel downfall. The episode thus depicts the necessity of social conservatism and strict hereditary conventions, in order that society and individuals be protected from the follies of personal ambition. It provides a fictional representation of the inappropriateness of such individualistic values as the right to compete for privileges.

In addition to works of history and *andarz*, at least one work bearing the title *ā'īnnāmag* ('Book of [Rules of] Conduct') was translated from Pahlavī into Arabic. From the excerpts quoted by Muslim authors, this book seems to have included descriptions of social and political organisation.[61] Various books with the title *Tājnāmag*, like the extant example attributed to al-Jāḥiẓ, seem similarly to have contained sections on social organisation.[62] In addition, al-Masʿūdī reports having seen a *Gāh-nāmag*, in which the official ranks of the Sasanian empire were recorded.[63] Finally, some collections of relevant anecdotes and sayings were apparently also translated; Ibn al-Nadīm lists one such collection under the title: 'Choice Anecdotes Concerning the Nobles, the Middling People, and the Low and Base'.[64]

Muslim accounts of Iranian social organisation

After the conquests of Iran and Iraq, the Arabs encountered the remnants of a hierarchical social system and a culture that was deeply conscious of Persian

[59] *Kalīla wa Dimna*, pp. 100–101. [60] *Kalīla wa Dimna*, pp. 105–106.

[61] Al-Thaʿālibī quotes the following passage from a certain *Kitāb al-ā'īn*: 'Under Jamshīd, the ranks of men (*marātib al-nās*) were according to age, with the oldest being highest in rank. Under Ẓaḥḥāk, men's ranks were assessed according to riches and wealth; under Farīdūn, according to men's ability and precedence; under Manūchihr, according to their origins and the ancientness of their stock; under Kay Kā'ūs, according to their intellect and wisdom; under Kay Khusraw, according to their strength and courage; under Luhrāsp, according to their religion and virtue; under the kings that followed, according to their meritorious deeds; and under Anūshīrvān, according to all of these factors, except for riches and wealth (*Ghurar akhbār mulūk al-Furs*, pp. 14–15). Cf. Ibn Qutayba, *'Uyūn al-akhbār*, vol. 1, pp. 8, 62; vol. 3, pp. 221, 278; vol. 4, p. 59. See also A. Tafazzoli, 'Ā'īnnāme', *Encyclopaedia Iranica*; Christensen, *L'Iran*, p. 62; Richter, *Studien*, pp. 40ff.

[62] Cf. Christensen, *L'Iran*, p. 66; Richter, *Studien*, pp. 40ff.

[63] *K. al-tanbīh wa'l-ishrāf*, ed. M.J. de Goeje (Leiden, 1967), pp. 103–104. [64] *Fihrist*, p. 316.

social ideals. But the first Arab settlers in Iraq and western Iran remained aloof from the native inhabitants, and to the limited degree that they came into contact with the Iranian and Persianised aristocracy they seem to have held its culture in contempt. Those who left Iraq for Khurāsān initially opted for isolation as well, but rather rapidly tended to develop common interests with the settled population there, and to find themselves tied to Khurāsānians of a similar social status. It was also in Khurāsān that Arabs were most likely to assimilate Persian culture.[65] This may have contributed to the increased importance of Iranian traditions in Islamic culture in the period after the ʿAbbāsid, Khurāsānian-led revolution. More significant, however, were the large numbers of Iranians who converted to Islam at an early date. Some of these converts were active in the perpetuation of Iranian culture in the new civilisation.

The first stage involved in the process of transmission and reception of Iranian social ideals was the creation of an extensive literature in translation. After the completion of the initial translations, the second stage in the process is marked by the appearance of accounts of Iranian social organisation in the writings of Muslim authors. This stage is represented by a fairly sizable literature, which will be considered here according to its treatment of the principal royal figures of Iranian legend and history. (The third stage, in which the ideas and vocabulary of Iranian social ideals were adopted for general purposes, will be discussed in subsequent chapters.)

Jamshīd

The association of the inauguration of a stratified society with the mythical king Jamshīd occurs frequently in Islamic historical works, whose authors probably encountered it in their principal source, the *Khwadāynāmag*.[66] One of the earliest extant histories in which the legend of Jamshīd appears is the *Ta'rīkh al-rusul wa'l-mulūk* of al-Ṭabarī (c. 224–310/838–923) who, like many later writers, describes Jamshīd's inauguration of four social categories as the third in a sequence of four institutions initiated by the monarch in obedience to divine instructions. Al-Ṭabarī is careful to distance himself from the account he presents:

According to one [Persian scholar] . . . from the first year of his reign until the fifth,[67] he [Jamshīd] ordered the manufacture of swords, coats of mail, steel weaponry, other types of armaments and iron tools for the artisans. From the fiftieth year of his reign until the hundredth, [he ordered] that silk, cotton and linen be spun, together with everything else that could be spun; that it be woven and dyed various colours, cut in various ways and worn. From the hundredth year until the hundred and fiftieth, he cat-

[65] Daniel, *Khurasan*, pp. 20–22; Crone, *Slaves*, pp. 61ff. See also ch. 4.
[66] A. Christensen, *Les types du premier homme*, vol. 2, p. 113.
[67] Ibn al-Athīr emends al-Ṭabarī's *khams* to read *khamsīn*, 'fifty' (see below).

egorised (*ṣannafa*) men into four strata (*ṭabaqāt*): a stratum of soldiers (*muqātila*), a stratum of religious scholars (*fuqahāʾ*), a stratum of secretaries (*kuttāb*), artisans (*ṣunnāʿ*) and cultivators (*ḥarrāthīn*), and he took a stratum of them as servants (*khadam*). He ordered each of these strata to stick to the occupation that he had assigned for it. From the hundred and fiftieth year until the two hundred and fiftieth, he battled against the demons and *jinn*, overcame them and humbled them, and they were subjected to him and compelled to follow his command. From the year 250 until the year 316, he forced the demons to cut stones and rocks from the mountains, to make marble, gypsum and chalk, and to build dwellings and baths by combining [these materials] with clay; to make lime; and to transport everything that was useful to men from the seas, mountains, mines and deserts: gold, silver and other precious metals that could be melted, types of perfumes, and medicines. They executed all that according to his command.[68]

Al-Ṭabarī was in no doubt that the Iranians had divided their society into four, but his description of the persons who made up the four groups perhaps reflects a certain confusion. The chief problem lies in the mention of Jamshīd's taking of a category of men as servants. Who belonged to this group? Possibly the statement should be taken to refer to one of the four categories already listed;[69] or, as in the case of the brief interpolation in the *ʿAhd Ardashīr*, the servants may be regarded as the fourth group itself;[70] alternatively, one may read the passage with Ibn al-Athīr (555–630/1160–1233), who follows al-Ṭabarī's version almost verbatim, but describes the four strata quite plainly: 'a stratum of soldiers, a stratum of religious scholars, a stratum of secretaries and artisans, and a stratum of agriculturalists; and he took servants from them [all]'.[71] Balʿamī (d. 363/974), the Sāmānid vizier responsible for the translation of al-Ṭabarī's history into Persian, interferes more drastically with al-Ṭabarī's text by including the secretaries (*dabīrān*) with the religious scholars (*dānāyān*) in the second group.[72]

Balʿamī's description of Jamshīd's social stratification is also of interest in another respect. It is followed by a passage that differs markedly from its counterpart in al-Ṭabarī. In al-Ṭabarī's account, Jamshīd wishes to prolong his kingship as long as possible and asks the scholars of the realm what he should do; they instruct him to obey God and to avoid all acts of disobedience.

[68] *Taʾrīkh al-rusul waʾl-mulūk*, vol. 1, p. 175.

[69] This is Christensen's reading: 'De la 100e à la 150e année il divisa les hommes en quatre classes: celle des guerriers, celle des savants, celle des scribes et celle des artisans et des laboureurs; une des classes il la prit à son service' (*Les types du premier homme*, vol. 2, p. 85, n. 3).

[70] ʿAbbās, *ʿAhd Ardashīr*, p. 63, and see above. See also Ibn al-Balkhī's account below.

[71] *Al-Kāmil fīʾl-taʾrīkh* (Beirut), vol. 1 (1965), p. 64. Fakhr-i Mudabbir, in his *Ādāb al-ḥarb waʾl-shujāʿat*, does not specify the number of groups into which Jamshīd classified people, but lists substantially the same functions: soldiers, religious scholars, secretaries, cultivators, artisans, servants; (*Ādāb al-ḥarb waʾl-shujāʿat*, ed. Aḥmad Suhaylī Khwānsārī (Tehran, 1346/1967), pp. 7–8).

[72] Balʿamī's list thus consists of soldiers; secretaries and religious scholars; cultivators (*kishtārvarzān*); and artisans (*pīsheh-varān*) (*Tārīkh*, vol. 1, p. 130). On the composition of Balʿamī's history, see B. Spuler, 'Die historische Literatur Persiens bis zum 13. Jahrhundert als Spiegel seiner geistigen Entwicklung', *Saeculum* 8 (1957), pp. 269–270.

Jamshīd heeds their advice successfully for four hundred years. But then Iblīs, unwilling to allow such a show of obedience to go untested, suggests to Jamshīd that his longevity is due to the monarch's divine status; Jamshīd is taken by this idea, asks his subjects to worship him, and is promptly decapitated.[73] Balʿamī presents a modified and much abridged rendition of this episode. 'After that, he [Jamshīd] gathered the scholars round him and asked them, "What will keep this realm lasting and permanent for me?" They replied, "Practise justice and benevolence among men" '.[74] Al-Ṭabarī's version of the legend is cast in a distinctly monotheistic mould; Jamshīd is admonished to obey God rather than to practise justice, and his final undoing is the result of overweening pride. Balʿamī's account, by contrast, is reminiscent of such sources as the *ʿAhd Ardashīr* and the *Tansarnāmeh*, in that it suggests that the proper treatment of the social categories, the practice of justice on earth, and the stability of rulership are all closely related. In this section of his translation, Balʿamī adapts al-Ṭabarī's text quite considerably, or possibly chooses to follow another source.

A generation later, when Firdawsī composed his *Shāhnāmeh* (completed c. 400/1010), he may have had access to sources translated into Persian from Pahlavī.[75] He even repeats the Pahlavī names of the four social categories instituted by Jamshīd, albeit in a garbled form.[76] Unlike most Muslim writers, Firdawsī reproduces the quadripartite model of Zoroastrian religious writings by restoring the priests to the first position in society and describing the cultivators in terms of respect. According to his account, the first group is composed of those who devote themselves to religious ceremonies, to whom Jamshīd assigned the mountains in which to worship God. The second category consists of the warriors, commanders of the armies and defenders of the throne. The third group are the cultivators, who toil, sow and reap, and who, though poor, obey no one and live freely, without enemies or quarrels. The fourth group, the artisans, are eager for gain and full of arrogance.[77] Firdawsī, who is clearly relying on quite different sources from those available to al-Ṭabarī, thus reiterates the Iranian contempt for commercial activity. Here as elsewhere he seems to be principally concerned with the preservation of Iranian legend, and his model makes no accommodation to the circumstances of his own time.

A general attribution of the initial stratification of society to Jamshīd is found in the *Kitāb al-wuzarāʾ waʾl-kuttāb* of al-Jahshiyārī (d. 311/942) and in Miskawayh's *Tajārib al-umam*. The former writer notes that Jamshīd was the

[73] Al-Ṭabarī, *Taʾrīkh*, vol. 1, p. 177. (Al-Ṭabarī also lists other accounts, in which Jamshīd comes to grief by being sawn in two.)
[74] Balʿamī, *Tārīkh*, vol. 1, pp. 130–132; cf. Christensen, *Les types du premier homme*, vol. 2, p. 90.
[75] Cf. Minorsky, 'The Older Preface to the *Shāh-nāma*', pp. 159–179.
[76] Firdawsī's Pahlavī terms have been reconstructed by Benveniste, 'Classes sociales', pp. 132–134, and Christensen, *Les types du premier homme*, p. 102, notes 1–4.
[77] Firdawsī, *Shāhnāmeh*, ed. and tr. J. Mohl, *Le livre des rois*, vol. 1, pp. 48–51.

first person to 'arrange the categories of people'; the latter relates that Jamshīd 'categorised, stratified and regulated (*ṣannafa*, *ṭabbaqa* and *rattaba*)' mankind, and insisted that each man stick to his own station and occupation. The only category either author names specifically is the one in which they both had a particular interest, namely that of the secretaries; they also report that these were internally divided into different ranks, since Jamshīd had 'regulated the stations of the secretaries (*rattaba manāzil al-kuttāb*)'.[78]

In the early fifth/eleventh-century *Ghurar akhbār mulūk al-Furs wa siyari-him* of al-Thaʿālibī, Jamshīd's general achievements are described as in al-Ṭabarī's history, but the author departs from al-Ṭabarī to follow unambiguously the quadripartite model of the Sasanian historiographical tradition in his enumeration of the various social categories inaugurated by the monarch. He recounts a speech, reminiscent in part of al-Ṭabarī's tone and in part of Balʿamī's, said to have been delivered by Jamshīd to the men and *jinn* of the seven climes over which he ruled: 'Indeed, I have come to rule over you by the favour with which God Almighty has distinguished me and by the light with which he has clothed me, that I should make the earth prosperous, make [his] creatures secure, spread justice, increase generosity, give freely, bring goodness to life, and cause evil to die.' Here al-Thaʿālibī implies a relationship between the inauguration of the social strata and the practice of justice, for his account continues with the narration of Jamshīd's series of four good works. After the manufacture of weapons and tools, and the making of fabrics and clothing, Jamshīd regulated mankind into various strata: the army, who defended the frontiers; physicians and religious scholars (*al-ʿulamāʾ biʾl-abdān waʾl-adyān*); secretaries and accountants; and merchants and artisans.[79] The prominence given by al-Thaʿālibī to the physicians (a group to which he himself belonged) is noteworthy. Also striking is the disappearance altogether of the cultivators, who are replaced by merchants.

Similar to al-Thaʿālibī's description of Jamshīd's four-fold stratification is that of Gardīzī in his *Zayn al-akhbār* (440–444/1049–1053). Gardīzī, unlike al-Thaʿālibī, places the men of religious learning (*dānāyān*) first in the hierarchy and the soldiers second. His third group consists of secretaries, doctors and astrologers, a combination that anticipates Niẓāmī Samarqandī's treatment, in his *Chahār maqāleh*, of the four categories regarded as indispensable to rulers.[80] Gardīzī's fourth group includes cultivators, merchants and artisans.[81]

Ibn al-Balkhī, author of the early sixth/twelfth-century *Fārsnāmeh*, follows

[78] Al-Jahshiyārī, *Kitāb al-wuzarāʾ waʾl-kuttāb*, p. 1; A. b. M. Miskawayh, *Tajārib al-umam*, (Leiden and London, 1909) vol. 1, pp. 8–9. Al-Jahshiyārī goes on to emphasise the importance that the Iranian kings had attached to the secretarial profession (p. 3).

[79] *Ghurar akhbār mulūk al-Furs*, pp. 11–12.

[80] Cf. Niẓāmī ʿArūḍī Samarqandī, *Chahār maqāleh*, ed. M.M. b. ʿAbd al-Wahhāb (London, 1910).

[81] Gardīzī, *Zayn al-akhbār=Tārīkh-i Gardīzī*, ed. ʿAbd al-Ḥayy Ḥabībī (Tehran, 1363), p. 33.

Balʿamī in emphasising the sacredness of Jamshīd's inauguration of the four categories and the close link between this act and justice. He opens his book, which is dedicated to Muḥammad b. Malikshāh (498–511/1104–1117), with a brief discussion of kingship, in which he impresses on his reader the need for the divinely appointed ruler to aspire towards knowledge and justice; when a king is adorned with these two virtues, God has vouchsafed him a fraction of prophethood.[82] When Ibn al-Balkhī comes to his treatment of Jamshīd, he uses him as a model of royal wisdom and equity: Jamshīd is endowed with 'knowledge, intellect and judgment to the degree of perfection', and addresses his subjects at Nawrūz with the words: 'God Almighty has made my dignity and splendour complete and has accorded me his support, and in response to these bounties, I have made it incumbent on myself to behave with justice and benevolence towards [my] subjects.'[83]

Jamshīd's bringing of order to mankind and his distinguishing of men one from another are again presented as the third in his sequence of four good works on earth. In this cosmic context, Ibn al-Balkhī gives a lengthy description of the social strata:

> The first category were those people who were marked by wit, wisdom, intelligence and knowledge. He ordered some of them to study the science of religion (*ʿilm-i dīn*), so that the laws of the community (*millat*) should be preserved by them. Others he ordered to study philosophy (*ḥikmat*), so that reference could be made to them in matters of material wellbeing, and so that by their clear judgment they might manage the affairs of the realm, because the interests of the realm can be served by philosophy, just as the interests of religion are served by religious knowledge . . . Others of this first category he ordered to learn the arts of secretaryship and accountancy, so that the arrangement of the kingdom, the management of money and transactions should be their affair. For the greatest tool in the preservation of the order of the kingdom, near and far, is an astute secretary with a prudent mind . . . As for the second category, he ordered those men in whom he discerned bravery, strength and manliness to learn the correct way of manipulating weapons and to be experts in war. He said that a kingdom that had risen to such a degree would not be free of enemies, and that enemies could not be repelled except by men of war. As for the third category, he ordered some to be artisans, such as bakers, greengrocers, butchers, builders and other such crafts as are found in the world; and others he ordered to practise cultivation, farming and the like. He distinguished the fourth category by a variety of services and made them attendants, such as domestic servants, muleteers, doormen and other assistants.[84]

Ibn al-Balkhī's is the most detailed description of the social strata to be attributed to Jamshīd. Its underlying quadripartite pattern may be perceived as priests and bureaucrats ('men of the pen', as in Balʿamī's list); soldiers; artisans and cultivators; and servants. Ibn al-Balkhī makes it clear that he considers the servants to constitute an independent category, and by enumerating

[82] Ibn al-Balkhī, *Fārsnāmeh*, eds. G. le Strange and R.A. Nicholson (London, 1921), p. 1. Ibn al-Balkhī's introduction is reminiscent of that of Niẓām al-Mulk to his *Siyar al-mulūk*, ed. H.S.G. Darke (Tehran, 1347), pp. 11ff. [83] *Fārsnāmeh*, pp. 30, 32. [84] *Fārsnāmeh*, pp. 30–31.

their tasks shows that their functions are not subsumed by members of the third grouping.

Although Ibn al-Balkhī quotes extensively from the *Tansarnāmeh* elsewhere in his book, this social model is quite different from that preserved in Ibn Isfandiyār's text. Ibn al-Balkhī devotes disproportionate attention to the first category, in which he includes both the men of religious learning and the philosophers, and to which he elevates both branches of the bureaucracy; this is perhaps related to the writer's official capacity as *mustawfī* of Fārs, although Balʿamī, another administrator, had already placed secretaries on a par with the men of religion. The third and fourth groups, who lack political power, receive the usual cursory treatment. It is also worth noting that the *Fārsnāmeh*, dedicated to its royal patron, has a distinctly didactic flavour. Its edifying tone is evident in the discussion of kingship with which Ibn al-Balkhī begins his book, and in the attention given to the role of each social category in the practice of statecraft. It is tempting to see in Ibn al-Balkhī's portrayal of Jamshīd as a model sovereign an indication of his personal sympathy for Iranian social ideals, which he hoped to communicate through subtle legendary–historical stories to Muḥammad b. Malikshāh.

In the Zoroastrian literature, Jamshīd's inauguration of the four social strata is portrayed as one event in a sequence of primeval acts through which the divine arrangement of the cosmos was accomplished. The importance of the legend lies in the fact that it establishes the quadripartite division as an essential element in the initial foundation of human civilisation. Most Muslim authors faithfully convey this point, which they presumably encountered in translations of Sasanian historiographical materials. The four social groupings that they describe vary considerably, however. The older Zoroastrian form of the model (priests, soldiers, cultivators, artisans) is preserved only by Firdawsī, who may have had additional translated Pahlavī sources available to him. The later model (priests, soldiers, secretaries, agriculturalists and artisans), preserved in the accounts of al-Thaʿālibī and others, was probably contained in the *Khwadāynāmag*. If this is correct, then the authors of the Sasanian sources themselves must have adapted the Jamshīd legend to make it consistent with the social ideal current in their time – a process of adaptation to new circumstances and ideological tastes that is continued in many of the Muslim accounts.

Ardashīr and Anūshīrvān

With the exception of Ibn al-Balkhī, who exploits the Jamshīd narrative for didactic purposes, most Muslim authors are content to list the mythical ruler's four categories, sometimes together with their component subcategories. It is Ardashīr and Anūshīrvān, the two kings taken to exemplify the Sasanian period, who are more usually connected with the ethico-political aspects of stratification. Here it can be said with confidence that the literature of the

Sasanian court, including works of *andarz*, must have presented these two monarchs as zealous upholders of social distinctions. Muslim treatments of Ardashīr and Anūshīrvān consistently follow Sasanian tradition in linking their names with lessons on the practical and moral dimensions of statecraft.[85]

Not surprisingly, the social model associated with Ardashīr and Anūshīrvān is almost invariably the later, 'bureaucratic' one. A very clear exposition of this model, associated with Anūshīrvān, appears in the *Kitāb al-sa'āda wa'l-is'ād* of al-'Āmirī (d. 381/992). Al-'Āmirī lists the men of religion (judges, priests, ascetics and teachers); the armed forces (cavalry and infantry); the secretaries (those for official correspondence, for the land-tax, and the recorders of contracts); and the servants, who were the cultivators, herdsmen, artisans and merchants.[86] The composition of this list suggests that the philosopher may have had access to the *Tansarnāmeh*.[87] The author of the *Kitāb al-tāj* and al-Bīrūnī, on the other hand, seem to have had the *'Ahd Ardashīr* at their disposal.[88]

One of the earliest extended treatments of Ardashīr's social stratification in an Islamic source occurs in the *Nihāyat al-arab fī akhbār al-Furs wa'l-'Arab*, a history composed by an unknown early third/ninth-century author and assumed to predate that of al-Ṭabarī by almost a century.[89] According to this text, Ardashīr delivered a speech to his ministers, provincial governors (*marāziba*), army leaders and nobles:

> You should know that men consist of four strata. One group of them have chosen the side of God . . . and strive to please and worship him. In this way, they have reached the noblest limit and attained the greatest and highest degree. Another group have elevated the side of the ruler to the limits of exaltation, and devote themselves to assisting him in the practice of equity among his subjects and the defence of his womenfolk. Another group are busy with logical reasoning and discussion in their administration of the affairs of the realm and in their attention to that by which benefit will accrue to the subjects, so that they are indispensable in the extreme to both the ruler and the subjects. Then there is a group amongst them who exert themselves in the attainment of, acquisition of and search for wealth by various means. And all of these co-operate with each other and help each other and need each other, just as one limb of the body needs another. I have categorised you according to your strata and ranks in your own interests, because, if you were entrusted with your own commerce and arranged your own fortunes, your affairs would be lost, your world would collapse around you and destroy you. For in neglecting the common people and failing to discipline them lies the great-

85 Their names are occasionally followed in such contexts by that of Bahrām Gūr (al-Jāḥiẓ, *K. al-tāj*, p. 149). 86 *Kitāb al-sa'āda wa'l-is'ād*, p. 209. 87 See above.

88 The author of the *K. al-tāj* reproduces the model of the *'Ahd Ardashīr* almost exactly (*K. al-tāj*, p. 25). According to Abū'l-Rayḥān al-Bīrūnī, Ardashīr categorised men into soldiers and the sons of vassal rulers; ascetics, temple guardians and men of religion; doctors, astrologers and scholars; and cultivators and artisans (*ṣunnā'*) (*Taḥqīq mā lil-Hind* (Hyderabad, 1958), p. 76).

89 See Grignaschi, 'La Nihāyatu-l-'arab fī aḫbāri-l-Furs wa-l-'Arab', *BEO* 22 (1969), pp. 15–67, and 'La *Nihāyatu-l-'arab fī aḫbāri-l-Furs wa-l-'Arab* et les *Siyaru mulūki-l-'Ağam* du Ps. Ibn-al-Muqaffa'', pp. 83–148; Grignaschi demonstrates that although the *Nihāyat al-arab* predates al-Ṭabarī's work, al-Ṭabarī had access to an earlier source than the unknown author of the earlier history.

est corruption for kings and the greatest danger to him who is in charge of their affairs.[90]

This extract illustrates the very common association of Ardashīr with a strict enforcement of social stratification in the interests of order and stability. Its didactic tone is reminiscent of such works as the *'Ahd Ardashīr* and the *Tansarnāmeh*, and is emphasised by its presentation in the form of a personal declaration from the throne. Also typical of Muslim (and presumably Sasanian) portrayals of Ardashīr's strong sense of social hierarchy is the paternalistic justification of stratification with which Ardashīr concludes his speech: after the ideal of harmony has been established, it is shown to be beyond attainment without the authoritarian control of an enlightened king, on whom the wellbeing of the subjects depends.[91]

Very similar ideals are associated with Anūshīrvān, who moreover is frequently said to have devoted a great deal of attention to the practices of his predecessors, and especially to those of Ardashīr, on whom he expressly modelled his own conduct.[92] Anūshīrvān is said to have been concerned above all with the maintenance of a basic distinction between the nobility and the commoners, and is in many accounts portrayed as a binarist.[93] But whereas Ardashīr is frequently associated with the negative consequences of the neglect of such a distinction, Anūshīrvān is linked with the happy and harmonious conditions enjoyed by the subjects as a result of his benevolent despotism. This is particularly evident in the following extract from the *Kārnāmaj fī sīrat Anūshīrvān* preserved by Miskawayh:[94]

When I [Anūshīrvān] realised that gratitude [to God] entailed both words and deeds, I considered what deed might be most pleasing to him, and found that it involved those

[90] Cambridge University Library, ms. Qq 225, f. 99a; cf. the abridged Persian translation, entitled *Tajārib al-umam*, made for Sa'd b. Zangī of Aleppo in the early seventh/thirteenth century (ms. AS 3115, f. 68b; on the relationship of the translation to the Arabic prototype, see Grignaschi, 'La *Nihāyatu-l-'arab fī aḫbāri-l-Furs wa-l-'Arab* et les *Siyaru mulūki-l-'Ağam*', pp. 83–105). Elsewhere (*Nihāyat al-arab*, f. 99b), the author has Ardashīr arrange his subjects into the following strata: men of religion and ascetics; soldiers; secretaries and men of culture (*udabā'*); cultivators and merchants. Several authors refer to comparable speeches or letters. Ibn Qutayba, for example, states that he came across such an address by Ardashīr in one of the *kutub al-'ajam* (*'Uyūn al-akhbār*, vol. 1, p. 7). The book in question may be a translation of the *Khwadāynāmag*, or possibly an epitome of that book, of the kind cited by Ibn Qutayba in his *K. al-Ma'ārif* (*al-Ma'ārif*, p. 652; cf. Lecomte, *Ibn Qutayba*, pp. 186–188; Richter, *Studien*, p. 40).

[91] Cf. Ardashīr's warnings that if men are allowed to exceed their stations, loss of sovereignty will be the inevitable result (*K. al-tāj*, p. 25, and the *'Ahd Ardashīr*, see above).

[92] Ibn Qutayba, *al-Ma'ārif*, p. 663; al-Tha'ālibī, *Ghurar akhbār mulūk al-Furs*, p. 606; Miskawayh, *Tajārib al-umam*, pp. 206, 459; Ibn al-Balkhī, *Fārsnāmeh*, p. 88. Cf. R. al-Sayyid, 'Naẓarāt fī jadaliyyāt al-'ilāqa bayn al-namūdhajayn', in *al-Umma wa'l-jamā'a wa'l-salṭa*, p. 114.

[93] Some accounts present Ardashīr in this way too (e.g. the *'Ahd Ardashīr* and the *Tansarnāmeh*; see above).

[94] Miskawayh reproduces extracts from what appears to have been an official chronicle of Anūshīrvān's reign, identified by Grignaschi as the *Kārnāmaj fī sīrat Anūshīrvān* cited by Ibn al-Nadīm (Grignaschi, 'Quelques spécimens', p. 13, n. 25).

things by which the skies and earth are made secure, mountains stand firm, rivers flow and the created world is made pure: truth and equity. So I stuck to those principles, and I saw that the fruit of truth and equity was the cultivation of the lands, by which men, animals, birds and [all] the inhabitants of the earth have their livelihood. When I pondered this, I realised that the soldiers are supported by the cultivators, and that the cultivators are likewise supported by the soldiers. The soldiers demand their wages from the land-taxpayers and those who live on the land, because they defend them and fight on their behalf against those who are behind them. It is therefore due that the cultivators reward them entirely, for their cultivation flourishes [only] because of them. If they delay in doing so, they cause [the army] to grow weak, and their enemies grow strong. Moreover, I considered it due that the land-taxpayers should keep only as much of their cultivated produce as would suffice for their subsistence and for the [further] cultivation of their lands. [On the other hand], I saw that it was not fitting to ruin them or to strip them of their possessions in order to [fill] the treasuries and [reward] the soldiers. If I did that, I would have committed injustice to the soldiers as well as to the taxpayers. For if the cultivator is ruined, his crop is ruined too – that is, those who live on the land, and the land [itself]. If the taxpayers have not enough on which to live and by which to cultivate their lands, the soldiers, whose strength derives from the cultivation of lands and from the cultivators, will perish. Land cannot be cultivated except by the surplus left in the hands of the taxpayers, and it is [therefore] out of generosity towards and respect for the soldiers that I treat the taxpayers well, allow them to cultivate their lands, and leave them a surplus for their livelihood. For those who live on the land and the land-taxpayers are the hands and strength of the soldiers and the army; the soldiers likewise are the hands and strength of the taxpayers. I have spent my efforts and endurance in thought and discernment, and have not seen fit to favour the latter over the former or the former over the latter; because I see them as two hands that co-operate with each other, or two feet that assist each other. By my life, he who harms the soldiers does not protect the taxpayers from injustice; and he who oppresses the taxpayers does not ward off injustice from the soldiers.[95]

The passage above makes clear one of the chief distinctions between the *khāṣṣa* and the *ʿāmma*: the former are tax-exempt, and the latter are the taxpayers who till the soil.[96] Anūshīrvān's renowned justice is understood principally in terms of taxation, and is linked to the observation of social differences.[97] This monarch, like Ardashīr, is credited with a strict insistence on a regulated pattern of social distinctions. In one well-known anecdote, Anūshīrvān is said to have needed money to finish his war against the Greeks. A rich shoemaker offered to lend the king a large sum of money, in the hope that the latter, in return, would elevate his son to the rank of the secretaries. Rather than grant

[95] Miskawayh, *Tajārib al-umam*, pp. 203–205; Grignaschi, 'Quelques spécimens', pp. 26–27. Cf. Ibn al-Athīr, *Kāmil*, vol. 1, pp. 456–457.

[96] Cf. A. b. Dāʾ¯ad al-Dīnawarī, *al-Akhbār al-ṭiwāl*, ed. ʿAbd al-Munʿim ʿĀmir (Cairo, 1960), p. 71.

[97] He is said, for instance, to have kept four seals for different administrative functions. The seal used for matters pertaining to the land-tax bore the motto 'equity' (al-Masʿūdī, *Murūj al-dhahab*, vol. 1, 294; cf. al-Jahshiyārī, *Kitāb al-wuzarāʾ waʾl-kuttāb*, p. 2; Ibn al-Athīr, *Kāmil*, vol. 1, p. 64; Ibn al-Balkhī, *Fārsnāmeh*, p. 93). On the idea of 'agricultural' justice, cf. J. Sadan, 'A "closed-circuit" saying on practical justice', *JSAI* 10 (1987), pp. 325–341.

this request, Anūshīrvān returned the money, lest this shoemaker's son, by his skill, assume the authority and privileges of those born into the higher category.[98] The king is also said to have forbidden the sons of commoners to receive education, for he believed that this would incite them to seek great things in affairs; and, again like Ardashīr, he is reputed to have held that if commoners were allowed to attain any position, they would rapidly debase the nobles. Al-Thaʿālibī, who reports this, adds to his account the verse:

How excellent a man was Anūshīrvān!
How knowledgeable he was of the low and base!
He forbade them from touching a pen thereafter,
So that they should not humiliate the sons of the nobles by their deeds.[99]

Several Muslim sources refer to a letter attributed to Ardashīr, in which the monarch addresses the four categories of his subjects and acknowledges their contributions to the welfare of the realm. The version recorded by al-Masʿūdī begins with 'the secretaries, responsible for the administration of the kingdom'; it then lists 'the religious scholars (*fuqahāʾ*), who are the support of religion'; 'the soldiers, who protect [the realm] in war'; and 'the cultivators, who make the land prosperous'.[100] Such examples demonstrate clearly that Sasanian quadripartite social models were intimately linked with the 'circles of justice' that formed the ideological basis of the state. These aphorisms, of which the maxim 'no ruler without men, no men without wealth, no wealth without prosperity, and no prosperity without justice and good administration' is a typical example, are also frequently placed in the mouths of Ardashīr, Anūshīrvān and occasionally lesser Sasanian characters,[101] although they were sometimes transplanted to enhance the political wisdom of other figures, including ʿAmr b. al-ʿĀṣ and ʿAlī.[102]

98 *Shāhnāmeh*, vol. 6, pp. 516–519; cf. Christensen, *L'Iran*, pp. 319–320. See also the amusing story of the shoemaker in *Shāhnāmeh*, vol. 5, pp. 578–581, and the illustration of the episode in M.B. Dickson and S.C. Welch, *The Houghton Shahnameh* (Cambridge, Massachusetts, 1981), vol. 2, plate 229. The social aspirations of shoemakers in Iranian cultural tradition contrast nicely with their anti-establishment views and activities in Western Europe (on which see E.J. Hobsbawn and J.W. Scott, 'Political Shoemakers', *Past and Present* 89 (1980), pp. 86–114).

99 Al-Thaʿālibī, *Ghurar akhbār mulūk al-Furs*, p. 608.

100 Al-Masʿūdī, *Murūj al-dhahab*, vol. 1, p. 272; cf. Ibn ʿAbd Rabbihi, *al-ʿIqd al-farīd*, vol. 1, p. 65; Ibn Qutayba, *ʿUyūn al-akhbār*, vol. 1, p. 7 (where the secretaries appear in the third position and are described as 'the adornment of the realm').

101 Al-Thaʿālibī, *Ghurar akhbār mulūk al-Furs*, p. 482; *Murūj al-dhahab*, vol. 1, p. 297. Cf. Morony, *Iraq*, p. 28, n. 5, where he suggests a Dumézilian interpretation of the division into ethical, military and economic factors.

102 J. Sadan, 'A "closed-circuit" saying on practical justice', pp. 330–336, and especially n. 17. See also the elaborate circle, combined with pronouncements on the duties of the just king towards the various social strata, contained in the pseudo-Aristotelian *Sirr al-asrār* (Badawī, *al-Uṣūl al-yūnāniyya*, pp. 126–127); cf. al-Mubashshir, *Mukhtār al-ḥikam*, p. 222, and Ṣāʿid al-Andalusī, *Ṭabaqāt al-umam*, tr. R. Blachère, *Le livre des catégories des nations*, p. 68. In a similar spirit, Ziyād, who is frequently associated with the reintroduction of Sasanian governmental practices in Islamic sources, is said to have advised his tax-collectors to treat the peasants well because 'as long as they are prosperous, you will be prosperous' (Ibn Qutayba, *ʿUyūn al-akhbār*, vol. 1, p. 10; cf. Morony, *Iraq*, pp. 34–36).

Knowledge of the Iranian past was widely disseminated among the educated élites of the early centuries, and this knowledge was frequently used for instructive purposes in the present. Iranians were thus able to maintain their culture to a considerable degree. Many of the accounts discussed in this chapter were the work of Iranians themselves, some of whom remained more or less attached to their cultural past, while others had lost that attachment.

Most authors do not overtly state their reactions to the ideas and practices they describe, although some, such as al-Ṭabarī, at least imply a certain scepticism as to the accuracy of the accounts they record, while others, such as Ibn al-Balkhī and the author of the *Kitāb al-tāj*, seem to identify strongly with their Persian roots. There are a few notable exceptions to this pattern that are of some interest. Al-Bīrūnī, for instance, gives an accurate description of the Sasanian 'bureaucratic' model, and proceeds to compare it with what he perceived as the quite different conception of social worth that characterised Islam, in which, he writes, 'all men are equal except in piety'; he also observes that the greatest obstacle between the Indian and Islamic civilisations lay in the former's attachment to a strictly hereditary social hierarchy.[103] Al-ʿĀmirī goes considerably further, and expresses stern disapproval of the assessment of social rank on the basis of birth. Al-ʿĀmirī's comments occur in his *Kitāb al-iʿlām bi-manāqib al-Islām*, a work written, as its title suggests, expressly to establish the superiority of Islam over other religions. It is significant that social organisation is among the topics that al-ʿĀmirī chooses in order to illustrate this superiority. How could the Avesta possibly be compared with the Qur'ān, he writes, given that 'it is known that human nobility (*al-sharaf al-insī*), for the Persian rulers, depended on family origins (*ansāb*), and that they forbade their subjects to progress from one rank to another? This practice prevents the distribution of pleasing characteristics, and discourages lofty souls from the attainment of high ranks. Had the religion of the Magians, like Islam, stressed the acquisition of fine moral qualities, the Persian rulers, eager to protect the religion, would not have ventured to oppose its injunction. Thus they would have associated human nobility with the rational soul and not with natural descent'.[104]

Al-ʿĀmirī's distaste for Iranian social organisation was apparently the result of meritocratic rather than egalitarian sympathies. It is clear that he accepts the existence of social distinctions, for he reports that for both the noble and the base, the strong and the weak, and friends and enemies, life under Islam

[103] *Taḥqīq*, pp. 75–76. A. Bausani sees in al-Bīrūnī's comments a nostalgia for the customs of the pre-Islamic Iranian kings ('L'India vista da due grandi personalità musulmane: Bābar e Bīrūnī', *Al-Bīrūnī Commemoration Volume, A.H. 362–A.H. 1362* (Calcutta, 1951), p. 69), but this is not entirely convincing; cf. al-Bīrūnī's express intention to remain dispassionate in his account (*Taḥqīq*, p. 5), and see also L. Marlow, 'Some Classical Muslim Views of the Indian Caste System' (*Muslim World* 85 (1995), pp. 15–16).

[104] Al-ʿĀmirī, *Kitāb al-Iʿlām bi-manāqib al-Islām*, ed. A. Ghorab (Cairo, 1387/1967), pp. 159–160. Cf. F. Rosenthal, 'State and Religion according to Abū l-Ḥasan al-ʿĀmirī, *IQ* 3 (1956), p. 52.

was preferable to every alternative.[105] But it is equally clear that he felt that the Persians' emphasis on heredity was misplaced. In this connexion al-ʿĀmirī quotes four *ḥadīth* in which nobility is associated not with family origins but with religious learning and piety, a praiseworthy life, and seniority.[106]

The Persians, however, according to al-ʿĀmirī, had been afflicted by two great torments. Firstly, their *mōbads* had forcibly prevented the common people from acquiring divine wisdom, and thus from attaining human perfection; secondly, all the social strata had been oppressed by the policy of subjugation practised by their rulers. The Iranian monarchs, he alleged, had declared themselves masters and everyone else their vassals. Forced to remain in one station, intelligent, freeborn men had been prevented from acquiring praiseworthy attributes and from striving for the dignity and prominence to which they naturally aspired.[107] Islam had therefore improved the lot of the Persians in three ways: it had relieved them from subjugation; it had guided them towards divine wisdom; and it had opened the path for them to the shade of the auspicious Islamic state (*hādhihi al-dawla al-maymūniyya*).[108]

A similar condemnation of rigid social stratification on the basis of birth appears in the *Mukhtār al-ḥikam wa maḥāsin al-kalim* (440/1048–1049) of al-Mubashshir b. Fātik. In this instance it is attributed to Plato, who is said to have claimed, 'Many rulers were deposed as a result of their zeal for ranks, whereby they assessed men's stations and prevented any man from leaving his category. This was a mistake on their [the rulers'] part, and its harmful effect were felt in that [unspecified] part of the world after a time, because the people, since they were all born into a certain rank or occupation, persisted in it until their virtues were extinguished. They were like a piece of land, the owner of which insists on cultivating only one type of crop; when the crop has been planted there for a long time, the species will perish. Occupations and offices of leadership grow strong only by the rotation of states and the transfer of stations.'[109]

Occasionally, then, Muslim writers were consciously stimulated by their investigations of pre- and non-Islamic systems of social organisation to draw

[105] It is tempting to see in this an indication of al-ʿĀmirī's complex attitude towards the Iranian past (cf. J.C. Vadet, 'Le souvenir de l'ancienne Perse chez le philosophe Abū l-Ḥasan al-ʿĀmirī (m. 381 H.)', *Arabica* 11 (1964), pp. 257–271).

[106] Al-ʿĀmirī, *al-Iʿlām*, p. 165. The *ḥadīth* reports are 'Let those of you with understanding and restraint be next to me, then those who are next to them, then those who are next to these last' (A. b. Shuʿayb al-Nasāʾī, *Sunan*, ed. M. ʿAlī Daʿʿās (Homs, 1388/1968), vol. 1, *imāma*, pp. 525–526, no. 23; Ibn Ḥanbal, *Musnad*, vol. 1, p. 457; vol. 4, p. 122); 'He who is best read in God's book and most learned in the *sunna* should lead you [in prayer]. If there are two such, then he whose goodness is more apparent [should lead you]; and if there are still two such, then it should be the elder of them' (al-Nasāʾī, *Sunan*, vol. 1, *imāma*, pp. 509–510, no. 3; Muslim, *Ṣaḥīḥ*, vol. 2, *ṣalāt*, *bāb man aḥaqq bi'l-imāma*, pp. 133–134); 'He who does not show indulgence for our young nor revere our elderly is not one of us' (Abū Dāʾūd, *Sunan*, vol. 4, *adab*, p. 286, no. 4943; Ibn Ḥanbal, *Musnad*, vol. 1, p. 657; vol. 2, pp. 185, 207, 222); and 'When the noble of a group comes to you, honour him' (see ch. 1).

[107] *Al-Iʿlām*, pp. 174–176.

[108] *Al-Iʿlām*, p. 176.

[109] *Mukhtār al-ḥikam*, p. 150.

comparisons with the conditions they perceived in their own society. More frequently, the author's estimation of the system he describes can be inferred only from the tone he adopts in portraying it.

In the chapters that follow, attention will be given to the ways in which this knowledge of the Iranian past permeated Islamic culture. In many cases, Muslim accounts of Iranian social organisation include partial justifications of the quadripartite model, some of which, such as the 'circle of justice', come to constitute part of the common stock of materials employed in the didactic literature of the Muslim courts. The traditional Iranian account of the origins of the social categories, however, is never transformed into an Islamic legend; when Muslim authors wished to provide divine sanction for social hierarchies in Islamic settings, they did so by theological rather than mythological means. Other elements, such as the quadripartite model itself, are gradually adopted to describe Islamic social conceptions, and inevitably assume new forms to coincide with their new applications. Even in their descriptions of pre-Islamic Iranian social organisation, many Muslim authors understand the quadripartite model in the light of the conditions of their own time.

The continued relevance of Iranian social models in Islamic civilisation is not a case of simple continuity or of straightforward revival. Instead it is an example of the endurance of a social ideal that proved at once to be embedded deeply enough to withstand the defeat of the political order that had provided its context, and flexible enough to find a respected place in the polity that replaced it. As the second half of this book will show, Islamic social description may thus be said to play a role in the gradual refinement and modification of Iranian cultural traditions in the context of changing circumstances.

PART II

The taming of Islamic egalitarianism

CHAPTER 4

The dissociation of egalitarianism and opposition

The second half of this book is devoted to the various ways in which the raw materials available to thinkers in classical times – the language of monotheistic-tribal egalitarianism, the Greek and Iranian traditions – were used in the visualisations of an ideal society produced by Muslims of the classical and early medieval periods. It traces the progressive watering down of the egalitarian impulse in various parts of the tradition, and seeks to demonstrate the important role played in this process by the *'ulamā'*.

Most of the conceptualisations to be considered in this section took shape between the second/eighth and seventh/thirteenth centuries in various regions of the Arab Middle East and the Perso-Islamic world. In other words, the environments in which they emerged were extremely diverse. There is nevertheless good reason, in my opinion, to consider these materials together. For while their immediate historical contexts may have differed substantially, these social imaginings contributed to a broader, living cultural and intellectual tradition, or rather set of traditions. Since it should not be assumed that any particular social model ever corresponded very closely to the historical realities of the environment, or environments, in which it was articulated, it is from this cultural and intellectual perspective that most of the examples under consideration here seem to make most sense. To some extent, the models of society to be discussed in what follows may have constituted a form of commentary on or criticism of the social arrangements that the author perceived in his own milieu. But for the most part it is difficult, even impossible, to demonstrate a clear and direct relationship between a social visualisation and the particular set of historical conditions in which it was produced, for while such a relationship probably exists, it is one of the utmost complexity, and our sources are often of limited assistance in the attempt to establish it. It is always the case that an individual's perceptions of his society are conditioned by numerous factors, including his own status and position, his intellectual and cultural background and interests, and his political leanings; in the case of the medieval Islamic world, an author's expression of his perceptions was also shaped to a substantial extent by literary considerations. For these reasons, my primary purpose in what follows is to situate each example of social thought within its intellectual, cultural and literary contexts, contexts that might be shared by educated persons across far-flung and in many respects very different areas within the Islamic world, rather than to attempt to assess, on the basis of what is in many cases rather flimsy evidence, its significance within its own immediate and local setting.

It has been argued that many of the Arab monotheists who participated in the initial conquests were motivated by the egalitarian orientation of their faith, and that their egalitarian expectations were social as well as religious. These expectations, as noted in the first chapter, left a marked residue on the literary remains of the first century and a half or so, some of which retain a nostalgic insistence on the social equality of the believers associated with ʿUmar and ʿAlī, while others constitute attempts to contain the social implications of egalitarian ideas. The endeavours of classical authors in a variety of literary genres to render the Islamic egalitarian ideal safe and innocuous will be discussed in a more systematic manner in the ensuing chapters. The purpose of the current chapter is to draw attention to the ways in which this taming was effected with respect to several issues and developments encountered in a preliminary fashion in the first section of this book: the exegetical history of the prime egalitarian Qurʾānic proof-text, 49:13; the changing relationship between ethnicity and social status in the second/eighth and third/ninth centuries; the beginnings of a court literature which drew to a considerable extent on non-Islamic, and especially Persian, ideas; and the active role played in the construction of social ideals by compilers and anthologists. The subsequent chapters will discuss aspects of Islamic social thought that emerged and crystallised after the general processes of sorting out and watering down examined in the present chapter had been largely accomplished.

In several respects, the current chapter is intended as a sequel to the first. It is therefore appropriate to draw attention to the differences in the materials under discussion in each of these two chapters, especially since the sources used in them are in some cases identical and in others perhaps contemporary. It will be remembered that the literature discussed in the first chapter was mostly of a fragmentary nature; it consisted of dicta, anecdotes and short pieces of description recorded in various compilations of classical times. In many cases these literary fragments were ascribed to figures of the first decades of the Islamic period, but it is likely that they reflect the ways in which Muslims of the second century and later came to think about their past. The materials under discussion in the present chapter, by contrast, are the works of known authors such as Ibn al-Muqaffaʿ, al-Jāḥiẓ and Ibn Qutayba. Although these writers naturally made use of the *ḥadīth* and *bons mots* discussed in the first chapter, their works are structured and extensive, and can be situated in their historical contexts far more easily and satisfactorily than the brief utterances they sometimes employ in their arguments. The writings of these classical authors are accordingly considered here not for the elements of retrospection that they may contain, for these have already been discussed, but for the ways in which such elements may be used by a writer to express his opinions on the social issues of his own time.

Egalitarianism and rebellion

Also relevant to a consideration of egalitarianism and its taming is the role that it may have played in the many insurrectionary movements of the late Umayyad and early ʿAbbāsid periods, and it is to this topic that I shall turn first. The revolts that took place in Khurāsān, Transoxania and northern Iran during the second/eighth and early third/ninth centuries were not of the same character; some were rural, others were urban, some were grounded in Islamic ideas, others were syncretistic and so on. They do, however, suggest widespread social discontent, and it is therefore appropriate to consider such evidence as can be mustered from the sources for egalitarian motives, and the use of egalitarian language, in such contexts.

Although they were not infrequently led by members of the Iranian aristocracy, the chief support for many of these revolts seems to have been among the poor, and often among peasants.[1] The ʿAbbāsid movement, which eventually gained support from many sections of the Khurāsānian population, was initially regarded by the native aristocracy as a popular uprising that threatened their own position. It seems quite likely that the agents of the ʿAbbāsid *daʿwa* in Khurāsān may have availed themselves of the language of Islamic egalitarianism in their efforts to exploit a variety of local dissatisfactions. They may also have incited revolts among slaves, although they probably had no intention of actually attempting to improve conditions for the latter.[2]

Even among the more syncretistic movements of this period, social grievances often seem to have played an important role. The revolt of Shurayk in Bukhārā in 133/750 may have been an expression of social divisions between city-dwellers and the rural population, and between the aristocracy and the down-and-outs.[3] The incipient revolt of Bih'āfarīd in the environs of Nīshāpūr may have had an egalitarian tendency; it was certainly concerned with social reform, and its attempt to promote a set of religious practices in a spirit of compromise between Zoroastrianism and Islam was intended to break the power and wealth of the Zoroastrian priestly hierarchy.[4] Social discontent was also a factor in the revolt of al-Muqannaʿ, most of whose followers were peasants or members of the poorer classes.[5] Bābak, on the other hand, may have

[1] Daniel, *Khurasan under Abbasid Rule*, pp. 125–126.

[2] Daniel, *Khurasan under Abbasid Rule*, pp. 53, 190, 192; see also p. 54, and p. 70, n. 152.

[3] Daniel, *Khurasan under Abbasid Rule*, p. 88.

[4] Al-Bīrūnī, *al-Āthār al-bāqiya ʿan al-qurūn al-khāliya*, ed. C.E. Sachau, *Chronologie orientalischer Völker* (Leipzig, 1923), pp. 210–211; Daniel, *Khurasan under Abbasid Rule*, pp. 91–92; B.S. Amoretti, 'Sects and Heresies', *Cambridge History of Iran*, vol. 4, ed. R.N. Frye (Cambridge, 1975), p. 490.

[5] Daniel, *Khurasan under Abbasid Rule*, pp. 137–147.

envisaged a social revolution, but there is no evidence that his vision was egalitarian, and the slaughter carried out by his followers was indiscriminate.[6]

The Khurramiyya, like their Mazdakite forebears, are occasionally said to have practised communal ownership of property, but there is little evidence to support this.[7] Communal access to women is frequently associated with the Khurramiyya and other rebellious groups and, given the social consequences of this practice, it is possible, though probably unlikely, that it derived from egalitarian ideals.[8] In any case, it is hard to imagine a situation in which the practice could have been justified by the use of egalitarian Qur'ānic proof-texts.

Thus it seems there is no firm evidence that any of these movements made use of egalitarian rhetoric, but it is conceivable and even probable that such language may have been used to gain the support of discontented Arabs and *mawālī* alike in some of the more 'Islamic' opposition movements of the period. Even if those involved in these revolts did not deliberately associate themselves with pious egalitarian vocabulary, the threat to the social order that their activities posed can only have intensified the sense of urgency with which contemporary authors set about limiting the scope of the Islamic egalitarian ideal to the next world.

The significance of 49:13

The realm of exegesis provides a useful example of the taming of egalitarianism, and suggests the prominent role of the *'ulamā'* in this process. Reference to the classical works of Qur'ānic commentary will be made throughout this second section of the book, but it is appropriate to begin with the exegetical history of Q. 49:13: 'O men! We have created you from male and female, and have made you into peoples and tribes that you may know one another. The most noble among you in the sight of God is the most pious.'[9] The *ḥadīths*

[6] Al-Maqdisī, *al-Bad' wa'l-ta'rīkh*, vol. 6, p. 116; see also B.S. Amoretti, 'Sects and Heresies', *Cambridge History of Iran*, vol. 4, pp. 505–508; Spuler, *Iran in früh-islamischer Zeit* (Wiesbaden, 1952), pp. 203, 437. There are some indications that Bābak himself was far from indifferent to the charisma of noble birth; see the accounts of al-Mas'ūdī, *Murūj al-dhahab*, vol. 3, p. 468, and Gh.H. Sadighi, *Les mouvements religieux iraniens au IIe et au IIIe siècle de l'hégire* (Paris, 1938), p. 267.

[7] See, for example, al-Baghdādī, *Kitāb al-farq bayn al-firaq*, ed. M. Badr (Cairo, 1323/1905), p. 347 (*al-nās kulluhum shurakā' fī'l-amwāl wa'l-nisā'*); cf. Sadighi, *Les mouvements religieux iraniens*, pp. 190, 204; W. Madelung, 'Khurramiyya', *EI2*. On Mazdak's communism, see ch. 3.

[8] The practice is associated with the Khurramiyya in general (al-Baghdādī, *Kitāb al-farq bayn al-firaq*, p. 347; al-Maqdisī, *al-Bad' wa'l-ta'rīkh*, vol. 4, p. 31), and with Khidāsh (al-Ṭabarī, *Ta'rīkh*, vol. 7, p. 109; al-Maqdisī, *al-Bad' wa'l-ta'rīkh*, vol. 6, p. 61; Daniel, *Khurasan under Abbasid Rule*, p. 36, and p. 65, n. 55) and perhaps al-Muqanna' (al-Bīrūnī, *al-Āthār al-bāqiya*, p. 211; Sadighi, *Les mouvements religieux iraniens*, pp. 181–182) in particular. On the corrupting effects of such practices to the social hierarchy, see Niẓām al-Mulk, *Siyar al-mulūk*, p. 266; tr. Darke, *The Book of Government*, pp. 202–203.

[9] The history of interpretation of this verse has been discussed at length in Mottahedeh, 'The Shu'ûbîyah Controversy', pp. 161–182, and al-Sayyid, 'Min al-shu'ūb wa'l-qabā'il ilā'l-umma', in *al-Umma wa'l-jamā'a wa'l-salṭa*, pp. 17–87 (see especially pp. 26–31). In these studies the

adduced by the various commentators suggest the range of interpretations the verse might have had in a particular milieu and in some cases reflect attempts to limit this range to the religious sphere.

Many of the major Qur'ānic commentators were at least ostensibly non-committal on the question of whether 49:13 applied only to equality before God in the next life or whether it also carried implications for social organisation in the here and now. It appears that an early school of interpretation regarded 49:13 as a reference only to differences in tribal genealogies, an interpretation which could have been applied by some to the question of social status in this world. But al-Ṭabarī (d. 310/923), who records this interpretation, paraphrases the clause 'the most noble among you in the sight of God is the most pious' in the following terms: 'the most noble of you in the sight of your Lord is he who is most zealous in the fulfilment of God's commands and in the avoidance of sins against him, and not he whose family is greatest or whose kinsfolk are most numerous'. There is no hint of social subversion in al-Ṭabarī's treatment of the verse. He also cites *ḥadīth* that in themselves have nothing to say about social rank: 'Men are the descendants of Adam and Eve, as if they fell short of a full measure (*ka-ṭaff al-ṣāʿ lam yamlaʾūhu*); on the Day of Judgment God will not ask after your inherited merit or genealogies; the most noble of you in God's sight is the most pious', and 'Your genealogies should not be a cause of shame for anyone; you are the descendants of Adam, as if you fell short of a full measure. No one has precedence over anyone else except on account of religion and good deeds. If a man is debauched, foul-mouthed, miserly or cowardly, it is reckoned up against him.'[10] It should be noted that although these *ḥadīth* are not obviously concerned with social status in this world, they were seen by some classical writers as having logical social implications.[11] Al-Ṭabarī's emphasis, however, is on genealogical concerns, and there is no reason to suppose from his discussion that he had anything other than religious equality in mind.

This narrow genealogical interpretation of 49:13 survived in the exegetical tradition long after the tribal identities of the early Arab Muslims had lost their meaning. As late as the seventh/thirteenth century, al-Bayḍāwī (d. c. 685/1286) wrote, '[We have created you . . .] from Adam and Eve; or, we have created each one of you from a father and a mother, so that all are equal in this respect, and there is no countenance for pride in one's lineage . . . It is piety by which souls become perfect and by which individuals differ in excellence, so that whoever desires nobility should seek it in piety. As the Prophet said: "Whoever takes pleasure in being the noblest of people, let him fear God", and

main emphasis is on the interpretation of the terms *shuʿūb* and *qabāʾil*; my principal concern here is with the significance of the verse's ultimate phrase (cf. ch. 1).

[10] Al-Ṭabarī, *Jāmiʿ al-bayān ʿan taʾwīl al-Qurʾān*, vol. 26, p. 140. Al-Ṭabarī also cites a third tradition, according to which Ibn ʿAbbās predicts that men will reject the Qur'ānic principle of basing precedence on righteousness and piety, and will insist instead that the 'most noble' are those who belong to the most illustrious families.

[11] See ch. 1 (*ṭaff al-ṣāʿ*).

"O men! There are only two kinds of people: the pious believer, who is noble in God's sight, and the miserable sinner, who is despicable in God's sight".'[12] In the following century, Ibn Kathīr (d. 774/1373) echoed this interpretation by quoting the passage, 'All people are equal in nobility in terms of their kinship in clay with Adam and Eve; they differ in excellence only in religious matters, that is, in obedience to God and in following his Prophet.' Furthermore Ibn Kathīr observed that '[People] differ in excellence in God's sight only in piety and not in their inherited merit (*aḥsab*).' He went on to cite several *ḥadīth* that restate or otherwise confirm the pious egalitarianism of 49:13: these include 'God looks not at your appearances and possessions, but at your hearts and deeds', and 'You are all the sons of Adam and Adam was made of clay; let a tribe abandon its boasting of its ancestors, or it will be more contemptible than a dung beetle in God's sight.'[13]

Al-Bayḍāwī and Ibn Kathīr are thus apparently as non-committal as al-Ṭabarī on the question of the nature of the equality affirmed by 49:13. But they too cite *ḥadīth* that emphasise the verse's religious relevance, and in addition, Ibn Kathīr adduces a *ḥadīth* that explicitly denies, or at least limits, the social relevance of the verse: 'the best of you in the Jāhiliyya are the best of you in Islam, as long as they possess religious understanding'.[14] Other commentators add similar qualifications to the nobility–piety equation. Most notably, Shaykh al-Ṭā'ifa al-Ṭūsī (d. 460/1067), in his discussion of 49:13, emphasises the – in his view – self-evident superiority of men of illustrious lineage, wealth or personal accomplishments over those who lacked such distinctions, as long as they were equal in religious merit.[15]

That al-Ṭūsī found it necessary to diminish explicitly the possible social significance of the egalitarianism implied in 49:13 is an indication that the verse had been understood by some to refer to equality in this world. Such interpretations are clearly attested for the third/ninth century, but had probably existed much earlier.[16] The writings of Ibn Qutayba (213–276/828–889) suggest that the verse was used to justify both ethnic and social egalitarianism in his day (the two were, of course, closely connected). In a response to what he regards as the over-literal interpretation of 49:13 by the *shuʿūbīs*, Ibn Qutayba argues that the Qur'ānic equation of nobility with piety refers only to the next world. Otherwise, he points out, there would be no distinction between superiority and inferiority among people, nor between the noble and

[12] *Anwār al-tanzīl*, vol. 2, p. 276.

[13] Ibn Kathīr, *Tafsīr*, vol. 6, pp. 386–389. The first *ḥadīth* appears in Ibn Māja, *Sunan*, vol. 2, *zuhd*, ch. 9, p. 1388, no. 4143, and Ibn Ḥanbal, *Musnad*, vol. 2, pp. 285, 539. The second appears in Ibn Ḥanbal, *Musnad*, vol. 2, pp. 361, 523–524. Ibn Kathīr also cites the second of the pair of traditions adduced by al-Bayḍāwī.

[14] Ibn Kathīr, *Tafsīr*, p. 387. See also Mottahedeh, 'The Shuʿûbîyah Controversy', pp. 176–177, and ch. 1.

[15] Al-Ṭūsī, *al-Tibyān*, vol. 9, pp. 352–353; the relevant passage is quoted in Mottahedeh, 'The Shuʿûbîyah Controversy', p. 176.

[16] See al-Sayyid, 'Min al-shuʿūb wa'l-qabā'il ilā'l-umma', in *al-Umma, wa'l-jamāʿa*, pp. 26–31.

the less noble, nor between the excellent and the less excellent, except in respect to the afterlife.[17] The anti-*shuʿūbī* context of Ibn Qutayba's remarks implies that ethnic considerations were uppermost in his mind, and it is evident from elsewhere in the surviving literature on the *shuʿūbiyya* controversy that the verse was frequently invoked as a proof-text to justify the equal status of Arabs and clients (*mawālī*).[18] The language employed in his argument, however, is suggestive of the degree to which ethnic identity and social status tended to be equated, and seems to indicate a lingering awareness that the verse 49:13 might also be taken to endorse egalitarianism on a social level.

Whether indirectly through the use of *ḥadīth* or explicitly through argument, a number of commentators and other writers took some trouble to demonstrate that 49:13 was not a prescription for social organisation in the present but represented an ideal to be brought about by divine wisdom in the next world. The Qurʾān commentaries are to some extent reflections of the immediate circumstances in which they were produced, and to some extent of the development of the classical interpretive tradition.[19] This tradition suggests that as the hierarchical aspects of Islamic societies found support in a growing range of hierarchical social ideals, the potentially subversive implications of 49:13 were still not forgotten.

The emergence of an Arabic court literature and the transposition of Iranian social ideals

It has been suggested that the earliest remnants of Islamic social thought reflect little of the wider Persian social context in which they are likely to have been produced.[20] To the extent that Iranian notions of social merit and organisation penetrated Arab-Islamic culture at all in the first and early second centuries, this seems to have been due more to the literary endeavours of Persian men of letters than to the general intermingling of ethnic groups in the cities of Iraq and Iran. The *dahāqīn* of Khurāsān and possibly elsewhere may have kept Iranian social ideals alive among themselves since the conquests, but it was their descendants in the late Umayyad and early ʿAbbāsid periods who, in their translations from Pahlavī into Arabic, placed their knowledge of Iranian culture at the disposal of the growing numbers of prosperous city-dwellers literate in Arabic, and thus communicated to them the importance of social organisation in the Iranian literary and historiographical traditions. The effects of this process of cultural transmission on Muslim treatments of the Iranian past have been discussed in the previous chapter. It is now

[17] As quoted in *al-ʿIqd al-farīd*, vol. 12, p. 181.

[18] Mottahedeh, 'The Shuʿûbîyah Controversy', pp. 167f. See also the roughly contemporary al-Sarakhsī, who refers only to the last phrase of 49:13 but interprets it as a recognition of the ethnic equality of Arab and non-Arab Muslims (*al-Mabsūṭ*, vol. 5, p. 23).

[19] The latter half of this point is made well by J.D. McAuliffe, *Qurʾānic Christians. An Analysis of Classical and Modern Exegesis* (Cambridge, 1991), especially pp. 28ff.

[20] See ch. 1.

appropriate to examine the appearance of Persian social conceptions in some early 'independent' compositions, that is, in works of literature that are not ostensibly concerned with the author's cultural ancestors but with his present historical situation.

One of the most important figures in the transmission of Iranian cultural traditions to Islamic civilisation is the former Persian nobleman and *mawlā*, Ibn al-Muqaffa' (d. 139/756 or later).[21] An Arabic court literature had already begun to take shape under Hishām (105–125/724–743) in the context of the expanding secretarial apparatus. This literary activity had included both translations into Arabic, such as that of the alleged *Letters of Aristotle to Alexander* (*Rasā'il Arisṭāṭālīs ilā'l-Iskandar*) by the caliph's secretary Sālim Abū'l-'Alā',[22] and the composition of original epistles by known authors, such as 'Abd al-Ḥamīd.[23] The extended literary compositions that now began to appear belong to the general category of *adab*, which presents, in an entertaining and didactic fashion, the broad mass of knowledge considered to constitute the necessary general culture of educated persons.[24]

Ibn al-Muqaffa''s works occupy an important place in early Arabic literary history and are highly distinctive.[25] Although his Persian noble background provided no guarantee of social recognition in Iraq in the mid-second/eighth century, Ibn al-Muqaffa''s career suggests that being Persian was no longer an automatic barrier to the acquisition of social status. Under the Umayyads Ibn al-Muqaffa' had been a secretary, and after the 'Abbāsid revolution he seems to have attained considerable social esteem, perhaps primarily as a result of his prodigious cultural knowledge and his literary activities. A certain prejudice against non-Arabs *per se* doubtless continued to exist in some quarters, but Ibn al-Muqaffa' was not overtly concerned with the social position of the *mawālī*. The industry with which he translated books from Pahlavī into Arabic is nevertheless indicative of his strong attachment to his cultural heritage and his desire to see it perpetuated.[26]

[21] See al-Sayyid, 'Naẓarāt fī jadaliyyāt al-'ilāqa bayn al-namūdhajayn', in *al-Umma wa'l-jamā'a wa'l-salṭa*, pp. 103ff; van Ess, *Theologie und Gesellschaft*, vol. 2, pp. 22–29.

[22] Grignaschi, 'Les «Rasā'il 'Arisṭāṭālīsa 'ilā-l-Iskandar»', pp. 7–52.

[23] See I. 'Abbās, *'Abd al-Ḥamīd ibn Yaḥyā al-Kātib*, pp. 25–60; J.D. Latham, 'The Beginnings of Arabic Prose Literature: The Epistolary Genre', in *Arabic Literature to the End of the Umayyad Period* (Cambridge, 1983), pp. 154–179; H.A.R. Gibb, 'The Social Significance of the Shuubiya', in *Studies on the Civilization of Islam*, eds. S.J. Shaw and W.R. Polk (Princeton, 1962), p. 63.

[24] Cf. F. Gabrieli, '*Adab*', *EI2*.

[25] They are not, however, quite as original as they might at first appear; for several examples of Ibn al-Muqaffa''s unacknowledged indebtedness to Sasanian sources, see S. Shaked, 'From Iran to Islam. Notes on Some Themes in Transmission', pp. 31–67.

[26] According to Ibn al-Nadīm, *Fihrist* (p. 118), Ibn al-Muqaffa' made translations of the *Khwadāynāmag* ('Book of Kings'); an *A'īnnāmag* ('Book of Rules of Etiquette') (cf. Richter, *Studien*, pp. 41ff); *Kalīla wa Dimna*; a work listed as *Tājnāmaj fī sīrat Anūshīrvān* (cf. Richter, *Studien*, pp. 60f); and the so-called *K. Mazdak* (on which see Tafazzoli, 'Observations sur le soi-disant Mazdak-Nāmag', *Acta Iranica* 23 (1984). With the exception of *Kalīla wa Dimna* (on which see ch. 3), none of these translations is extant, although many of them are quoted frequently in the works of other writers.

Given his aristocratic background, it is not surprising that Ibn al-Muqaffaʿ should have taken the desirability of a social hierarchy for granted. Writing shortly after the founding of the ʿAbbāsid dynasty, Ibn al-Muqaffaʿ saw an urgent need for the creation of imperial structures, social and otherwise, and his vision included the maintenance, or at least acknowledgement, of an Arab aristocracy linked in its culture and interests to the ruler and his court. Furthermore, the advent of the ʿAbbāsids coincided with the reintroduction of several features of the Sasanian imperial style and the frequent appointment of *mawālī* to prominent posts and, although the degree to which the Khurāsānians had assimilated aspects of Persian culture may have been less extensive than has sometimes been supposed,[27] their forceful presence at the political centre helped to create an environment in which the integration of Iranian culture into Islamic civilisation was not only possible, but also necessary.[28]

Of Ibn al-Muqaffaʿ's original writings, the most significant for its treatment of social organisation is his *Risāla fī'l-ṣaḥāba*, for it is here that he addresses the need for a dignified aristocracy most directly and comprehensively. His aristocratic inclinations can also be detected in some of his other works. In one place, he distinguishes between the nobles and the common people, the *aḥrār* and the *sifla*, and admonishes the ruler not to let the former go hungry while the latter have full stomachs.[29] He is also one of the first authors to employ the categories of *khāṣṣa* and *ʿāmma*.[30] But it is in the *Risāla fī'l-ṣaḥāba* that Ibn al-Muqaffaʿ presents systematically his plan for an Islamic empire, in which certain Iranian social ideals are reproduced, albeit transposed entirely into an Arab-Islamic frame of reference.[31] The epistle takes its name from the caliph's companions or *ṣaḥāba*, a group attested only for al-Manṣūr (136–158/754–775) and al-Mahdī (158–169/775–785), and probably an Islamised form

27 See A. Arazi and A. El'ad, '«L'Épître à l'armée» Al-Ma'mūn et la seconde *daʿwa*', *SI* 66 (1987), pp. 61ff; Daniel, *Khurasan under Abbasid Rule*, pp. 20f.

28 Crone, *Slaves*, pp. 61f, 67–68, 74–76; Daniel, *Khurasan under Abbasid Rule*, p. 60.

29 *Al-Adab al-kabīr*, in Ibn al-Muqaffaʿ, *Āthār Ibn al-Muqaffaʿ*, p. 286; cf. Richter, *Studien*, p. 7. On the probable Iranian background of the use of the term *ḥurr* to mean both 'free' and 'noble', see F. de Blois, '"Freemen" and "Nobles" in Iranian and Semitic Languages', *JRAS* (1985), pp. 5–15. On the attribution of this text to Ibn al-Muqaffaʿ, see I. ʿAbbās, 'Naẓra jadīda fī baʿḍ al-kutub al-mansūba li-bn al-Muqaffaʿ', *Majallat majmaʿ al-lugha al-ʿarabiyya bi Dimashq* 52 (1397/1977), pp. 540–541.

30 *Risāla fī'l-ṣaḥāba*, in Ibn al-Muqaffaʿ, *Āthār Ibn al-Muqaffaʿ*, *passim*; *al-Adab al-kabīr*, p. 301; *al-Adab al-ṣaghīr*, p. 324. Cf. P. Charles-Dominique, 'Le système éthique d'Ibn al-Muqaffaʿ d'après ses deux épîtres dites «*al-ṣaġīr*» et «*al-kabīr*»', *Arabica* 12 (1965), pp. 53–54; Beg, 'al-Khāṣṣa wa'l-ʿāmma', *EI2*; Shaked, 'From Iran to Islam. Notes on Some Themes in Transmission', pp. 36–37.

31 The work was probably intended for al-Manṣūr, and must therefore have been composed between the accession of that caliph in 136/754 and the author's death. The earliest date given for Ibn al-Muqaffaʿ's death (or, according to most accounts, execution) is 139/756, although a later date seems more likely (cf. S.D. Goitein, 'A Turning Point in the History of the Muslim State', *Studies in Islamic History and Institutions* (Leiden, 1966), p. 153, n. 3). There is good reason to suppose that the epistle was written towards the beginning of al-Manṣūr's reign (Crone, *Slaves*, p. 252, n. 530; van Ess, *Theologie und Gesellschaft*, vol. 2, p. 24).

of the military companionship of the Marwānid period.[32] The group included Umayyad princes, scholars and in particular Syrian generals who had lent their services to the new régime.[33] The *Risāla fī'l-ṣaḥāba* is best known for its proposal that the caliph, regarded as the source of both religious and political authority, impose religious and legal uniformity at the expense of the *ʿulamāʾ*.[34]

Also part of Ibn al-Muqaffaʿ's imperial scheme was the protection of social privilege for those properly deserving of it. He considered it necessary that those who shared the caliph's intimacy possess special characteristics, which were not required in those whom the caliph appointed to posts and to whom he subsequently gave orders. These desired characteristics included both respectable ancestry and praiseworthy personal qualities. Ibn al-Muqaffaʿ found that the current caliph's associates included men 'whose names were contemptible, who were not of ancient ancestry, and who had not proved themselves (in combat) in recent times . . . those who had failed to attain the education fit for an eminent man, were without well-known inherited merit, of poor judgement, notorious for immorality among the people of their cities, and who had passed most of their lives as artisans working with their hands, but had nevertheless failed to acquire experience (*balāʾ*) or wealth'.[35] Such men, he reported with disapproval, were admitted to the presence of the caliph before many of the descendants of the Muhājirūn and Anṣār, before the caliph's own family, and before the great Arab families (*ahl buyūtāt al-ʿarab*); furthermore, they were awarded double the stipends and grants given to Banū Hāshim and other leaders of Quraysh.[36] Ibn al-Muqaffaʿ, then, recognised a nobility composed of both old Arab families, whose social position was based on the traditional tribal principles of *nasab* and *ḥasab*, and the descendants of those with precedence in Islam. He was not attempting to restore the Persian aristocracy from which he stemmed, and did not argue, as the *shuʿūbī*s would a century later, that Iranians who had been considered noble in pre-Islamic times should be able to retain that social status under the new polity. The aristocracy that Ibn al-Muqaffaʿ envisaged would buttress the power of the ʿAbbāsid dynasty and it is this, as well as his contempt for trade and manual labour, that illustrates the Persian conditioning of his thought.

Concerning the current caliph's companions, Ibn al-Muqaffaʿ continues: 'Neither respect for kinship (*riʿāyat raḥim*) nor religious understanding (*fiqh fī'l-dīn*) placed [them] in that position; [they owe their rank] not to experience in a well-known, respected confrontation with an enemy in the past, nor to

[32] On which see Crone, *Slaves*, pp. 38, 55f.

[33] Crone, *Slaves*, p. 67, where it is suggested that the purpose of the institution may have been to conciliate the defeated Syrians.

[34] *Idem*, *Slaves*, p. 69; Goitein, 'Turning Point', p. 157.

[35] *Risāla fī'l-ṣaḥāba*, in *Āthār Ibn al-Muqaffaʿ*, p. 357; tr. Goitein, 'Turning Point', pp. 160f.

[36] In this passage Ibn al-Muqaffaʿ is perhaps reminding the ʿAbbāsids of their own genealogical propaganda, in which the Hāshimite and ʿAbbāsid lines were often placed in opposition to other groups within Quraysh (cf. ch. 1).

recently acquired riches; not to the fact that they are indispensable for any purpose whatsoever, nor on account of any aptitude which they possess; they are not horsemen, preachers or great scholars; [they owe their positions merely to the fact that] they have served as secretaries or chamberlains.'[37] In this section of his epistle, then, Ibn al-Muqaffaʿ appears to consider kinship, religious learning, military skill and wealth to be possible grounds for inclusion in the aristocracy. He goes on to list explicitly the types of people whom he considers worthy of the caliph's companionship: those who, by virtue of kinship (*qarāba*) or military experience, enjoyed a favoured position with him; those whose nobility, judgement and deeds were worthy of the caliph's assembly, of conducting conversation with him, and of offering counsel; men well known for bravery, who combined merit (*ḥasab*) and probity (*ʿafāf*) with their valour, and deserved to be promoted from the army to the companionship of the caliph; worthy religious scholars, whose good behaviour and religious knowledge would be beneficial to society; and men of noble birth, who did not corrupt themselves or others.[38] Wealth is not included in this list of positive attributes, although, as noted above, lack of economic means appears as a disqualification in Ibn al-Muqaffaʿ's description of the sundry nature of the caliph's present companions.[39]

It was part of Ibn al-Muqaffaʿ's imperial plan, then, that social rank be recognised and protected by isolating the caliph from contact with those beneath his dignity and ensuring that positions were given only to men who were entitled to them by their social status. These were thoroughly Sasanian concerns. On the other hand, Ibn al-Muqaffaʿ was willing to admit the social value of a fairly wide range of people: those with established nobility of birth; those whose nobility stemmed from their descent from members of the early Muslim community; and those who had achieved a reputation as a result of their personal abilities, in such areas as warfare and scholarship. For him, then, aristocratic status was hereditary, although only men who lived up to the standards of gentility associated with their noble birth were actually worthy of the caliph's company; similarly, ordinary men could become worthy of elevation to the ranks of the caliph's companions in cases of extraordinary and proven individual merit.

The ʿAbbāsids did in fact attempt to construct a service aristocracy.[40] They created a three-tiered nobility out of those associated, or those whose

[37] *Risāla fī'l-ṣaḥāba*, in Ibn al-Muqaffaʿ, *Āthār Ibn al-Muqaffaʿ*, p. 357. Ibn al-Muqaffaʿ's low opinion of these professions is also apparent on p. 358.

[38] *Risāla fī'l-ṣaḥāba*, in Ibn al-Muqaffaʿ, *Āthār Ibn al-Muqaffaʿ*, p. 358; summarised by Goitein, 'Turning Point', p. 161.

[39] Ibn al-Muqaffaʿ also addresses the question of the ruler's companions in his mirror for princes *al-Adab al-kabīr*, where the two qualities that receive most attention are religion and, as in *Kalīla wa Dimna*, manliness (*muruwwa*) (*al-Adab al-kabīr*, in *Āthār Ibn al-Muqaffaʿ*, pp. 282, 309–10). On *muruwwa*, cf. Goldziher, *Muslim Studies*, vol. 1, pp. 11–44; Ibn al-Ḥaddād, *al-Jawhar al-nafīs*, pp. 117–120, and al-Sayyid's comments in his introduction to the latter text, pp. 29–30, 49ff.

[40] Crone, *Slaves*, pp. 65–73.

forebears had been associated, with the ʿAbbāsid revolution, and they added to this Khurāsānian aristocracy the caliph's companions and clients. These measures did not, however, succeed in creating the kind of social category prescribed by Ibn al-Muqaffaʿ. Al-Manṣūr apparently made little effort to assert himself against the *ʿulamāʾ* or to integrate the latter into a composite aristocracy tied to the dynasty, along the lines of the Sasanian model; and his successors were eventually forced to yield moral and religious authority to the scholars and to accept, at least nominally, the latter's political and social ideals. The fifty-odd years following the execution of Ibn al-Muqaffaʿ were characterised by the emergence of two cultures, one identified with secretaries, the other identified with scholars and soldiers. The ʿAbbāsids themselves, with the exception of al-Maʾmūn (198–218/813–833), generally found it expedient to take the side of the *ʿulamāʾ* and the army rather than that of the bureaucracy.[41] In his purported testament, al-Manṣūr is said to have advised his son al-Mahdī, 'Think the best of your Lord but the worst of your tax collectors and secretaries.'[42] Despite the fact that the secretaries were probably almost always loyal supporters of the caliphate, it is likely that the spate of insurrectionary movements in Iran and Transoxania in the second/eighth and early third/ninth centuries exacerbated the ʿAbbāsids' suspicion of Iranian culture.[43]

The *shuʿūbiyya*

The concerns of the *shuʿūbi*s have left a noticeable mark on much of the material already treated in this book. But it is appropriate to discuss the full-blown literary controversy of the *shuʿūbiyya*, which reached its greatest intensity in the third and subsequent centuries, here, in the context of the transmission of Iranian and other non- and pre-Islamic ideals to Islamic culture and the adaptation of such ideals to a setting in which equality was associated with piety. According to Gibb's well-known and convincing argument, at the heart of the *shuʿūbiyya* was a struggle among competing parties over the cultural orientation of Islamic civilisation.[44] The controversy was thus not primarily concerned with the issue of social precedence. A century or so after the death of Ibn al-Muqaffaʿ, the Iranian secretaries whose views are of principal relevance here had, in fact, risen considerably from the lowly social position to which they had been reduced under the earlier Umayyads, and had won for themselves a position of importance in the administration of the state. Indeed, had they not achieved such stature, their opinions would not have caught the attention of caliphs and the educated élites and consequently would not have been recorded in such detail. But in complex ways, the subject of social pre-emi-

[41] Hārūn's elimination of the Barmakids is the most dramatic example; see further Crone, *Slaves*, pp. 70–71.

[42] Al-Ṭabarī, *Taʾrīkh*, vol. 8, p. 106. The saying does not appear in al-Yaʿqūbī's version of the testament; cf. A. Dietrich, 'Das politische Testament des zweiten ʿAbbāsidenkalifen al-Manṣūr', *Der Islam* 30 (1952), pp. 133–65.

[43] Gibb, 'Social Significance', p. 66, and see above.

[44] Gibb, 'Social Significance'.

nence was entangled in the *shuʿūbiyya* controversy, and ethnic and social interpretations of egalitarianism were thus once again intimately bound up together. Part of what was involved in the struggle over cultural orientation, from an Iranian point of view, was a desire to ensure the recognition of hierarchy and the respect due to nobility, since these values were so clearly emphasised in the Iranian intellectual and literary tradition. Yet at the same time, the *shuʿūbiyya* managed to pass themselves off as egalitarians (as their unlikely soubriquet of *ahl al-taswiya*, 'the partisans of equality', attests), and they seem to have been able to do this on the basis of their adoption of the by now standard equation of nobility with piety.[45]

One of the ways in which the struggle for the orientation of Islamic culture manifested itself was in the often vituperative literary expression given to the competition for social esteem between secretaries and merchants. Such literature sometimes seems to reflect a cultural antipathy between Iranians (and other peoples) and Arabs, and sometimes the cultural distance between courtly and urban environments;[46] and, since secretaries were in the employ of rulers, they were perceived as belonging to the world of the court. Sometimes, however, cultural and ethnic differences were perceived to overlap, as is suggested in the case of an opinion ascribed to the pro-Persian al-Maʾmūn: 'The people of the marketplace are base, craftsmen are vile, merchants are avaricious, and the secretaries are kings over the people.'[47] In this example, the contempt for commerce and crafts on the one hand and the elevation of the secretaries on the other are compatible with the Iranian cultural attitudes associated with the secretaries.[48] Antipathy towards secretaries, who evidently had acquired considerable prestige, is associated particularly with the figure of al-Jāḥiẓ (160–255/776–868), who apparently saw in the merchants of his time a perpetuation of the Arab egalitarian ideal,[49] and to whom is attributed (almost certainly incorrectly) the contemptuous *Risāla fī dhamm akhlāq al-kuttāb*.[50] The author of this text aims to prove that the secretaries are

[45] See for example Ibn ʿAbd Rabbihi's account of the *shuʿūbiyya*, in which he associates them with arguments based on the last phrase of Q. 49:13, the Prophet's speech on the occasion of his farewell pilgrimage, and other stock materials that give expression to the egalitarian point of view (*al-ʿIqd al-farīd*, vol. 12, p. 172); see also Ibn Qutayba's comments on the misuse of these texts by the *shuʿūbīs* (*al-ʿIqd al-farīd*, vol. 12, pp. 181–182, and see above). The oddity of the term *ahl al-taswiya* in its application to the *shuʿūbīs* has been noted by Mottahedeh, 'The Shuʿûbîyah Controversy', p. 177.

[46] See I.M. Lapidus, *A History of Islamic Societies* (Cambridge, 1988), pp. 120–125.

[47] Al-Bayhaqī, *al-Maḥāsin wa'l-masāwī*, p. 103; al-Jāḥiẓ, *al-Maḥāsin wa'l-aḍdād*, p. 148; al-Rāghib al-Iṣfahānī, *Muḥāḍarāt al-udabāʾ*, vol. 2, p. 459; Ibn Ḥamdūn, *al-Tadhkira al-Ḥamdūniyya*, vol. 2, p. 71, no. 137. This saying reverses the normal sequence of the descriptive formula discussed in ch. 1 by listing a number of worthless social groups first and then singling out one group for their excellence. [48] Cf. Crone, *Slaves*, p. 257, n. 600.

[49] S. Enderwitz, *Gesellschaftlicher Rang und ethnische Legitimation. Der arabische Schriftsteller Abū ʿUṯmān al-Ǧāḥiẓ (gest. 868) über die Afrikaner, Perser und Araber in der islamischen Gesellschaft* (Freiburg, 1979), pp. 178–184.

[50] On the question of al-Jāḥiẓ's authorship, see Pellat, 'Une charge contre les secrétaires d'état attribuée à Ǧāḥiẓ', *Hespéris* 48 (1956), pp. 29–31, and 'Nouvel essai d'inventaire de l'oeuvre ǧāḥiẓienne', *Arabica* 31 (1984), p. 145. Al-Jāḥiẓ is also said to be the author of a *Risāla fī madḥ al-kuttāb* (Pellat, 'Charge contre les secrétaires', p. 29, notes 2 and 3).

unworthy of the respect they have come to enjoy. He rejects the idea that the secretarial art is a noble and excellent one; after all, the Prophet had had no gift for it, and kings and tribal leaders were known to have had atrocious handwriting.[51] Secretaryship, in his opinion, was a base occupation, in that it placed people in a subordinate and servile position. In some respects, indeed, the secretary had less freedom of action than a slave, and despite his high opinion of himself, his position was that of an ignorant fool.[52]

The author of this text does not make it clear whether it is the profession that corrupts otherwise worthy men or whether it is only people who are base by nature who become secretaries.[53] He cites a statement ascribed to al-Zuhrī in which the science of *ḥadīth* is declared to be a manly interest of no appeal to the effeminate. Having already called the religious credentials of the secretaries into question, the author pronounces al-Zuhrī's statement especially applicable to them.[54] He notes that certain Muʿtazilites regard the tendency of the common people to idolise secretaries as a mark of intellectual weakness.[55] The author then observes that there is some merit in every profession, except that of the secretary, who is prone to deceive and betray his fellows. He proceeds, rather hypocritically, to criticise those who claim to recognise the weaknesses of men on the basis of their livelihoods and their trades, and who consider a man whose occupation is noble to be generally noble in his actions. In the author's professed opinion, it was a sign of the error of this tendency that the secretarial art was regarded as extremely noble among the *khāṣṣa*, when in fact secretaries were servile and deceitful.[56]

Such tracts are, whatever else, reflections of the high status that secretaries were perceived to enjoy in third/ninth-century Iraq, and the resentments occasioned by the rise in their fortunes.[57] Yet the *shuʿūbī*s still sought greater control over the direction of cultural matters, and in asserting their claims to exercise such control resorted to Q. 49:13 and associated materials. Some based their claim to inclusion in the élite on the view that 'Social rank (*rutba*)

[51] *Dhamm akhlāq al-kuttāb*, in *Rasāʾil al-Jāḥiẓ*, vol. 2, pp. 189–90.

[52] *Dhamm akhlāq al-kuttāb*, pp. 190–91. In his *Risāla fī madḥ al-tujjār wa dhamm ʿamal al-sulṭān*, al-Jāḥiẓ specifically compares the undignified subordination of the secretaries to the honoured independence of the merchants (Enderwitz, *Gesellschaftlicher Rang*, pp. 180–181). For a counterattack on the part of the secretaries against merchants, see al-Tawḥīdī, *Kitāb al-imtāʿ wa'l-muʾānasa*, eds. A. Amīn and A. al-Zayn (Beirut, 1966), p. 61; cited in Enderwitz, *Gesellschaftlicher Rang*, p. 179.

[53] On the confusion of social and moral baseness in the writings of al-Jāḥiẓ, see Enderwitz, *Gesellschaftlicher Rang*, pp. 72–73, and ch. 7.

[54] *Dhamm akhlāq al-kuttāb*, p. 194. The author also points out the heretical tendencies of several secretaries of the past; *Dhamm akhlāq al-kuttāb*, pp. 202ff; tr. Pellat, 'Une charge contre les secrétaires', pp. 41ff.

[55] *Dhamm akhlāq al-kuttāb*, pp. 196–97; tr. p. 38. The author specifically includes al-Jāḥiẓ among the Muʿtazilites who held this view, a strange reference which casts doubt on al-Jāḥiẓ's authorship of the text. The author's defence of the *muḥaddithūn* also seems uncharacteristic of al-Jāḥiẓ.

[56] *Dhamm akhlāq al-kuttāb*, pp. 199–201.

[57] For further materials that reflect the rivalry between merchants and secretaries, see Ibn Qutayba, *ʿUyūn al-akhbār*, vol. 1, *Kitāb al-sulṭān*, pp. 42ff.

is [like] a genealogical tie (*nasab*) which unites its possessors, so that the noble among the Arabs is closer to the noble among the non-Arabs than to the base among the Arabs, and the noble among the non-Arabs is closer to the noble among the Arabs than to the base among the non-Arabs. For the nobles of the people form a single stratum (*ṭabaqa*), just as the base among them form a stratum.'[58] In this effort to gain recognition for an élite composed of Arab and non-Arab nobles, the *shuʿūbīs* were apparently moderately successful; Ibn Qutayba, whose refutation of the *shuʿūbiyya* has been mentioned, himself supported this kind of assimilation, and reported the view that 'Nobility is a single tie, for the noble man of any people is well-born "inna 'l-sharaf nasab mufrad fa'l-sharīf min kulli qawmin nasīb".'[59]

Some *shuʿūbīs* perhaps showed their true intentions by asserting the superiority of Iranians over Arabs.[60] Al-Jāḥiẓ, who refutes this claim to ethnic superiority in his *Risāla fī'l-nābita*,[61] emphasises the damage brought about by the competition (*mufākhara*) between *shuʿūbīs* and Arabs, which he considers a destructive form of solidarity (*ʿaṣabiyya*).[62] He reports that, according to the *shuʿūbīs*, the *mawlā* becomes an Arab through the institution of clientage, in the same way that an ally (*ḥalīf*) of Quraysh becomes a Qurashī.[63] The *shuʿūbī* claim to superiority, however, according to al-Jāḥiẓ, rested on the dual grounds of their possession of kingship and prophethood in the past, and their ties to the Arabs (to whom God had since transferred those privileges) in the present.[64] What, he asks, could be more irritating than to find your slave claiming to be nobler than you are, while at the same time admitting that he had become noble by your act of manumission?[65]

[58] Ibn Ḥamdūn, *al-Tadhkira al-Ḥamdūniyya*, vol. 2, pp. 70–71, no. 136; al-Rāghib al-Iṣfahānī, *Muḥāḍarāt al-udabāʾ*, vol. 1, p. 349. (This statement is also attributed to al-Maʾmūn.)

[59] Ibn Qutayba, *ʿUyūn al-akhbār*, vol. 1, *Kitāb al-suʾdad*, p. 228; see also Lecomte, *Ibn Qutayba*, pp. 344–347; Mottahedeh, 'The Shuʿûbîyah Controversy', p. 180.

[60] Gibb, 'Social Significance', pp. 66–67; Goldziher, 'The Shuʿūbiyya', *Muslim Studies*, vol. 1, pp. 137–163.

[61] Also known under the title *Risāla fī Banī Umayya*, this epistle was probably composed in c. 225/839–840 under al-Muʿtaṣim (Pellat, 'Un document important pour l'histoire politico-religieuse de l'Islam: La «Nâbita» de Djâhiz', *AIEO* 10 (1952), p. 304). On the *nābita* in the works of al-Jāḥiẓ and elsewhere, see W. al-Qāḍī, 'The Earliest "Nābita" and the Paradigmatic "Nawābit"', *SI* 78 (1993), pp. 27–61. In this text, al-Jāḥiẓ refers to a work in progress (apparently lost) on the excellence and deficiency of the *mawālī*, and the nobility of the Arabs (*Risāla fī'l-nābita*, in *Rasāʾil al-Jāḥiẓ*, vol. 2, p. 22; tr. Pellat, 'La «Nâbita» de Djâhiz', p. 325). He probably dealt with the relative excellence of Arabs and *mawālī* in several of his writings (cf. Pellat, 'Ǧāḥiẓiana III. Essai d'inventaire de l'oeuvre ǧāḥiẓienne', *Arabica* 3 (1957), nos. 22, 23, 104, 156), but the *Risāla fī'l-nābita* is one of his few extant works on the subject. Not all of al-Jāḥiẓ's works suggest a wholly anti-*shuʿūbī* orientation, however; cf. Pellat, 'Ǧāḥiẓiana, II: Le dernier chapitre des *Avares* de Ǧāḥiẓ', *Arabica* 2 (1955), pp. 322–52.

[62] Al-Jāḥiẓ, *Risāla fī'l-nābita*, pp. 20, 22; tr. Pellat 'La «Nâbita»', pp. 305, 324, 325.

[63] The *shuʿūbīs* based their claim on the *ḥadīths*, 'The client of a people belongs to them (*mawlā al-qawm minhum*)' and 'Clientage constitutes kinship, like that based on common genealogy (*al-walāʾ luḥma ka-luḥmat al-nasab*); it cannot be sold or given away'. On the latter, see Crone, *Roman, Provincial and Islamic Law*, p. 40.

[64] Cf. *al-ʿIqd al-farīd*, vol. 12, pp. 173–175.

[65] Al-Jāḥiẓ, *Risāla fī'l-nābita*, pp. 21–22; tr. Pellat, 'La «Nâbita»', pp. 324–25.

Given his extraordinary interest in human nature and its frailties, it is not surprising that the list of works attributed to al-Jāḥiẓ includes several items that deal with the similarities and differences between people, the characteristics of particular social groups, and the merits and faults of specific occupations and their practitioners.[66] Other examples of al-Jāḥiẓ's social thought will be discussed in the following chapters.

Taming egalitarianism in the classical anthologies

The remainder of this chapter is concerned with the literary elements in the classical anthologies pertaining to the roles of heredity, ethnicity and wealth in the assessment of status. It will be remembered that the first chapter of this book also dealt with a considerable amount of material culled from anthologies. That material consisted of literary fragments purported to have originated in the first century or so, and these fragments, it has been argued, shed some light on the kind of society that Muslims of the second/eighth century came to associate with the earliest period of their history. The materials to be treated in the remainder of the present chapter are often more extensive than these earlier fragments, and are sometimes attributed to well-known classical authors and poets. Of particular concern here, however, are the ways in which the anthologists arranged their materials and, through their arrangements, contributed to the process of taming dangerous but morally appealing ideas.

Anthologies frequently seem to reflect conservative and commonplace ways of thinking. They present a selection of materials pertaining to well-known categories of general interest, and although some of these materials may be remarkable for their literary qualities and wit, the categories into which they are arranged are unlikely to have startled their audiences. It is thus of interest to note that several of the classical anthologies contain sections devoted to differences and similarities among people. In such sections it is clear that for compiler and reader, such concepts as *karam* and *sharaf*, and *nasab* and *taqwā*, have become the subjects of pleasing anecdotes and witty poetry, rather than expressions of social grievances and religio-political opposition.

A good deal of the anthologised material is ostensibly meritocratic or egalitarian in nature. Al-Rāghib al-Iṣfahānī, for example, includes in his anthol-

[66] For those books that have not come down to us, of course, our impression of their contents is based only on their titles and extracts quoted elsewhere. Nevertheless, even allowing for the questionable authorship of certain books, and for the probable identity of some titles with works known under other names, the list compiled by Pellat ('Ǧāḥiẓiana III', pp. 147–80; cf. Pellat, 'Nouvel essai') includes a large number of works that appear to deal with professions, as well as a *Risāla fī waṣf al-ʿawāmm* (cf. Rescher, *Excerpte und Übersetzungen*, pp. 550ff). For an example of al-Jāḥiẓ's interest in practitioners of lowly professions, see Sadan, 'Kings and Craftsmen. A Pattern of Contrasts', *SI* 56 (1982), pp. 10ff, and *SI* 62 (1985), pp. 91ff. On al-Jāḥiẓ's use of the terms *khāṣṣa* and *ʿāmma*, see Enderwitz, *Gesellschaftlicher Rang*, pp. 196–197, n. 24.

ogy a section that deals with the subject of 'nobility as piety'. He opens it with the Qur'ānic verse 49:13, and notes that, though a man might be of noble parentage, he will not be spared on that account. He proceeds to record that, in the Jāhiliyya, nobility had consisted of eloquence, valour and generosity, while in Islam, it consisted of religion and piety; as for paternity, it was of no significance. Al-Rāghib also quotes a (possibly *shu'ūbī*) poem, in which reference is made to the *taqwā-nasab* equation:

By your life, a man's (worth) derives only from his religion,
So do not abandon piety in reliance on *ḥasab*.
Faith adorned Salmān of Persia,
While polytheism debased the noble Abū Lahab.[67]

In the anthologies of al-Bayhaqī and Pseudo-Jāḥiẓ, a similar example is ascribed to a generic sage (*ḥakīm*): 'Nobility is not in inherited merit (*ḥasab*) and lineage (*nasab*). Consider the fact that, of two brothers born to the same father and mother, one is more noble than the other. If that were the result of lineage, neither one of them would be more excellent than the other, because their lineage is the same. On the contrary, it is the result of deeds, for nobility derives only from deeds and not from lineage.'[68] The two authors go on to quote an (unidentified) poet who expresses the same sentiment in the following verse: 'Your father is mine too, and there is no doubt that we have the same grandfather; / Yet we are of two different woods, myrtle and the castor-oil-plant.'[69]

What is striking about all of these examples is that, despite the boldness with which they are expressed, they appear in such a generalised form that it is impossible to reconstruct the context in which they may have been produced. Unlike much of the material discussed in the first chapter, none of these examples is attributed to a specific person, and the compiler of the anthology has made no effort to convey any context, even a spurious one, in which such sayings were initially uttered. This, together with the stylised nature of many of these sayings, suggests that the ideas and vocabulary found in them were already entirely familiar. On the one hand, the generality of this form of expression elevates these apparently egalitarian and meritocratic values to the status of universal ideals, but on the other, the omission of all information concerning their application to any actual situation removes the threat of subversion with which such ideals may once have been associated.

A second implication of this lack of context is that the once exclusively Arab

67 *Muḥāḍarāt al-udabā'*, vol. 1, p. 340.

68 *Al-Maḥāsin wa'l-masāwī*, p. 102; *al-Maḥāsin wa'l-aḍdād*, p. 126 (*ḥasab* is omitted in the first line). Cf. the similar pieties ascribed to Sindbad ('Noble rank lies in humility, nobility in piety, and greatness in doing good') and Buzurgmihr ('There is no lineage like good character, no knowledge like foresight, and no virtue like refraining from injury') in the *Tuḥfat al-mulūk dar ādāb* (Tehran, 1317/193) of 'Alī Iṣfahānī (pp. 88, 92).

69 *Al-Maḥāsin wa'l-masāwī*, p. 102; *al-Maḥāsin wa'l-aḍdād*, p. 126. On the metaphorical use of the term *'ūd*, cf. Goldziher, *Muslim Studies*, vol. 1, p. 150, n. 7.

significance of such terms as *nasab* and *ḥasab* has been lost. The sharpness of these terms has been dulled to the point that they seem to have come to stand for any hereditary or closed social system. At the same time, the concept of *taqwā* provides the justification for an open system based on personal merit according to a variety of criteria. Many of the materials recorded in classical anthologies take the form of reinterpretations of the traditional, once potent terms, and thus they are comparable to the reworkings of ideas expressed also in the form of *ḥadīth*.[70] Such materials ostensibly deny the significance of lineage, but the force of the denial is undermined by the presentation of the anthologists.

Classical anthologies also include a number of verses in which the normal, hereditary understanding of nobility is apparently inverted. Such examples attest to the increased status that one could hope to gain by passing oneself off as the descendant of a noble Arab tribe well into the third/ninth century, but at the same time they also indicate that rejection of the principle of heredity had become a well-established literary motif. The Baghdadi poet Ibn al-Rūmī (c. 221–283/836–896), himself the son of a Byzantine freedman and a woman of Persian origin, dedicated a panegyric poem to al-Muʿtamid's Persian vizier, Ismāʿīl b. Bulbul (d. 278/892), who claimed to be a descendant of the Banū Shaybān. In the poem, Ibn al-Rūmī claims that it is not the vizier who seeks to increase his status by associating himself with Shaybān, but Shaybān that is honoured by him:

How many a father has been elevated in nobility by his son who descended from him,
As ʿAdnān was elevated by the Apostle of God?
Men are elevated by their ancestors; only occasionally
Are they elevated and adorned by their sons.[71]

Al-Mutanabbī (303–354/915–965) also refused to take credit for his ancestors and inverted the customary direction of the transfer of merit:

I am not ennobled by my people;
It is rather they who are ennobled by me.
I have reason to be proud of myself
And not of my ancestors.[72]

In a well-known poem addressed to Muḥammad b. ʿAbd Allāh b. Ṭāhir (d. 253/867), Ibn al-Rūmī again belittles the importance of ancestors and emphasises the value of personal achievements. His words may have been intended as a response to those who criticised the Ṭāhirids for boasting of their con-

[70] See ch. 1.
[71] ʿAlī b. al-ʿAbbās Ibn al-Rūmī, *Dīwān*, ed. Ḥusayn Naṣṣār (Cairo), vol. 6 (1981), p. 2425, 11.87–88; al-Rāghib al-Iṣfahānī, *Muḥāḍarāt al-udabāʾ*, vol. 1, p. 335 (second line); Ibn al-Ṭiqṭiqā, *Kitāb al-fakhrī fī'l-ādāb al-sulṭāniyya wa'l-duwal al-islāmiyya* (Cairo, 1317/1899), p. 299 (first line only); Goldziher, *Muslim Studies*, vol. 1, pp. 133–34 (first line only).
[72] ʿAbd al-Raḥmān al-Barqūqī, *Sharḥ Dīwān al-Mutanabbī* (Beirut, 1965), vol. 2, p. 46; *Muḥāḍarāt al-udabāʾ*, vol. 1, p. 334.

nexions with Khuzāʿa when they were not in fact genuine members of the tribe but merely its clients:[73]

Inherited merit (*al-ḥasab al-mawrūth*) – may it not thrive! – is not worthy of esteem (*muḥtasab*)
Unless it is accompanied by something else that has been earned (*muktasab*).
If the branch does not bear fruit, though it is a branch
Of the fruit-bearing kind, men regard it as mere fire-wood.
You, by my life, are a scion of those endowed with greatness
So do not allow yourself to be counted among the lowliest of branches!
There are people who compete for dignity by [their] noble souls,
And they are not content [merely to indicate] a mother or a father.
Do not rely on anything other than what you yourself have done,
And do not consider dignity to be that which is inherited by genealogy.
A man achieves eminence only by his own [merit],
Even if he can count noble ancestors endowed with merit through their deeds.[74]

This verse illustrates not only the continued appearance of prejudice against *mawālī* but also the general importance of heredity in determining a man's social position. According to a very common phrase, positive traits, and above all nobility, are said to be inherited 'by one eminent man from another (*kābiran ʿan kābirin*)';[75] in the context of a boasting match (*mufākhara*) between Muḍar and Yaman, Ibrāhīm b. Makhrama al-Kindī of Yaman flatters the caliph Abū'l-ʿAbbās al-Saffāḥ (132–136/750–754) on his genealogy by saying of his maternal uncles that 'they will never cease to be rulers and masters, and they will inherit leadership one eminent man from another and the last from the first'.[76] While the common view that heredity played a crucial role in shaping an individual's character and capacities thus came to be expressed in formulaic terms, pious objections to the prevalence of such hereditary conceptions of hierarchy and privilege also came to form part of the

[73] On the Ṭāhirids' pretensions to Arab lineage, see Bosworth, 'The Interaction of Arabic and Persian Literature and Culture in the 10th and Early 11th Centuries', *al-Abḥāth* 27 (1978–9), p. 59. On Ibn al-Rūmī's connexion with the Ṭāhirid family, see Bosworth, 'The Tahirids and Arabic Culture', *JSS* 14 (1969), p. 72.

[74] Ibn al-Rūmī, *Dīwān*, vol. 1, no. 111, pp. 150–151; *Muḥāḍarāt al-udabāʾ*, vol. 1, p. 335; cf. the anonymous anthology *Rawḍat al-nāẓir wa nuzhat al-khāṭir*, ms. Fatih 5324, which appends to the poem the frequently cited couplet: 'The orphan is not he whose father has died / The orphan is the orphan of intellect and culture.' For further verses which express the same sentiment, see Rosenthal, *Knowledge Triumphant* (Leiden, 1970), p. 322.

[75] *Al-ʿIqd al-farīd*, vol. 12, p. 10 (here in reference to Quraysh); Abū Isḥāq Ibrāhīm b. ʿAlī al-Ḥuṣrī, *Zahr al-ādāb wa thamar al-albāb*, ed. ʿAlī Muḥammad al-Bajāwī (Cairo, 1372/1953), vol. 1, p. 95; Nāṣir al-Dīn Kirmānī, *Simṭ al-ʿulā lil-ḥaḍrat al-ʿulyā* (Tehran, 1328/1949), p. 9; Ḥamd Allāh Mustawfī, *Tārīkh-i guzīdeh*, GMS XIV (1910–1913), p. 6; Maḥmūd b. Muḥammad al-Iṣfahānī, *Dastūr al-vizāra* (Tehran, 1364), p. 66; Nāṣir al-Dīn Kirmānī, *Nasāʾim al-asḥār min laṭāʾim al-akhbār*, ed. Jalāl al-Dīn Muḥaddith (Tehran, 1338s/1378q), p. 102; Muḥammad b. Ibrāhīm, *Tārīkh-i Kirmān*, ed. M. Th. Houtsma, *Recueil de textes relatifs à l'histoire des Seljoucides*, vol. 1 (*Histoire des Seljoucides du Kermân*) (Leiden, 1886), p. 146.

[76] Al-Bayhaqī, *al-Maḥāsin wa'l-masāwī*, pp. 94–95; cf. al-Ḥuṣrī, *Zahr al-ādāb*, vol. 2, pp. 815–816. The reference is to Banū'l-Ḥārith b. Kaʿb, the caliph's mother's tribe (*Zahr al-ādāb*, p. 815).

general vocabulary of literary men. Literary forms based on an opposition between the two outlooks were removed from any specific context and elevated to the level of abstraction. The result was that far from appearing to undermine the status quo, such materials were now deemed fit to be incorporated into the larger body of belletristic literature that catered to the cultural tastes of the educated élites.

Wealth, knowledge and social status in classical *adab*

A similar adjustment is evident in the treatment of wealth in classical anthologies and other works of *adab. Ḥadīth* that deal with wealth reflect a lively debate on the subject of the compatibility of an abundance of wealth with moral precedence.[77] Again, the anthologists reduce the discussion to stylised and generalised statements and exchanges; the social ambitions and the sense of deprivation that seem to underlie at least some of the fragmentary materials disappear into the witticisms and moralising of classical times. Many of these examples draw comparisons between wealth and knowledge, and ascribe greater value to the latter than the former.[78]

The generalising tendency of the classical tradition is apparent in the very arrangement adopted by the authors of anthologies. For instance, several writers devote separate, sequential sections to the excellences and deficiencies of wealth and poverty.[79] The effect of this is to create an appearance of symmetry which all but emasculates the literary items included in each section, even those that might in other contexts have had considerable force. The

[77] Kinberg, 'Compromise of Commerce', pp. 193–212. For a discussion of the conflict between asceticism and admiration for wealth, see al-Māwardī, *Tashīl al-naẓar*, introduction, pp. 48–73. On contrasting attitudes towards trade and wealth in some selected sources of the classical period, see also Lambton, 'The Merchant in Medieval Islam', in W. Henning (ed.), *A Locust's Leg. Studies in Honour of S.H. Taqizadeh* (London, 1962), pp. 121–130.

[78] In various and complex ways the acquisition of knowledge could, of course, be associated with social status; for a discussion of how this might have occurred in at least one context, see R. Bulliet, *The Patricians of Nishapur* (Cambridge, Massachusetts, 1972), pp. 47ff.

[79] See, for example, Ibn Qutayba, *'Uyūn al-akhbār*, vol. 1, *K. al-su'dad*, pp. 239–249; al-Rāghib al-Iṣfahānī, *Muḥāḍarāt al-udabā'*, vol. 2, pp. 498ff; Abū Ya'lā Muḥammad Ibn al-Ḥabbāriyya, *Falak al-ma'ānī*, ms. AS 4157, ff. 19ff (cf. O. Rescher, 'Über arabische Handschriften der Aja Sofia', *WZKM* 26 (1912), p. 75).

According to another opinion, poverty and wealth were equally detrimental to an individual's moral well-being. Only a few of the rich or poor were able to transcend the consequences of their economic circumstances in order to attain virtue. This point of view is articulated by the Baṣran Mu'tazilite (and druggist) Mu'ammar b. 'Abbād al-Sulamī (d. 215/830). Mu'ammar, a *mawlā*, was proud of his position between the rich and the poor, and claimed, 'People are of three sorts: the rich, the poor and the middling people. The poor are [as good as] dead, with the exception of those whom God has enriched by the strength of contentment; the rich are drunk, except for those whom God protects by preparing them for changes [in their fortune]. The better part of goodness thus lies with the middling people, and the greater part of wickedness with the poor and the rich, on account of the folly induced by poverty and the vanity of wealth' (Ibn Qutayba, *'Uyūn al-akhbār*, vol. 1, *K. al-su'dad*, p. 331; quoted in van Ess, *Theologie und Gesellschaft*, vol. 3 p. 63).

Qur'ānic verse 18:47, 'Wealth and sons are the adornments of earthly life', appears not as a reminder of the fleeting nature of worldly pleasures but in a positive context in discussions of the admirable aspects of affluence.[80] Ibn al-Ḥabbāriyya (d. 509/1115), in his anthology *Falak al-maʿānī*, goes on to extol the virtues of wealth:

Wealth elevates its possessor even if he is of low origin and little education. It renders him perceptive, even if he is cowardly. It loosens his tongue, even if he is distraught. It directs him towards fine characteristics. [By wealth], relationships are established, good reputations protected, manliness (*muruwwa*) becomes apparent, leadership arises, the world receives bounties, aims are achieved, and desires are fulfilled. Wealth creates a connexion with people when they cut one off, brings one victory when people undermine one, and makes slaves of the free to one's own advantage. Were it not for wealth, the nobility of the noble man would not be apparent, nor the avarice of the mean; the generous man would not receive thanks, nor would the miser be vilified; womenfolk would find no protection, and bounties would not be attained.[81]

Such passages, however decontextualised, seem to convey a frank admiration for riches and the status, respectability and enjoyment they bring. Other examples seek to justify affluence by arguing for its compatibility with piety and knowledge. In one instance, Luqmān's son is said to have asked his father to name the best quality that a man could possess. 'Religion', Luqmān replies. The sage's son then asks which two qualities are best, and receives the answer, 'Religion and wealth'. In response to his son's repeated questioning, Luqmān finally enumerates five qualities: religion, wealth, modesty, fine character and generosity. 'Anyone who combines these five qualities,' he states, 'is pure, pious, close to God, and immune from the Devil.'[82]

In a further case of the reduction of a genuine social and moral issue to the pleasing compactness of a literary formula, wealth and knowledge appear in many classical compilations as a standard pair of rivals. According to a common maxim, knowledge and education are the best possible bequests, since wealth can be dissipated, whereas education is a means to the acquisition of wealth, and thus to the highest ranks in society.[83] ʿAlī Iṣfahānī, the seventh/eleventh-century author of a *Tuḥfat al-mulūk*, attributes to Apollonius the view that 'The value of men is in knowledge, and their adornment is in

80 Ibn ʿAbd Rabbihi, *al-ʿIqd al-farīd*, vol. 8, p. 144; Ibn al-Ḥabbāriyya, *Falak al-maʿānī*, f. 19b. Such usages of the verse are in contrast to the interpretations recorded in works of classical *tafsīr* (see Introduction).

81 Ibn al-Ḥabbāriyya, *Falak al-maʿānī*, ff. 19b–20a; cf. Ibn ʿAbd Rabbihi, *al-ʿIqd al-farīd*, vol. 8, pp. 144–151.

82 Al-Ghazālī, *Iḥyā'*, vol. 3, p. 51; Sirāj al-Dīn Urmavī, *Laṭā'if al-ḥikma*, ed. Gh.Ḥ. Yūsufī (Tehran, 1351), p. 174.

83 Al-Kulīnī, *al-Kāfī*, vol. 8, p. 150; al-Bayhaqī, *al-Maḥāsin wa'l-masāwī*, p. 400; al-Mubashshir b. Fātik, *Mukhtār al-ḥikam*, p. 18 (attributed to Idrīs). Cf. Ibn Qutayba, *ʿUyūn al-akhbār*, vol. 2, *K. al-ʿilm wa'l-bayān*, p. 120, and Ibn Ḥamdūn, *al-Tadhkira al-Ḥamdūniyya*, vol. 2, pp. 23–24, no. 22, where a similar view is attributed to Buzurgmihr; see also Shihāb al-Dīn M. b. A. al-Ibshīhī, *al-Mustaṭraf fī kull fann mustaẓraf* (Beirut, 1406/1986), vol. 1, p. 57, where the same saying is attributed to 'a wise man'; and Rosenthal, *Knowledge Triumphant*, p. 327.

wealth.'[84] Naturally, moralistic authors insist on the superiority of knowledge to wealth, often on the grounds that knowledge is a lasting inner attribute, while wealth is transitory and external to the soul; but they perpetuate the convention of associating the two. The prominent Shāfiʿī scholar Sirāj al-Dīn Urmavī (594–682/1198–1283), chief *qāḍī* of the Seljuks of Rum at Konya, enumerates five proofs for the superiority of knowledge over wealth. In the first of these proofs, he adduces a saying attributed to ʿAlī b. Abī Ṭālib: 'Knowledge is better than wealth, because knowledge protects you, whereas you must protect wealth; because wealth is destroyed when spent, whereas knowledge is purified when imparted; and because knowledge rules, while wealth is ruled.'[85]

The general and stylised nature of these passages suggests that what originated in a struggle for social recognition by men who were well-to-do but not well connected had, by the middle of the third/ninth century or so, lost its urgency. Such materials no longer seem to reflect genuine disagreements, but rather the taste of the literary élites for clever, balanced forms of expression. The ideas articulated in such examples have been made to conform to the conventional, 'safe' modes of presentation typified by the anthologists, and this exercise seems effectively to have nullified the radical element inherent in their contents.

This chapter has attempted to begin delineating the processes whereby the Islamic egalitarian ideal was stripped of its social implications. These

[84] *Tuḥfat al-mulūk dar ādāb* (Tehran, 1317), p. 59; cf. similar quotations in Rosenthal, *Knowledge Triumphant*, pp. 325–326.

[85] This aphorism is usually quoted as part of ʿAlī's exhortation to Kumayl b. Ziyād al-Nakhaʿī; al-Bayhaqī, *al-Maḥāsin wal'-masāwī*, p. 400; Ibn Qutayba, *ʿUyūn al-akhbār*, vol. 2, *K. al-ʿilm wa'l-bayān*, p. 120; al-Māwardī, *Adab al-dunya wa'l-dīn*, ed. M. Karīm Rājiḥ (Beirut, 1401/1981), p. 43; al-Ṭurṭūshī, *Sirāj al-mulūk*, p. 121; Ibn Abī'l-Ḥadīd, *Sharḥ nahj al-balāgha*, vol. 5 (1964), pp. 434–436; al-Ghazālī, *Iḥyā'*, vol. 1, p. 8; Quṭb al-Dīn Shīrāzī, *Durrat al-tāj*, ed. Sayyid M. Mishkāt (Tehran, 1317–20), vol. 1, pp. 39–40; Rosenthal, *Knowledge Triumphant*, p. 256, n. 5. Sirāj al-Dīn goes on to present the four remaining proofs. According to the second, wealth turns friends into enemies, while knowledge transforms enemies into friends. According to the third, knowledge detaches men from this world and delivers them to the Lord, while wealth detaches them from the Lord and delivers them to the world. Fourthly, wealth does not accompany a man past the grave, whereas knowledge remains with him in both worlds. Fifthly, Qārūn is said to have possessed wealth, and God caused him to sink into the ground (Q. 28:81); Idrīs, on the other hand, was endowed with knowledge, and was elevated to an exalted position (Q. 19:57). If knowledge is superior to wealth, Sirāj al-Dīn then asks, why is it that scholars are constantly seen at the doors of the wealthy, while rich men are seldom seen at the doors of scholars? In answer to his question, which may have been on some level inspired by Plato's 'the wise going to the doors of the rich' (*Republic*, 489B; noted by Rosenthal, *Knowledge Triumphant*, pp. 325–6), Sirāj al-Dīn notes that scholars recognise the value of wealth, and consequently pursue it; the rich, however, do not appreciate the value of knowledge, and therefore do not seek it. He then lists a further six reasons why a believer should seek knowledge: in order to demonstrate obedience, to refrain from sin, to show gratitude for bounties, to practise patience in adversity, to be able to administer justice, and to banish the devil when he incites him to lapse (*Laṭā'if*, pp. 20–21). For similar discussions of the superiority of knowledge to wealth, see Shīrāzī, *Durrat al-tāj*, vol. 1, pp. 39–40; ʿAlī al-Iṣfahānī, *Tuḥfat al-mulūk*, pp. 19–20; and Rosenthal, *Knowledge Triumphant*, pp. 324–328.

processes took place in the context of the social changes taking place during the second/eighth and third/ninth centuries. Among the most relevant developments were the increasing ethnic and social diversity of the Muslim community in the main urban centres; the diminishing emphasis placed on tribal identities in the course of the second/eighth century;[86] the emergence of new and more internally diverse élites, both military and civil; and, in connexion with these changes, the gathering strength of the trend against the conflation of ethnic and social status.

Under these conditions, the egalitarian vocabulary that had come to be associated with moral rectitude and potential political opposition was put to new uses. It was employed, for example, in the struggles of ambitious non-Arab Muslims for full inclusion in the circles of the powerful. Yet even after the late second/eighth century, when Iranians and others had largely succeeded in gaining admission to the new élites, the *shuʿūbī*s among them continued to use such language. Their ostensible purpose was to argue for the equality of Arabs and non-Arabs – they were able, in fact, to take advantage of the moral high ground that egalitarianism had already successfully made its own. Their real design, however, seems to have been to direct the orientation of Islamic civilisation towards their own cultural traditions, and in this, doubtless partially in response to their own position, they were opposed by those who felt the civilisation's proper focus should be on Arab culture.[87] It is apparent from the literature of the classical period that members of both the secretarial and the religious scholarly élites succeeded in co-opting and laundering the egalitarian language of the Islamic tradition in such a way that it was left with very little social meaning. In their writings these men made use of the terms *nasab* and *taqwā* in a generalised sense, to refer to any form of hereditary privilege and personal merit respectively. This trend is a mark of the process whereby the nobility–piety equation was gradually deprived of its potency, the egalitarian ideal stripped of its subversive connotations, and its utopian vision restricted to the next life.[88]

A further development that seems to be reflected in some of this literature is the growth in the position of the *ʿulamāʾ*, both as sources of moral authority and as social leaders. By the late second/eighth century, those involved in the life of the courts had no choice but to accept that the *ʿulamāʾ* had gained

86 In Baṣra, this is reflected in the decrease in numbers of *mawālī* and the increase in personal *nisba*s that denote characteristics other than tribal affiliation (Donner, 'Tribal Settlement in Basra', pp. 97–120).

87 Cf. al-Sayyid, 'Naẓarāt fī jadaliyyāt al-ʿilāqa bayn al-namūdhajayn', in *al-Umma wa'l-jamāʿa wa'l-salṭa*, pp. 101ff.

88 For a theoretical and comparative treatment of the transition from the first phase in the creation of a new society, when a new social stratification emerges, to a second phase, in which social classification is institutionalised, see Mousnier, *Social Hierarchies*, pp. 50ff, 61ff; of particular interest is his discussion of new interpretations of 'nobility' by the Roman Catholic League in sixteenth-century France (pp. 58–59). (Mousnier does not include the emergence of Islamic civilisation among his examples.)

incontestable possession of the moral high ground, but in return they could reasonably expect that the *'ulamā'* would not seek to translate the anti-hierarchical and anti-authoritarian moral at the heart of their scholarly tradition into active social and political opposition. In fact, as will be seen increasingly in the following chapters, the *'ulamā'* in many cases lent support to the notion of hierarchy itself.

CHAPTER 5

The didactic literature of the courts

On occasion a small number of Muslim groups may have hoped for an egalitarian social structure in which their own members would be equally entitled to the available resources; but with these exceptions it seems that few Muslims of the classical and early medieval periods could envisage a society that was organised other than as a hierarchy of degrees.[1] The degree to which a hierarchical consciousness took precedence over the possible social implications of Islamic egalitarianism is suggested, as discussed in the preceding chapter, in the work of the classical anthologists, whose collections reflect the tastes of a wide spectrum of educated persons. The present chapter is devoted to the ways in which an ideal hierarchy of degrees was visualised, and the way these visualisations interacted with the egalitarian tradition, in the advice literature that flourished in the courts of classical and early medieval times.

The materials to be considered here are homiletic and paraenetic writings, in the form of testaments and 'mirrors for princes'. The 'political' epistle (*risāla*) and testament (*waṣiyya*, *ʿahd*), compositions of advice and admonishment ostensibly addressed to rulers or those about to assume authority, are among the earliest Arabic literary forms of Islamic times; they incorporated elements from several sources, including Byzantine, Hellenistic and especially Sasanian wisdom literature.[2] The epistle and testament are the predecessors of mirrors for princes,[3] a genre that also absorbed elements from numerous other Islamic and non-Islamic sources.[4]

[1] On the communist experiments of the Qarmaṭī state in Baḥrayn, see introduction, n. 26, and the references cited there. On the possibility of egalitarian motivation in certain Iranian rebellions of the second/eighth and third/ninth centuries, see ch. 4. On the nature of Khārijite egalitarianism, which seems to have been limited to the rejection of genealogical requirements for the caliphate, see Madelung, *Religious Trends in Early Islamic Iran* (Albany, New York, 1988), pp. 54ff.

[2] Dietrich, 'Das politische Testament', pp. 133–136; D. Gutas, 'Classical Arabic Wisdom Literature: Nature and Scope', *JAOS* 101 (1981), pp. 57–62.

[3] I use the term loosely to denote any work that offers advice on the subject of government and is dedicated to a ruler or high-ranking official; for the distinctions between various kinds of mirrors, see Lambton, 'Islamic Mirrors for Princes', *La Persia nel medioevo* (Rome, 1971), pp. 419–442; L.A. Karp, 'Sahl b. Hârûn: The Man and his Contribution to *'Adab*', unpublished Ph.D. thesis (Harvard University, 1992), pp. 124ff. See also Gutas, 'Ethische Schriften im Islam', *Neues Handbuch der Literaturwissenschaft* (Frankfurt), vol. 5 (1990), pp. 346–365.

[4] Richter, *Studien*, p. 64, n. 1; Dietrich, 'Das politische Testament', p. 135, n. 10; p. 136, n. 11;

Two general observations may be made concerning the diverse body of texts that make up Islamic advice literature. Firstly, works of this kind are overtly didactic: by varied means, they seek to instruct their audiences and often to inculcate certain political and moral values. Secondly, most examples of this form of literary expression are products of court circles. Sometimes a book was written for a specific occasion or to address a specific problem;[5] more frequently, such works are of a more general nature, and were written by statesmen, men of letters, and other persons who participated in the life of the court, sometimes, one senses, in a desire to attract the monarch's attention and receive a reward from him. Such books were popular in almost all regions of the Islamic world throughout much of the pre-modern period, and it seems that, especially in areas where Islamic culture was carried in the Persian language, books of advice on government formed a recognised part of the trappings of kingship. It is difficult to gauge how much attention rulers paid to them, but that they must have been regarded as important elements in the political culture is evident from the sheer number that survive.

In examining the treatment of the themes of hierarchy and social differentiation in the didactic literature of the classical courts, four trends are particularly noteworthy. Firstly, many authors display an unabashed attachment to noble birth. Secondly, the cultivators, conspicuously absent from some other forms of social description in the Islamic world, occupy a prominent position, and a marked emphasis is placed on the need to protect peasants in order to ensure the welfare of society as a whole. Thirdly, one notices an attempt to elevate the position of particular groups in the minds of the audience; this is especially common among *'ulamā'* who found themselves in the service of kings as well as of religion. Fourthly, expressions of pious egalitarianism retain their moral importance in this literature, but seem to do so more as reminders to the holders of power that they are answerable to a higher authority than as implicit social criticism.

Testaments

The testament, which purports to represent the considered advice of an experienced ruler to his son and successor, delivered either shortly before the death of the former or on some other occasion of gravity, not surprisingly lays considerable emphasis on righteous behaviour and piety. Even when not associated with imminent death, a ruler's words of wisdom for his sons tend to accentuate religious virtues over worldly distractions. For instance, 'Abd al-Malik (65–86/685–705), writing for the benefit of his five sons, is said to have encouraged them to seek knowledge, by which they might become 'the beauty

A.H. Dawood, *A Comparative Study of Arabic and Persian Mirrors for Princes from the Second to the Sixth Century A.H.*, unpublished Ph.D. thesis (London, 1965).

5 This is especially likely in the case of epistles on political subjects; cf. Latham, 'The Beginnings of Arabic Prose Literature', pp. 154–179.

of the age, for the conditions of the world have changed, and learning is [now] the finest of all conditions, in such a way that, although lineage is great, it is still greater when accompanied by learning and knowledge'.[6] In this example, which appears in an early seventh/thirteenth-century mirror,[7] the caliph combines political pragmatism and loyalty to Arab tradition with a recognition of the changes brought about by Islam and an expression of pious wisdom.

In addition to such anecdotal communications from fathers to sons, a number of longer 'political' testaments survive, and these often contain reflections on the question of social status. An important early example of such a testament is that written by the secretary ʿAbd al-Ḥamīd on behalf of Marwān II to the latter's son ʿUbayd Allāh.[8] Although the letter was ostensibly composed for a specific occasion, much of the advice contained in it is of a general nature. Much of the letter deals with military matters.[9] On several occasions, however, the author refers to the caliph's close companions or entourage (*biṭāna*), as well as to the offices of secretary, chamberlain, judge and chief of police. In these and other places he shows himself to be quite conscious of a social hierarchy in which birth and ability, often linked, seem to have been the most important principles. The author stipulates that the caliph's closest companions ought to be men of understanding and piety drawn from among the élite members of his own family,[10] and urges generosity towards people possessed of *sharaf* and *ḥasab*.[11] He also refers several times to the categories of *ʿāmma* and *khāṣṣa*, and uses the latter to designate those associated with the king's service.[12] He shows a modest concern for the former, and notes that consideration shown to the common people is beneficial both in this world and the next.[13] He frequently uses the term *sharaf*, but not always to refer to lineage, since he notes, for example, that the caliph can attain the highest levels of *sharaf* through principled and magnanimous behaviour.[14] He notes that the officer in charge of the caliph's police force and army should be possessed of *ḥasab*.[15]

6 ʿAlī al-Iṣfahānī, *Tuḥfat al-mulūk*, pp. 56–57; cf. the saying ascribed to ʿAbd al-Malik cited in Rosenthal, *Knowledge Triumphant*, p. 327.

7 The *Tuḥfat al-mulūk* is discussed in C.-H. de Fouchécour, *Moralia: les notions morales dans la littérature persane du 3e/9e au 7e/13e siècle* (Paris, 1986), pp. 162–71, and Marlow, 'Kings, Prophets and the *ʿUlamāʾ* in Medieval Islamic Advice Literature', *SI* 81 (1995), pp. 5–24.

8 The letter, which was composed on the occasion of ʿUbayd Allāh's campaign against Khārijite rebels, is dated 129/746–747. It has come down to us in the anthology *Kitāb al-manthūr waʾl-manẓūm* of Ibn Abī Ṭāhir Ṭayfūr (204–280/819–893).

9 For a summary of the contents of the letter, see H. Schönig, *Das Sendschreiben des ʿAbdalḥamīd b. Yaḥyā (gest. 132/750) an den Kronprinzen ʿAbdallāh b. Marwān II* (Stuttgart, 1985), pp. 13–16.

10 ʿAbbās, *ʿAbd al-Ḥamīd ibn Yaḥyā al-Kātib*, p. 222; tr. Schönig, *Sendschreiben*, p. 25.

11 ʿAbbās, *ʿAbd al-Ḥamīd ibn Yaḥyā al-Kātib*, p. 221; tr. Schönig, *Sendschreiben*, p. 24.

12 *ʿAbd al-Ḥamīd ibn Yaḥyā al-Kātib*, pp. 220, 225, 229, 233, 237, 263 (*ʿāmma*); see also pp. 225, 229 (*raʿiyya*), and p. 232 (*sūqa*, contrasted with *ahl al-adab*); pp. 226, 229, 233 (*khāṣṣa*).

13 *ʿAbd al-Ḥamīd ibn Yaḥyā al-Kātib*, p. 233; tr. Schönig, *Sendschreiben*, pp. 36–37.

14 *ʿAbd al-Ḥamīd ibn Yaḥyā al-Kātib*, p. 229; tr. Schönig, *Sendschreiben*, p. 32.

15 *ʿAbd al-Ḥamīd ibn Yaḥyā al-Kātib*, pp. 243, 249; tr. Schönig, *Sendschreiben*, pp. 48, 55.

Another important example of this genre is the testament of Ṭāhir b. al-Ḥusayn (159–207/775–822) to his son ʿAbd Allāh, said to have been written on the occasion of the latter's appointment as governor of Diyār Rabīʿa in 206/821.[16] This letter takes up many issues of government in a general way and, given its scope and approach, resembles a short mirror as much as an epistle or testament.

Ṭāhir's letter is one of the principal surviving products of the Ṭāhirid taste for cultural and literary activities in Arabic.[17] It contains very little evidence of an affection for Persian political ideals; it is, in fact, thoroughly steeped in the piety and ethics of the Islamic religious tradition.[18] This is evident in its treatment of matters pertaining to social rank. Naturally, Ṭāhir recognises and accepts the general distinction between the *khāṣṣa* and the *ʿāmma*, although this is not particularly emphasised.[19] But nowhere does the author list the groups that make up the social body, nor does he discuss to any great extent the ruler's behaviour towards various functionaries, or on what basis the latter should be appointed. Ṭāhir discusses the importance of the office of *qaḍāʾ*,[20] but not the qualities of those who should be appointed as *qāḍī*s. He discusses the qualities of officials who should be chosen to administer districts, and the need to see that they are adequately paid.[21] The ruler or governor should seek out and heed the advice of the learned, and make a fixed time to see each of his officials and secretaries every day.[22] He should supervise the affairs of the army, the soldiers' pay registers, and the government departments concerned with military matters, and ensure that the soldiers' salaries are adequate and their allowances generous.[23] One respect in which Ṭāhir's letter may perhaps reflect Iranian concepts of the workings of government is in the recommendation that the ruler assign a trusted person to report to him on the affairs of tax-collectors.[24] Respect for descent is evident in Ṭāhir's advice that the ruler keep an eye on the well-born and noble (*aḥrār al-nās wa dhawī al-sharaf*) and that, as long as he is satisfied that their intentions towards him are good, he should promote their welfare and act kindly towards them; similarly he should

[16] The earliest extant version of this epistle again appears in a work of Ibn Abī Ṭāhir Ṭayfūr, in this case the *Taʾrīkh Baghdād*. Ibn Abī Ṭāhir's compositions reflect an interest in literary and cultural subjects and include a number of works in the *Fürstenspiegel* tradition. His literary career in Baghdad brought him into contact with many of the outstanding littérateurs and high government officials of his time (cf. Rosenthal, 'Ibn Abī Ṭāhir Ṭayfūr', *EI*2). Al-Ṭabarī, who made use of Ibn Abī Ṭāhir's work in his history, reproduced Ṭāhir's letter (*Taʾrīkh*, vol. 8, pp. 582ff). The letter subsequently appeared also in the works of Ibn al-Athīr and Ibn Khaldūn (cf. Rosenthal, *The Muqaddimah*, vol. 2, p. 139, n. 751).

[17] Cf. Arazi and El'ad, '«L'Épître à l'armée» Al-Maʾmūn et la seconde *daʿwa*', p. 67. On the Ṭāhirids' attitudes towards Persian literature, see W. Barthold, 'Ṭāhirids', *EI*1, and Bosworth, 'The Ṭāhirids and Persian Literature', *Iran* 7 (1969) pp. 103–106.

[18] Cf. Bosworth, 'An Early Arabic Mirror for Princes: Ṭāhir Dhū l-Yamīnain's Epistle to his Son ʿAbdallāh (206/821)' *JNES* 29/1 (1970), p. 27.

[19] Ibn Abī Ṭāhir Ṭayfūr, *Baghdād*, p. 21; cf. the contrasts between *wulāt* and *ʿāmma*, pp. 23, 26; *ashrāf* and *duʿafāʾ*, p. 22; *jund* and *raʿiyya*, p. 24.

[20] Ibn Abī Ṭāhir Ṭayfūr, *Baghdād*, pp. 24–25. [21] *ibid.*, p. 25. [22] *ibid.*, pp. 23, 28.

[23] *ibid.*, p. 24. [24] *ibid.*, p. 26; cf. 27–28; cf. Bosworth, 'An Early Arabic Mirror', p. 29.

look after the members of high-born families (*ahl al-buyūtāt*) when they fall into need.[25]

Much of this advice appears in some form in later mirrors for princes, including those that seek to perpetuate Iranian political ideals. But there is a pious tone to Ṭāhir's epistle as a whole that appears only occasionally in the well-known Persian mirrors of the fifth/eleventh century. To the extent that Ṭāhir refers to political customs that may have had an Iranian origin, it is probably because these had been adopted by the ʿAbbāsid court rather than because he identified with the larger social ideals behind them.

One particularly noteworthy feature of Ṭāhir's letter is its emphasis on the welfare of the common people. Ṭāhir, at the same time that he advises his son to cultivate and assist men of noble lineage, also admonishes him to a pious and possibly even somewhat egalitarian attitude: he should distribute the *kharāj* revenues fairly and equally for all entitled to them ('wazziʿhu bayna aṣḥābihi bi'l-ḥaqq wa'l-ʿadl wa'l-taswiya wa'l-ʿumūm bihi'), and not exempt a noble from full taxation on account of his *sharaf*, nor a rich man on account of his wealth, nor one of his secretaries, nor any of his personal retainers (*khāṣṣa*);[26] he should not be harsh towards any human being, nor should he turn away a poor petitioner;[27] he should look after the poor and wretched, and even seek out those who are unable to bring their complaints to him directly, or who do not know how to do so;[28] he should attend to those who have suffered injuries, their orphans and widows, and allot them stipends from the treasury; he should also award pensions to the blind, and allocate a larger amount for those who know the Qur'ān and have memorised most of it; he should establish hospices for the sick and provide them with attendants and doctors to treat their illnesses;[29] he should regard as the noblest (*akram*) of his associates he who is not afraid to point out a shortcoming or error to him in private;[30] he should see that the non-Muslim members of the polity, as well as the Muslims, are treated with justice and decency (*ʿadl* and *ṣalāḥ*).[31] Ṭāhir also reminds his son several times of the importance of the wellbeing of the *ʿāmma* and of his duties towards the *raʿiyya*.[32]

These passages suggest that Ṭāhir's idea of government included the active promotion of the welfare of the weaker members of society. This ideal, however, is expressed not in terms of social egalitarianism – on the contrary, Ṭāhir takes social distinctions for granted – but in terms of the moral virtues of charity and compassion towards the poor and disadvantaged. The view that the ruler should not spare himself in seeing to the welfare of the subjects in his charge, itself consistent with the paternalistic understanding of the monarch's role in Iranian political culture, found sanction in the Qur'ānic appeals for decent treatment and kindness towards the weak. This emphasis on moral

[25] Ibn Abī Ṭāhir Ṭayfūr, *Baghdād*, p. 26. [26] *ibid.*, p. 25. [27] *ibid.*, p. 23.
[28] *ibid.*, pp. 26–27. [29] *ibid.*, p. 27. [30] *ibid.*, p. 28. [31] *ibid.*, p. 28.
[32] *ibid.*, *ʿāmma*, pp. 25, 26; *raʿiyya*, pp. 19, 21, 22, 23, 24, 25, 26, 28.

guidance rather than social protest is also apparent in the letter said to have been composed by al-Ḥasan al-Baṣrī (21–110/642–728) for ʿUmar b. ʿAbd al-ʿAzīz, where al-Ḥasan, rather than arguing for social equality, reminds the caliph of God's concern for the weak, particularly orphans and the poor, and admonishes him that the just *imām* shows compassion towards such persons.[33] The idea that the poor members of the community have a certain religious significance is also reflected in several *ḥadīth*,[34] and assistance to the poor, widows and orphans is regarded as especially meritorious.[35]

A much greater inclination towards the Iranian social ideal is evident in the two recensions of the composition known as ʿAlī's letter to Mālik b. al-Ḥārith al-Ashtar al-Nakhaʿī (d. 38/658), which appears to be based on Ṭāhir's testament.[36] The first recension is preserved in the *Daʿāʾim al-Islām*, the compendium of Ismāʿīlī law composed by al-Qāḍī al-Nuʿmān in c. 347/957.[37] The second version is preserved in the *Nahj al-balāgha* compiled by al-Sharīf al-Raḍī in 400/1009.[38]

The letter to Mālik, in both versions, differs from Ṭāhir's epistle in some significant respects. It is apparently conditioned by Iranian forms of social description to a far greater extent than the Ṭāhirid text, although it retains the concern for the common people apparent in the earlier epistle. The author pays a certain lip-service to the pious ideal of equality when he notes that the subjects are 'your brethren by origin (*nisba*) and your equals by creation' (according to the *Daʿāʾim* text), or 'your brethren in religion (*dīn*)' (according to the *Nahj*).[39] But both versions of the letter ascribed to ʿAlī, like that of Ṭāhir, take the distinction between the *khāṣṣa* and the *ʿāmma* for granted, although they sometimes display an exaggerated preference for the latter over the former:

[33] *Al-ʿIqd al-farīd*, vol. 1, pp. 54ff; cf. Ritter, 'Studien zur Geschichte der islamischen Frömmigkeit', i, 'Ḥasan al-Baṣrī', *Der Islam* 21 (1933), pp. 21ff. See also Abū Yūsuf, *Kitāb al-kharāj* (Cairo 1382/1962), tr. B. Lewis, *Islam from the Prophet Muhammad to the Capture of Constantinople* (New York and Oxford, 1987), vol. 1, pp. 152f.

[34] 'This community will only be saved by the supplication, prayer and devotion of the weak' (*Kanz al-ʿummāl*, vol. 3, p. 174, no. 6017; cf. variants on p. 175) is one of the clearest examples.

[35] Al-Muttaqī, *Kanz al-ʿummāl*, vol. 3, p. 175, no. 6020; pp. 176ff.

[36] Al-Qāḍī, 'An Early Fāṭimid Political Document', pp. 91–94; Richter, *Studien*, p. 86. According to the *Nahj al-balāgha*, the testament was written by ʿAlī to Mālik on the occasion of the latter's appointment as governor of Egypt in 38/658. None of the standard histories knows of such a letter, and the earliest references to (and quotations from) it appear in al-ʿĀmirī's *al-saʿāda wa'l-isʿād* (al-Qāḍī, 'An Early Fāṭimid Political Document', pp. 75–76).

[37] This version appeared in the Maghrib in the early fourth/tenth century, and is seemingly attributed to the Prophet and ʿAlī simultaneously (*Daʿāʾim al-Islām* (Cairo, 1383/1963), vol. 1, p. 350; cf. al-Qāḍī, 'An Early Fāṭimid Political Document', pp. 73–74). It is inserted into the *Kitāb al-jihād*, although it is almost entirely irrelevant to the contents of this section. A partial translation of the entire testament has been made by G. Salinger, 'A Muslim Mirror for Princes', *Muslim World* 46 (1956), pp. 24–39.

[38] This version, which appeared in Iraq, is definite in its attribution to ʿAlī (Ibn Abī'l-Ḥadīd, *Sharḥ Nahj al-balāgha*, vol. 17, p. 30; al-Qāḍī, 'An Early Fāṭimid Political Document', pp. 71–108).

[39] *Daʿāʾim*, p. 354 (Salinger, 'A Muslim Mirror for Princes', p. 27); Ibn Abī'l-Ḥadīd, *Nahj*, p. 32.

May the most precious affair in your sight be the most equitable in what is right (*wa-l-yakun aḥabbu'l-umūr ilayka awsaṭahā fī'l-ḥaqq*),[40] the most universal in the way of justice, and the most conducive to the contentment of the subjects; for the displeasure of the common people impairs the contentment of the élite, while the displeasure of the élite is pardonable as long as the common people are content.[41] None of the subjects is a more troublesome burden to the ruler in times of ease and less support to him in adversity, has greater contempt for justice and is more importunate in demanding, is less grateful upon receiving and slower to excuse a deprivation, and is weaker in enduring the vicissitudes of time than the élite; whereas the pillar of religion, the collective strength of the Muslims, and the readiness to [confront] enemies reside in the common people of the community; so direct your goodwill and inclination towards them.[42]

This goes further than the normal egalitarian pieties that had become palatable in court circles. By contrast, the social model that follows this expression of distaste for court life is reminiscent of the Sasanian circles of justice in its mood and of Sasanian social models in its constituent elements:

Know that the people are of five strata, none of which can prosper except in conjunction with the others. Among them are the soldiers; the assistants of the ruler, such as the judges, tax-collectors, secretaries and the like; the land-taxpayers, the cultivators and others; the merchants and artisans; and the lowest stratum, that is, the needy and destitute. The soldiers are the strength of the subjects by the permission of God, the adornment of the realm, the glory of Islam, the cause of security and protection. The army cannot subsist other than by the land-tax and booty which God produces for them and from which they derive strength for the war against their enemies. They depend on it for their welfare, as do those members of their families whose support is their responsibility. The army and land-taxpayers cannot subsist without the judges, tax-collectors and secretaries [who] manage their affairs, collect their benefits, and are depended on in general and specific matters. None of them can subsist without the merchants and artisans, [who] produce benefits by their occupations, establish markets, and provide for [the rest of society] by practising crafts to which their skills do not extend. And the last stratum, that of the needy and destitute, is afflicted by need of all the people, and in God each one has a livelihood. Each one has a claim on the ruler in proportion to that which is fitting for him, and he [the ruler] cannot acquit himself of the duty which God has decreed for him except by [constant] attention, seeking God's aid on his behalf, and adjusting himself to the demands of his duty, whether it is in accordance with or in opposition to his own desire.[43]

Despite its expression of concern for the welfare of the common people, this social model is in striking contrast to the numerous egalitarian maxims placed in ʿAlī's mouth,[44] and even to the predominantly pious tone of Ṭāhir's letter. Far from implying an alienation from political authority and the social order it endorsed, the model attributed to ʿAlī here emphasises those groups that

[40] An echo of the Prophetic *ḥadīth* that runs *khayr al-umūr awsaṭuhā*; or, perhaps, of Ṭāhir's exposition on the virtues of moderation (*iqtiṣād, qaṣd*), on which see Bosworth, 'An Early Arabic Mirror', p. 28. [41] Cf. al-ʿĀmirī, *al-saʿāda wa'l-isʿād*, p. 297.

[42] *Nahj*, pp. 34–35; cf. *Daʿā'im*, vol. 1, p. 355, which adds to the last line, 'to the exclusion of others'. [43] *Daʿā'im*, p. 357; cf. *Nahj*, pp. 48–49. [44] See ch. 1.

stood in a direct relationship to the ruler and contributed to the functioning of the state. The first two categories (soldiers and officials) are responsible for the operation of the state in its military and civil branches respectively; the third and fourth (cultivators, merchants and artisans) form the tax-base for these functions. The model is arranged in a hierarchical fashion, and the cultivators appear in a relatively prominent position. All of the first four groups are said to be directly or indirectly dependent on one another, in the same way that the component elements in the Sasanian circle of justice co-existed in harmony on the basis of their mutual need. The attention to the peasants apparent in both the circle of justice and the letter to Mālik is not only ethical but also pragmatic, since, as the passage in question indicates, it is an element in the assertion of social control by the ruler. The inclusion of the fifth category, that of the needy and destitute, reflects the Islamic ethic of compassion towards the weak that had entered the vocabulary of kingship. Although in some contexts this last group might be invested with a certain religious significance, from a social point of view it is portrayed as parasitic.[45]

There are some considerable differences between the two recensions,[46] although this particular passage does not vary a great deal. In the *Nahj* version, unlike that of the *Daʿāʾim*, the number of strata is not given at the outset; the secretaries, judges and tax-collectors are listed separately; the 'armies' are called 'the armies of God'; secretaries are described as 'for general and specific affairs'; and the taxpayers include the *ahl al-dhimma* who pay the poll-tax as well as the Muslims who pay the land-tax.[47] In both recensions, the section quoted above is followed by separate descriptions of each category, in which several variations occur between the two versions. According to the *Daʿāʾim*, the stratum of secretaries is said to consist of multiple substrata (*manāzil*), each with its own functions and rights.[48] With a single exception, the *Nahj* refers not to the *wuzarāʾ* but to the *kuttāb*.[49]

Other differences are of a more general nature. For example, the attribute of

[45] It is also worth noting the passage, 'Do not abandon a beneficial custom (*sunna ṣāliḥa*), which has been maintained by good men before you, has secured concord (*ulfa*), and worked for the welfare of the common people; and do not introduce a new custom which violates in any way the ancient traditions of justice that have been established before you, lest the reward go to him who founded them and you be guilty of sin by destroying part of them' (*Daʿāʾim*, pp. 356–57; Salinger, 'A Muslim Mirror for Princes', p. 30; *Nahj*, p. 47). A similar exhortation to follow the examples of past rulers and former peoples appears in Ṭāhir's letter (cf. Bosworth, 'Early Arabic Mirror', p. 27); unlike the later testament, Ṭāhir's makes no mention of the role of such customs in preserving social harmony or protecting the common people.

[46] Al-Qāḍī, 'An Early Fāṭimid Political Document', pp. 81ff.

[47] These two groups are also conflated in Ṭāhir's letter (see Bosworth, 'An Early Arabic Mirror', p. 37, n. 22, and *The History of al-Ṭabarī*, vol. 32 (*The Reunification of the ʿAbbāsid Caliphate*), tr. C.E. Bosworth (Albany, New York, 1987), p. 121, n. 369).

[48] *Daʿāʾim*, p. 364; Salinger, 'A Muslim Mirror for Princes', pp. 35–36.

[49] On this point, see al-Qāḍī, 'An Early Fāṭimid Political Document', p. 85. In his commentary, Ibn Abī al-Ḥadīd interprets ʿAlī's *kātib* as the equivalent of the *wazīr* familiar to later generations (*Sharḥ*, p. 79). (On the transition from *kātib* to *wazīr*, see R.A. Kimber, 'The Early Abbasid Vizierate', *JSS* 37/1 (1992), pp. 65–85.)

religious knowledge is emphasised throughout the *Daʿāʾim*'s version; it is listed among the required qualifications for the commander of the army, the chief *qāḍī* and his assistants, and the tax-collectors.[50] It is absent from the *Nahj* in all these cases. Moreover, the version of the testament preserved in the *Nahj* often ascribes less significance to piety and religious understanding and more to hereditary qualities than the Maghribi recension.[51] The *Daʿāʾim* version advises the audience to associate with 'men of religious understanding, piety, and fine actions in the past; then with the brave among them, for in such men are combined generosity, a portion of greatness, and a sign of good opinion in God and faith in Him'.[52] The *Nahj*, by contrast, seems to reflect al-Sharīf al-Raḍī's own social circle in its advice that Mālik associate with 'men of personal honour (*muruwwāt*) and inherited merit (*aḥsāb*), members of worthy families (*al-buyūtāt al-ṣāliḥa*) and fine past actions; then the people of courage, bravery, generosity and munificence, for they combine together nobility (*karam*) and beneficence (*ʿurf*)'.[53] It is not difficult to understand why al-Qāḍī al-Nuʿmān (or the author of his source) might have added these elements to the Maghribi version of the testament, but it is hard to imagine that they were deliberately omitted in the Iraqi recension, and it seems possible that the two recensions do not stem immediately from a common source.

'Alī's letter to Mālik should also be compared with the *sīra* of the Zaydī imām al-Manṣūr bi'llāh al-Qāsim b. 'Alī al-'Iyānī, who ruled over northern Yemen from 389/999 to 393/1003. The *sīra*, composed by al-Manṣūr's secretary, includes quotations in full from the ruler's official correspondence. One of the letters reproduced in this work is from al-Manṣūr to the Sharīf al-Qāsim b. al-Ḥusayn al-Zaydī on the occasion of the latter's appointment in 390/1000 as governor of the southern parts of the realm. In this letter, al-Manṣūr describes the people as consisting of seven categories: the scholars of the law (*fuqahāʾ*); the local lords (*salāṭīn*); the soldiers (*junūd*); the tribes (*ʿashāʾir*), both nomadic and sedentary; the merchants (*tujjār*); the craftsmen (*ṣunnāʿ*); and the scum of the towns and base people (*ḥashw al-qurā wa ardhāl al-nās*). Al-Manṣūr then discusses each of these groups in turn. It is striking that his attitude towards the last three categories differs markedly from his treatment of the first four. The ruler needed the support of the first four groups, and consequently was obliged to respect their privileges. The merchants, craftsmen and urban poor, however, carried little political weight, and the task of government was merely to control and discipline them; it had no need to consider their aspirations.[54]

Al-Manṣūr's letter may shed further light on the two recensions of the letter associated with 'Alī. Its enumeration of the social categories, and its

[50] *Daʿāʾim*, pp. 358, 360, 361. [51] But see n. 39, for an exception to this.
[52] *Daʿāʾim*, p. 358. [53] *Nahj*, p. 51.
[54] Madelung, 'Al-Hamdānī's Description of Northern Yemen in the Light of Chronicles of the 4th/10th and 5th/11th Centuries', *Religious and Ethnic Movements in Medieval Islam* (Hampshire, 1992), pp. 131–135.

description of the ruler's responsibilities towards and fair expectations from each, again appear in a letter composed for a governor on his appointment to an important regional post. In this context, such social description no doubt served to bolster the legitimacy of the ruler in whose name the letter was written and that of his representative, the addressee. Unlike the letters associated with ʿAlī, however, al-Manṣūr's letter is clearly linked to the specific circumstances of his rule; certain local princes are even mentioned by name. The texts ascribed to ʿAlī, and especially that contained in the *Nahj*, have been made to reflect universal ethical norms of government rather than the circumstances in which they were purportedly written. A further point of contrast lies in the urban-pastoral context for al-Manṣūr's model and the agrarian-based description that appears in the *Daʿāʾim al-Islām* and the *Nahj al-balāgha*.

Probably roughly contemporary with the two recensions of ʿAlī's letter is the similar model contained not in a testament but in the *Rasāʾil* composed in the first half of the fourth/tenth century by the Ikhwān al-Ṣafāʾ. Like other Muslim philosophers, the authors envisage a rational universe composed of numerous preordained and immutable hierarchies. These various hierarchical orders sometimes overlap with each other; the social model in the *Rasāʾil*, for example, is not merely a categorisation of functions but a hierarchy of intellects by which men were linked with the Universal Intellect. Although they considered men's intellects to be of countless degrees, the Ikhwān al-Ṣafāʾ limit their description to nine. It was as a result of their differing intellects that men necessarily adopted certain functions in society.

In our opinion, this [superiority] is apparent among them [the intelligent] and becomes known from them according to their strata in worldly affairs and their ranks in the matter of religion. These [strata and ranks] are many; their number can be counted only by God Almighty. But we shall gather them all into the [following] nine divisions to facilitate understanding, and we shall condense them for the purpose of memorisation. Accordingly, in our opinion, there are among them [the intelligent] the men of religion, divine ordinances, and prophecies (*ahl al-dīn waʾl-sharāʾiʿ waʾl-nubuwwāt*), founders of laws (*aṣḥāb al-nawāmīs*). Below them are those entrusted with the observation of their rules and the preservation of their traditions (*sunan*), and those known for their devotion to them. Among them also are the religious scholars and philosophers (*ahl al-ʿilm waʾl-ḥukamaʾ*), the men of culture (*udabāʾ*), and those involved in spiritual exertions (*aṣḥāb al-riyāḍāt*), who are entrusted with teachings (*taʿālīm*), discipline (*taʾdīb*), spiritual exercises (*riyāḍāt*), and the branches of knowledge (*maʿārif*). Also among them are kings, rulers, commanders, leaders, those who manage affairs (*aṣḥāb al-siyāsāt*), and those attached to their service, such as troops, guards (*aʿwān*), secretaries, tax-collectors, treasurers, trustees (*wukalāʾ*) and those like them. Then there are among them the builders, farmers, cultivators, shepherds, cattle-herders and keepers of animals of all kinds. Among them also are the artisans, craftsmen (*aṣḥāb al-ḥiraf*) and those who furnish all objects and necessities (*al-muṣliḥūn lil-amtiʿa waʾl-ḥawāʾij jamīʿan*). Also among them are the merchants, sellers, travellers and traders in objects and necessities from distant parts. Then there are among them those who eke out a living by serving others and carrying out their daily errands. Among them also are the weak, mendicants and beggars, and other such poor and wretched persons.[55]

This model aims at a comprehensive description of the orders of human existence, ranked in terms of men's intellectual levels, which are inevitably reflected in their occupations. It suggests the idea that humanity constitutes a microcosm in which the first stratum of humanity, composed of prophets and founders of divine laws, are the representatives of the supreme law.[56] Beneath them are the embodiments of the next highest human intellect, and so on. It is noticeable that those learned in the religious sciences and philosophy are grouped together, as are those involved in the military and the civilian branches of government. The cultivators, artisans and merchants are clearly differentiated from one another, however, and, together with the stratum of rulers and their servants, may reflect the common quadripartite ranking of occupations: rulership, agriculture, craftsmanship and commerce.[57] The inclusion of a category of servants may suggest the notion, attested elsewhere in the philosophical tradition, of a category of mankind who were 'slaves by nature' and fit only to serve others.[58] Given the Ikhwān's apparent desire to give a comprehensive account of the social categories, the poor and weak may be included primarily for the sake of completeness; but one may perhaps discern here a respect for the Islamic duty of charity towards the helpless and dependent elements of society, since the Ikhwān al-Ṣafā' go on to devote a special section to the excellence of the poor and wretched, in which they describe these persons as a token of divine mercy and a warning for the rich and affluent.[59] All of humanity is thus envisaged in a hierarchical structure, and even within each category, the Ikhwān point out that every individual is in the position of a master to others or a subordinate (*ra'īs sā'is, mar'ūs masūs*).[60]

The social model of the Ikhwān al-Ṣafā' is meant to demonstrate a coherence in the universe that only the intellectual élite could perceive. That it is not primarily intended to mirror the functions of government is suggested by its grouping together of rulers, soldiers and bureaucrats in one generalised category, whereas the document associated with 'Alī distinguishes between the

[55] *Rasā'il*, vol. 3, p. 428.

[56] Cf. al-Fārābī, *Talkhīṣ*, p. 13; al-'Āmirī, *al-Sa'āda wa'l-is'ād*, pp. 212–213. (Such ideas are reminiscent of Ismā'īlī thought; on the Ismā'īlī associations of the Ikhwān al-Ṣafā', see S.M. Stern, 'The Authorship of the Epistles of the Ikhwān-aṣ-Ṣafā', *IC*, 20 (1946), pp. 367–372, and *idem*, 'New Information about the Authors of the "Epistles of the Sincere Brethren"', *Islamic Studies*, 3 (1964), pp. 405–428.)

[57] See ch. 7. The distinction between cultivators, artisans and merchants is also reminiscent of the theories expounded by Aristotle in his *Politics* (*Pols.*, IV, 4 and VII, 8); in Aristotle's conception, however, the cultivators and craftsmen were deemed unworthy of citizenship.

[58] Cf. Ibn Sīnā, *Ilāhiyyāt*, p. 453; Naṣīr al-Dīn Ṭūsī, *Akhlāq*, pp. 284, 288 (tr. Wickens, pp. 214, 217); Ritter, 'Handbuch', p. 14; and ch. 2.

[59] *Rasā'il*, vol. 3, pp. 429ff.

[60] *Rasā'il*, vol. 3, p. 428. On the hierarchical vision of the Ikhwān al-Ṣafā', see further ch. 2.

military and bureaucratic functions. While the model contained in the *Da'ā'im* and the *Nahj* gives first place to the soldiers, that of the Ikhwān places intellectual and spiritual figures above rulers, soldiers and those involved in administration. It resembles the model associated with 'Alī in the low position it assigns to merchants, and its inclusion of the poor and destitute. It seems that such models were in circulation in various forms in fourth/tenth-century Iraq. The Ikhwān articulated a model that reflected their esoteric vision of human society as a microcosm of a rational universe, and al-Sharīf al-Raḍī articulated one that resembles a theory of practice more than a philosophical outlook.[61]

Mirrors for Princes

Social rank and organisation are recurring themes not only in the testament but also in the later literary development of the mirror. The mirror for princes offers advice to a ruler or high-ranking official on the practical and ethical aspects of government, whereas the testament purports to represent the wisdom accumulated by a ruler or other figure of authority in the course of his many years of experience, communicated in a mood of reflection to his son and successor. The mirror for princes is typically longer and consists of chapters or sections devoted to particular issues. It also tends to be oriented towards the practical and ethical aspects of government in the present – with an eye to remaining on the right side of God, certainly – rather than focusing on the pious humility with which all men should approach the next world. To a large extent mirrors draw on a common stock of materials of mixed origins. In many cases, and especially in the case of those written in Persian, they provide a channel for the continuing transmission of the Iranian tradition to the courts of Muslim rulers, especially those that adopted Perso-Islamic culture.

The formulation of full social models is, however, relatively uncommon in the well-known fifth/eleventh-century mirrors for princes in Arabic and Persian. It is more usual in the works of authors whose interests were abstract and philosophical rather than (or as well as) practical, and consequently it is a significant feature of those later mirrors that are also works of political philosophy and ethics. Much of the content of the earlier mirrors has implications for conceptions of social organisation, however. Authors of mirrors were concerned with the relationship of various social categories to the king and their behaviour in his presence, they devoted a good deal of attention to the qualifications and duties of various government officials, they showed a marked concern for the tax-paying peasantry, and they rarely failed to include a circle of justice in their books. Individual authors sometimes make a case for the

[61] It is perhaps of some interest to note that the *Rasā'il* themselves were ascribed not only to Ismā'īlī imāms, but also, on occasion, like the letter to Mālik, to 'Alī, or to Ja'far al-Ṣādiq; Stern, 'New Information', pp. 419f.

social precedence of their own particular hereditary or occupational groups, and even the circle of justice is, at least in part, a means of justifying social domination.

One feature common to many mirrors for princes is their unapologetic respect for noble birth, although they often emphasise the desirability of cultivating personal virtues in addition to it. Niẓām al-Mulk (408–485/1018–1092), for example, in his famous *Siyar al-mulūk* or *Siyāsatnāmeh*, places great emphasis on the necessity for a clear social hierarchy, and pays little attention to egalitarian pieties. To the extent that he is concerned with religious commitment at all, his concern is that positions of authority should only be given to those whose convictions will not undermine the stability of the state: for him, the most important qualifications for social recognition and for appointment to high office are nobility, capability and acceptable religious beliefs, rather than religiosity.[62] In a passage reminiscent of the *Testament of Ardashīr* and the *Letter of Tansar*, he describes the supremacy of the noble over the base, under the surveillance of the ruler, as the human state most pleasing to God, and considers the inversion of this order with considerable alarm. It is a sign of troubled times, in Niẓām al-Mulk's opinion, when men of noble birth are crushed, while the least of men become *amīr*s and the basest of persons become chief secretaries (*ʿamīd*),[63] and the noble (*aṣīlān*) and learned (*fāḍilān*) are dispossessed, while the base (*furūmāyeh*) adopt the titles of rulers and viziers. In such times, all affairs fall short of their proper order and organisation.[64] When it pleased God to end this time of disturbance, a just and intelligent ruler of princely stock would emerge and, having informed himself of the rightful order of things by inquiring into the practice of past rulers, he would restore the proper order. He would make the precise degree of each person apparent (*andāzeh-yi darajeh-yi har kasī padīdār kunad*). He would reinstate the worthy (*arzānīyān*), and dismiss the unworthy, whom he would then appoint to their proper tasks and trades (*kār, pīsheh*).[65] The idea of such a monarch, who would embody numerous themes of Persian political culture, was attractive to many members of the élites, and did much to influence their perceptions of real rulers.[66]

62 Cf. Lambton, 'The Dilemma of Government in Islamic Persia: The *Siyāsat-Nāma* of Niẓām al-Mulk', *Iran* 22 (1984), p. 56.

63 Probably *ʿamīd-i dīvān-i rasāʾil*, 'chief secretary'; Ḥ. Anvarī, *Iṣṭilāḥāt-i dīvānī-yi dawreh-yi Ghaznavī va Saljūqī* (Tehran, 1335), pp. 256–257.

64 Niẓām al-Mulk, *Siyar al-mulūk*, p. 190; tr. Darke, *The Book of Government*, p. 143; cf. Minovi (ed.), *Tansarnāmeh*, p. 2, and see ch. 3.

65 Niẓām al-Mulk, *Siyar al-mulūk*, p. 190; tr. Darke, *The Book of Government*, p. 144; see also Lambton, 'Dilemma of Government', p. 59.

66 ʿAḍud al-Dawla (d. 372/983) is often said to have conformed to this royal ideal. Al-Rūdhrāwarī praises the Būyid king for not giving any of his followers more than that to which his station entitled him (cited in Mottahedeh, 'The Shuʿûbîyah Controversy', p. 177). On the Būyids' own presentation of their claim to royal authority, see Madelung, 'The Assumption of the Title Shāhānshāh by the Būyids and "the Reign of the Daylam (*dawlat al-Daylam*)"', *JNES* 28 (1969), pp. 84–108, 168–183; see also Bosworth, 'The Interaction of Arabic and Persian

Niẓām al-Mulk goes still further in his expression of respect for nobility when he notes that rulers of all ages have undertaken to preserve ancient families (*abnā-yi mulūk*), to ensure that they are neither neglected nor debarred from their rightful positions. It was true that other persons, most of whom were considered worthy on the basis of personal rather than hereditary principles, had been protected too: the scholars, the descendants of ʿAlī, the worthy (*muṣliḥān*), the frontier-soldiers, the guardians of the frontiers, and the expositors of the Qurʾān. In those days, according to Niẓām al-Mulk, no one had been deprived of his rightful position.[67] In his own age, however, this ideal had been lost. No one paid any attention any longer to the correct awarding of titles; consequently, there were too many of them, and their value and importance had been debased, so that they no longer bore any relation to the holder's rank (*martabat*) and importance (*andāzeh*). Instead, bazaar merchants and peasants had the same titles as chief secretaries and well-known persons, so that there was no difference between the positions of the well known and the unknown.[68] In a good age, the vizier and officers (*pīshkārān*) are virtuous and noble (*nīk, aṣīl*); every task is allotted to its proper practitioner; tasks are not entrusted to those without excellence and noble origin; all things are restored to their proper order; and each man's rank is visible, so that religious and worldly affairs are well-arranged, and every man has a task according to his capability.[69]

In its strong attachment to hierarchy, the importance it ascribes to noble birth, its ideal of the king who keeps everyone in his proper place, and its horror of social mobility, the *Siyāsatnāmeh* recapitulates the late Sasanian social ideal with little modification. Niẓām al-Mulk does not prescribe a social model, beyond his acceptance of the dichotomy between *lashkar* and *raʿiyyat*,[70] but his social outlook is clearly very much in the Iranian tradition, which in his view, as doubtless in that of the majority of Iranian Muslims by his time, was completely compatible with and indeed found support in Islam. Although he recognises the entitlement of some other groups, especially those with religious credentials, to social privilege, he insists that those born into families that had a long history of greatness – for non-religious reasons – should be allowed to maintain their position and, if necessary, be assisted in doing so.

This social outlook also appears in other mirrors whose authors inclined principally towards a Perso-Islamic cultural orientation. Afḍal al-Dīn

Literature and Culture', pp. 62ff; J.L. Kraemer, *Humanism in the Renaissance of Islam. The Cultural Revival during the Būyid Age*, 2nd edition (Leiden and New York, 1992), pp. 212, 272ff, 284). Ibn Khaldūn also considers the ability to assign all persons to their proper station a mark of legitimate royal authority (tr. Rosenthal, vol. 1, pp. 293–294).

67 *Siyar al-mulūk*, pp. 190–191; tr. p. 144.

68 *Siyar al-mulūk*, pp. 200–201; tr. p. 152. For a similar description of how the world had gone to the dogs, see ʿAlāʾ al-Dīn ʿAṭā Malik Juvaynī, *Tārīkh-i jahān-gushā*, ed. M.M. Qazvīnī (Leiden and London), vol. 1 (1912), pp. 4–5.

69 *Siyar al-mulūk*, p. 241; tr. p. 184.

70 Cf. Lambton, 'Dilemma of Government', p. 62.

Kirmānī, historian, secretary and author of the late sixth/twelfth-century mirror *ʿIqd al-ʿulā lil-mawqif al-aʿlā*,[71] also envisaged the ideal ruler as one who would keep every stratum in its place and every individual in the situation appropriate to him. He lists the following social categories: 'princes, those of noble birth, those of high lineage and inherited merit; the religious scholars, men of learning, worshippers of God and men of righteous conduct;[72] cultivators and landowners; and merchants and artisans'.[73] This description does not set out to present the social categories from the ruler's point of view: there is no mention of the secretaries or (unless one follows a variant) of the army either. The description is not a reformulation of the circle of justice. Instead, it is presented as the definition of 'good government', and the emphasis is on the privileges of high birth. Men of noble birth are placed in a category of their own at the apex of society, while the remaining strata are somewhat reminiscent of those of the pre-Islamic Iranian 'priestly' model of the ninth- and tenth-century Zoroastrian texts.[74] (It is noteworthy that the merchants again occupy the lowest position.) Afḍal al-Dīn adduces several texts, all of which he interprets with reference to the proper status of men of lineage: the Qurʾānic verse 26:215 ('Lower your wing to those of the Muslims who follow you');[75] the *ḥadīth* 'When the noble of a group comes to you, honour him';[76] a saying attributed to Aristotle: 'Protect those endowed with manly qualities (*muruwwāt*) and those with a long record of goodness, even if their conditions have declined, and do not disclose the secrets of men of substance';[77] and a poem by al-Mutanabbī in praise of Sayf al-Dawla:

If you honour the noble man, you possess him;
But if you honour the base man, he will become insolent.
The bestowal of generosity with high rank where the sword is appropriate
Is as harmful as the use of the sword where generosity is fitting.[78]

On the basis of these and other proof-texts, Afḍal al-Dīn observes that failure to maintain the men of noble birth and established houses and the men of learning in the positions of respect due to them might cause them to become

[71] Dedicated to Malik Dīnār, the leader of the Ghuzz who conquered Kirmān in 581–583/1185–1187; cf. M. Th. Houtsma, 'Zur Geschichte der Selǵuqen von Kermân', *ZDMG* 39 (1885), pp. 392–395. On Afḍal-i Kirmānī, see Muḥammad b. Ibrāhīm, *Tārīkh-i Saljūqīyān-i Kirmān* (Houtsma, *Recueil*, vol. 1), pp. 35–36 (Muḥammad b. Ibrāhīm also quotes several times from Kirmānī's memoir *Badāʾiʿ al-azmān fī vaqāʾiʿ Kirmān* in his own history); M.E. Bāstānī Pārīzī, 'Afżal-al-Dīn Kermānī', *Encyclopaedia Iranica*; Lambton, 'Islamic Mirrors for Princes', pp. 436–438; C.A. Storey, *Persian Literature, A Bio-Bibliographical Survey* (London, 1936), vol. 1, part 1, fasc. 3, p. 357.

[72] *ahl-i ṣalāḥ*; according to a variant, *ahl-i silāḥ*, 'men of weapons' (*ʿIqd al-ʿulā*, p. 58, n. 2).

[73] *ʿIqd al-ʿulā*, p. 58.

[74] The quadripartite 'priestly' model may be summarised briefly as priests, soldiers, cultivators and artisans; see ch. 3.

[75] This interpretation finds little or no support in classical *tafsīr*; see for example Fakhr al-Dīn al-Rāzī, *al-Tafsīr al-kabīr*, vol. 24, p. 173, and al-Bayḍāwī, *Anwār al-tanzīl*, vol. 2, p. 61.

[76] See ch. 1. [77] Cf. *K. al-saʿāda waʾl-isʿād*, p. 378; and see ch. 2.

[78] Nāṣīf al-Yāzijī, *al-ʿArf al-ṭayyib fī sharḥ dīwān Abīʾl-Ṭayyib* (Beirut, 1384/1964), vol. 2, p. 183.

disaffected.[79] Elsewhere, he deplores the prevailing social disorder when, he claims, persons of low birth and otherwise unsuitable individuals occupied high office.[80]

The circumstances under which Niẓām al-Mulk and Afḍal al-Dīn wrote their books were quite different from those under which the authors of the testaments discussed earlier in this chapter composed theirs. Niẓām al-Mulk lived through the first large-scale wave of migration of Turkish peoples into the Middle East, and wrote his mirror in the brief period during which the eastern Islamic world was once more unified in the empire of the Seljuks. Afḍal al-Dīn wrote after the disintegration of the Seljuk empire and after the continued migrations from the steppes had transformed the economic, social and political conditions of much of the eastern Islamic world. The economic and demographic situation of Iraq and Iran had proved unable to support the Seljuks' attempt to create a centralised government, and the Seljuks themselves had soon adopted the Ghaznavid practices of relying on slave armies and allocating revenue and other types of grants (*iqṭā ʿāt*) in place of salaries.[81] A notable feature of the material considered here is that Niẓām al-Mulk and Afḍal al-Dīn were both anxious to win from their Turkish royal masters recognition for the standing of the aristocracy. The Turks, unlike the Arabs, had their own royal traditions, and were no strangers to stratification and hierarchy; furthermore, they speedily became great patrons of Perso-Islamic culture. These developments, which are reflected in the works of men such as Niẓām al-Mulk and Afḍal al-Dīn, are related to the Turkish rulers' need to establish a centralised government, against the interests of their Turkoman followers.

Other authors of didactic literature attached a similar value to noble birth, but also gave greater expression to Islamic egalitarian pieties. It is no surprise that Kay Kāʾūs, penultimate ruler of the Ziyārid dynasty in the Caspian provinces in the second half of the fifth/eleventh century and author of the *Qābūsnāmeh*,[82] took the distinction between élites and the common people for granted, or that he advocated that people should seek to cultivate different abilities depending on the group to which they belonged. In general, he notes, there is no better legacy for the children of the élite than accomplishment (*hunar*), culture (*adab*) and learning (*farhang*), while for the children of commoners, nothing is better than mastering a craft (*pīsheh*). He adds, however, that in his opinion mastering a craft is an accomplishment in itself, and that if children of members of the élite were to master a hundred crafts, as long as they did not make use of them for gain, each one would be an accomplishment and would one day prove worthwhile.[83] Kay Kāʾūs may have advised his son

[79] *ʿIqd al-ʿulā*, pp. 58–61.
[80] *ʿIqd al-ʿulā*, pp. 14–15; cf. Lambton, *Continuity and Change*, p. 222.
[81] For a discussion of the various types of grant and assignment to which the term *iqṭāʿ* was applied under the Seljuks and Īlkhāns, see Lambton, *Continuity and Change*, pp. 97–129.
[82] Composed in 475/1082–83 and addressed to his son and intended successor Gīlānshāh.
[83] *Qābūsnāmeh*, ed. Gh.Ḥ. Yūsufī (Tehran, 1368), p. 135.

to master a profession because he realised that the latter might not necessarily rule until his death, and thus might at some time find himself in need of practical skills and professional knowledge in order to support himself (Gīlānshāh was indeed overthrown by the Ismāʿīlīs of Alamūt in c. 483/1090).[84] As an example, he relates how the deposed Kayānid monarch Gushtāsp had been forced to flee incognito to the land of the Greeks, but was able to eke out a living there through his proficiency in smithery; on his return to Iran, Gushtāsp had encouraged others to master a craft, and consequently the custom had arisen that each Iranian of high status had knowledge of a craft, however little he needed it to ensure his livelihood.[85] Despite this attempt to associate practical skills with noble birth, Kay Kāʾūs's entire discussion of professional knowledge suggests that the Iranian aristocracy still held the practice of crafts in contempt.

Elsewhere, again drawing attention to the attitudes of the high-born, Kay Kāʾūs instructs his son that noble descent alone is not enough, and that the cultivation of personal qualities brings a deeper kind of nobility:

> Know, boy, that people without lasting accomplishments are without value, in the same way that a thorn tree has a trunk but casts no shade, and is of no benefit to itself or to others. [It is true that] men of noble origin and descent, though they may lack accomplishments, will not remain without a portion of men's respect; worse off is he who possesses neither descent nor accomplishments. But an effort should be made, so that, although you are of noble origin and descent, you should also possess a [noble] quality in your person; for noble qualities in a person are superior to nobility of origin. As they have said: 'Nobility is in intellect and education, and not in origin and descent.' Do not be content with the name that your mother and father gave to you, for that name is only an [external] sign. [Your true] name is that which you acquire for yourself through your accomplishments, so that you attach to the name of Jaʿfar, Zayd, ʿAmr, ʿUthmān or ʿAlī the title of 'Teacher', 'Learned One' or 'Sage'. If men do not possess, in addition to noble origin, noble qualities in themselves, then they are unfit for any man's company. But if you encounter a man endowed with both kinds of qualities, seize hold of him and do not let him out of your hands, for he is of use to everyone.[86]

The point, then, is that although high birth entitles its possessor to social esteem and is an essential part of nobility, the truly noble man combines his birthright with personal qualities and skills. Nobility of birth is not insignificant and cannot be disregarded, but it does not allow its possessors to neglect the cultivation of personal virtues.

The view that knowledge and piety might replace noble lineage and in fact themselves constituted the only true entitlement to social esteem entered the corpus of materials used in mirrors for princes at an early date. The Middle Turkish didactic poem *Kutadgu bilig*, for example, composed by Yūsuf Khāṣṣ Ḥājib in 463/1069 for the Qarakhānid ruler, Tavghach Bughra Khān, contains many statements to this effect: 'Know that wisdom and intellect are noble

[84] *Qābūsnāmeh*, p. 158; Bosworth, 'Kay Kāʾūs b. Iskandar', *EI2*.
[85] *Qābūsnāmeh*, pp. 135–136. [86] *Qābūsnāmeh*, pp. 27–28.

things and they ennoble the chosen servant . . . Wherever there is intellect, there is greatness, and whoever has wisdom achieves nobility'; 'Honour and esteem are all for the intelligent. The ignorant is a mere handful of clay. Any man may don a cloak of honour, but true nobility belongs to the man of wisdom and intellect. Whoever possesses intellect is nobly born, and whoever possesses wisdom has attained the level of princes.'[87] The Qarakhānids had taken Transoxania in the late fourth/tenth century, before the great wave of Turkish migration into the Middle East, and had quickly assimilated the Perso-Islamic traditions of the region. It has been suggested that Yūsuf was attempting to establish a place in Islamic culture for the Turkish tradition, and thus to repeat what Firdawsī had accomplished for the Iranian cultural tradition. He attempted to do this, however, not on the basis of the traditions of Turkish legend and saga but of the Irano-Islamic ideals of statecraft that he found in Arabic and Persian literature. These he sought to integrate with the Turkish traditions of royalty and wisdom.[88] In the passages cited here, he has adopted the pious and egalitarian attitude that had become part of the mainstream Irano-Islamic cultural tradition, and was not incompatible with an attachment to a hierarchy of degrees.

Other authors of advice literature emphasised the claims of groups identified in religious terms to the highest social positions. A more religiously conditioned understanding of society's constituent parts is implied by Najm al-Dīn Dāya al-Rāzī (573–654/1177–1256), the famous Ṣūfī of the Kubrawī order, in his *Mirṣād al-'ibād min al-mabda' ilā'l-ma'ād* (618–620/1221–1223). In the fifth chapter of this work, inspired by the Qur'ānic references to 'eight pairs' (6:143; 39:6), Najm al-Dīn proceeded from 'the elucidation of the ways of rulers and those endowed with authority' to 'the elucidation of the condition of rulers and of their conduct with each group of the subjects'. He then enumerated the subjects as ministers, men of the pen and deputies; religious scholars, including *muftī*s, preachers and judges; those endowed with bounties and wealth; farmers, village headmen and peasants; merchants; and artisans and craftsmen.[89]

Another list of the functional groups among the king's subjects appears in Shihāb al-Dīn Aḥmad b. Muḥammad b. Abī'l-Rabī''s mirror for princes dedicated perhaps to the caliph al-Musta'ṣim (640–656/1242–1258), entitled *Sulūk al-mālik fī tadbīr al-mamālik*.[90] Shihāb al-Dīn lists four bases of the realm: the

[87] R. Dankoff (tr.), *Wisdom of Royal Glory (Kutadgu Bilig): A Turko-Islamic Mirror for Princes* (Chicago, 1983), pp. 44, 49.

[88] Dankoff, *Wisdom of Royal Glory*, p. 1; cf. Inalcik, 'Turkish and Iranian Political Theories and Traditions in *Kutadgu Bilig*', in *The Middle East and the Balkans under the Ottoman Empire* (Bloomington, Indiana, 1993), pp. 1–18; Dankoff, 'Inner Asian Wisdom Traditions in the Pre-Mongol Period', *JAOS* 101 (1981), pp. 87–95.

[89] *Mirṣād al-'ibād min al-mabda' ilā'l-ma'ād*, ed. Ḥusayn al-Ḥusaynī al-Ni'matullāhī (Tehran, 1312), pp. 411ff; tr. H. Algar, *The Path of God's Bondsmen from Origin to Return* (New York, 1982), pp. 411ff.

[90] On the reading of 'al-Musta'ṣim' for 'al-Mu'taṣim' (218–227/833–842), see J. Zaydān, *Ta'rīkh ādāb al-lugha al-'arabiyya* (Cairo, 1957), vol. 2, p. 252, and Plessner, *Der Oikonomikos des Neupythagoräers Bryson* (Heidelberg, 1928), pp. 31ff. Although there is no positive evidence

ruler, the subjects, justice and administration.[91] He goes on to subdivide the subjects into several parts. These include, firstly, the 'worthy' (*muta'ahhilūn*), or those who confine themselves to worship and austerity and admonish the world by their threats and promises. The second group consists of the philosophers, or those familiar with the sciences of wisdom (*al-ʿulūm al-ḥikmiyya*), such as medicine, astrology, accountancy, geometry and suchlike. Thirdly, Shihāb al-Dīn lists the religious scholars, who are the bearers of traditions (*ḥamalat al-āthār*) and the successors of the prophets, whose assistance is to be sought in distinguishing the lawful from the unlawful, and for exoteric and esoteric exegesis. Fourthly, he refers to the men of lineage (*dhawū ansāb*), who are the people of nobility, rank and stature (*sharaf, jāh, qadr*), and who constitute the support of the realm. The fifth group are the men of war, or the protectors of the realm, who provide defence against enemies and security against the disasters wrought by them, and through whom cities and realms are conquered. The sixth category consists of the inhabitants of the marketplaces: artisans and servants, by whom the affairs of men are made complete, and their requisites speedily attained. Seventhly, Shihāb al-Dīn lists the inhabitants of the villages, who make the land fruitful by ploughing, cultivating and sowing, and on whom the rest of mankind are dependent.[92]

Shihāb al-Dīn's list suggests that his chief concern was with the intellectual and spiritual élites to whom he assigns the first three positions in his hierarchy. He was not interested, it would seem, in the bureaucracy. The remainder of Shihāb al-Dīn's model is not dissimilar from that of Afḍal al-Dīn, except that the former places the cultivators at the bottom of the list. In every case, Shihāb al-Dīn explains the value of each group to society as a whole; he does not appear to be pleading the case of any particular group over another. Although its structure is less symmetrical than that of Naṣīr al-Dīn al-Ṭūsī, Shihāb al-Dīn's model reflects the same general order of its component functional groups.[93]

Authors of advice literature who were themselves scholars were particularly likely to emphasise the respect in which the king should hold men of religious learning. Such scholarly authors frequently owed their positions to the ruling authorities, and therefore had an immediate interest in the ways in which rulers treated and rewarded scholars. For the ruler himself, showing deference and generosity to scholars was a necessary element in the establishment of his government's legitimacy. The anonymous author of the *Baḥr al-favā'id*,

that the work was dedicated to the later caliph, its contents are not dissimilar to those of other works written in the same period. The geographical setting in which the text was composed remains uncertain. The *Sulūk al-mālik fī tadbīr al-mamālik* was identified by Brockelmann with *al-Akhlāq al-mushajjar*, a work written under al-Mustaʿṣim in 655/1256 (*GAL* SI, p. 372).

91 Shihāb al-Dīn Ibn Abī'l-Rabīʿ, *Sulūk al-mālik fī tadbīr al-mamālik*, ed. Nājī al-Takrītī (Beirut, 1978), p. 138.

92 Ibn Abī 'l-Rabīʿ, *Sulūk al-mālik*, pp. 147–148; cf. al-Fārābī, *Fuṣūl al-madanī*, pp. 136–137.

93 This list of the main groupings of men in terms of their social function is followed by another, tripartite one which distinguishes between them on the basis of their innate propensities to good and evil (Ibn Abī 'l-Rabīʿ, *Sulūk al-mālik*, pp. 148–149).

dedicated to the atabeg ruler of Marāgheh, Arslān Aba b. Āq Sunqur, and probably composed between 1159 and 1162,[94] was apparently an Ashʿarī Shāfiʿī scholar.[95] He complained that the religious scholars, together with the other elements of society who were eligible to receive an allowance from the treasury (judges, Qur'ān reciters, the poor, orphans and warriors for the faith), were being deprived of the money to which they were entitled; instead, this money was being spent on astrologers, physicians, musicians, jesters, cheats, wine-merchants and gamblers.[96] The author also recommends that the errors of the *ʿulamāʾ* should be overlooked, and claims that God will overlook seventy of their sins, but not one sin of the ignorant.[97] Elsewhere in his book, when enumerating the rights of various sectors of the population, the author lists the commanders and rulers, the subjects, and the religious scholars;[98] in this minimalistic piece of social description, he nevertheless recognises the *ʿulamāʾ* as a third category, in addition to the rulers and the ruled.[99] To justify his vision of the elevation of the religious scholars above the rest of society, the author also cites several *ḥadīth*, such as the Prophet's prayer for the *ʿulamāʾ*, 'O God, have mercy on my successors (*khulafāʾ*)',[100] and 'If two categories of the people are morally upright, then all the people will be – the religious scholars and the rulers.'[101] An anonymous (and undated) mirror entitled *al-Durr al-thamīn fī manāhij al-mulūk wa'l-salāṭīn* offers an extended version of the same piece of social description, also in the form of a Prophetic *ḥadīth*:

> 'My community will not be morally upright unless its élites (*khawāṣṣ*) are upright.' 'And who are the élites of your community, Apostle of God?' 'Four [groups]: the commanders (*umarāʾ*), the religious scholars (*ʿulamāʾ*), the worshippers (*ʿubbād*) and the merchants (*tujjār*). The commanders are the shepherds of the people; and if the shepherd is negligent, who will protect the sheep? As for the religious scholars, they are the physicians of the people; if the physician is ill, who will cure the sick? The worshippers are the guides of the people; if the guide is errant, who will lead him who seeks guidance? As for the merchants, they are the trusted ones of God; if the trusted one is treacherous, on whom shall one depend?'[102]

This model emphasises the indispensable role played by each category; the four groups singled out reflect the urban social values of the *ʿulamāʾ*.

94 J.S. Meisami, *The Sea of Precious Virtues (Baḥr al-favāʾid)* (Salt Lake City, 1991), pp. vii–xii.

95 Lambton, 'Islamic Mirrors for Princes', p. 426; Meisami, *Sea of Precious Virtues*, p. xii.

96 *Baḥr*, p. 310. 97 *Baḥr*, p. 174. 98 *Baḥr*, pp. 172–174.

99 On the various social roles played by the *ʿulamāʾ* in many regions in the post-ʿAbbāsid period, see Lapidus, 'The Evolution of Muslim Urban Society', *Comparative Studies in Society and History* 15 (1973), pp. 40ff.

100 The author also cites a *ḥadīth* calling for respect to be shown to kings (p. 428; Meisami, *Sea of Precious Virtues*, p. 294). 101 *Baḥr*, p. 428.

102 Ms. Kadizade Mehmed 291, f.13b. In the introduction to this work, a dedication to *Mawlānā al-Sulṭān* . . . is followed by a lacuna, in which an unknown hand has inscribed 'Tughril'. The first part of the book deals with 'what distinguishes rulers and is incumbent upon them, and the mention of those qualities which are the foundations of the realm and the basis of dominion, by which the earth endures and the lands are cultivated'; the second part consists of *mawāʿiẓ* attributed to the four *Rāshidūn*, the later caliphs, rulers and so on.

Sirāj al-Dīn Urmavī (594–682/1198–1283), the Shāfiʿī scholar and eminent logician who dedicated his *Laṭāʾif al-ḥikma* (655/1257) to ʿIzz al-Dīn Kay Kāʾūs of the Seljuks of Rūm, consistently emphasises the ruler's duties towards the *ʿulamāʾ*. The latter were God's elect (*khavāṣṣ-i ḥaqq*), according to the *ḥadīth*, 'The people of the Qurʾān are the people of God and His elect.'[103] If those who have memorised the Qurʾān are the people of God, he asserts, then anyone learned in both the exoteric and esoteric sense of the Qurʾān must certainly be among the elect of the elect (*khāṣṣ al-khawāṣṣ*). The degree of respect due to any particular member of the *ʿulamāʾ* depended on the nobility of the branch of his studies and the extent of his learning in it, but since knowledge was superior to deeds, all religious scholars were greater in merit than ascetics and other worshippers.[104] Just as for some authors, those of noble blood deserved exemption from harsh judgement in the case of minor wrongdoings, so for Sirāj al-Dīn, an eccentric member of the *ʿulamāʾ*, regardless of his manner or behaviour, should be given the benefit of the doubt, as long as he did not transgress the *sharīʿa* or hold objectionable doctrines.[105] Sirāj al-Dīn also interprets the Qurʾānic *ūlīʾl-amr* (4:59) as a reference to 'rulers and scholars'; he subdivides the latter into 'the men of religious knowledge and the men of the pen'. He proceeds to explain:

> The ruler's authority is [achieved] by the rule of the sword and government, while the authority of the scholar is [achieved] through the rule of the pen and legal opinion. These two are tied to each other, because were it not for the legal opinions of the men of religious knowledge, the ruler could not exercise his government, and were it not for the ruler's government, the legal opinions of the people of religious knowledge could not be put into effect. Since these two are dependent upon each other, or rather, since they both appear to be the same thing, inevitably God brought them together in one line in his words 'those with authority among you'.[106]

In this unusual piece of interpretation, Sirāj al-Dīn thus emphasises the interdependence of kings and scholars.[107] The insistence on the need for the king

[103] Ibn Māja, *Sunan*, vol. 1, *muqaddima*, ch. 16, p. 78, no. 215; Ibn Ḥanbal, *Musnad*, vol. 3, pp. 127, 128, 242. [104] *Laṭāʾif*, pp. 258–259. [105] *Laṭāʾif*, p. 259.

[106] *Laṭāʾif*, pp. 226–227.

[107] Sirāj al-Dīn's exegesis of this passage differs considerably from that of most classical commentators. Al-Ṭabarī, for example, records various views on the correct understanding of the phrase *ūlīʾl-amr*, and favours the opinion that it refers to the holders of political authority, to whom obedience is due only in so far as their commands are in accordance with God's (*Jāmiʿ al-bayān*, vol. 8, pp. 495ff). Similar interpretations appear in al-Zamakhsharī (*al-Kashshāf*, vol. 1, pp. 535f.) and al-Bayḍāwī (*Anwār al-tanzīl*, vol. 1, pp. 214f); Ibn Kathīr, however, prefers to interpret the phrase as a reference to the *ʿulamāʾ* (*Tafsīr*, vol. 2, p. 326). Sirāj al-Dīn's commentary follows, in a simplified form, one of the arguments put forward by Fakhr al-Dīn al-Rāzī, on whose works the *Laṭāʾif al-ḥikma* is to some extent dependent and to whom its author refers occasionally in his text (see Urmavī, *Laṭāʾif*, introduction, p. 15). In Fakhr al-Dīn's interpretation, however, the chief significance of 4:59 is that it confirms, in order, the four Shāfiʿite *uṣūl*: the Qurʾān, *sunna*, *ijmāʿ* and *qiyās*. The words *aṭīʿūʾllāha wa aṭīʿūʾl-rasūl* connote for him the Qurʾān and *sunna*; the continuation of the verse (*fa-in tanāzaʿtum fī shayʾin fa-ruddūhu ilāʾllāhi waʾl-rasūl* ('And if you disagree on anything, refer the matter to God and his messenger')), he argues, is a reference to *qiyās*. (Al-Bayḍāwī, another Shāfiʿite judge and a

to recognise and abide by the supremacy of the *sharīʿa*, substantiated by reference to rulers who had succeeded in doing so, is a further indication of Sirāj al-Dīn's desire to establish the legitimacy of the government he served.[108]

The inclusion of pious egalitarian motifs in the literature of the courts, and the recognition of the *ʿulamāʾ* as one of the groups most deserving of social esteem, are indicative of the extent of the scholars' success. Their alienation from the state is accepted as the morally correct position even by the representatives of the state itself. Yet the expressions of egalitarianism that entered the corpus of *belles-lettres* lost their threatening implications, and were incorporated as pious exercises into the literature of high culture. Mirrors for princes, like the anthologies discussed in the preceding chapter, include a large number of verses that resemble the following rather trite example:

When learning (*dānishī*) becomes apparent upon you,
The nobles (*aḥrār*) will hold their heads low in your presence;
Acquire *adab*, and you will become all you wish,
For *adab* is more highly praised than *nasab*.[109]

The inclusion of such materials in works addressed to rulers and their high-ranking officials suggests how mainstream the respect for knowledge had become. The high esteem in which knowledge was held could not be ignored, and the constant injunctions to men of privilege that they recognise the ultimate equality of great and small in God's eyes were powerful reminders to them to exercise their powers in full awareness of a higher authority. It is also worth noting that al-Ghazālī, in a work of a quite different ilk, emphasises not only the benefits that knowledge brings its possessors in their preparation for the next life, but also the high social esteem that accompanies it in the present:

When I considered knowledge, I saw that it was pleasurable in itself, with the result that it was pursued for its essence (*ladhīdhan fī nafsihi . . . maṭlūban li-dhātihi*). I found it a path towards the abode of the other world and its happiness, and a means towards proximity to Almighty God; [indeed], there is no access to him other than by it. [Moreover], the greatest of things in rank (*rutba*) for man is eternal happiness, and the best of things for him is that which is a means towards [that happiness]. There can be no access to this other than by knowledge and works, nor can works themselves be accomplished without knowledge of how to perform them. The root of happiness in this world and the next, then, is knowledge, which is therefore the best of works. Indeed,

contemporary of Sirāj al-Dīn, offers a similar interpretation (*Anwār al-tanzīl*, vol. 1, p. 215).) The phrase *ūlīʾl-amr*, in al-Rāzī's view, does not refer to the Rāshidūn or any other rulers, and still less to the Imāms, as the Shīʿites claim; it refers to *ahl al-ḥall waʾl-ʿaqd min al-umma*, that is, to the *ʿulamāʾ*, whose consensus (*ijmāʿ*) it therefore renders binding. He argues, among other points, that since this verse makes obedience to *ūlīʾl-amr* absolutely necessary, they must consequently be *maʿṣūm*; the duty of obedience to rulers, on the other hand, was conditional on their just behaviour, which was in fact exceedingly rare. In any case, he maintains, the acts of rulers were dependent on the *fatwās* of the *ʿulamāʾ*, who were therefore, as it were, *umarāʾ al-umarāʾ* (al-Rāzī, *Tafsīr*, vol. 10, pp. 143–48). Sirāj al-Dīn has thus adopted some of Fakhr al-Dīn's arguments, and indeed some of his language, but for a quite different purpose.

108 *Laṭāʾif*, pp. 270–272, 287–288.

109 ʿAlī al-Iṣfahānī, *Tuḥfat al-mulūk*, p. 18.

how could it not be so, since one recognises the excellence of a thing by the nobility of its fruit, and observes that the fruits of knowledge are proximity to the Lord of the Worlds, approaching the horizon of angels, and association with the heavenly host? These [fruits] are in the next world. As for the fruits of knowledge in this world, [they are] grandeur, dignity, the influence of one's judgement on rulers, and the demand for respect (*iḥtirām*) from [all] natures (*ṭibāʿ*). Even the most ignorant of the Turks and the most boorish of the Arabs find their natures compelled to revere their elders for their exclusive possession of superior knowledge acquired by experience; indeed, it is even in the nature of the beast to respect man, because it senses that man is distinguished by a perfection which exceeds its own level (*daraja*).[110]

It seems fairly clear that many of the *ʿulamāʾ* felt entitled to both moral authority and social recognition from the holders of power. In cases where they found themselves in the position of servants of the state, they insisted that those whom they served were respectful of their moral rank and generous in their support. They interpreted the Qurʾānic equation of nobility and piety to their advantage, and the appearance, in a watered-down form, of materials in which the significance of nobility and lineage are denied attests to their success.

Commentaries on ʿAlī's sayings

Another body of material that may have arisen against a background of political opposition and social protest and yet became innocuous over time consists of the numerous egalitarian and meritocratic sayings attributed to ʿAlī.[111] These too were quickly incorporated into the belletristic tradition, and became popular subjects for commentaries dedicated to rulers as a variation on the genre of the mirror for princes. These commentaries, which seem to have been especially popular in the Perso-Islamic world, were designed for the articulation of wisdom on matters of social and political significance.

One example of such a commentary is Muḥammad b. Ghāzī Malaṭyavī's *Barīd al-saʿāda* (composed in 609–610/1212–1214), which consists of the author's reflections on selected Qurʾānic verses, *ḥadīth*, *āthār* and other passages, dedicated to Abūʾl-Muẓaffar ʿIzz al-Dīn Kay Kāʾūs I (608–618/1211–1220) of the Seljuks of Rūm. Malaṭyavī's comments on the aphorism 'The value of each man is that in which he is proficient' are entirely shaped by the contemporary tradition of court literature:

It is necessary that the protective shadow of the ruler be the centre of eternal happiness and the abode of everlasting dominion, so that both the learned and the ignorant, in order to attain their desire, turn towards that Kaʿba of auspicious fortune. When they are granted the nobility of access and the glory of audience, [the ruler] should invite each person to approach in accordance with his attainment of good qualities and his achievement of hopes and desires, and should generously welcome him without regard for the nobility of his paternity. If a competent man has an obscure assistant, he should not deny the children of the latter proximity on account of the obscurity of their father,

[110] *Iḥyāʾ*, vol. 1, p. 13. [111] See ch. 1.

because sweetness comes from unripe dates, while ash is born of fire. Therefore he should know that esteem should be given to things of precious value, and not to things of noble descent, and he should recognise that pride should be taken only in what exists now, and not in one's ancestors . . . In our audience hall, let honour be in proportion to a man's attainment, patronage according to knowledge, and guardianship in agreement with perspicacity.[112]

Malaṭyavī takes up the themes of access to the ruler's person and confidence, and expresses the egalitarian ideal in language that is reminiscent of *Kalīla wa Dimna*.[113] The importance of nobility and paternity is denied, but in language that echoes the idiom of the court where heredity and clearly differentiated social ranks were an important part of the political culture. The inclusion of such materials and such language in the context of the Seljuk court suggests that their purpose was to emphasise the virtue of humility, since on the Day of Judgement even kings would not be entitled to special treatment. It was certainly not intended to imply an egalitarian view of society.

The suitability of ʿAlī's maxims for the edification and entertainment of rulers and their companions is evident from the dedication of another commentary on the *Mi'at kalima*, this time by the eminent Shīʿī scholar Kamāl al-Dīn Mītham b. ʿAlī b. Mītham (d. 679/1280),[114] to Shihāb al-Dīn Masʿūd b. Garshāsp-Shāh.[115] In his commentary on the phrase, 'Nobility is in excellence and education, and not in inherited merit and lineage',[116] Mītham associates the terms 'excellence' and 'education' with the perfection of the theoretical and practical faculties of the soul respectively. These virtues alone, he maintains, are cause for pride; only lasting spiritual perfection constitutes true nobility. Pride in wealth or ancestors is therefore false pride. In the case of wealth, this is for two reasons. Firstly, it is not a spiritual virtue and consequenty does not lead towards happiness in the next world (but indeed often leads towards its opposite); moreover, it is external to the human soul, so that whoever boasts of it boasts of something that he does not truly possess. Secondly, it is not enduring, and indeed how can something endure when it is exposed to damage and is liable to disappear at any moment, so that its owner is never secure? As for pride in genealogy, whoever invokes it, boasts of it, and claims nobility on its account may indeed have forebears and ancestors whose virtues and perfections were worthy of pride and had earned them nobility; however, if those men were present now and were to say: 'The excellence which

[112] Muḥammad b. Ghāzī Malaṭyavī, *Barīd al-saʿāda*, ed. M. Shīrvānī (Tehran, 1351/1972), pp. 269–270. [113] See chs. 1, 3.

[114] Al-Sayyid Ḥasan al-Ṣadr, *Ta'sīs al-shīʿa* (Tehran, n.d.), pp. 169, 393–395; ʿAbd Allāh al-Iṣfahānī, *Riyāḍ al-ʿulamā' wa ḥiyāḍ al-fuḍalā'*, ed. al-Sayyid Aḥmad al-Ḥusaynī (Qumm), vol. 1 (1401/1981), p. 52.

[115] Mītham also dedicated commentaries on the *Nahj al-balāgha* to members of the Juvaynī family (Yūsuf b. Aḥmad al-Baḥrānī, *Lu'lu'at al-baḥrayn* (Qumm, n.d.), pp. 255–256; M.T. Dānishpazhūh (ed.), *Farmān-i Mālik-i Ashtar* (Tehran, 1359/1400), p. 18).

[116] Cf. Kay Kā'ūs, *Qābūsnāmeh*, p. 27; Rashīd al-Dīn, *Mukātabāt-i Rashīdī*, no. 22; ʿAlī al-Iṣfahānī, *Tuḥfat al-mulūk*, p. 11 ('Nobility is in fine *adab*, not in superior *ḥasab*').

you claim in us is ours, not yours; we alone possess it; what do you have of it that others do not have?' then you would find their boastful descendant nonplussed, silent and embarrassed. This is why the Prophet said: 'Do not bring me your genealogies; bring me your deeds.'

[O you] who boast of wealth and genealogy:
Our only reason for pride is knowledge and education.
There is no good in a noble man without education,
No good in him [at all], even though he may walk on gold.[117]

So popular did ʿAlī's maxims become that ʿAbd al-ʿAzīz al-Kāshī, author of the seventh/thirteenth-century anthology *Rawḍat al-nāẓir wa nuzhat al-khāṭir* devotes a section to 'the fact that nobility is in excellence and education, not in origin and descent', and attributes to ʿAlī a versified expression on the same theme:

Men are equals with respect to the material out of which they have been fashioned;
Their father is Adam and their mother, Eve.
If they have a noble origin
About which they can boast, it is clay and female semen.
Excellence belongs only to those with knowledge;
They are guides for the direction of those who seek the right path.
The worth of a man is that in which he is proficient
And the ignorant are enemies of those endowed with knowledge.[118]

The classical and early medieval authors of didactic literature contributed very significantly to the taming of Islamic egalitarianism. Like the anthologies discussed in the previous chapter, mirrors for princes and testaments referred frequently to the pious ideal of equality, but they did so in ways that plainly allow for no social or political relevance. The implications of egalitarianism, in these materials as in others, were restricted to the afterlife, while in the present it was a hierarchical consciousness that set the norm. This development is in part a reflection of the degree to which scholars, the custodians of the religious tradition in which Islamic egalitarianism was rooted, had acquiesced in the face of political authority, although the degree to which they were incorporated into it varied from place to place and from time to time. The role of the *ʿulamāʾ* in providing explicit justification for social inequalities will be discussed further in the following chapter.

Also noteworthy in the didactic literature studied in this chapter is the

[117] *Sharḥ Kamāl al-Dīn Mītham b. ʿAlī b. Mītham al-Baḥrānī ʿalāʾl-miʾat kalima*, ed. Jalāl al-Dīn Muḥaddith (Tehran, 1349sh/1390q), pp. 65–67. See also Vaṭvāṭ, *Maṭlūb kull ṭālib min kalām Amīr al-Muʾminīn ʿAlī b. Abī Ṭālib*, ed. Jalāl al-Dīn Muḥaddith (Tehran, 1342sh/1382q), p. 39, and ʿAbd al-Wahhāb, *Mā namaqahu ʿAbd al-Wahhāb fī sharḥ kalimāt Amīr al-Muʾminīn*, ed. Jalāl al-Dīn Muḥaddith (Tehran, 1349sh/1390q), p. 56.

[118] *Rawḍat al-nāẓir wa nuzhat al-khāṭir*, TS 2452, f.67a. (See Ḥājjī Khalīfa, *Kashf al-ẓunūn ʿan asāmī al-kutub waʾl-funūn* (Istanbul), vol. 1 (1941), p. 587; Rescher, 'Arabische Handschriften des Top Kapú Seraj', *RSO* 4 (1912), pp. 703–704.)

attention it gives to peasants. Despite the important links between cities and the surrounding countryside in many parts of medieval Islamic Middle East,[119] cultivators are ignored or treated with contempt in several parts of the tradition.[120] The culture of the courts of Iraq, Iran and elsewhere, however, was now firmly rooted in the recognition of the agrarian base to the state. This must be considered in part a mark of the success of Iranian statesmen and men of letters in their transmission of social, political and economic ideals, a success which becomes particularly apparent with the establishment of Turkish political and military dominance in the eastern regions of the Islamic world. The attention devoted to the peasants in mirrors for princes is linked to the circles of justice that are frequently found in the same literature, since both express the ideal of social harmony as a means through which social domination can be exercised.

[119] See Lapidus, 'Muslim Cities and Islamic Societies', in *Middle Eastern Cities*, ed. I.M. Lapidus (Berkeley and Los Angeles, 1969), pp. 47–79.

[120] This is especially apparent in *ḥadīth* (see for example Kister, 'Land Property', pp. 284–285). Of course traditions favourable to agriculture can also be found (see, for example, Kister, 'Land Property'; al-Shaybānī, *Kitāb al-kasb*, ed. S. Zakkār (Damascus, 1400/1980), p. 63; al-Kulīnī, *al-Kāfī*, vol. 5, pp. 260ff; al-Muttaqī, *Kanz al-ʿummāl*, vol. 4, p. 31, no. 9348; p. 32, no. 9354; p. 33, no. 9359).

CHAPTER 6

Rationalisations of inequalities

If the culture of the courts had to come to some accommodation with the pious egalitarian ethic embedded in the religious tradition, religious scholars also felt the need to come to terms with the continued existence of hierarchy. The efforts of Sunnī scholars to demonstrate the righteousness of the community in an area where it seemed to have strayed from Islamic ethical principles were related to, and largely contemporary with, the desire felt by the same scholars to establish the legitimacy of seemingly inadequate governments. In their justifications of social differences on religious grounds, such scholars frequently availed themselves of philosophical arguments, categories and methods of reasoning. They also made copious use of passages from the Qur'ān and *sunna*, which they presented as evidence for a divine logic that underlay social hierarchy.

In their desire to perceive an order to the universe, Muslim philosophers postulated a hierarchy among men on the basis of intellectual and spiritual aptitude.[1] They were less interested in the question of social stratification for its own sake than in uncovering the rational principles by which the known cosmos, including human societies, were governed. Muslim philosophers almost invariably subscribed to the view that men were incapable of supplying all their needs in isolation; mutual co-operation was therefore essential for human survival. The necessity of co-operation led to the formation of communities, in which each man was responsible for the provision of a single common need.[2] The particular function of an individual within the community was dictated by his natural disposition; it was therefore imperative that men should differ in their innate dispositions in order to ensure that all the community's needs were met.

This commonplace point of view is fully exemplified in the thought of the

[1] See ch. 2.

[2] This theory is put forward particularly clearly by Ibn Khaldūn (*The Muqaddimah*, tr. Rosenthal, vol. 2, pp. 271ff). A contrasting, possibly somewhat anti-philosophical view is expressed by Najm al-Dīn Dāya Rāzī (573–654/1177–1256), who regards trades and crafts as an aperture through which the intelligent man can gaze on God's activity and creative work (Najm al-Dīn Dāya al-Rāzī, *Mirṣād al-'ibād min al-mabda' ilā'l-ma'ād*, pp. 532ff; tr. H. Algar, *The Path of God's Bondsmen From Origin to Return* (New York, 1982), pp. 482ff).

Ikhwān al-Ṣafā'. According to the Ikhwān, whose view of the cosmos was intensely hierarchical, social stratification was divinely ordained. The Ikhwān took for granted not only the general categories of *khāṣṣ* and *'āmm*, but also innumerable intermediate ranks. They considered it one of the characteristics of prophethood to establish laws for the élite, the commoners and all the strata in between these two groups. Rulers, who were the successors and deputies of prophets, were responsible for upholding the order (*niẓām*) and hierarchy (*tartīb*) inaugurated by their inspired predecessors. It was their task to divide their subjects into categories, strata, levels and ranks, so that each individual was duly assigned to the group appropriate to him, just as each of the cardinal numbers had its inalienable place in an immutable series.[3]

The moralists

For many Muslim philosophers, the question of social hierarchy is linked to the issue of larger differences among individuals. Several writers address the problem of the relative importance of innate (we might say genetic) and environmental factors in accounting for various types of differences among people, such as differences of intelligence.[4] Miskawayh seems inclined to give more importance to nature than to nurture: among the factors that may account for human differences, he lists men's natural dispositions; their customs; their stations and positions with regard to knowledge and understanding; their aspirations, desires and concerns; and (in the opinion of some people, he notes) their ancestors.[5] Al-Rāghib al-Iṣfahānī, whose writings were perhaps approximately contemporary with those of Miskawayh, appears to give more or less equal attention to both innate and environmental factors and, unlike Miskawayh, supports his choice of differentials by reference to the Qur'ān, *sunna* and Arabic maxims. His list of relevant factors consists of individual temperament, disposition and character; the relative wholesomeness or corruption of an individual's parents; the sperm and blood from which an individual is conceived; the woman who suckles him in infancy; education, instruction, discipline and conditioned habits; the influence of the people who

[3] Ikhwān al-Ṣafā', *Rasā'il Ikhwān al-Ṣafā'*, vol. 3, p. 495; cf. vol. 1, p. 321; and see ch. 5.

[4] For a discussion of classical views on the innate or acquired nature of intelligence and the social implications of such views, see al-Māwardī, *Tashīl al-naẓar wa ta'jīl al-ẓafar fī akhlāq al-malik wa siyāsat al-mulk*, ed. al-Sayyid (Beirut, 1987), introduction, pp. 37ff, especially p. 41, and al-Sayyid, 'al-'Aql wa'l-dawla fī'l-Islām, in *al-Umma wa'l-jamā'a wa'l-salṭa*, p. 195.

[5] *Tahdhīb al-akhlāq*, ed. C.K. Zurayk (Beirut, 1966), p. 87; tr. C.K. Zurayk, *The Refinement of Character* (Beirut, 1968), p. 78. In the light of the wide scope assigned to heredity by most Muslim philosophers (see ch. 2), Miskawayh probably regarded the third and fourth factors as innate rather than conditioned; cf. Fakhr al-Dīn al-Rāzī's discussion of knowledge, on which see below. A slightly different list of factors is given by Naṣīr al-Dīn Ṭūsī in his Persian paraphrase of this section of Miskawayh: Ṭūsī mentions the differences in men's natures; their customs; their knowledge, cogniscence and understanding; their aspirations; and their capacities for desire and endurance. According to some, Ṭūsī records, men also differ as a result of fortune and coincidence (*bakht*, *ittifāq*) (*Akhlāq*, p. 89; tr. Wickens, *Nasirean Ethics*, p. 66).

care for an individual; and the extent of a person's own efforts to purify himself through knowledge and works.[6] A century-and-a-half or so later, Fakhr al-Dīn al-Rāzī (543–606/1149–1209), who, like al-Rāghib, combined the disciplines of *falsafa* and *'ilm*, emphasises the significance of environmental factors in his description of the effects of age, noble lineage, wealth, and geographical and climatic conditions on men's temperaments.[7]

For Fakhr al-Dīn and his seventh/thirteenth-century follower, Sirāj al-Dīn Urmavī, the differences between people and their relative superiority and inferiority depend on the quality of the individual human soul. On this issue Sirāj al-Dīn records disagreements between the adherents of his own school and other unnamed philosophers. He writes that in the view of 'the philosophers', all human souls are alike (*mutasāvī*) in essence (*māhiyyat*), but different in their attributes (*ṣifāt*) and conditioning (*infi'āl*), on account of their various temperaments (*mizāj*); the school of Fakhr al-Dīn, on the other hand, held that human souls were alike not in essence but in genus (*jins*), and unlike in their differentia (*fuṣūl*). According to Sirāj al-Dīn, 'the philosophers' justified their position by arguing that man was a compound of body and soul. If men's souls differed in essence, then no two people would be alike in their human essence, and the term 'human' would be without meaning. Fakhr al-Dīn, by contrast, advanced several proofs from sacred sources to justify his position. Firstly, he quoted the Qur'ānic verse: 'God knows best with whom to place His message' [6:124] as evidence that the prophet's soul was different from that of other men. Secondly, as proof of the differences of human souls, he adduced the Prophetic *ḥadīth* 'Men are sources [to be mined for their qualities], like deposits of gold and silver'[8] and 'Souls are enlisted soldiers; those of them who become acquainted with each other are sympathetic to each other (*i'talafa*), and those who have no knowledge of each other differ.'[9] Thirdly, Fakhr al-Dīn observed that while some men strove and exerted themselves to learn but gained little understanding as a result of their endeavours, others made little effort yet became fully knowledgeable. This was due to the difference in their natural dispositions (*fiṭrat*).[10]

The notion that individual souls differ in quality forms the premise for many rationalisations of hierarchy. Authors who wished to justify differences of status among men often derived a defence of hierarchy by combining the idea of differing innate dispositions with the view that men were obliged to co-operate in order to fulfil the complex needs of an entire community. Thus several writers perceived the disparities among men as the result of different aspirations (*himam*) created in them by God. These various aspirations

[6] *Tafṣīl al-nash'atayn wa taḥṣīl al-sa'ādatayn*, pp. 115–118.
[7] Youssef Mourad, *La physiognomie arabe et le Kitāb al-firāsa de Fakhr al-Dīn al-Rāzī* (Paris, 1939), pp. 48–58. [8] See ch. 1, n. 69.
[9] Muslim, *Sunan*, vol. 8, *birr*, pp. 41–42; Abū Dā'ūd, *Sunan*, vol. 4, *adab*, p. 260, no. 4834; Ibn Ḥanbal, *Musnad*, vol. 2, pp. 295, 527, 539.
[10] Urmavī, *Laṭā'if al-ḥikma*, pp. 132–133; cf. pp. 239, 451.

directed each man towards a single occupation, and consequently the needs of society as a whole were fulfilled. For some, this determination of men's aspirations, while apparently leaving them free to choose their occupations, was a sign of God's wisdom. The differences between men were therefore inevitable, necessary and divinely ordained.

This kind of outlook is evident in several places in the works of al-Māwardī (364–450/974–1058). Al-Māwardī opens his *Tashīl al-naẓar wa taʿjīl al-ẓafar* with the observation, 'God . . ., in the profundity of his wisdom and the justice of his decree, has made men different in their categories and diverse in their levels ('jaʿala al-nās aṣnāfan mukhtalifīn wa aṭwāran mutabāyinīn'), so that they might be linked to one another through their difference and made mutually compatible in their diversity; and moreover so that both those who follow and those who are followed might be sympathetic to each other in affection, and so that both those who issue commands and those who are subject to them might render one another assistance in co-operation.'[11] In his *Adab al-dunyā wa'l-dīn*, al-Māwardī makes the essential helplessness of human beings in isolation from their fellows the basis for his entire exposition on the wellbeing of the world. He asserts that man is, according to the Qur'ānic phrase, *ḍaʿīf* (weak), but that this neediness is in fact a mark of God's bounty and favour (*niʿma, luṭf*).[12] The need for mutual assistance, moreover, is at the base of individual differences, for if everyone were the same, no one would be in a position to come to the aid of anyone else. Here al-Māwardī cites the Qur'ānic verse, 'lā yazālūna mukhtalifīna illā man raḥima rabbuka wa li-dhālika khalaqahum' (11:117–118). Extrapolating from a somewhat unusual piece of exegesis, according to which the verse refers to differences in sustenance (*rizq*), al-Māwardī interprets it as a divine injunction for economic differences; the fact that, as he observes, some are rich while others are poor is thus the consequence of divine intention.[13] Al-Māwardī makes this point as part of his larger argument that the welfare of the world itself demands that not everybody may prosper equally. Thus it seems that he regards human inequalities as inevitable and, from a perspective that transcends that of the individuals caught in them, desirable. Al-Māwardī does not embark here on a list of the groups he regards as essential social constituents, but his view of society and its relationship to authority is clearly a strongly hierarchical one.[14] It is noteworthy that he takes the relevance of genealogy, as a condition for ties of

[11] *Tashīl al-naẓar*, p. 97. For a discussion of this and similar passages in al-Māwardī's *oeuvre*, see also the editor's introduction, pp. 8ff, 26f.

[12] *Adab al-dunyā wa'l-dīn*, p. 144. The Qur'ānic phrase is *khuliqa 'l-insānu ḍaʿīfan* (4:28).

[13] *Adab al-dunyā wa'l-dīn*, p. 147. This is one of six recognised interpretations listed by al-Māwardī in his own commentary (*al-Nukat wa'l-ʿuyūn, Tafsīr al-Māwardī*, ed. al-Sayyid b. ʿAbd al-Maqṣūd b. ʿAbd al-Raḥīm (Beirut, 1412/1992), vol. 2, p. 511); see further below. In the passage under discussion here, al-Māwardī also adduces the verse *wa'llāhu faḍḍala baʿḍakum ʿalā baʿḍin fī'l-rizq* (16:71). See also his *Adab al-dunyā wa'l-dīn*, pp. 222–230, where al-Māwardī makes a similar argument on the basis of a number of other proof-texts in his discussion of various means of earning a living.

[14] See *Adab al-dunyā wa'l-dīn*, pp. 154–156.

friendship as well as marriage, for granted.[15] The existence of poverty and its attendant social frictions nevertheless disturbed him, and he regarded abundance, which helped to minimise the ill effects of inequality, as one of the six principles essential for wellbeing in the affairs of this world.[16]

In his *Qawānīn al-wizāra wa siyāsat al-mulk*, al-Māwardī employs this conception of predetermined aspirations expressly to justify men's different functions in society. He discusses this issue in his description of the executive duties of the vizier of delegation (*wazīr al-tafwīḍ*).[17] These duties include 'the execution of the subjects' affairs in accordance with their accustomed practices and transactions, in which they differ and by which they are linked together (*wa-khtalafū fīhā ḥattā 'talafū bihā*)'. The explanation for this state of harmony through diversity is that human beings need many sorts of commodities, not all of which can be provided by one man alone; therefore, men's aspirations differ, each group of men being particularised by one aspiration with the result that all men are linked together by mutual need. In this way, farmers attend to their cultivation, artisans labour with their crafts, and merchants devote themselves to their commercial enterprises.[18] Al-Māwardī proceeds to describe a quadripartite social model: 'Men are of four strata. One of them is for horsemanship (*furūsiyya*); admit men to it on account of their nobility. One is for the upholding of religiosity (*iqāmat al-diyāna*); admit men to it on account of their competence. One is for agriculture and cultivation; reward its members according to equity. One is for the crafts (*mihan*); do not deprive its members of goodwill.'[19] In its quadripartite form, its placement of cultivators above artisans, its omission of merchants altogether, and its emphasis on nobility, this schema is reminiscent of the Iranian 'priestly' model, and thus it is apparent here as elsewhere that al-Māwardī did not perceive any deep contradiction between Sasanian and Islamic notions of political organisation.[20] It is nevertheless somewhat surprising that the author fails to invoke the Qur'ān or *sunna* in support of his argument.[21]

15 *Adab al-dunyā wa'l-dīn*, pp. 164, 172. See also al-Māwardī, *Tashīl al-naẓar*, pp. 12–13.

16 *Adab al-dunyā wa'l-dīn*, p. 159.

17 On this office, see al-Māwardī, *al-Aḥkām al-sulṭāniyya*, pp. 25–26; see also Sourdel, *Le vizirat 'abbāside de 749 à 939 (132 à 324 de l'hégire* (Damascus, 1960), pp. 714–718, and al-Sayyid, 'Naẓarāt fī jadaliyyāt al-'ilāqa bayn al-namūdhajayn', in *al-Umma wa'l-jamā'a wa'l-salṭa*, pp. 91ff.

18 *Qawānīn al-wizāra wa siyāsat al-mulk*, ed. al-Sayyid (Beirut, 1979), p. 142; cf. A.Ḥ. al-Baghdādī, *al-Fikr al-siyāsī 'inda Abī'l-Ḥasan al-Māwardī* (Beirut, 1984), p. 90.

19 *Qawānīn al-wizāra*, pp. 142–143. In an earlier edition of the text (Cairo, 1348/1929), this model is attributed to Ḥimyar, according to tradition the first of the kings descended from Qaḥṭān to rule over Yemen (Ibn Qutayba, *al-Ma'ārif*, p. 626; al-Mas'ūdī, *Murūj al-dhahab*, vol. 2, p. 48; al-Khwārazmī, *Kitāb mafātīḥ al-'ulūm*, ed. G. van Vloten (Leiden, 1895), p. 107); al-Sayyid's emendation of Ḥimyar to Jam[-shīd] is doubtless correct.

20 See further al-Sayyid, 'Naẓarāt fī jadaliyyāt al-'ilāqa bayn al-namūdhajayn', in *al-Umma wa'l-jamā'a wa'l-salṭa*, pp. 118ff, and *idem*, 'al-Salṭa wa'l-ma'rifa', in *al-Umma wa'l-jamā'a wa'l-salṭa*, p. 271.

21 The style and content of the text may suggest that it was written early in al-Māwardī's career (al-Baghdādī, *al-Fikr al-siyāsī*, pp. 70ff); for further discussion of the place of this and similar works in al-Māwardī's *oeuvre*, see al-Māwardī, *Tashīl al-naẓar*, pp. 29–31, 82–83.

Like al-Māwardī, al-Rāghib al-Iṣfahānī and after him al-Ghazālī (450–505/1058–1111)[22] were preoccupied principally with economic differences. Disparities of wealth seemed to threaten the notion of divine fairness, and it was partly their moral and theological sensibilities that compelled al-Rāghib and al-Ghazālī to address this question. They were also motivated, however, by Muslims' practical need for knowledge of the licit means for the acquisition of wealth through commerce and the practice of crafts. What is most striking in much of al-Rāghib's varied *oeuvre* is his integration of traditional religious scholarship into a conceptual framework based on philosophical viewpoints and categories. Both al-Rāghib and al-Ghazālī have assimilated the philosophical arguments for the necessity of human society, and they justify these ideas not only by logical deduction, but also (and primarily) by divine and Prophetic pronouncements, such as the Prophetic proverb 'Men will not cease to prosper as long as they differ; if they become equal, they will perish'[23] and the *ḥadīth* 'Difference within my community is a blessing.'[24] Al-Rāghib and al-Ghazālī interpret these texts as references to differences in men's social functions and economic status, in most cases following little-known interpretations. This is evident in the following extract from the *Tafṣīl al-nash'atayn wa taḥṣīl al-sa'ādatayn* of al-Rāghib al-Iṣfahānī:[25]

On the difference and diversity of men.

All things are equal and not dissimilar insomuch as they are formed by wisdom. God Almighty alerted [mankind] to this when he said: 'You see no difference among the creatures of the Merciful' [67:3].[26] They are different, however, insomuch as each sort is distinguished by a special advantage, and although every sort is different, nothing differs as much as men, as God Almighty said: 'And he created you in stages (*aṭwāran*)' [71:14],[27] and 'And we elevated some of you above others by degrees'

[22] On al-Ghazālī's debt to al-Rāghib, see Madelung, 'Ar-Rāġib al-Iṣfahānī', pp. 152–155. Despite the paucity of biographical information available for al-Rāghib, it seems probable that, like many Iṣfahānīs of this day, he was a Shāfi'ī (Madelung, 'Ar-Rāġib al-Iṣfahānī', p. 158; Rowson, 'al-Rāghib al-Iṣfahānī', *EI2*); it is also worth noting that it appears to have been predominantly Shāfi'īs who followed him (Fakhr al-Dīn al-Rāzī and al-Bayḍāwī as well as al-Ghazālī).

[23] Al-Rāghib al-Iṣfahānī, *Tafṣīl al-nash'atayn*, p. 114; *idem, K. al-dharī'a ilā makārim al-sharī'a* (Beirut, 1400/1980), p. 264. On this *ḥadīth*, see ch. 1.

[24] Al-Ghazālī, *Iḥyā'*, vol. 2, p. 84. The latter *ḥadīth* originally referred to a difference of opinion among legal scholars (Goldziher, *Introduction to Islamic Theology and Law*, trs. A. and R. Hamori (Princeton, 1981), p. 48 (=*Vorlesungen über den Islam* (Heidelberg, 1910), p. 52); Goldziher, 'Catholic Tendencies and Particularism in Islam', in *Studies on Islam*, tr. and ed. M.L. Swartz (New York and Oxford, 1981), pp. 126–127).

[25] *Tafṣīl al-nash'atayn*, pp. 111–114. The idea that men's occupations, just like other aspects of their lives and destinies, are predetermined in accordance with divine wisdom is articulated throughout al-Rāghib's *oeuvre*; see also *Tafṣīl al-nash'atayn*, pp. 107–108; *al-Dharī'a*, pp. 262ff; *Mufradāt alfāẓ al-Qur'ān*, ed. Ṣafwān 'Adnān Dāwūdī (Damascus and Beirut, 1412/1992), pp. 184–185 (under the term *jabbār*).

[26] This interpretation is not inconsistent with al-Rāghib's brief discussion of the Qur'ānic use of the term *tafāwut* in his *Mufradāt*, p. 646, where he defines it as 'difference in characteristics'.

[27] For the standard commentators, the sense of *aṭwāran* is temporal: God's creation progressed from simple to increasingly compound substances (al-Zamakhsharī, *al-Kashshāf*, vol. 4 (1385/1966), p. 163; al-Bayḍāwī, *Anwār al-tanzīl*, vol. 2, p. 359; Ibn Kathīr, *Tafsīr*, vol. 7, p. 124).

[43:32].[28] God Almighty has also said: 'Behold how we favoured some of them over others, and the next world will be greater in degrees and greater in favour' [17:21].[29] He also said: 'Had God wished, he would have made you one community, yet he [made you as you are] that he might try you by that which he has given you' [5:48],[30] and 'It is he who made you viceroys in the earth and raised some of you above others in degrees, so that he might try you in that which he has given you' [6:165].[31] And he said also: 'Had your lord wished, he would have made mankind one community, yet they

This sense is also noted by al-Rāghib in his *Mufradāt*, where he finds support for it in Q. 22:5; but al-Rāghib's characteristic openness to wider interpretations is suggested by his view, expressed in the same work, that the phrase *aṭwāran* may denote differences in people's physical and moral dispositions (*khalq* and *khuluq*); in this latter connexion he links it with Q. 30:22, *wa-khtilāfu alsinatikum wa alwānikum* (*Mufradāt*, p. 528). Both senses are also noted by Abū'l-Futūḥ Rāzī, according to whom the term *aṭwāran* may be understood in a temporal sense or as a reference to the different categories (*aṣnāf*) and modes of existence (*akvān*) by which men are characterised, such that they may be black, white, red or yellow, Arab or non-Arab, tall or short, attractive or ugly, intelligent or stupid, and so on (*Rawḥ al-jinān*, vol. 11, p. 276). Al-Māwardī records the same pair of interpretations: the standard one, involving temporal development; and the secondary one, according to which the text refers to differences of stature, strength, aspiration and demeanour, wealth and poverty, disposition and deeds (*al-Nukat wa'l-'uyūn*, vol. 6, p. 102).

[28] For al-Bayḍāwī, the difference in divine favour is in sustenance and other unspecified matters (*Anwār al-tanzīl*, vol. 2, p. 238); for Ibn Kathīr, in wealth, sustenance, intellect, understanding, and other external and internal faculties (*Tafsīr*, vol. 6, p. 225). Al-Māwardī records five interpretations for the verse, the first three of which refer to differences in moral standing, such that one man is *fāḍil* while another is *mafḍūl*; to freedom and slavery; and to wealth and poverty (*al-Nukat wa'l-'uyūn*, vol. 5, pp. 223–224). In his *Mufradāt*, al-Rāghib notes that the verse may also refer to differences in station (*manzila*) (p. 361). Thus he appears here to reflect the general tenor of the mainstream commentaries, but to apply it to a specifically social context.

[29] According to al-Bayḍāwi, this verse refers to God's different favours in regard to sustenance, and to the greater differences among people in the afterlife, where people are consigned to the various levels of paradise and hell (*Anwār al-tanzīl*, vol. 1, p. 536). For Fakhr al-Dīn al-Rāzī, it refers to unspecified worldly goods which are bestowed on or withheld from believers and polytheists impartially in this world, although the different stations of the two categories will be clearly apparent in the next life (*al-Tafsīr al-kabīr*, vol. 20, p. 181). Ibn Kathīr interprets the verse as a reference to worldly differences of wealth and poverty, good looks and ugliness, early death and a long life, and so on (*Tafsīr*, vol. 4, p. 297). There is therefore some support in classical *tafsīr* for al-Rāghib's interpretation of this verse as a reference to social differences.

[30] The standard interpretation of this passage is that it refers to religious identity: God would have made all people in all periods followers of a single religion and a single law; or, had he wished all people to follow Islam, he would have compelled them to do so (al-Ṭabarī, *Jāmi' al-bayān*, vol. 10, pp. 389–390; al-Māwardī, *al-Nukat wa'l-'uyūn*, vol. 2, p. 45; al-Zamakhsharī, *al-Kashshāf*, vol. 1, p. 618; al-Bayḍāwī, *Anwār al-tanzīl*, vol. 1, pp. 260–261; Ibn Kathīr, *Tafsīr*, vol. 2, pp. 588–589). Al-Rāghib's use of 5:48 in this context is therefore rather contrived.

[31] Here al-Rāghib's interpretation is closer to those of the standard commentaries. For al-Ṭabarī, God elevates some men over others by favouring them in sustenance, wealth and riches, or strength (*Jāmi' al-bayān*, vol. 12, pp. 287–289). For al-Māwardī, he distinguishes some men by wealth, the nobility of their ancestors, and the strength of their bodies (*al-Nukat wa'l-'uyūn*, vol. 2, p. 197). For Fakhr al-Dīn al-Rāzī, he elevates them in nobility, intellect, rank (*jāh*) and sustenance (*al-Tafsīr al-kabīr*, vol. 14, p. 13). For al-Zamakhsharī, he raises some men above others in nobility and sustenance in order to test their gratitude for the wealth and rank that he has bestowed on them (*al-Kashshāf*, vol. 2, p. 65). For al-Bayḍāwī, God raises some men above others in terms of nobility and riches, so that he can test them in the degree of rank and wealth that he has given them (*Anwār al-tanzīl*, vol. 1, p. 317).

do not cease to differ, except him on whom your Lord has mercy' [11:118–119].[32] Similarly, God Almighty alerted mankind when he said: 'And in the earth are neighbouring tracts, vineyards and ploughed lands, and date-palms, both like and unlike, which are watered with one water. And we have favoured some over others in fruit. In this are portents for those who have sense' [13:4].[33]

The wisdom that should necessarily be inferred from this is that, since in his solitariness man cannot be self-sufficient, even if he were able to exist alone, his survival, even for the shortest time, would be impossible or difficult. For the first thing that man needs is something with which to cover himself and by which to nourish himself. He will not find such covering ready-made, nor such nourishment fully prepared, as is the case for many animals. Instead, he is forced to manufacture them. This manufacture requires tools, which are likewise not readily available. Thus one man has not the means to prepare all that he needs to live a praiseworthy life. So men have no option but to share and co-operate. Therefore God assigns a task to each group, together with a condition unsuitable for other occupations. In this way, men divide occupations amongst themselves, each adopts a category of occupations and practises [his own] with enthusiasm. As God has said: 'But they [mankind] have broken their religion among them into sects, each group rejoicing in its tenets' [23:53].[34] Wisdom requires that their bodies, faculties and aspirations differ, and 'each one is enabled to do that for which he was created'.[35] God Almighty said: 'Say: each one does according to his

32 Again, the more usual interpretation refers to religion: had God willed, he would have made all men Muslims, but instead some follow truth and others falsehood (al-Ṭabarī, *Jāmiʿ al-bayān*, vol. 15, pp. 531ff; al-Zamakhsharī, *al-Kashshāf*, vol. 2, p. 298, where the verse is taken as evidence that God has given human beings the capacity to choose truth or falsehood for themselves; Fakhr al-Dīn al-Rāzī, *al-Tafsīr al-kabīr*, vol. 18, pp. 76ff; al-Bayḍāwī, *Anwār al-tanzīl*, vol. 1, p. 450, where the verse is taken as proof that faith is not voluntary but divinely created; Ibn Kathīr, *Tafsīr*, vol. 3, p. 586). It is worth noting that in his *Mufradāt*, al-Rāghib himself refers only to faith in his discussion of this verse (p. 86). Fakhr al-Dīn al-Rāzī understands the verse to refer to differences in religion, moral disposition and deeds, and thus reflects a somewhat broader interpretation of the verse; he nevertheless argues against an understanding of the passage as a reference to differences in colour, language, sustenance and occupations (*aʿmāl*) (*al-Tafsīr al-kabīr*, p. 77). Al-Ṭabarī and Ibn Kathīr report – and then reject – a view ascribed to al-Ḥasan al-Baṣrī, according to which the verse refers to difference in sustenance and to the subjugation of some people by others (*yusakhkhir baʿḍuhum baʿḍan*; cf. Q.43:32) (al-Ṭabarī, *Jāmiʿ al-bayān*, vol. 15, pp. 534–535; Ibn Kathīr, *Tafsīr*, vol. 3, p. 586). These interpretations suggest that al-Māwardī (see above) and al-Rāghib were not alone in seeing a reference to social differences in this verse, although they were hardly following the mainstream interpretation. (It is of interest that in his own work of commentary, al-Māwardī does not refer to such an interpretation (*al-Nukat wa'l-ʿuyūn*, vol. 2, p. 511).)

33 For al-Zamakhsharī, al-Bayḍāwī and Ibn Kathīr, the references are to the differences in the natural properties of the earth and in the vegetation it produces, and these differences are signs of God's power and wisdom; they draw no analogies with differences among human beings (*al-Kashshāf*, vol. 2, p. 349; *Anwār al-tanzīl*, vol. 1, pp. 475–476; *Tafsīr*, vol. 4, pp. 67–68). For al-Ṭabarī, however, the phrase *ṣinwān wa ghayr ṣinwān* may refer to the different moral dispositions of men (*Jāmiʿ al-bayān*, vol. 16, pp. 338ff).

34 For Shaykh al-Ṭā'ifa al-Ṭūsī and al-Bayḍāwī, the significance of this verse does not extend beyond the religious sphere: people differ in religion, and all are certain that they possess the truth (al-Ṭūsī, *al-Tibyān*, vol. 7, p. 375; al-Bayḍāwī, *Anwār al-tanzīl*, vol. 2, pp. 8, 107; for another use of this verse, see ch. 2). Al-Māwardī also records a secondary interpretation, according to which the verse refers to each group's enjoyment of its wealth and offspring (*al-Nukat wa'l-ʿuyūn*, vol. 4, p. 57).

35 This is one of al-Rāghib's favourite *ḥadīth*s in this connexion; cf. *Tafṣīl al-nash'atayn*,

rule of conduct (*'alā shākilatihi*)' [17:84],[36] so that [the provision of] men's livelihoods is divided among them as God has recounted in the verses quoted above. And the Almighty said: 'Had your lord wished, he would have made mankind one community, yet they do not cease to differ, except him on whom your lord has mercy' [11:118–119].[37] The resulting difference is evident. And men, when the difference of their goals and aspirations is considered, are more-or-less predestined in their occupations, even though they are apparently free to choose. The Prophet . . . has indicated the wellbeing that is dependent on their difference and the diversity of their strata in his words: 'Men will not cease to prosper as long as they differ; if they become equal, they will perish.'[38]

The ways in which al-Rāghib uses these passages from the Qur'ān can be considered in three ways. Firstly, he may make use of a verse that can, without too great a stretch of the imagination, be made to yield a socio-economic significance within the tradition of formal *tafsīr*, such as 43:32, which, according to many commentators, may refer among other things to wealth (this also applies to 17:21 and 6:165). Here, then, al-Rāghib is expanding on an interpretation that is generally recognised as plausible. Secondly, he may take a verse that all agree refers to differences among people, such as 11:118–119; but whereas the classical commentators interpret such verses as references to differences in religion, al-Rāghib uses them to make his argument about socio-economic and occupational differences (the same applies to 5:48, 23:53 and 17:84). Thirdly, he sometimes takes a verse which is generally regarded as referring neither to wealth nor to socio-economic differences, such as 71:14, and expands its meaning in a way that might be regarded as rather contrived (this is true also of 13:4).

Al-Rāghib al-Iṣfahānī discusses the issues of social and economic differences at greater length in his *al-Dharī'a ilā makārim al-sharī'a*, where he

pp. 107–108; *al-Dharī'a*, p. 263; *Mufradāt*, pp. 462–463. For its more usual predestinarian uses, see van Ess, *Zwischen Ḥadīṯ und Theologie* (Berlin, 1975), pp. 39–47.

36 This is one of al-Rāghib's favourite Qur'ānic passages in his treatments of human differences, and he frequently adduces it, as here, in conjunction with the *muyassar ḥadīth*. In his *Mufradāt*, al-Rāghib paraphrases the verse by saying that each person acts according to the limitations of his nature (*'alā sajiyyatihi allatī qayyadathu*); he also refers the reader to his discussion of the verse in his *Dharī'a* (*al-Dharī'a*, p. 264; *Mufradāt*, pp. 462–463). Elsewhere in his *Tafṣīl al-nash'atayn* (pp. 107–108), al-Rāghib uses the verse to argue that God creates a known position (*maqāman ma'lūman*) for each type of human being, just as he does for the angels. The standard commentaries see in this verse a reference to religious differences, not to social or professional ones. For al-Zamakhsharī and al-Bayḍāwī, everyone acts according to his own way (*madhhab*, *ṭarīqa*), which is conditioned by divine guidance or its opposite, leading astray (*al-Kashshāf*, vol. 2, p. 464; *Anwār al-tanzīl*, vol. 1, p. 549). Al-Bayḍāwī also records an alternative interpretation that fits rather better with al-Rāghib's use of the text: according to this view, one's *ṭarīqa* might be formed by the essence of one's soul and the consequences of one's bodily composition; in addition, al-Bayḍāwī notes that the term *shākila* has been interpreted to mean one's nature (*ṭabī'a*), custom and religion. Ibn Kathīr records some of the same interpretations, but concludes that they all amount to the same thing: a warning and threat to the polytheists (Ibn Kathīr, *Tafsīr*, vol. 4, p. 344).

37 Repeated from above.

38 Al-Rāghib quotes the same aphorism, which appears in many collections of proverbs, in *al-Dharī'a*, p. 264.

devotes a chapter to occupations and means of acquiring wealth.[39] Here, too, he assumes that man is incapable of providing for the least of his needs without the help of other members of his species, and that therefore it is essential for men to gather together in groups in order to support each other. Since man is by nature a social being, men need each other for their religious and worldly interests. Al-Rāghib supports this philosophical premise by adducing the *ḥadīth*, 'The believers are like a single edifice, one part bracing the other',[40] and 'The believers, in their mutual love, affection and sympathy, are like a single body; when one part suffers pain, the other parts respond to it.'[41]

Also in this chapter, al-Rāghib expands on the theory that God has determined the various occupations that men adopt: 'Since men are in need of each other, God has designated each one of them without exception for some occupation that he can practise, and has created hidden correspondences and divine conformities between their own natures and their occupations, so that each one in his turn prefers a certain profession, delights in being associated with it, and devotes his powers to its pursuit.'[42] Had God not thus determined men's interests, all men would have chosen the same occupation; they would have chosen only the best things for themselves, only the most pleasant places to live, only the cleanest of occupations, and only the most exalted of tasks. This would have led inevitably to strife. In his wisdom, however, God had created men in such a way that the weaver was satisfied with his occupation and considered that of the cupper blameworthy, while the cupper was content with his own occupation and deemed that of the weaver contemptible.[43] In support of this view, al-Rāghib adduces several of the same Qur'ānic passages and *ḥadīth* that he uses in the *Tafṣīl al-nash'atayn*.[44] 'For in such a matter, to be distinct from one another, dissimilar and different is a cause of cohesion, joining and agreement; in just this way, without difference between them, the shapes used in writing would have no order.' Therefore, it was the duty of anyone whom God had led to a lawful occupation to maintain it, as the Prophet had said: 'Whoever gains his livelihood from something should stick to it.'[45]

A brief statement to the same effect is also found in al-Ghazālī's 'Book of Good Conduct in the Acquisition of Wealth and Earning a Livelihood'. Here, as in many parts of the *Iḥyā'*, al-Ghazālī apparently bases his account on that contained in the *Dharī'a*. He advises merchants and other men involved in professions to persist in their trades, 'for if occupations and trades were aban-

[39] I am grateful to Roy Mottahedeh for making available to me his unpublished translation of this chapter of the *Dharī'a*. I have followed his felicitous wording in the passages quoted below.

[40] Al-Bukhārī, *Ṣaḥīḥ*, vol. 1, *ṣalāt*, p. 122; vol. 8, *adab*, p. 14; Ibn Ḥanbal, *Musnad*, vol. 4, pp. 405, 409.

[41] Ibn Ḥanbal, *Musnad*, vol. 4, pp. 268, 270, 271, 274, 276. This and the preceding *ḥadīth* are cited in *al-Dharī'a*, p. 262.

[42] *Al-Dharī'a*, p. 263.

[43] Here al-Rāghib's argument closely resembles the view of al-Jāḥiẓ in his *Ḥujaj al-nubuwwa*, *Rasā'il*, vol. 3, pp. 242–243.

[44] Q. 23:53; 43:32; 25:20; 17:84; the *ḥadīth* reports 'Each one is enabled to do that for which he was created' and 'Men will not cease to prosper as long as they are distinct from one another; if they become equal, they will perish'; *al-Dharī'a*, pp. 263–264.

[45] *Al-Dharī'a*, p. 264.

doned, livelihoods would be lost, and most men would perish; for the order of things in general derives from the co-operation of all, and the assigning of a specific task to each group. If all were to engage in one craft, the rest would fall idle and perish'. It was for this reason, al-Ghazālī claimed, that certain (unspecified) people interpreted the *ḥadīth*, 'Difference within my community is a blessing' as a specific reference to 'the difference in their aspirations for occupations and professions'.[46] The same argument appears in a Shīʿite context in the *Akhlāq-i Nāṣirī*. Naṣīr al-Dīn Ṭūsī reasons that in order to fulfil men's several needs, divine wisdom creates a diversity of human purposes, aspirations and opinions, so that some men aspire to noble occupations, and others to base ones. He also considers the disparities of wealth and intelligence among people to be preordained, in order that all, rich and poor, intelligent and stupid, should become mutually dependent, since 'if all men were equal, they would all perish'.[47]

Also in his *Dharīʿa*, al-Rāghib al-Iṣfahānī seeks to justify the seeming injustice of God's creation of discrepancies in wealth among the members of the community. Only poverty or the fear of it, he maintains, could induce men to strive, endure hard work, and perform services of benefit to other people, whether by choice or by necessity. If each man could meet his own needs alone, no one would undertake any task for anyone else, and this would result in the decay of the world and universal poverty.[48] Only three occupations subsisted on the basis of wealth: rulership, commerce and the secretarial art. All the remainder were founded on poverty or the fear of it; for otherwise, who would undertake such tasks as weaving, cupping, dyeing and sweeping, and the transport of provisions and clothes? In support of his argument for the necessity of poverty, al-Rāghib then quotes the Qur'ānic verse: 'And if God were to enlarge the provision for his servants, they would surely rebel in the earth, [but he sends down in the measure that he wills]' (42:27); to this verse he refers anyone who is perplexed by the fact that the generous and all-providing God chooses some of his creatures for wealth and others for poverty.[49]

[46] *Iḥyā'*, vol. 2, p. 84. Here al-Ghazālī anticipates a common modernist interpretation (Goldzhiher, 'Catholic Tendencies and Particularism', p. 136).

[47] *Akhlāq*, pp. 249–251; tr. Wickens, *Nasirean Ethics*, pp. 189–190.

[48] A similar argument is proposed by Isḥāq b. Ibrāhīm al-Kātib (writing after 335/946), who states that if God gave each person what he wanted, then everyone would belong to the highest social category and the noblest rank, and no one would need anyone else any more, so that they would cease to support each other and to co-operate with one another (*al-Burhān fī wujūh al-bayān*, eds. A. Maṭlūb and Kh. al-Ḥadīthī (Baghdad, 1387/1967), pp. 271–272; I owe this reference to Michael Cook).

[49] *Al-Dharīʿa*, pp. 264–265. In this case al-Rāghib's interpretation matches the views of mainstream commentators; cf. al-Bayḍāwī, *Anwār al-tanzīl*, vol. 2, p. 231, and al-Ṭūsī, *al-Tibyān*, vol. 9, p. 162, where the somewhat curious argument is made that if God had bestowed his bounty equally on all people, they would not be content with what they had but would compete with each other and seek to dominate one another, with the result that human existence would be fraught with corruption, killing, attempts at subjugation and securing financial assistance; instead, God had made some people rich and others poor, for the sake of the common good (*maṣlaḥa*). Al-Jāḥiẓ also assumes that disparities of wealth are part of the divine plan (*Ḥujaj al-nubuwwa*, *Rasā'il*, vol. 3, p. 242).

Al-Rāghib goes on to discuss God's equipping of human beings with the necessary intellectual and physical instruments to enable them to pursue the professions towards which he has already directed their aspirations. To those whom he has destined for the pursuit of religious knowledge and the preservation of religion, he gives pure hearts and intellects with the appropriate skills, subtle temperaments, and delicate and suitable bodies; to those destined for worldly professions, such as agriculture and construction, he gives hard hearts, rigid intellects, harsh temperaments and tough bodies. Those created for a practical profession will therefore never be suited to philosophy. Whatever their preordained task, the highest type of men are those who strive for skill in their occupations, apply themselves to their work, and seek the pleasure of God to the best of their abilities. This point is emphasised by the Qur'ānic quotations: 'Men whom commerce and sale do not distract from the remembrance of God' [24:37] and '(The angels) . . . who do not disobey God in that which he has commanded them, but do as they have been commanded' [66:6], and the *ḥadīth*, 'God loves the skilful worker.'[50]

Al-Rāghib also sets out to establish the earning of one's livelihood as a duty. He recounts the well-known anecdote concerning 'Umar b. al-Khaṭṭāb, in which, on encountering a man of substance, 'Umar is reported to have asked, 'Has he got a profession?'; if the answer was negative, the man fell in 'Umar's estimation.[51] Similarly, the Prophet is said to have asked the delegation from 'Abd al-Qays what passed for manliness (*muruwwa*) among them, and to have approved of their reply: 'Temperance and a profession (*al-'iffa wa'l-ḥirfa*).'[52] The Prophet is alleged to have said, 'God loves the believing craftsman (*al-mu'min al-muḥtarif*)',[53] and 'God loves the honest merchant and the sincere artisan, for he is wise.'[54]

Al-Ghazālī, whose discussion of the subject of social inequalities in many places parallels that of al-Rāghib, establishes the excellence of acquiring wealth, by reference to the Qur'ān, *ḥadīth* and *āthār*, at the beginning of his book on occupations. In his opinion, only four groups of men are exempt from the requirement to provide for themselves: those whose bodies are occupied with the worship of God; mystics; those who instruct others in the external aspects of religion, such as *muftī*s, Qur'ān reciters, traditionists and so on; and

50 *Al-Dharī'a*, pp. 265–266; al-Ghazālī, *Iḥyā'*, vol. 2, p. 63.

51 *Al-Dharī'a*, p. 267. Elsewhere, 'Umar is said to have expressed the opinion that earning one's livelihood through the practice of a craft is superior to begging (al-Jāḥiẓ, *al-Bayān wa'l-tabyīn*, vol. 2, p. 81).

52 *Al-Dharī'a*, p. 267; *Muḥāḍarāt al-udabā'*, vol. 2, p. 459; cf. al-Jāḥiẓ, *al-Bayān wa'l-tabyīn*, vol. 2, p. 176, where the saying is ascribed to al-Aḥnaf, but the Prophet is not mentioned. R. al-Sayyid has suggested reading *ḥurma* for *ḥirfa* (Ibn al-Ḥaddād, *al-Jawhar al-nafīs*, p. 50).

53 Al-Kulīnī, *al-Kāfī*, vol. 5, p. 113 (ascribed to 'Alī); al-Muttaqī, *Kanz al-'ummāl*, vol. 4, p. 4, no. 9199; p. 10, no. 9239; al-Ghazālī, *Iḥyā'*, vol. 2, p. 63.

54 Al-Rāghib al-Iṣfahānī, *Muḥāḍarāt al-udabā'*, vol. 2, p. 459. Cf. the several *ḥadīth* which praise the man who lives by the labour of his own hands (al-Muttaqī, *Kanz al-'ummāl*, vol. 4, p. 4, nos. 9195, 9196; p. 8, nos. 9220, 9222, 9223; p. 9, nos. 9228, 9229, 9234; p. 13, no. 9253).

those engaged in effecting the good of the Muslim community, such as rulers, judges, witnesses and so on. He observes that in these cases, it is desirable that such persons receive nourishment from the hands of others.[55]

Having established that the differences between men's possessions and occupations are natural, advantageous and ordained by God, al-Rāghib al-Iṣfahānī and al-Ghazālī go on to discuss 'the divisions of occupations, their ranks and specific excellences'. Al-Rāghib's discussion of this subject is of an abstract and philosophical nature; al-Ghazālī, on the other hand, focuses chiefly on the cleanliness of the various professions. These subjects will be treated in the following chapter.

The authors considered in this chapter were able to combine philosophical explanations of human differences with their own predestinarian understanding of the social order, and thus to produce rational theologies in order to substantiate hierarchical realities. One striking feature of these theologies is that although the moralists took great pains to prove that a diversity of occupations was necessary for the common good, they never considered why it was that equality of need did not coincide with equal social esteem. They did not ask, for example, why it should be that weavers and cuppers were despised while those who practised non-manual occupations were honoured, although both were equally vital to the functioning of society. In many instances, this difference in the social standing that accompanied different tasks is simply ignored. Elsewhere, the lowly nature of the 'base' occupations is taken for granted, and the only issue is why anyone should be motivated to adopt such a craft: were such persons base by nature, or was it poverty that compelled them to undertake such repellent tasks? In short, the arguments for social inequalities presented by the moralists are largely vindications of the status quo; in this respect they echo and complement to some extent the better-known discussions of the legitimacy of government found in the writings of Sunnī political thinkers.

55 *Iḥyā'*, vol. 2, pp. 63–66; cf. Ritter, 'Handbuch', p. 32.

CHAPTER 7

Hierarchies of occupations

This chapter is devoted to the perceptions held by those who lived in the pre-modern Middle East of various crafts and occupations. Occupation was among the most significant principles for social differentiation in Muslim societies as elsewhere.[1] From varying perspectives, philosophers, legal scholars, officials and men of letters addressed the question of the social prestige attached to certain crafts and professions. The impact of such judgements was enhanced by the fact that, although it was neither a legal requirement nor a universal practice, there was a strong tendency in pre-modern societies for sons to enter the professions of their fathers, and this was widely considered to be socially desirable.[2]

The materials discussed in this chapter are drawn from a particularly wide geographical area and cover several centuries. The fact that so many ways of thinking about occupations, some of them amounting to prejudices, reappear in several parts of the Islamic world and in several areas of the tradition should not, however, be taken to suggest that the societies from which they were drawn were all alike or that they were unchanging. Instead, they give some impression of the common constraints under which members of pre-modern societies functioned. Assessing people's social status on the basis of their occupations was a part of life, as indeed it is today; in addition, occupations were widely regarded as indicators of a person's moral standing, in spite of a strong religious principle that gave no sanction to this trend. The actual degree of contempt in which any particular craft or occupation was held naturally varied from one region to another. But in societies in which a person's livelihood depended in large part on the esteem in which he was held by those around him, it was impossible to ignore the general principle that occupations were associated with social and moral stature for almost everyone.

[1] Cf. Rodinson, 'Classes sociales', p. 143; Karpat, 'Some Historical and Methodological Considerations', pp. 83–84.

[2] See for example Ikhwān al-Ṣafā', *Rasā'il Ikhwān al-Ṣafā'*, vol. 1, pp. 291–292, and al-Ḥasan b. 'Abd Allāh al-'Abbāsī, *Āthār al-uwal fī tartīb al-duwal* (Cairo, 1295/1878), p. 41; cf. S.D. Goitein, 'The Working People of the Mediterranean Area during the High Middle Ages', *Studies in Islamic History and Institutions* (Leiden, 1966), pp. 260–61, 267–69, 278, and al-Sayyid, *Mafāhīm al-jamā'āt*, p. 106.

For the most part, the literature under discussion here is concerned with manual occupations and crafts (variously termed *ṣināʿa*, *ḥirfa*, *mihna*), and was generated not by the practitioners of such crafts themselves but by rather better-off men who were in a position to be able to observe them. In the Islamic world as elsewhere, manual occupations were frequently despised (cf. *m.h.n*, 'to be low, base, menial').[3] But this contempt was somewhat tempered by the widespread view that crafts spanned a spectrum in which those at one end were despicable while those at the other were at least relatively 'noble'. The tendency to differentiate precisely between various means of earning a livelihood seems to be consistent with what may have been a common attitude among craftsmen themselves. Although circumstances might sometimes bring them together, artisans and manual workers did not typically constitute unified social groups with a sense of a shared professional identity and common interests. In eleventh- and twelfth-century Cairo (and doubtless elsewhere) there were significant distinctions between the masters of the higher crafts, who often worked with their own capital or formed partnerships, and those of little means, hired labourers and the poor.[4] There was also no firm distinction between merchants and artisans as those who produced commodities were often also responsible for selling them, and even large-scale merchants resorted to craftsmanship when business was slow.[5] Yet despite the lack of a general *esprit de corps* or of organised professional structures in the period under discussion, observers frequently referred to the practitioners of specific crafts as collectivities. In this connexion, it is worth noting the common recommendation that certain crafts should be concentrated in special areas of the market.[6]

If the literature on occupations reflects a tendency to belittle and even vilify manual occupations, it also preserves elements that point to a respect for earning an honest living through the practice of a craft. Such down-to-earth sentiments, which seem to have been intended to counter ascetic trends rather

[3] Cf. Goldzhiher, 'Die Handwerke bei den Arabern', *Globus* 46 (1894), pp. 203–205; Sadan, 'Kings and Craftsmen: A Pattern of Contrasts', *SI* 62 (1985), p. 90. An amusing example of the prejudice against practitioners of manual crafts may be found in a story told about al-Sakkākī, who was originally a metal-worker (see F. Krenkow, 'al-Sakkākī', *EI*1; I owe this reference to W. Heinrichs). On the evolution of attitudes towards manual labour, see M. Shatzmiller, *Labour in the Medieval Islamic World* (Leiden, 1994), pp. 369–398, and al-Sayyid, *Mafāhīm al-jamāʿāt*, pp. 82ff.

[4] Goitein, 'Working People', pp. 277–78; on the division of labour and specialisation, see further Shatzmiller, *Labour*, pp. 200ff.

[5] Goitein, 'Working People', pp. 273–74; Shatzmiller, *Labour*, p. 261.

[6] See, for example, the views of two twelfth-century authors, the Syrian al-Shayzarī and the Spanish Ibn ʿAbdūn (*Nihāyat al-rutba fī ṭalab al-ḥisba*, p. 11; *Risālat Ibn ʿAbdūn fī'l-qaḍā' wa'l-ḥisba*, ed. É. Lévi-Provençal, *Trois traités hispaniques de ḥisba* (Paris, 1955), p. 43). Their recommendation is apparently intended as a general rule, although most authors of *ḥisba* manuals are concerned chiefly with the matter of safety when they stipulate that certain professions should be practised at a distance from others. For some examples of the confinement of crafts to separate areas of the market in practice, see al-Sayyid, *Mafāhīm al-jamāʿāt*, pp. 86–87, and also Goitein, 'Working People', pp. 258–60.

than the general élitist contempt for labour,[7] are often articulated in the form of traditions attributed to the Prophet and the early caliphs. Also common are associations of the prophets and esteemed figures of the early Islamic period with specific occupations.[8]

Theoretical classifications of crafts

One of the most widely attested classifications of occupations from the classical period enumerates four valuable social functions: rulership (*siyāda*, *imāra*), craftsmanship, commerce and agriculture. As Radwan al-Sayyid has shown, this model seems to have originated in early Ḥanafī circles in response to certain interpretations of the Ṣūfī ideal of *tawakkul* and as an attempt to demonstrate the legitimacy of government and government service.[9] It appears in the work of al-Shaybānī (132–189/749–805), for whom the four occupations are equal in value;[10] it is also attested in the writings of al-Jāḥiẓ.[11] Later authors cite the classification as a *bon mot*, frequently attributed to al-Ma'mūn, and add the common refrain that anyone who did not practise one of these four professions was dependent on those who did, muddied the waters, and caused prices to rise.[12] It is striking that while these four kinds of occupation are often mentioned together, they are not always valued equally. The *Kitāb al-ḥathth ʿalā al-tijāra* of the Ḥanbalī Aḥmad al-Khallāl (d. 311/942) refers only to commerce and manual crafts; this is in keeping with the strong urban following of the Ḥanbalīs.[13] Al-Māwardī emphasises the importance of commerce and craftsmanship, but also discusses the merits of agriculture and animal husbandry, and describes agriculture as the base of the other three occupations.[14] Here he follows the line of thought said by al-Shaybānī to have been espoused by the majority of the scholars of his circle, that agriculture was superior to commerce on account of its greater useful-

[7] See al-Māwardī, *Tashīl al-naẓar*, pp. 50–52; Kinberg, 'Compromise of Commerce' pp. 193–212; R. Gramlich, *Die Nahrung der Herzen* (Stuttgart, 1994), vol. 2, pp. 330ff; van Ess, *Die Gedankenwelt des Ḥāriṯ al-Muḥāsibī* (Bonn, 1961), pp. 99ff; F. Khuri, 'Work in Islamic Thought', *al-Abhath* 21 (1968), pp. 3–13.

[8] Al-Shaybānī, *Kitāb al-kasb*, pp. 34ff; Ibn Qutayba, *al-Maʿārif*, pp. 575–577; al-Bayhaqī, *al-Maḥāsin wa'l-masāwī*, p. 103; al-Jāḥiẓ, *al-Maḥāsin wa'l-aḍdād*, p. 127; Ibn al-Jawzī, *Talbīs Iblīs* (Cairo, n.d.), pp. 281–282. See also al-Sayyid, *Mafāhīm al-jamāʿāt*, pp. 83, 89, 104.

[9] Al-Māwardī, *Tashīl al-naẓar*, pp. 49–52; al-Sayyid, *Mafāhīm al-jamāʿāt*, pp. 83, 89. See also Brunschvig, 'Métiers vils', pp. 146–147.

[10] Al-Shaybānī, *Kitāb al-kasb*, p. 63 (reading *imāra* for *ijāra*).

[11] *Ḥujaj al-nubuwwa*, in *Rasā'il al-Jāḥiẓ*, vol. 3, p. 242.

[12] Al-Rāghib al-Iṣfahānī, *Muḥāḍarāt al-udabā'*, vol. 2, p. 459 (without attribution); al-Bayhaqī, *al-Maḥāsin wa'l-masāwī*, p. 103 (attributed to al-Ma'mūn); *al-Maḥāsin wa'l-aḍdād*, p. 127 (attributed to al-Ma'mūn); al-Māwardī, *Adab al-dunyā wa'l-īn*, p. 224 (attributed to al-Ma'mūn); Ibn al-Fuwaṭī (attrib.), *al-Ḥawādith al-jāmiʿa wa'l-tajārib al-nāfiʿa fī'l-miʾa al-sābiʿa*, ed. M. Jawād (Baghdad, 1351/1932), p. 343 (attributed to Naṣīr al-Dīn al-Ṭūsī). For the appearance of this aphorism in an Ottoman source, see Inalcik, 'Comments on "Sultanism"', pp. 69–70, n. 45.

[13] Al-Māwardī, *Tashīl al-naẓar*, pp. 52–53; Shatzmiller, *Labour*, pp. 377ff.

[14] *Adab al-dunyā wa'l-dīn*, pp. 224–226.

ness.[15] Al-Māwardī divides occupations into those involving thought (*ṣināʿat fikr*), those involving action (*ṣināʿat ʿamal*), and those that combine thought and action (*ṣināʿa mushtarika bayn al-fikr waʾl-ʿamal*), and clearly does not attach equal value to these types. The crafts of thought, among which he classifies the arts of government and learning, are at the apex of the hierarchy of crafts.[16] It is interesting to note that he regards commerce as a subdivision of the two basic activities of agriculture and production, despite his obvious urban inclinations and the stance of much of the Islamic tradition.[17] He ranks the secretarial art, together with the builder's craft, among those occupations that combine action and thought, although he notes that in the former it is thought that predominates and in the latter, action.[18]

According to a second configuration, found principally in the works of philosophers and those who adopted philosophical ideas, the three essential occupations were those that fulfilled universal human requirements most directly: agriculture, weaving and building. These three occupations appear together in the works of al-Jāḥiẓ, the Ikhwān al-Ṣafāʾ and Ibn Taymiyya.[19] Again, to these three, many writers add a fourth occupation: leadership (*siyāsa*), which is considered the noblest of all. In accordance with the philosophical impulse to demonstrate logical correspondences among the various known phenomena, several thinkers subdivide these four categories into lesser hierarchies. Al-Rāghib al-Iṣfahānī, al-Ghazālī and Quṭb al-Dīn Shīrāzī divide the category of leadership into four levels of authority, corresponding to the ranks of prophets, rulers, philosophers (*ḥukamāʾ*), and preachers and religious scholars.[20] They employ the metaphor of the human body to portray the relative ranks of each type of occupation: agriculture, weaving and building correspond to the heart, liver and brain (the 'roots' of the body); secondary occupations correspond to the subordinate organs of the stomach, veins and arteries; tertiary activities correspond to the hands and eyebrows, which complete and adorn the body.[21] According to the Ikhwān al-Ṣafāʾ, for each of the essential occupations, there are several subsidiary and subordinate (*tābiʿ*, *khādim*) ones. According to this system, agriculture requires irrigation, canal-digging, carpentry, smithery and so on; weaving requires spinning and

[15] *Kitāb al-kasb*, pp. 64–65. Al-Shaybānī cites as a *ḥadīth* the saying, 'The best of people is he who is most useful to others' (p. 65). The same view is expressed by al-Rāghib al-Iṣfahānī, *al-Dharīʿa*, p. 272.

[16] *Adab al-dunyā waʾl-dīn*, pp. 226–227; see also the diagram in al-Sayyid, *Tashīl al-naẓar*, p. 56, and al-Sayyid's comments, pp. 58ff. On al-Māwardī's treatment of knowledge, see pp. 63ff.

[17] *Adab al-dunyā waʾl-dīn*, p. 226; al-Māwardī, *Tashīl al-naẓar*, p. 57.

[18] *Adab al-dunyā waʾl-dīn*, p. 227; al-Māwardī, *Tashīl al-naẓar*, pp. 54–55, p. 61.

[19] *Ḥujaj al-nubuwwa*, in *Rasāʾil al-Jāḥiẓ*, vol. 3, p. 243; *Rasāʾil Ikhwān al-Ṣafāʾ*, vol. 1, p. 284; Ibn Taymiyya, *al-Ḥisba fīʾl-Islām* (Beirut, 1412/1992), pp. 26, 29. Cf. al-Māwardī, *Tashīl al-naẓar*, pp. 55–56, 59.

[20] *Al-Dharīʿa*, pp. 270–271; *Iḥyāʾ*, vol. 1, pp. 13–14; *Durrat al-tāj*, vol. 1, pp. 50–51. Fakhr al-Dīn al-Rāzī distinguishes between only three levels of government: that of kings and their deputies, that practised by the *ʿulamāʾ*, and that of prophets (*Jāmiʿ al-ʿulūm*, ed. M. Ḥ. Tasbīḥī (Tehran, 1346), p. 205).

[21] *Al-Dharīʿa*, p. 271; *Iḥyāʾ*, vol. 1, p. 14; *Durrat al-tāj*, vol. 1, pp. 50–51.

carding. Beneath these subsidiary occupations is a third level of tasks by which they are completed and perfected, such as cookery, sewing, bleaching, mending and embroidery. The Ikhwān al-Ṣafā' include a fourth level of occupations, the sole purpose of which is adornment; in this category they list lace-making, the manufacturing of silk, perfume-making and so on.[22]

Within these major occupational categories, the Ikhwān al-Ṣafā' make several further distinctions of rank based on the materials used in each profession, the products created by it, the need for such products, the benefits they bring about, and the intrinsic nature of an occupation.[23] The material used by those who practised different professions might be either spiritual (*rūḥānī*), as in intellectual occupations, or corporeal (*jismānī*), as in practical crafts. If corporeal, it might be simple – that is, it might use one of the four primary elements, or a combination of them; or compound – that is, it might use mineral, vegetable or animal matter.[24] Crafts might also be distinguished by the tools and instruments they required. Some occupations needed only various organs of the human body; some demanded one tool, others two, still others required many tools.[25]

In his commercial handbook *al-Ishāra ilā maḥāsin al-tijāra*, a work of a more practical orientation, the fifth/eleventh-century author Ja'far b. 'Alī al-Dimashqī, who was probably a merchant based in Fāṭimid Egypt, also presents a philosophical classification of the professions.[26] He distinguishes between theoretical and practical occupations; among the former he includes jurisprudence, grammar, geometry and the like, and among the latter (which he describes as 'crafts' (*mihan*)), weaving, agriculture, wool- and cotton-carding and so on.[27] A man could earn his living by commerce, the practice of

[22] Ikhwān al-Ṣafā', *Rasā'il*, vol. 1, pp. 284–285; cf. Lewis, 'An Epistle on Manual Crafts', *IC* 17 (1943), pp. 142–151. See also the discussion of Ibn Khaldūn, tr. Rosenthal, *The Muqaddimah*, vol. 2, pp. 355–356.

[23] The view that a craft's nobility depends partially on the nobility of the materials employed in it is a common one; see al-Rāghib al-Iṣfahānī, *al-Dharī'a*, p. 272, and Ṣalāḥ al-Dīn al-Nāhī, *al-Khawālid min ārā' al-Rāghib al-Isfahānī* (Amman and Beirut, 1407/1987), pp. 118–119; and Ja'far b. 'Alī al-Dimashqī, *Kitāb al-ishāra ilā maḥāsin al-tijāra* (Cairo, 1318/1900), p. 42, where one reads that the doctor is superior to the carpenter, because the material on which the former works is the human body rather than wood, and because his purpose is to preserve and restore health rather than to fashion beds and doors.

[24] Ikhwān al-Ṣafā', *Rasā'il*, vol. 1, pp. 280–282; cf. Miskawayh, *Tahdhīb al-akhlāq*, p. 37, tr. Zurayk, *The Refinement of Character*, p. 34.

[25] Ikhwān al-Ṣafā', *Rasā'il*, vol. 1, pp. 282–284.

[26] Ritter, 'Handbuch', pp. 2–3; C. Cahen, 'A propos et autour d'"Ein arabisches Handbuch der Handelswissenschaft"', *Oriens* 15 (1962), pp. 160–62. The author of this text owes much to the Arabic translation of *Bryson*, and perhaps to other translated philosophical sources; see Ritter, 'Handbuch', pp. 8–14; Plessner, *Der Oikonomikos*, pp. 29–39; Cahen, 'A propos', pp. 167ff.

[27] *Ishāra*, pp. 39, 43. Cf. Kay Kā'ūs, 'There are many occupations . . . yet, regardless of the particular characteristics of an occupation, it falls into one of three types: it may involve a body of knowledge that is applied to a practical craft; it may involve a practical skill from which a body of knowledge is derived; or it may consist of a practical skill (independent of any theoretical knowledge).' Among the occupations of the first type Kay Kā'ūs lists medicine, astrology, geometry, surveying, poetics and the like; among the second, he lists minstrelsy, veterinary science, construction and canal-digging (*Qābūsnāmeh*, (ed.) Gh. M. Yūsufī (Tehran, 1368), pp. 157–158).

an occupation, or a combination of both. In what appears to have been a theoretical distinction rather than a reference to recognised professional categories, al-Dimashqī states that those whose earnings were acquired by commerce included the travelling merchant (*rakkāḍ*), the wholesaler (*khazzān*) and the exporter (*mujahhiz*).[28] The practical occupations reflected men's needs, which were of two sorts: necessary and natural, such as the needs for housing, clothing and food, and incidental and circumstantial (*waḍʿiyya*), such as the need for some means of defence against enemies, and medicines. The fulfilment of any one of these needs entailed a number of occupations, both for production and for completion. A crop, for example, had to be sown, watered, tended during its growth and reaped, after which a further series of activities was necessary depending on the use to which the crop was to be put. In this way, various occupations were linked: the builder needed the services of the carpenter, the carpenter those of the ironsmith, the ironsmith those of the miner; and carpenters, ironsmiths and miners all depended on the services of the builder. It was this mutual need, al-Dimashqī notes, that led to the foundation of cities.[29]

Naṣīr al-Dīn Ṭūsī divides occupations into three ranked categories: noble, base and intermediate.[30] The highest category is that of the 'occupations of noble and manly persons' (*ṣināʿāt-i aḥrār va arbāb-i muruvvat*), who are themselves of three kinds. The first subcategory consists of occupations that depend on the substance of the intellect, such as sound opinion, apposite counsel and good administration; these are the occupations of ministers. The second group consists of occupations that depend on cultivation and learning, such as writing, rhetoric, astrology, medicine, accountancy and surveying; these are the occupations of men of culture and learning. The third subcategory comprises occupations that depend on strength and courage, such as horsemanship, military command, the control of the frontiers, and defence against enemies; these are the occupations of chivalry.

Ṭūsī also subdivides the base occupations into three kinds. The first group includes activities repugnant to the general welfare, such as practising a monopoly and sorcery; these are the occupations of the wicked. The second group comprises activities repugnant to virtue, such as tomfoolery, minstrelsy and gambling; these are the occupations of fools. The third subcategory consists of activities repugnant to human nature, such as cupping, tanning and street-sweeping; these are the occupations of the abject. Ṭūsī notes that such base occupations, though repugnant to human nature, are not abhorrent to

[28] *Ishāra*, p. 40; Ritter, 'Handbuch', pp. 6, 15, 58; Cahen, 'A propos', p. 166.

[29] *Ishāra*, p. 4; cf. Ritter, 'Handbuch', pp. 10–11, where the similarities between this passage and a comparable one in Ibn Abīʾl-Rabīʿ's *Sulūk al-mālik* are noted, and a common source for the two texts is posited. The passage echoes closely the exposition of the author of *Bryson* (Plessner, *Der Oikonomikos*, p. 148).

[30] *Akhlāq*, pp. 211–212; tr. Wickens, *Nasirean Ethics*, p. 158. Cf. Plessner, *Der Oikonomikos*, pp. 65–66.

the intelligence, since it was, after all, necessary that some men perform these tasks.

Any occupation that belongs neither to the noble nor to the base group of categories is of intermediate status. This rank of professions includes necessary occupations, such as agriculture, and unnecessary ones, such as dyeing; simple occupations, such as carpentry and blacksmithery, and compound ones, such as scale-making and the cutler's trade.

Probably the most striking feature of this material is its banality. These efforts to classify and rank occupations may perhaps be considered in conjunction with the rather apologetic philosophical–theological outlook discussed in the previous chapter, since they too could be used to justify the status quo. In some cases, however, these classifications seem to bear little relation to social realities. Certainly they could have been of little comfort or indeed interest to the street-sweeper and the tanner, whose professions, in the opinion of many, marked them as socially, intellectually and morally base.

Prejudices against 'base' occupations

As suggested above, the literature on occupations contains many instances in which authors tend to equate social status with intellectual and moral qualities. Perhaps most notably, al-Jāḥiẓ, in several of his works, implies that men who practise 'base' occupations are themselves morally corrupt. In his *Risāla fī manāqib al-turk*, probably composed during the reign of al-Muʿtaṣim (218–227/833–842), he observes that every cupper on earth, regardless of his race (*jins*) and the region from which he originates, loves wine; in the same way, rag-sellers, fishmongers, cattle dealers and weavers are in all cases the worst of God's creation when it comes to the conclusion of contracts and transactions. Al-Jāḥiẓ suggests, then, that this kind of moral deficiency is a natural and inseparable part of these trades, so that those who practise them are predisposed to develop such flaws.[31] He echoes a similar prejudice when he claims that Christians are popular with the common people because they engage in elevated professions and become secretaries to rulers, servants to kings, doctors to the notables, druggists and money changers; Jews, on the other hand, are found in the base professions, as dyers, tanners, cuppers, butchers or repairers of cracked utensils.[32] Al-Jāḥiẓ also notes the power of religion to transcend such distinctions in status: religion makes the weaver and the peasant equal, and creates equality among people of different lineages and

[31] *Risāla fī manāqib al-turk*, in *Rasāʾil al-Jāḥiẓ*, vol. 3, pp. 209–210. See also *Kitāb fīʾl-awṭān waʾl-buldān*, *Rasāʾil al-Jāḥiẓ*, vol. 4, pp. 127–28, where the same crafts, and especially weaving, are associated with dishonesty; al-Jāḥiẓ again insists that weaving is the same thing no matter where it is practised, and this implies that it is the craft itself that engenders the propensity to swindle.

[32] *Al-radd ʿalā al-naṣārā*, *Rasāʾil al-Jāḥiẓ*, vol. 3, p. 316. On the ethnic aspects of labour, see Shatzmiller, *Labour*, pp. 327–346.

from different regions; it was this sense of equality, based on strong religiosity, that made the Khawārij such ferocious fighters.[33]

Despite the absence of any religious prohibition, weaving and cupping appear in many parts of the tradition to represent paradigmatically base occupations. The degree of contempt in which cuppers and weavers were held varied from region to region and from time to time, and they were not the only groups singled out as despicable. But weaving and cupping are frequently mentioned together to connote the lowest of all occupations. In Baghdad, Abū'l-ʿAtāhiya (130–210/748–825), himself a cupper's son, insisted that piety ennobled even the weaver and the cupper.[34] On the basis of the Prophetic *ḥadīth*, 'Men are equal (*al-nās akfāʾ*), except for the weaver and the cupper', some legal scholars, particularly those of the Ḥanafī school, accorded weavers and cuppers a lower status in marriage equality (*kafāʾa*) and the capacity to give legal testimony (*ʿadāla*).[35] ʿAlī, elsewhere the spokesman for egalitarian and meritocratic principles, is said to have regarded weavers as hostile to religion and positively sinister.[36] Other *ḥadīth* reflect efforts to rehabilitate weavers and cuppers, however; at least some attempt was made to counter the prevailing distaste for the latter profession by having the Prophet pay his cupper.[37] The shame cast upon weaving in popular Iraqi culture contrasts with the high value attached to that craft in the philosophical tradition, where agriculture, weaving and building supply the three fundamental needs of mankind. It might perhaps belong to a cultural continuum that also included the brāhmanic contempt for weaving and other manual crafts; certainly it appears to have been less pronounced in the western Islamic world, and in medieval Alexandria, weavers became well-to-do and were apparently regarded as respectable.[38]

There is also evidence in many parts of the Islamic tradition of a prejudice against hirelings. One of the chief criticisms levelled against the secretaries by

[33] Al-Jāḥiẓ, *Manāqib al-turk*, p. 209.

[34] Abū'l-Faraj al-Iṣfahānī, *Kitāb al-aghānī* (Cairo), vol. 4 (1350/1931), p. 5; Goldziher, 'Handwerke', p. 205, n. 33.

[35] Brunschvig, 'Métiers vils', pp. 150, 159–164; and see below.

[36] Goldziher, 'Handwerke', p. 205; Brunschvig, 'Métiers vils', p. 156. Similar examples are cited in van Ess, *Theologie und Gesellschaft*, vol. 2, p. 239.

[37] The reports on cupping reflect both popular contempt for the profession and attempts to counter it; see al-Bukhārī, *Ṣaḥīḥ*, vol. 1, pt. 3, *buyūʿ*, pp. 78–79, 115; Abū Dāʾūd, *Sunan*, vol. 2, *nikāḥ*, p. 233, no. 2102; *buyūʿ*, vol. 3, p. 266, nos. 3423, 3424, and contrast p. 266, no. 3421; Ibn Māja, *Sunan*, *tijārāt*, ch. 10, p. 731, nos, 2162, 2163, 2164, although contrast p. 732, no. 2165; al-Kulīnī, *al-Kāfī*, vol. 5, pp. 115–116, but see also p. 114, no. 5, and p. 115, no. 6; al-Muttaqī, *Kanz al-ʿummāl*, vol. 4, p. 128, no. 9873; p. 137, no. 9899. See also al-Ḥārith b. Asad al-Muḥāsibī, *al-Makāsib*, ed. ʿAbd al-Qādir Aḥmad ʿAṭā (Beirut, 1407/1987), pp. 88–89; Brunschvig, 'Métiers vils', p. 153. On weaving, the *ḥadīth* reports again reflect some attempts to present the craft in a positive light. According to one *ḥadīth*, weaving is considered the best occupation for women, and sewing for men (al-Muttaqī, *Kanz al-ʿummāl*, vol. 4, p. 31, no. 9347; Brunschvig, 'Métiers vils', p. 149). See also Sadan, 'Kings and Craftsmen', *SI* 62 (1985), p. 95, n. 148, and Serjeant, 'Social Stratification in Arabia', *The Islamic City* (ed. R.B. Serjeant) (Paris, 1980), pp. 130, 141, n. 1, on the disagreements over the status of weaving in South Arabian sources.

[38] Brunschvig, 'Métiers vils', p. 158, n. 3; p. 161; Goitein, 'Working Class', p. 263; cf. Sadan, 'Kings and Craftsmen', *SI* 62 (1985), p. 90, n. 133.

the author of the *Dhamm akhlāq al-kuttāb*, as has already been noted, was that they were servile.[39] Contempt for persons who worked for others, as suggested by the saying 'A free man does not live under the constraint of another', seems to have been widespread.[40]

Jaʿfar b. ʿAlī al-Dimashqī reflects the common urban view that a man's occupation is of considerable importance in determining his social status. He holds that some occupations ennoble and elevate those who practise them, and goes so far as to claim that such professions enable men to dispense with lofty connexions and noble offices which can only be acquired through rivalry and competition. Other occupations debase and weaken those who practise them, so that they have no prospect of achieving rank or social eligibility for marriage (*kafāʾa*), even if they are the descendants of old families and trace their lineage to well-known ancestors.[41] Jaʿfar cites here the meritocratic maxims 'The value of a man is that in which he is proficient', and 'Men are the sons of that in which they are proficient.'[42] He observes that the occupations deemed reprehensible by the 'best philosophers' are those that necessitate frequent association with women and children, since this impairs men's intellects and judgement; those that demand attention to putrefying objects, fish and dirt, since this has a detrimental effect on both mind and body; arduous tasks, such as conveying burdens; and menial services, which bring disgrace to all who undertake them.[43]

Jaʿfar apparently regards these aspects of professional activity as merely socially disabling; many contemporary legal scholars consider them morally disabling as well. In the introduction to his 'Book of Good Conduct in the Acquisition of Wealth and Earning a Livelihood', al-Ghazālī divides men into three groups according to the spiritual value of their occupations: those whose work provides for their earthly livelihood but at the cost of their ultimate salvation (these people are bound for perdition); those whose work ensures their salvation but does not provide for their earthly livelihood (these are among the saved); and those whose work provides for their earthly livelihood and at the same time directs them towards their salvation (this is the middle path). He regards this last type of occupation as most suitable for the majority of mankind.[44] Al-Ghazālī's further discussion of the moral values of various professions reflects many of the popular perceptions and prejudices apparent in al-Jāḥiẓ's and Jaʿfar's enumerations of reprehensible occupations.

In his fifth chapter,[45] al-Ghazālī describes several desirable and undesirable professions. He recommends the adoption of an 'important' occupation, rather than a 'dispensable' one (that is, one that has as its purpose worldly

39 See ch. 4. 40 Crone, *Pre-Industrial Societies*, pp. 31–32.
41 *Ishāra*, p. 41. Cf. Ritter, 'Handbuch', p. 60; Ziadeh, 'Equality (*Kafāʾa*)', pp. 512–514; Brunschvig, 'Métiers vils', pp. 159–164; Goitein, 'Working People', p. 263.
42 *Ishāra*, p. 41; Ritter, 'Handbuch', p. 60; see ch. 1.
43 *Ishāra*, p. 43; Ritter, 'Handbuch', pp. 61–62.
44 *Iḥyāʾ*, vol. 2, p. 62; Ritter, 'Handbuch', p. 31.
45 Much of this chapter is reproduced from the *Qūt al-qulūb* of Abū Ṭālib al-Makkī (d. 386/996); see Gramlich, *Die Nahrung der Herzen*, vol. 3, pp. 610ff, and Brunschvig, 'Métiers vils', p. 149.

bounties and adornment). He advocates the avoidance of painting, goldsmithery, plastering, and all activities by which the world is adorned, since such things are despised by men of religion. Naturally, the manufacture of musical instruments and other forbidden items should also be abandoned.[46] Al-Ghazālī considers the sale of foodstuffs and shrouds reprehensible, since they cause inflation and induce men to desire the death of their fellows; he also disapproves of butchery and goldsmithery, because they harden the heart and lead to the adornment of the world with gold and silver respectively.[47]

In his preoccupation with the cleanliness of professions, and also reflecting popular prejudice, al-Ghazālī discourages the despised occupations of the tanner, cupper and sweeper.[48] According to some authorities, he notes, the professions of brokerage, selling animals and money-changing[49] are also undesirable. Dealing in cloth, the trade of Abū Bakr, is considered especially praiseworthy on account of its cleanliness. According to a *ḥadīth*, 'If the people of paradise practised a trade it would be in cloth, and if the people of Hell practised a trade, it would be money-changing.'[50] The ten most frequent occupations among the best of the *salaf* are listed as leatherwork, commerce, transporting, tailoring, cobbling, fulling, making slippers, ironsmithery, making spindles, hunting and fishing, and copying. Aḥmad b. Ḥanbal is said to have asked ʿAbd al-Wahhāb al-Warrāq (d. c. 251/865) his occupation, and on learning that he was a copyist, said: 'A good means of earning; if I worked with my hands, I would adopt your craft.'[51]

46 Cf. Serjeant, 'A Zaidī Manual of Ḥisbah of the Third Century', *RSO*, 28 (1953), p. 17; Abū Ya'lā Muḥammad b. al-Ḥusayn al-Farrā', *al-Aḥkām al-sulṭāniyya* (Beirut, 1403/1983), p. 294; al-Māwardī, *Aḥkām*, p. 282; Ibn al-Ukhuwwa, *Ma'ālim al-qurba fī aḥkām al-ḥisba*, ed. R. Levy (London, 1938), pp. 35, 12.

47 *Iḥyā'*, vol. 2, pp. 75, 85; Gramlich, *Die Nahrung der Herzen*, vol. 3, p. 622; cf. al-Kulīnī, *al-Kāfī*, vol. 5, p. 144, no. 4. On the reprehensible nature of selling foodstuffs, cf. al-Muttaqī, *Kanz al-ʿummāl*, vol. 4, p. 33, no. 9361; Ibn al-Ukhuwwa, *Ma'ālim al-qurba*, pp. 67, 22; Ritter, 'Handbuch', pp. 29, 42; Brunschvig, 'Métiers vils', p. 150.

48 These occupations are also linked in a medieval Yemeni source (Serjeant, 'Social Stratification in Arabia'). See also Gerholm, *Market, Mosque and Mafraj*, pp. 131–132, and Crone, *Roman, Provincial and Islamic Law*, p. 50, where it is suggested that the low esteem in which these crafts are held in Islamic law may perpetuate a pre-Islamic prejudice.

49 This last profession is considered particularly dangerous (see, for example, al-Shayzarī, *Nihāyat al-rutba fī ṭalab al-ḥisba*, p. 74).

50 Numerous *ḥadīth* express praise for traders in cloth (e.g. al-Muttaqī, *Kanz al-ʿummāl*, vol. 4, p. 31, no. 9346; p. 32, nos. 9349 [with spices], 9356 [with straw]; p. 33, nos. 9360, 9361; cf. Ritter 'Handbuch', p. 29; Brunschvig, 'Métiers vils', p. 149). Abraham is said to have been a cloth merchant, and the Prophet is reported to have encouraged Muslims to adopt the same profession (Goitein, 'The Rise of the Middle Eastern Bourgeoisie in Early Islamic Times', *Studies in Islamic History and Institutions* (Leiden, 1966), p. 222, n. 3). Cf. the aphorism quoted by al-Jāḥiẓ: 'The best craft (*ṣinā'a*) is in silk cloth (*khazz*), and the best commerce (*tijāra*) is in cloth (*bazz*)' (*Kitāb al-tabaṣṣur bi'l-tijāra* (Cairo, 1966), p. 13 (see Pellat, 'Ǧāḥiẓiana, I: Le *kitāb al-tabaṣṣur bi-l-tiǧāra* attribué à Ǧāḥiẓ', *Arabica* I (1954), pp. 153–54)). Expressions of contempt for money-changing are extremely common, although a somewhat more tolerant view is attributed to the imām al-Bāqir (al-Kulīnī, *al-Kāfī*, vol. 5, pp. 113–114).

51 *Iḥyā'*, vol. 2, p. 85; Gramlich, *Die Nahrung der Herzen*, vol. 3, p. 623. (The exchange is not recorded in Ibn Abī Ya'lā, *Ṭabaqāt al-Ḥanābila*, ed. M.Ḥ. al-Fiqī (Cairo, 1371/1952), vol. 1, pp. 209–212.)

Al-Ghazālī reflects common prejudices in his disdain for 'base' occupations. He notes that the practitioners of four crafts are generally associated with weak judgement: weavers, cotton manufacturers, spinners and teachers. He suggests that the reason for this phenomenon is that such people associate mostly with women and children, whose judgement is similarly weak.[52] He also cites the tradition according to which Mary cursed weavers, because one (or several) of them had shown her the wrong path in her search for Jesus.[53]

The *ḥisba* literature

Authors of treatises and manuals on *ḥisba* (market inspection) are generally less interested in theoretical expositions of the classifications of professions than in the practical difficulties presented to the *muḥtasib* (market inspector) by each craft.[54] They assume that not only weavers and dyers, but practitioners of all professions are liable to behave disreputably, and the *muḥtasib* should therefore be vigilant with merchants and artisans of all kinds. Nevertheless, some authors on the subject of *ḥisba* seem to take for granted the popular prejudices against practitioners of certain trades, and their writings suggest an acute consciousness of social rank.

One author who emphasises the need for the *muḥtasib* to understand the social differences among those with whom he comes into contact is the still unidentified North African writer al-Jarsīfī, who wrote after the year 1278 and appears to have lived in Spain.[55] In his opinion, those who followed 'low' trades were not like the practitioners of delicate crafts, and they should therefore be given more severe punishments; by drawing a parallel with the distinction between a bold, reckless man and a stupid, ignorant man, al-Jarsīfī appears to associate the practice of a low craft with lack of intellect and understanding, and perhaps with meanness of character and general wickedness as well.[56] Al-Jarsīfī also urges the *muḥtasib* to be particularly alert to offences involving persons of rank.[57] His list of importunate persons who should not be permitted to enter people's houses includes barbers (*ḥajjāmūn*,

[52] *Iḥyā'*, vol. 2, p. 85; Gramlich, *Die Nahrung der Herzen*, vol. 3, p. 623; cf. al-Dimashqī, *Ishāra*, p. 43. Al-Shayzarī and Ibn al-Ukhuwwa advise that cotton-spinners, flax-spinners and spindle-makers should be forbidden to allow women to sit at their doors and to converse with them, presumably for fear that sexual indiscretions may result from such contact (*Nihāyat al-rutba fī ṭalab al-ḥisba*, pp. 69, 70; *Ma'ālim al-qurba*, pp. 142, 143, 225, 46, 90). On the role of women themselves in spinning, see Shatzmiller, 'Aspects of Women's Participation in the Economic Life of Later Medieval Islam: Occupations and Mentalities', *Arabica* 35 (1988), pp. 45–46.

[53] Ibn Ḥanbal, *Musnad*, vol. 5, p. 382; *Iḥyā'*, vol. 2, p. 85; Brunschvig, 'Métiers vils', pp. 156–157.

[54] On the information to be gleaned from the *ḥisba* literature on the organisation of crafts, see al-Sayyid, *Mafāhīm al-jamā'āt*, pp. 98ff.

[55] Wickens, 'Al-Jarsīfī on the *ḥisba*', *IQ* 3 (1956), p. 176, n. 1; J.D. Latham, 'Observations on the Text and Translation of al-Jarsifi's Treatise on "Hisba"', *JSS* 5 (1960), p. 125.

[56] Al-Jarsīfī, *Risāla fī'l-ḥisba*, in *Trois traités hispaniques de ḥisba*, ed. É. Lévi-Provençal (Paris, 1955), p. 127; tr. Wickens, 'Al-Jarsīfī', p. 186.

[57] Al-Jarsīfī, *Risāla fī'l-ḥisba*, p. 123; Wickens, 'al-Jarsīfī', p. 182, n. 1.

'cuppers')[58] and spinners as well as fortune-tellers, soothsayers, herbalists, clowns, effeminate perverts, people of loose morals and so on, and thus reflects popular distaste for certain professions as well as for dissolute characters.[59]

Ibn al-Ukhuwwa (d. 729/1329), whose *Ma'ālim al-qurba fī aḥkām al-ḥisba* appears to be an enlarged version of al-Shayzarī's *Nihāyat al-rutba* adapted to an Egyptian enviroment,[60] is also noticeably concerned with questions of social rank. Water-carriers, he writes, when giving customers water to drink, should give them pots appropriate to their stations, and men of high rank should be given new pots from which no one else has drunk.[61] He also states that, since wearing one's hair in long, loose locks is the mark of noble families (*ahl al-sharaf*), no one who does not belong to such a family should be allowed to imitate this fashion; otherwise, it is a form of deception.[62] Furthermore Ibn al-Ukhuwwa takes up the issue of the fitness of practitioners of base professions (among whom he includes cuppers, weavers, watchmen, bath-attendants, refuse collectors, butchers, fishmongers and other men who come into contact with unclean things) to serve as witnesses. He notes that according to one opinion, the practice of a base profession precludes the acceptance of evidence, since it is an indication of inferior intelligence.[63] According to another view, their testimony can be accepted, since these people practise their professions out of necessity rather than choice. A third opinion distinguishes between occupations considered contemptible on religious grounds, and those – such as weaving – which are regarded as base from a worldly point of view only; according to this view, the testimony of those who practise professions of the latter sort is valid. Ibn al-Ukhuwwa notes that some scholars introduce a further distinction between a man born into an occupation and one who has chosen it for himself.[64] This last idea suggests that the social opprobrium attached to certain professions might be mitigated in the light of the common tendency for occupations to be hereditary.

If authors on *ḥisba* reflect popular prejudices against certain professions, they single out others for praise. Al-Shayzarī and Ibn al-Ukhuwwa describe veterinary medicine (*bayṭara*), elsewhere regarded as contemptible, as a noble

[58] For the occupation of the *ḥajjām* in Andalusia, see Lévi-Provençal, *Séville musulmane au début du xiie siècle* (Paris, 1947), p. 154, n. 136a; Latham, 'Observations', p. 137.

[59] Al-Jarsīfī, *Risāla fī'l-ḥisba*, p. 123; Wickens, 'Al-Jarsīfī', p. 182; Latham, 'Observations', pp. 136–137. [60] Cahen, 'Ibn al-Ukhuwwa', *EI2*. [61] *Ma'ālim al-qurba*, pp. 239, 97.

[62] *Ma'ālim al-qurba*, pp. 199, 77.

[63] *li-anna ikhtiyārahum li-hādhihi al-ṣinā'a . . . dalīl 'alā khasfi 'uqūlihim* (*Ma'ālim al-qurba*, p. 215).

[64] *Ma'ālim al-qurba*, pp. 215, 86; cf. Brunschvig, 'Métiers vils', pp. 161–162. Ibn 'Abd al-Ra'ūf includes many of the same categories in his list of practitioners of unclean professions, and notes that they should not be permitted to sell bread, nor to perform their work next to bakers and sellers of bread and milk (*Risāla fī ādāb al-ḥisba wa'l-muḥtasib*, ed. É. Lévi-Provençal, *Trois traités hispaniques de ḥisba* (Paris, 1955), pp. 90, 92; cf. Lévi-Provençal, 'Un document sur la vie urbaine et les corps de métiers à Séville au début du XIIe siècle: le traité d'Ibn 'Abdūn', *JA* 224 (1934), pp. 177–192).

science (*ʿilm jalīl*) worthy of considerable scholarly attention.[65] They also consider medicine a valuable profession, since it involves both theoretical and practical knowledge and is permitted by the law.[66] Ibn al-Ukhuwwa regrets the fact that many Muslims prefer the study of jurisprudence, so that in many towns *dhimmī* doctors, whose testimony cannot be accepted, are the only ones available.[67] But he also regards teaching as the noblest of the professions, a view for which he invokes the *ḥadīth* 'The best of you are those who learn the Qur'ān and teach it', and 'The best men who walk the earth are the teachers, who, when religion deteriorates, renew it.'[68]

Naturally enough, Ibn al-Ukhuwwa follows *sharʿī* principles in insisting on the equality of all free Muslim men before the law. In his chapter on judges and witnesses, he quotes ʿUmar as saying, 'Make all men equal in your sight, in your court and in your equity, so that the strong may not hope to procure your unjust dealing nor the weak despair of your justice.'[69] It is interesting to note, however, that in cases of misdemeanours for which there are no statutory penalties, Ibn al-Ukhuwwa recommends disparity in punishment according to the social rank of the offender. The punishment (*ta'dīb*) for persons of high social standing who are otherwise respectable (*dhaw[ū] al-hay'a min ahl al-ṣiyāna*) should be milder than that for people characterised by disgusting language and stupidity. Punishment should be graded according to the social rank of the miscreant: a man of high rank should be ostracised; a man of lesser rank should be rebuked verbally; members of the lower classes should be imprisoned according to the status (*rutba*) of the offender and the nature of the offence.[70] Here Ibn al-Ukhuwwa, despite his reference to the general religious principle of equality before the divine law, goes well beyond the legal inequality of slaves and free Muslims sanctioned by the *sharīʿa*. This is a clear indication of the distinction between the principles of equality in God's eyes and hierarchy in this world.

The sword and the pen

A rather different method of classifying professions is that which distinguishes between the occupations of the 'sword' and those of the 'pen', emblems of the military and civilian functions of government respectively. These categories are a standard feature of social models from the seventh/thirteenth century

[65] *Nihāyat al-rutba fī ṭalab al-ḥisba*, p. 80; *Maʿālim al-qurba*, pp. 150, p. 49. For the opposite point of view, see for example al-Jāḥiẓ, *Ḥujaj al-nubuwwa*, *Rasā'il*, vol. 3, p. 242; Brunschvig, 'Métiers vils', p. 160. [66] *Nihāyat al-rutba fī ṭalab al-ḥisba*, p. 97.

[67] *Maʿālim al-qurba*, pp. 165–166, 56–57. [68] *Maʿālim al-qurba*, p. 170.

[69] *Maʿālim al-qurba*, pp. 202, 79; cf. pp. 218, 87.

[70] *Maʿālim al-qurba*, pp. 191, 73–74. Ibn ʿAbdūn instructs the *muḥtasib* to overlook misdemeanours only in the case of men of rank, and cites the *ḥadīth* that runs *aqīlū dhawī'l-hay'āt [ʿatharātihim]* (*Risāla fī'l-qaḍā' wa'l-ḥisba*, ed. É. Lévi-Provençal, *Trois traités hispaniques de ḥisba* (Paris, 1955), p. 17).

onwards, especially in the Perso-Islamic world,[71] but they appear together in poetry as early as the early third/ninth century.[72] The pen is initially regarded as the symbol of secretaries and the *adab* cultural tradition, but by the fifth/eleventh century it seems to have been widely understood to include the *'ulamā'* and the world of religious learning as well. According to Jaʿfar b. ʿAlī al-Dimashqī, for example, the professions associated with the sword and the pen are the most illustrious of occupations, since it is by the sword and pen that the world is ruled. Among those whose leadership is exercised through the sword Jaʿfar lists rulers, military governors, chamberlains, military commanders, the heads of families and the chiefs of tribes; among those whose leadership is exercised through the pen he lists viziers, secretaries, judges, preachers and so on. Jaʿfar describes the former as 'protectors (*ḥumāt*)', and the latter as 'men of competence (*kufāt*)'.[73] The anonymous sixth/twelfth-century author of the *Baḥr al-favā'id*, anxious to establish the legitimacy of government, also writes that 'the stability of the faith and of Islam depends on the religious scholars, who determine what is lawful and unlawful. The stability of religion and of the community depends on rulers, who distinguish between justice and injustice. For this reason, it has been said, "The pen and the sword are brothers, and neither can dispense with the other".'[74] The inclusion of both scribal and religious functionaries among the 'men of the pen' may reflect the breakdown in many settings by early medieval times of the once clear distinction between clerks and scholars.

For some, despite the partial erosion of the cultural division between scholars and bureacrats, a sharp disparity between the world of the court and that of religious scholarship appears to have remained. Ḥasan b. ʿAbd al-Mu'min al-Khū'ī, whose commitment to the secretarial art was strong enough for him to compose two manuals on the subject in the late seventh/thirteenth century, perceives a fundamental distinction between those associated with political power (*arkān-i dawlat*) and those dedicated to upholding religion (*aʿyān-i dīn*). In both his compositions, he lists secretaries and bureaucrats attached to the central government (*aṣḥāb-i qalam, ṣudūr-i dīvān*) in the first category, together with sultans, kings, viziers and military commanders (*umarā'*);[75] he also

[71] Naṣīr al-Dīn Ṭūsī's social model, discussed in the introduction, is the best example; and elsewhere, Ṭūsī reports that 'the foundations of the kingdom depend on two things, the sword and the pen, of which the former is in the hand of the military, and the latter in the hand of the scribes' (Minovi and Minorsky, 'Naṣīr al-Dīn Ṭūsī on Finance', pp. 756, 770).

[72] Goldziher, 'Über Dualtitel', *WZKM* 13 (1899), p. 322; G.J. van Gelder, 'The Conceit of Pen and Sword: On an Arabic Literary Debate', *JSS* 32 (1987), pp. 340f, n. 44.

[73] Cf. Goldziher, 'Über Dualtitel', pp. 326–327. Jaʿfar goes on to make the rather surprising remark that anyone whose occupation did not fall into either of these two categories would not be remembered with honour (*Ishāra*, pp. 42–43). Cf. the advice, 'Do not let your son concern himself with anything other than the sword and the pen' (al-Mubārak b. Khalīl al-Mawṣilī, *Adab al-siyāsa bi'l-ʿadl*, ms. Köpr, 1200, f.46a).

[74] *Baḥr al-favā'id*, p. 428; Meisami, *Sea of Precious Virtues*, p. 294.

[75] *Ghunyat al-kātib*, pp. 13–14; *Rusūm al-rasā'il wa nujūm al-faḍā'il*, published in the same volume, pp. 12–13.

includes provincial officials and master craftsmen (*muḥtarifeh*) in this group, although he assigns them to a lower level.[76] Ḥasan places religious figures and functionaries of all kinds in the second category. Rather surprisingly, he also lists physicians, astronomers, poets and men of letters in this group, despite the fact that such persons were frequently attached to royal and other high-placed patrons.

Throughout the Islamic world, the sword and pen were used as symbols of the military and civilian branches of government at least since the third/ninth century, when they appear both in court protocol and in courtly literature. Ceremonial swords or pens were frequently bestowed as marks of honour on prominent servants of the state; al-Muʿtaḍid (279–289/892–902), for example, bestowed two swords on his general Isḥāq b. Kandaj, who consequently acquired the soubriquet *dhū'l-sayfayn*,[77] while the vizier Mu'ayyad al-Dīn b. al-ʿAlqamī (d. 656/1258) received a set of pens from the caliph al-Mustaʿṣim (640–656/1242–1258).[78] Under the Īlkhāns, the vizier Rashīd al-Dīn Faḍl Allāh (697–717/1298–1317) is alleged to have continued this tradition by sending, together with other gifts, a ceremonial ink-pot to Ṣadr al-Dīn Muḥammad Turka, who had dedicated a book to him.[79]

Rulers also bestowed on their officials titles in which the two symbols were mentioned or suggested. Although it was in many contexts unusual for viziers to hold permanent military command, several titles for viziers, such as *dhū'l-riyāsatayn*,[80] *dhū'l-kifāyatayn*[81] and *dhū'l-wizāratayn*,[82] referred to the combination of the military and civilian functions.[83] Sometimes these two functions were called 'the two virtues'; Abū'l-Ḥusayn al-ʿUtbī, the vizier of the Sāmānid Nūḥ b. Manṣūr (366–387/977–997), was called *ṣāḥib faḍīlatay al-sayf wa'l-qalam*, and Abū Bakr Mu'ayyad al-Mulk, a son of Niẓām al-Mulk, was said to 'combine the virtue of the sword with the manners (*ādāb*) of the pen'.[84] The combination of the military and civilian functions, described by the sword and the pen, was sometimes identified as the distinguishing feature of the vizierate of delegation (*wizārat al-tafwīḍ*); the vizierate of execution (*wizārat al-tanfīdh*)

[76] *Ghunyat al-kātib*, pp. 9–11; *Rusūm al-rasā'il*, pp. 8–9.
[77] Goldziher, 'Über Dualtitel', p. 325, n. 3.
[78] M. b. Shākir al-Kutubī, *Fawāt al-wafayāt wa'l-dhayl ʿalayhā*, ed. I. ʿAbbās (Beirut), vol. 3 (1973), p. 253; Ibn al-Fuwaṭī (attrib.), *al-Ḥawādith al-jāmiʿa*, p. 249.
[79] Rashīd al-Dīn, *Mukātabāt-i Rashīdī*, pp. 240–244.
[80] Held by al-Faḍl b. Sahl (Goldziher, 'Über Dualtitel', p. 325, n. 2; cf. Goitein, 'The Origin of the Vizierate and its True Character', *Studies in Islamic History and Institutions* (Leiden, 1966), p. 186).
[81] Ibn al-ʿAmīd (Goldziher, 'Über Dualtitel', pp. 326–328).
[82] Goldziher, 'Über Dualtitel', pp. 324, 325, n. 4; Goitein, 'Origin of the Vizierate', p. 189.
[83] Khālid b. Barmak is said to have been the first person 'to combine the duties of military governor and civil collector of taxes' (al-Thaʿālibī, *Laṭā'if al-maʿārif*, p. 20; tr. Bosworth, *The Book of Curious and Entertaining Information*, p. 49; Goldziher 'Über Dualtitel', pp. 327f). Yaḥyā the Barmakid was both *wazīr* and *amīr*, and was described by al-Ṭabarī as combining 'the two vizierates' (Goitein, 'Origin of the Vizierate', p. 183, n. 5). Ismāʿīl b. Bulbul (d. 278/892) was also said to combine the sword and pen (Ibn al-Ṭiqṭiqā, *K. al-fakhrī*, p. 298; cf. van Gelder, 'Conceit', p. 345, n. 59).
[84] Nāṣir al-Dīn Kirmānī, *Nasā'im al-asḥār*, pp. 36, 52.

required lesser qualifications.[85] Major officials other than viziers might also acquire such titles; in 539/1144–1145, the governor of Hurmuz, Muḥammad b. al-Marzubān, was known as 'master of the sword and the pen'.[86]

The metaphors of the sword and pen are prominent in the court literature of the medieval period. They may be presented as equals, or one may be placed in a superior rank to the other. These various positions are summarised by Ibn al-Ṭiqṭiqā in his *Kitāb al-fakhrī*, dedicated to Fakhr al-Dīn 'Īsā of Mawṣil and completed in 701/1301:

The realm is guarded by the sword and administered by the pen. There is difference of opinion concerning which of the two, the sword or the pen, is superior and more worthy of favour (*taqdīm*). One group considers the pen dominant over the sword; they argue that the sword protects the pen, and is therefore its guardian and servant; another group considers the sword to be dominant and argues that the pen serves the sword, because it procures sustenance for those who wield swords, as a servant would. Another group maintains that the two are equal, and that neither one can dispense with the other. They hold that the realm is made fertile by generosity and made prosperous by justice, made firm by the intellect, preserved by courage, and ruled by leadership. They say, 'Courage is for the possessor of the state.'[87]

In a discussion of the same topic, Ibn Khaldūn analyses the importance of the sword and pen at various stages in the development of a dynasty.[88]

Authors of mirrors for princes frequently exemplify Ibn al-Ṭiqṭiqā's third position, and portray the military and bureaucratic functions in government as partners, neither of the pair being able to dispense with the other. Yūsuf Khāṣṣ Ḥājib, for example, records the following verse:

It is a virtue to know wisdom
And a plus to wield the sword:
The sword it is that conquers
And the pen that reaps reward.[89]

Similarly, in his *Chahār maqāleh* (c. 550/1155), Niẓāmī 'Arūḍī Samarqandī writes in his introduction: '[God] adorned [this world] with the order and prohibition of prophets and saints, and entrusted it to the sword and pen of rulers and ministers.'[90]

The opinion that 'God created the world for the sword and the pen, and he placed the sword beneath the pen' (sometimes quoted as a Prophetic *ḥadīth*),[91] seems to reflect genuine differences of opinion on the relative standing of the bureaucratic administration and force of arms. The same disagreement is

[85] Al-Māwardī, *Qawānīn al-wizāra*, p. 138. [86] Ibn Ḥawqal, *Kitāb ṣūrat al-arḍ*, p. 49.
[87] *Kitāb al-fakhrī*, pp. 45–46. [88] *The Muqaddimah*, tr. Rosenthal, vol. 2, pp. 46–48.
[89] *Kutadgu bilig*, tr. Dankoff, *Wisdom of Royal Glory*, p. 129. [90] *Chahār maqāleh*, p. 1.
[91] Al-Māwardī, *Qawānīn al-wizāra*, p. 138; Goitein sees in this *ḥadīth* the recognition of the placement of the vizier over all other officials, including the highest military commanders, although he remained an officer of the civil administration ('Origin of the Vizierate', p. 188).

sometimes evident in the 'contention' (*munāẓara*, *mufākhara*), another literary genre in which the metaphors of the sword and pen appear frequently. Works of this sort, composed usually in verse or rhyming prose, take the form of stylised boasting contests between personifications of pairs such as spring and autumn, the rich and the poor, Damascus and Cairo, and so on; speaking in turn, each object or topic proclaims its superiority over the other by means of praise and blame.[92] The earliest recorded example of a full-blown *munāẓara* between the sword and the pen appears in Spain, and is written by Aḥmad b. Burd (d. 445/1053–54).[93] While some examples of contentions, such as that between musk and civet, were simply vehicles for poets to display their literary virtuosity, that between the sword and the pen may sometimes reflect real tensions and conflicting interests.[94] That the genre was popular is attested by the large number of such works preserved in anthologies and as independent compositions.[95] In the Mongol and post-Mongol periods, these *munāẓarāt* seem to have become even more popular.[96]

The categorisation of certain posts as belonging to the realm of the sword or that of the pen is primarily a feature of court circles. Most authors who discuss occupations in terms of the functions of government are associated with or patronised by holders of government appointments; they may even hold such posts themselves. The fact that the merchant Jaʿfar notes the distinction between the sword and the pen and, in one instance, describes all other occupations as unworthy may suggest that he was prominent and wealthy enough to have ties with members of government circles. He makes no attempt to integrate this binary division of occupations into the larger philosophical framework of his discussion, however, and apparently considered it quite separate from his own urban environment.

As noted at the beginning of this chapter, the materials discussed above were produced in many different regions of the medieval Islamic world, and they cover a relatively long period of time. Despite the striking prevalence of certain ways of thinking about specific crafts and about the earning of a livelihood in general, it is evident that even the most widespread and entrenched prejudices were far from uniformly held. The prestige or lack of it associated with a

92 Steinschneider, *Rangstreit-Literatur. Ein Beitrag zur vergleichenden Literatur und Kulturgeschichte* (Vienna, 1908); E. Wagner, 'Die arabische Rangstreitdichtung und ihre Einordnung in die allgemeine Literaturgeschichte', *Abhandlung der Akademie der Wissenschaft und der Literatur in Mainz* 8 (1962), pp. 435–476; van Gelder, 'Conceit', pp. 329–360.

93 Wagner, 'Rangstreitdichtung', p. 450; van Gelder, 'Conceit', pp. 348ff.

94 Cf. Wagner, 'Rangstreitdichtung', p. 450; van Gelder, 'Conceit', p. 337.

95 Al-Ḥuṣrī, *Zahr al-ādāb*, vol. 1, pp. 431ff; L. Cheikho (ed.), *Majānī al-adab fī ḥadā'iq al-ʿarab* (Beirut), vol. 4 (1884), pp. 162ff; Goldziher, 'Über Dualtitel', p. 322, n. 2, n. 3.

96 Cf. Steinschneider, *Rangstreit-Literatur*, nos. 94–102; Goldziher, 'Über Dualtitel', p. 322, n. 4, n. 5. There are also examples of *muwāzana* between different types of secretary, e.g. in the *maqāmāt* of al-Ḥarīrī and al-Qalqashandī (cf. Bosworth, 'A *Maqāma* on Secretaryship: al-Qalqashandī's *al-Kawākib al-durriyya fī'l-manāqib al-Badriyya*', *BSOAS* 27 (1964), pp. 293–94, 296–97).

particular occupation varied from place to place and from time to time. But it is clear that a person's occupation affected the way in which he was perceived, in social, intellectual and even moral terms, by those around him throughout the medieval Islamic world. In this respect, despite the generally informal character of social hierarchies in Islamic contexts, medieval Islamic societies were no different from the more systematically structured societies of India, China and the West.

Conclusion

In the preceding chapters I have attempted to show the diversity of the social visualisations produced in Islamic societies of the classical and early medieval periods, and have suggested that some of these visualisations respond in part to the moral issues posed by the co-existence of highly stratified societies with an emphatically egalitarian religious ideology. To achieve these ends I have drawn on a varied body of literary sources produced in different regions of the Arab Middle East and the Perso-Islamic world over some six centuries. The lack of uniformity in these materials and in the visualisations articulated in them is obvious. Not all Muslims, even in any single environment, saw their world in any of the ways described in this book, and even the most widely popular of social ideals, such as the quadripartite society of orders envisaged by Naṣīr al-Dīn Ṭūsī, was never universally accepted. It is equally obvious that none of these social imaginings is ever likely to have corresponded very closely to historical realities.

What is evident, however, is that certain ways of thinking about the good of society tended to constitute recognisable intellectual and cultural traditions, and that there was a great deal of cross-pollination among these traditions. In this way, the branch of utopian thought considered in this book contributes to several areas of study which are rarely considered together, such as historiography and political writings, philosophical and geographical compositions, advice literature and the larger corpus of *adab*, legal works and the writings of moralists, and so on. For example, some expressions of Islamic social thought echo and perhaps even anticipate certain characteristics of better known branches of Islamic political thinking. Just as Sunnī scholars found themselves forced to accept governments that were less than ideal, they also found it necessary to justify social differences and inequalities. If it was essential to establish the legitimacy of government in order to ensure that the *umma* had not gone astray, it was at least equally important to demonstrate the correspondence of its social arrangements to divine intention. Once scholars were engaged not only in accepting but also in justifying the existence of unofficial social hierarchies in Islamic terms, the realisation of the egalitarian ideal was increasingly postponed to the next world.

It has been argued, however, that some groups among the early Muslim community may have expected that Islam's religious egalitarianism would also have an effect on social arrangements in this world. In the early period, an individual's social status was largely inseparable from his ethnic identity, and it was only in the course of the late second/eighth and third/ninth centuries that social and ethnic conceptions of equality began to diverge. Accordingly, calls for equality were frequently expressed in ethnic terms. Whenever it was used to articulate a grievance (of whatever nature), the egalitarian ideal represented opposition to the status quo. Consequently, in the first and second centuries expressions of pious egalitarianism had a dangerous edge to them; they were manifestations of deeply felt social grievances and profound moral disenchantment in a period in which the distribution of power and privilege were not yet set and prevailing patterns were thus vulnerable to challenges.

In the course of the third/ninth and fourth/tenth centuries, the egalitarian ideal associated with the Qur'ān and the tribal past came to lose its subversive connotations. This is reflected in the tradition of formal *tafsīr* itself, but still more so in the popular forms of interpretation represented by poetry, *adab*, and didactic and moralistic literature. The Qur'ānic equation of nobility and piety (49:13, 'the most noble of you in the sight of God is the most pious') was adopted so widely that it became essentially symbolic; it served to remind rulers and other men of privilege that they too would one day face God alone, but no longer suggested the prevalence of social injustice in the present world. The fact that Ṭūsī's model achieved such popularity is a mark of the extent to which this taming of Islamic egalitarianism was successful.

To a significant extent, Islamic conceptions of hierarchy took shape as non-Islamic and pre-Islamic understandings of social ranking came into contact with the compound tribal and monotheistic ethos in the particular historical circumstances in which Islamic civilisation was formed. In examining the trends in social description that culminated in Ṭūsī's model, the question of the degree to which a non-Islamic, and expecially an Iranian cultural environment conditioned Muslim understandings of social organisation is therefore of considerable importance. There is no evidence of direct continuity, or even of straightforward subsequent revivals, of Sasanian social ideals among Muslims in the early Islamic period. Channels for the transmission of Iranian culture to Islamic civilisation were certainly available to Muslims in Iraq and Iran in the first and second centuries, but the earliest surviving specimens of Islamic social description from these regions seem to show little trace of the larger Persian milieu. In fact, there are indications of considerable distaste for and resentment of the luxurious practices and distinguishing features of the upper levels of the Iranian hierarchy. The coexistence of early Arab Muslims and peoples of Persian culture did not lead to the spontaneous adoption by the former of the social ideals of the latter, and the earliest indigenous Muslim pronouncements on social stratification reflect the ambitions and disappointments of particular groups within the new polity.

From the late Umayyad period onwards, however, the literary activities of Iranian converts and others introduced Iranian social ideas into the culture of the educated élites. Iranian forms of social organisation attracted the interest of Muslim writers, who increasingly modified their descriptive reports in the light of the conditions of their own time, so that eventually these reports ceased to be mere curiosities and acquired a relevance in the present. It is possible to trace three main stages in this process: firstly, the translation of historiographical and didactic texts from Pahlavī into Arabic; secondly, the appearance of accounts of Iranian social organisation in the works of Muslim authors, whose representations were progressively adapted as they grew further removed from the original translated materials; and thirdly, the appearance of such social ideals in didactic, ethical and other works of literature. In this final stage, the Iranian roots of some ways of expressing social ideals were rarely entirely forgotten (in some contexts, in fact, their Iranian associations may have added to their cultural prestige), but such visualisations transcended mere regional significance and were presented as part of a universal wisdom. Ṭusī's model is a significant landmark in this long process of cultural adaptation.

Although the legacy of Greek political philosophy was ultimately less influential than the Iranian tradition, it too left its impress on Muslim understandings of social stratification. Plato's tripartite conception of the ideal society, and a later Greek five-fold development from it, were reproduced in certain philosophical texts, and very occasionally elsewhere. Furthermore, educated Muslims of the classical and early medieval periods, like their counterparts in other pre-industrial societies, shared many of the principles underlying the Platonic view: these principles include the importance of contributing one's talents and labour to the larger community, the significance of heredity, a conservative social attitude, the association of intellectual and moral qualities with certain professions, and the ideal of social harmony based on a division of labour. Muslims of these times had no need of Plato and Aristotle to introduce them to such ideas, but their acceptance of them facilitated a broad adoption of philosophical categories. The Greek tradition contributed a complex of philosophical premises on which social ideas could be based, and these were taken up by Muslim moralists, who wished to demonstrate the legitimacy of the social (as well as political) realities of their time.

Social models are expressions of ideals by their very nature; even in the Ottoman Empire, the ruler's power to create an ideal society was restricted in innumerable ways.[1] In this respect it is worth drawing a comparison with the Indian context, in which the four Vedic *varṇas* are of enormous religious and cultural importance, but, for all the brahmans' attempts to accommodate the reality within the theory, thousands of variously defined *jāti*s have in fact constituted the effective units of social interaction in much of India for at least a

[1] See Inalcik, 'Comments on "Sultanism"', pp. 58–59.

millennium. But there is a crucial difference between the Indian and the Islamic situations. Unlike their Indian counterparts, and despite their proponents' frequent attempts to portray them as part of the divinely ordained pattern of things, the hierarchical social models produced in classical and early medieval Islamic societies were never fully and convincingly able to acquire the unassailable authority of religious sanction.[2] On the contrary, although its existence was accepted, the entire notion of social differentiation – so clearly endorsed in the Vedic model – was placed on the defensive by the egalitarian orientation of the religious tradition.

[2] A comparable situation arose in Sri Lanka, where a modified system of castes survived despite the presence of Buddhism and the consequent erosion of the religious justification for hierarchy (R. Gombrich, *Precept and Practice. Traditional Buddhism in the Rural Highlands of Ceylon* (Oxford, 1971), pp. 294ff).

Bibliography

Abarqūhī, Shams al-Dīn Ibrāhīm, *Majma' al-baḥrayn*, ed. N.M. Haravī, Tehran 1364/1406

'Abbās, I., *'Abd al-Ḥamīd ibn Yaḥyā al-Kātib wa mā tabaqqā min rasā'ilihi wa rasā'il Sālim Abī'l-'Alā'*, Amman 1988

Dīwān shi'r al-Khawārij, Beirut 1402/1982

'Naẓra jadīda fī ba'ḍ al-kutub al-mansūba li-bn al-Muqaffa'', *Majallat majma' al-lugha al-'arabiyya bi Dimashq* 52, 1397/1977

Ta'rīkh bilād al-Shām min mā qabl al-Islām ḥattā bidāyat al-'aṣr al-umawī, Amman 1410/1990

(ed.), *'Ahd Ardashīr*, Beirut 1387/1967

al-'Abbāsī, al-Ḥasan b. 'Abd Allāh, *Āthār al-uwal fī tartīb al-duwal*, Cairo 1295/1878

'Abd al-Wahhāb, *Mā namaqahu 'Abd al-Wahhāb fī sharḥ kalimat amīr al-mu'minīn*, ed. Jalāl al-Dīn Muḥaddith, Tehran 1349/1390

Abū Dā'ūd, Sulaymān b. al-Ash'ath al-Sijistānī, *Sunan*, ed. M. Muḥyī'l-Dīn 'Abd al-Ḥamīd, 4 vols., Cairo 1935

Abū'l-Faẓl, *Ā'īn-i Akbarī*, ed. H. Blochmann, 2 vols., Calcutta 1872–1877

Abū Ghānim Bishr b. Ghānim al-Khurāsānī al-Ibāḍī, *al-Mudawwana al-kubrā*, ed. M. b. Yūsuf Aṭfayyish, Beirut 1394/1974

Abū 'Ubayd al-Qāsim b. al-Sallām, *Kitāb al-amthāl*, ed. 'Abd al-Majīd Qaṭāmish, Damascus 1400/1980

Abū Yūsuf, *Kitāb al-kharāj*, Cairo 1382/1962

Ahmad, I., 'Caste and Kinship in a Muslim Village of Eastern Uttar Pradesh', *Family, Kinship and Marriage among Muslims in India*, ed. I. Ahmad, New Delhi 1976

Ahmed, R., *The Bengal Muslims 1871–1906. A Quest for Identity*, Delhi and Oxford 1988

al-Amâsî, Ahmed b. Hüsamüddin, *Mir'ât ül-mülûk*, Süleymaniye Kütüphanesi, ms. Esed Efendi 1890

al-'Āmirī, Abū'l-Ḥasan, *Kitāb al-i'lām bi-manāqib al-Islām*, ed. A. Ghorab, Cairo 1387/1967

Kitāb al-sa'āda wa'l-is'ād, ed. M. Minovi, Wiesbaden 1957–8

Amoretti, B.S., 'Sects and Heresies', *Cambridge History of Iran*, vol. 4, ed. R.N. Frye, Cambridge 1975

Anvarī, Ḥ., *Iṣṭilāḥāt-i dīvānī-yi dawreh-yi Ghaznavī va Saljūqī*, Tehran 1335

Arazi, A. and A. El'ad, '«L'Épître à l'armée» Al-Ma'mūn et la seconde *da'wa*', *SI* 66, 1987

Arberry, A.J., 'Some Plato in an Arabic Epitome', *IQ* 2, 1955
'The Nichomachean Ethics in Arabic', *BSOAS* 17, 1955
Aristotle, *Nicomachean Ethics*, tr. J.A.K. Jackson, Harmondsworth, 1955
al-ʿAskarī, Abū Hilāl, *Jamharat al-amthāl*, eds. M. Abū'l-Faḍl Ibrāhīm and ʿAbd al-Majīd Qaṭāmish, 2 vols., Cairo 1384/1964
pseudo-Aṣmaʿī, *Nihāyat al-arab fī akhbār al-Furs wa'l-ʿArab*, Cambridge University Library, ms. Qq 225. Abridged Persian tr., *Tajārib al-umam*, ms. Aya Sofya 3115
Āvī, Ḥusayn b. Muḥammad, *Farmān-i Mālik-i Ashtar*, ed. M.T. Dānishpazhūh, Tehran 1359/1400
Badawī, ʿAbd al-Raḥmān, *al-Uṣūl al-yūnāniyya lil-naẓariyyāt al-siyāsiyya fī'l-Islām*, Cairo 1954
al-Baghdādī, *Kitāb al-farq bayn al-firaq*, ed. M. Badr, Cairo 1323/1905
al-Baghdādī, A.Ḥ., *al-Fikr al-siyāsī ʿinda Abī'l-Ḥasan al-Māwardī*, Beirut 1984
Bagnall, R.S., *Egypt in Late Antiquity*, Princeton 1993
Baḥr al-favā'id, ed. M.T. Dānishpazhūh, Tehran 1345/1966–67. Tr. J.S. Meisami, *The Sea of Precious Virtues*, Salt Lake City 1991
al-Baḥrānī, Yūsuf b. Aḥmad, *Lu'lu'at al-baḥrayn*, Qumm n.d.
al-Bakrī, *Faṣl al-maqāl fī sharḥ kitāb al-amthāl*, eds. I. ʿAbbās and ʿAbd al-Majīd ʿĀbidīn, Beirut 1403/1983
Balʿamī, *Tārīkh-i Balʿamī*, ed. M.T. Bahār, 2 vols., Tehran 1353/1974
al-Barqī, Aḥmad b. Muḥammad, *Kitāb al-maḥāsin*, Najaf 1384/1964
al-Barqūqī, ʿAbd al-Raḥmān, *Sharḥ dīwān al-Mutanabbī*, 4 vols., Beirut 1965
Barth, F., 'The System of Social Stratification in Swat, North Pakistan', *Aspects of Caste in South India, Ceylon and North-West Pakistan*, ed. E.R. Leach, Cambridge 1969
Barthold, W., 'Ṭāhirids', *EI*1
Bāstānī Pārīzī, M.E., 'Afżal-al-Dīn Kermānī', *Encyclopaedia Iranica*
Bausani, A., 'L'India vista da due grandi personalità musulmane: Bābar e Bīrūnī', *Al-Bīrūnī Commemoration Volume, A.H. 362–A.H. 1362*, Calcutta 1951
al-Bayḍāwī, *Anwār al-tanzīl wa asrār al-ta'wīl*, 2 vols., ed. H.O. Fleischer, Leipzig 1846–1848
Bayhaqī, Abū'l-Faḍl, *Tārīkh-i Masʿūdī*, eds. Q. Ghanī and A.A. Fayyāḍ, Tehran 1324/1945
al-Bayhaqī, Ibrāhīm b. Muḥammad, *al-Maḥāsin wa'l-masāwī*, Beirut 1380/1960
Beg, M.A.J., 'al-Khāṣṣa wa'l-ʿāmma', *EI*2
Benveniste, E., 'Les classes sociales dans la tradition avestique', *JA* 221, 1932
Le vocabulaire des institutions indo-européennes, 2 vols., Paris 1969
'Traditions indo-iraniennes sur les classes sociales' *JA* 230, 1938
al-Bīrūnī, Abū'l-Rayḥān, *Taḥqīq mā lil-Hind*, Hyderabad 1958
al-Āthār al-bāqiya ʿan al-qurūn al-khāliya, ed. C.E. Sachau, *Chronologie orientalischer Völker*, Leipzig 1923
Bosworth, C.E., 'A *Maqāma* on Secretaryship: al-Qalqashandī's *al-Kawākib al-durriyya fī'l-manāqib al-Badriyya*', *BSOAS* 27, 1964
Al-Maqrīzī's 'Book of Contention and Strife Concerning the Relations between the Banū Umayya and the Banū Hashim', Manchester 1980
'An Early Arabic Mirror for Princes: Ṭāhir Dhū l-Yamīnain's Epistle to his Son ʿAbdallāh (206/821)', *JNES* 29, 1970
'Kay Kā'ūs b. Iskandar', *EI*2

The Ghaznavids. Their Empire in Afghanistan and Eastern Iran, 994–1040, Edinburgh 1963
'The Interaction of Arabic and Persian Literature and Culture in the 10th and Early 11th Centuries', *al-Abḥāth* 27, 1978–9
The Mediaeval Islamic Underworld: The Banū Sāsān in Arabic Society and Literature, 2 vols., Leiden 1976
'The Tahirids and Arabic Culture', *JSS* 14, 1969
'The Ṭāhirids and Persian Literature', *Iran* 7, 1969
(tr.), *The History of al-Ṭabarī*, vol. 32, *The Reunification of the ʿAbbāsid Caliphate*, Albany, New York 1987
Bowersock, G., *Hellenism in Late Antiquity*, Ann Arbor 1990
Boyce, M., *A History of Zoroastrianism*, Leiden 1975–
The Letter of Tansar, Rome 1968
'The Bipartite Society of the Ancient Iranians', *Societies and Languages of the Ancient Near East*, ed. M.A. Dandamayev, Warminster 1982
Boylan, P., *Thoth the Hermes of Egypt. A Study of Some Aspects of Theological Thought in Ancient Egypt*, London and Bombay 1922
Briant, P., 'Class system', ii, *Encyclopaedia Iranica*
Brock, S., 'From Antagonism to Assimilation: Syriac Attitudes to Greek Learning', *East of Byzantium: Syria and Armenia in the Formative Period*, eds. N.G. Garsoïan, T.F. Mathews and R.W. Thomson, Washington 1982
Brockelmann, C., 'al-Bayhaḳī, Ibrāhīm b. Muḥammad', *EI2*
Geschichte der arabischen Literatur, 3 vols. and 2 supplements, Leiden 1937–42
'Kalīla wa-Dimna', *EI2*
Brown, P., *The Body and Society. Men, Women and Sexual Renunciation in Early Christianity*, New York 1988
The World of Late Antiquity, A.D. 150–750, London 1971
Brunschvig, R., 'Métiers vils en Islam', *Études d'islamologie*, vol. 1, Paris 1976
Bucci, O., 'Caste e classi sociali nell'antico diritto iranico', *Apollinaris* 45, 1972
al-Bukhārī, M. b. Ismāʿīl, *al-Jāmiʿ al-ṣaḥīḥ*, 9 vols., Cairo n.d.
Bulliet, R.W., *The Patricians of Nishapur*, Cambridge, Massachusetts 1972
Cahen, Cl., 'A propos et autour d'"Ein arabisches Handbuch der Handelswissenschaft"', *Oriens* 15, 1962
'Ibn al-Ukhuwwa', *EI2*
Cameron, Averil, 'Byzantium and the Past in the Seventh Century: The Search for Redefinition', *Le septième siècle. Changements et continuités*, eds. J. Fontaine and J.N. Hillgarth, London 1992
Christianity and the Rhetoric of Empire. The Development of Christian Discourse, Berkeley 1991
'New Themes and Styles in Greek Literature: Seventh-Eighth Centuries', *The Byzantine and Early Islamic Near East*, vol. 1, *Problems in the Literary Source Material*, eds. Averil Cameron and L.I. Conrad, Princeton 1992
Procopius and the Sixth Century, Berkeley 1985
'The Eastern Provinces in the Seventh Century A.D. Hellenism and the Emergence of Islam', *Hellenismos. Quelques jalons pour une histoire de l'identité grecque*, ed. S. Saïd, Leiden and New York 1991
The Mediterranean World in Late Antiquity, A.D. 395–600, London and New York 1993

Charles-Dominique, P., 'Le système éthique d'Ibn al-Muqaffa' d'après ses deux épîtres dites «*al-ṣaġīr*» et «*al-kabīr*»', *Arabica* 12, 1965
Cheikho, L. (ed.), *Majānī al-adab fī ḥadā'iq al-'arab*, 4 vols., Beirut 1884–7
Christensen, A., 'Abarsām et Tansar', *Acta Orientalia* 10, 1932
Les gestes des rois dans les traditions de l'Iran antique, Paris 1936
Les Kayanides, Copenhagen 1931
Les types du premier homme et du premier roi dans l'histoire légendaire des Iraniens, 2 vols., Leiden 1934
L'Iran sous les Sassanides, 2nd edn, Copenhagen 1944
Conrad, L.I., 'The Plague in Bilād al-Shām in Pre-Islamic Times', *Proceedings of the Symposium on Bilād al-Shām during the Byzantine Period*, eds. M.'A. Bakhīt and M. 'Aṣfūr, Amman 1986
'The Plague in the Early Medieval Near East', unpublished Ph.D. dissertation, Princeton 1981
Cook, M.A., 'Activism and Quietism in Islam: The Case of the Early Murji'a', *Islam and Power*, eds. A. Cudsi and A. Dessouki, Baltimore 1981
Crone, P., 'Kavād's Heresy and Mazdak's Revolt', *Iran* 29, 1991
Pre-Industrial Societies, Oxford 1989
Roman, Provincial and Islamic Law, Cambridge 1987
Slaves on Horses. The Evolution of the Islamic Polity, Cambridge 1980
'The Tribe and the State', *States in History*, ed. J.A. Hall, Oxford 1986
Daniel, E., *The Political and Social History of Khurasan Under Abbasid Rule, 747–820*, Minneapolis and Chicago 1979
Dānishpazhūh, M.T. (ed.), *Farmān-i Mālik-i Ashtar*, Tehran 1359/1400
Dankoff, R., 'Inner Asian Wisdom Traditions in the Pre-Mongol Period', *JAOS* 101, 1981
Wisdom of Royal Glory (Kutadgu Bilig): A Turko-Islamic Mirror for Princes, Chicago 1983
al-Dārimī, 'Abd Allāh b. 'Abd al-Raḥmān, *Sunan*, 2 vols., ed. 'Abd Allāh Hāshim Yamānī, Medina 1386/1966
Davvānī, Jalāl al-Dīn, *Lavāmi' al-ishrāq fī makārim al-akhlāq=Akhlāq-i Jalālī*, Lucknow 1377/1957. Tr. W.F. Thompson, *Practical Philosophy of the Muhammadan People*, London 1839
Dawood, A.H., 'A Comparative Study of Arabic and Persian Mirrors for Princes from the Second to the Sixth Century A.H.', unpublished Ph.D. thesis, London 1965
de Blois, F., '"Freemen" and "Nobles" in Iranian and Semitic Languages', *JRAS* 1985
de Fouchécour, C.-H., *Moralia. Les notions morales dans la littérature persane du 3e/9e au 7e/13e siècle*, Paris 1986
de Menasce, J.P., 'Andarz Literature', *Cambridge History of Iran*, vol. 3 (2), ed. E. Yarshater, Cambridge 1983
Dēnkard (vol. 47), ed. F. Max Müller, *Sacred Books of the East*, Oxford 1897. Tr. E.W. West, *Pahlavi Texts*, Part V, Oxford 1897
Derchain-Urtel, M.T., *Thot à travers ses épithètes dans les scènes d'offrandes des temples d'époque gréco-romaine*, Brussels 1981
Dickson, M.B. and S.C. Welch, *The Houghton Shahnameh*, 2 vols., Cambridge, Massachusetts, 1981
Dieterici, F. (tr.), *Die Staatsleitung*, Leiden 1904
Dietrich, A., 'Das politische Testament des zweiten 'Abbāsidenkalifen al-Manṣūr', *Der Islam* 30, 1952

al-Dimashqī, Ja'far b. 'Alī, *Kitāb al-ishāra ilā maḥāsin al-tijāra*, Cairo 1318/1900
al-Dīnawarī, A. b. Dā'ūd, *al-Akhbār al-ṭiwāl*, ed. 'Abd al-Mun'im 'Āmir, Cairo 1960
Doniger, W. (tr.), *The Rig Veda*, Harmondsworth 1981
Doniger, W. and B.K. Smith (trs.), *The Laws of Manu*, London 1991
Donner, F.M., *The Early Islamic Conquests*, Princeton 1981
'Tribal Settlement in Basra during the First Century A.H.', *Land Tenure and Social Transformation in the Middle East*, ed. T. Khalidi, Beirut 1984
Dresch, P., *Tribes, Government, and History in Yemen*, Oxford 1989
Dumézil, G., *L'Idéologie tripartie des Indo-Européens*, Brussels 1958
Mythe et épopée, 3 vols., Paris 1968–1973
al-Durr al-thamīn fī manāhij al-mulūk wa'l-salāṭīn, Süleymaniye Kütüphanesi, ms. Kadizade Mehmed 291
Enderwitz, S., *Gesellschaftlicher Rang und ethnische Legitimation. Der arabische Schriftsteller Abū 'Uṯmān al-Ǧāḥiẓ (gest. 868) über die Afrikaner, Perser und Araber in der islamischen Gesellschaft*, Freiburg 1979
Fakhr-i Mudabbir, *Ādāb al-ḥarb wa'l-shujā'at*, ed. Aḥmad Suhaylī Khwānsārī, Tehran 1346/1967
al-Fārābī, Abū Naṣr, *al-Siyāsa al-madaniyya*, Beirut 1964. Tr. F. Dieterici, *Die Staatsleitung*, Leiden 1904
Fuṣūl al-madanī, ed. and tr. D.M. Dunlop, *Aphorisms of the Statesman*, Cambridge 1961
Kitāb taḥṣīl al-sa'āda, Rasā'il al-Fārābī, Hyderabad 1345/1946
Mabādi' ārā' ahl al-madīna al-fāḍila, ed. and tr. R. Walzer, *Al-Fārābī on the Perfect State*, Oxford and New York 1985
Risāla fī'l-akhlāq, Süleymaniye Kütüphanesi, ms. Aya Sofya 1957
Talkhīṣ Nawāmīs Aflāṭūn, ed. F. Gabrieli, London 1952
Festugière, A.-J., *La révélation d'Hermès Trismégiste*, 4 vols., Paris 1949–54
Firdawsī, *Shāhnāmeh*, ed. and tr. J. Mohl, *Le livre des rois*, 7 vols., Paris 1976
Fleischer, C.H., *Bureaucrat and Intellectual in the Ottoman Empire. The Historian Mustafa Âli (1541–1600)*, Princeton 1986
'Royal Authority, Dynastic Cyclism, and "Ibn Khaldûnism" in Sixteenth-Century Ottoman Letters', *JAAS* 18, 1983
Fowden, G., *Empire to Commonwealth. Consequences of Monotheism in Late Antiquity*, Princeton 1993
Freytag, G.W., *Arabum Proverbia*, 3 vols., Bonn 1838–43
Frye, R.N., 'Feudalism in Sasanian and Early Islamic Iran', *JSAI* 9, 1987
The Heritage of Persia, Cleveland 1963
Fyzee, A.A.A., 'Qadi al-Nu'man, the Fāṭimid Jurist and Author', *JRAS* 1934
Gabrieli, F., 'Adab', *EI2*
'La «*Risāla*» di al-Ǵāḥiẓ sui Turchi', *RSO* 32, 1957
'L'Opera di Ibn al-Muqaffa'', *RSO* 13, 1932
Galston, M., *Politics and Excellence. The Political Philosophy of Alfarabi*, Princeton 1990
Gardīzī, *Zayn al-akhbār=Tārīkh-i Gardīzī*, ed. 'Abd al-Ḥayy Ḥabībī, Tehran 1363
Gerholm, T., *Market, Mosque and Mafraj. Social Inequality in a Yemeni Town*, Stockholm 1977
Gériès, I., 'al-Maḥāsin wa-'l-masāwī', *EI2*
Un genre littéraire arabe, al-Maḥāsin wa-l-masāwī, Paris 1977

al-Gharawī, M., *al-Amthāl al-nabawiyya*, 2 vols., Beirut 1401/1980
al-Ghazālī, *Iḥyā ʿulūm al-dīn*, 4 vols., Cairo n.d.
Gibb, H.A.R., 'The Social Significance of the Shuubiya', *Studies on the Civilization of Islam*, eds. S.J. Shaw and W.R. Polk, Princeton 1962
Goichon, A.-M., 'Ibn Sīnā', *EI2*
Goitein, S.D., 'A Turning Point in the History of the Muslim State', *Studies in Islamic History and Institutions*, Leiden 1966
'The Origin of the Vizierate and its True Character', *Studies in Islamic History and Institutions*, Leiden 1966
'The Rise of the Middle Eastern Bourgeoisie in Early Islamic Times', *Studies in Islamic History and Institutions*, Leiden 1966
'The Working People of the Mediterranean Area during the High Middle Ages', *Studies in Islamic History and Institutions*, Leiden 1966
Goldziher, I., 'Catholic Tendencies and Particularism in Islam', in *Studies on Islam*, tr. and ed. M.L. Swartz, New York and Oxford 1981
'Die Handwerke bei den Arabern', *Globus* 46, 1894
Introduction to Islamic Theology and Law, trs. A. and R. Hamori, Princeton 1981;= *Vorlesungen über den Islam*, Heidelberg 1910
Muslim Studies, eds. and trs. C.R. Barber and S.M. Stern, 2 vols., London and Chicago 1967–1971;=*Muhammedanische Studien*, 2 vols., Halle 1889–1890
'Über Dualtitel', *WZKM* 13, 1899
Gombrich, R., *Precept and Practice. Traditional Buddhism in the Rural Highlands of Ceylon*, Oxford 1971
Gramlich, R., *Die Nahrung der Herzen*, 3 vols., Stuttgart 1992–5
Griffini, E. (ed.), *'Corpus Iuris' di Zaid ibn ʿAlī*, Milan 1919
Grignaschi, M., 'La Nihāyatu-l-'arab fī aḫbāri-l-Furs wa-l-ʿArab', *BEO* 22, 1969
'La *Nihāyatu-l-'arab fī aḫbāri-l-Furs wa-l-ʿArab* et les *Siyaru mulūki-l-ʿAǧam* du Ps. Ibn-al-Muqaffaʿ', *BEO* 26, 1973
'La «*Siyāsatu-l-ʿāmmiyya*» et l'influence iranienne sur la pensée politique islamique', *Acta Iranica*, 2e série, *Hommages et Opera Minora* 3, 1975
'Le roman épistolaire classique conservé dans la version arabe de Sâlim Abû-l-ʿAlâ'', *Muséon* 80, 1967
'Les «Rasā'il 'Arisṭāṭālīsa 'ilā-l-Iskandar» de Sālim Abū-l-ʿAlā' et l'activité culturelle à l'époque omayyade', *BEO* 19, 1965
'Quelques spécimens de la littérature sassanide conservés dans les bibliothèques d'Istanbul', *JA* 254, 1966
Gutas, D., 'Classical Arabic Wisdom Literature: Nature and Scope', *JAOS* 101, 1981.
'Ethische Schriften im Islam', *Neues Handbuch der Literaturwissenschaft*, vol. 5, Frankfurt 1990
Haddad, Y.Y. and A.T. Lummis, *Islamic Values in the United States. A Comparative Study*, New York and Oxford 1987
Ḥājjī Khalīfa, Katip Çelebi, *Kashf al-ẓunūn ʿan asāmī al-kutub wa'l-funūn*, 6 vols., Istanbul 1941–55
Haldon, J.F., *Byzantium in the Seventh Century*, Cambridge 1990
'Ideology and Social Change in the Seventh Century: Military Discontent as a Barometer', *Klio* 68, 1986
'*Ḥasab wa-nasab*', *EI2*

Herrin, J., *The Formation of Christendom*, Princeton 1987
Hinds, M., 'Kūfan Political Alignments and their Background in the Mid-Seventh Century A.D.', *IJMES* 2, 1971
Hobsbawm, E.J. and J.W. Scott, 'Political Shoemakers', *Past and Present* 89, 1980
Hodgson, M.G.S., *The Venture of Islam*, 3 vols., Chicago and London 1974
Hornus, J.-M., 'Le corpus dionysien en syriaque', *Parole de l'Orient* 1, 1970
Houtsma, M.Th, 'Zur Geschichte der Selǵuqen von Kermân', *ZDMG* 39, 1885
al-Ḥuṣrī, Abū Isḥāq Ibrāhīm b. ʿAlī, *Zahr al-ādāb wa thamar al-albāb*, ed. ʿAlī Muḥammad al-Bajāwī, 2 vols., Cairo 1372/1953
Ibn ʿAbd al-Barr, Yūsuf b. ʿAbd Allāh, *al-Inbāh ʿalā qabāʾil al-ruwāh*, Cairo 1350/1931
Ibn ʿAbd Rabbihi, Aḥmad b. Muḥammad, *al-ʿIqd al-farīd*, 31 vols., ed. K. al-Bustānī, Beirut 1952–3
Ibn ʿAbd al-Raʾūf, *Risāla fī ādāb al-ḥisba waʾl-muḥtasib*, ed. É. Lévi-Provençal, *Trois traités hispaniques de ḥisba*, Paris 1955
Ibn ʿAbdūn, *Risālat Ibn ʿAbdūn fīʾl-qaḍāʾ waʾl-ḥisba*, ed. É. Lévi-Provençal, *Trois traités hispaniques de ḥisba*, Paris 1955
Ibn Abīʾl-Ḥadīd, ʿIzz al-Dīn, *Sharḥ nahj al-balāgha*, ed. M. Abūʾl-Faḍl Ibrāhīm, 20 vols., Cairo 1959–1964
Ibn Abīʾl-Rabīʿ, Shihāb al-Dīn, *Sulūk al-mālik fī tadbīr al-mamālik*, ed. Nājī al-Takrītī, Beirut 1978
Ibn Abī Ṭāhir Ṭayfūr, Abūʾl-Faḍl Aḥmad, *Baghdād fī taʾrīkh al-khilāfa al-ʿabbāsiyya*, Baghdad 1388/1968
Ibn Abī Uṣaybiʿa, A. b. al-Qāsim, *ʿUyūn al-anbāʾ fī ṭabaqāt al-aṭibbāʾ*, ed. A. Müller, 2 vols., Göttingen 1884
Ibn Abī Yaʿlā, *Ṭabaqāt al-Ḥanābila*, ed. M.Ḥ. al-Fiqī, Cairo 1371/1952
Ibn al-Athīr, Majd al-Dīn, *al-Nihāya fī gharīb al-ḥadīth*, 5 vols., Cairo n.d.
Ibn al-Athīr, ʿIzz al-Dīn, *al-Kāmil fīʾl-taʾrīkh*, 13 vols., Beirut 1965–1967
Ibn Bābawayh, M. b. ʿAlī, *Man lā yaḥḍuruhu ʾl-faqīh*, ed. al-Sayyid Ḥasan al-Mūsawī, 4 vols., Najaf 1377–1378/1957
Ibn Bājja, M. b. Yaḥyā, *Risālat al-wadāʿ*, ed. M. Asín Palacios, *Andalus* 8, 1943
Tadbīr al-mutawaḥḥid, ed. M. Asín Palacios, Madrid-Granada 1946
Ibn al-Balkhī, *Fārsnāmeh*, eds. G. le Strange and R.A. Nicholson, London 1921
Ibn al-Faqīh, *Kitab al-buldān*, ed. M.J. de Goeje, Leiden 1967
Ibn al-Farrāʾ, Abū Yaʿlā Muḥammad b. al-Ḥusayn, *al-Aḥkām al-sulṭāniyya*, Beirut 1403/1983
Ibn al-Fuwaṭī (attrib.), *al-Ḥawādith al-jāmiʿa waʾl-tajārib al-nāfiʿa fīʾl-miʾa al-sābiʿa*, ed. M. Jawād, Baghdad 1351/1932
Ibn al-Ḥabbāriyya, Abū Yaʿlā Muḥammad, *Falak al-maʿānī*, Süleymaniye Kütüphanesi, ms. Aya Sofya 4157
Ibn al-Ḥaddād, M. b. Manṣūr, *al-Jawhar al-nafīs fī siyāsat al-raʾīs*, ed. R. al-Sayyid, Beirut 1983
Ibn Ḥajar al-ʿAsqalānī, A. b. ʿAlī, *Fatḥ al-barī bi-sharḥ al-Bukhārī*, 17 vols., Cairo 1378/1959
Tahdhīb al-tahdhīb, 12 vols., Hyderabad 1325–7
Ibn Ḥamdūn, M. b. al-Ḥasan, *al-Tadhkira al-Ḥamdūniyya*, 2 vols., ed. I. ʿAbbās, Beirut 1983–1984
Ibn Ḥanbal, Aḥmad, *Musnad*, 6 vols., Beirut n.d.
Ibn Ḥawqal, Abūʾl-Qāsim, *Kitāb ṣūrat al-arḍ*, ed. J.H. Kramers, Leiden 1967

Ibn Ḥazm, ʿAlī b. Aḥmad, *al-Muḥallā*, 11 vols., ed. A.M. Shākir, Beirut 1969

Ibn al-Jawzī, *Talbīs Iblīs*, Cairo n.d.

Ibn Juljul, Sulaymān, *Ṭabaqāt al-aṭibbā' wa'l-ḥukamā'*, ed. F. Sayyid, Cairo 1955

Ibn Kathīr, *Tafsīr al-Qur'ān al-ʿaẓīm*, 7 vols., Beirut 1966

Ibn Khallikān, Shams al-Dīn Aḥmad b. Muḥammad, *Wafayāt al-aʿyān wa anbā' abnā' al-zamān*, ed. I. ʿAbbās, 8 vols., Beirut 1397/1977

Ibn Manẓūr, M. b. Mukarram, *Lisān al-ʿarab*, 15 vols., Beirut 1374/1955

Ibn Māja, M. b. Yazīd, *Sunan*, ed. M. Fu'ād ʿAbd al-Bāqī, 2 vols., Cairo 1372–1373/1952–1954

Ibn Mītham, Kamāl al-Dīn Mītham b. ʿAlī, *Sharḥ Kamāl al-Dīn Mītham b. ʿAlī b. Mītham al-Baḥrānī ʿalā'l-mi'at kalima*, ed. Jalāl al-Dīn Muḥaddith, Tehran 1349sh/1390q.

Ibn al-Muqaffaʿ, *Āthār Ibn al-Muqaffaʿ*, ed. ʿUmar Abū'l-Naṣr, Beirut 1966

Ibn al-Nadīm, M. b. Isḥāq, *Kitāb al-fihrist*, ed. G. Flügel, 2 vols., Beirut 1966

Ibn al-Qifṭī, ʿAlī b. Yūsuf, *Ta'rīkh al-ḥukamā'*, ed. J. Lippert, Leipzig 1903

Ibn Qutayba, ʿAbd Allāh b. Muslim, *al-Maʿārif*, ed. Tharwat ʿUkāsha, Cairo 1388/1969

ʿUyūn al-akhbār, 4 vols., Cairo 1925–30

Ibn al-Rūmī, ʿAlī b. al-ʿAbbās, *Dīwān*, 6 vols., ed. Ḥ. Naṣṣār, Cairo 1973–81

Ibn Rushd, M. b. A., *Bidāyat al-mujtahid wa nihāyat al-muqtaṣid*, 2 vols., Cairo 1386/1966

Ibn Saʿd, M., *al-Ṭabaqāt al-kubrā*, 9 vols., Beirut 1377–88/1957–88

Ibn Shākir al-Kutubī, M., *Fawāt al-wafayāt wa'l-dhayl ʿalayhā*, ed. I. ʿAbbās, Beirut 1973

Ibn Sīnā, Abū ʿAlī al-Ḥusayn b. ʿAbd Allāh, *al-Ilāhiyyāt*, Cairo 1380/1960

al-Najāt, Beirut 1405/1985

Ibn Taymiyya, *al-Ḥisba fi'l-Islām*, Beirut 1412/1992

Ibn al-Ṭiqṭiqā, *Kitāb al-fakhrī fi'l-ādāb al-sulṭāniyya wa'l-duwal al-islāmiyya*, Cairo 1317

Ibn al-Ukhuwwa, *Maʿālim al-qurba fī aḥkām al-ḥisba*, ed. R. Levy, London 1938

al-Ibshīhī, Shihāb al-Dīn M. b. A., *al-Mustaṭraf fī kull fann mustaẓraf*, 2 vols., Beirut 1406/1986

Ikhwān al-Ṣafā', *Rasā'il Ikhwān al-Ṣafā'*, 4 vols., Beirut 1376–77/1957

Inalcik, H., *The Ottoman Empire. The Classical Age 1300–1600*, New York and Washington 1973

'Comments on "Sultanism": Max Weber's Typification of the Ottoman Polity', *Princeton Papers* 1, 1992

'Turkish and Iranian Political Theories and Traditions in *Kutadgu Bilig*', *The Middle East and the Balkans under the Ottoman Empire*, ed. H. Inalcik, Bloomington, Indiana 1993

al-Iṣfahānī, ʿAbd Allāh, *Riyāḍ al-ʿulamā' wa ḥiyāḍ al-fuḍalā'*, ed. al-Sayyid Aḥmad al-Ḥusaynī, 6 vols., Qumm 1401/1980–1

al-Iṣfahānī, Abū'l-Faraj, *Kitab al-aghānī*, Cairo 1350/1931

al-Iṣfahānī, Abū'l-Shaykh, *K. al-amthāl fi'l-ḥadīth al-nabawī*, ed. ʿAbd al-ʿAlī al-Ḥamīd, 2 vols., Bombay 1402/1982

al-Iṣfahānī, ʿAlī, *Tuḥfat al-mulūk dar ādāb*, Tehran 1317/1938

al-Iṣfahānī, Ḥamza, *Ta'rīkh sinī mulūk al-arḍ wa'l-anbiyā'*, Beirut 1961

al-Iṣfahānī, Maḥmūd b. Muḥammad, *Dastūr al-vizāra*, Tehran 1364

al-Iṣfahānī, al-Rāghib, *K. al-dharīʿa ilā makārim al-sharīʿa*, Beirut 1400/1980
Muḥāḍarāt al-udabāʾ wa muḥāwarāt al-shuʿarāʾ waʾl-bulaghāʾ, 4 vols., Beirut 1961
Mufradāt alfāẓ al-Qurʾān, ed. Ṣafwān ʿAdnān Dāwūdī, Damascus and Beirut 1412/1992
Tafṣīl al-nashʾatayn wa taḥṣīl al-saʿādatayn, ed. ʿAbd al-Majīd al-Najjār, Beirut 1408/1988

Itzkowitz, N., *Ottoman Empire and Islamic Tradition*, New York 1972

al-Jāḥiẓ, ʿAmr b. Baḥr, *al-Bayān waʾl-tabyīn*, 4 vols., ed. ʿAbd al-Salām Muḥammad Hārūn, Cairo 1405/1985
Kitāb al-bukhalāʾ, Beirut 1399/1979
K. al-tarbīʿ waʾl-tadwīr, ed. C. Pellat, Damascus 1955
Rasāʾil, 4 vols., ed. ʿAbd al-Salām Muḥammad Hārūn, Cairo 1399/1979

al-Jāḥiẓ, ʿAmr b. Baḥr (attrib.), *al-Maḥāsin waʾl-aḍdād*, Beirut n.d.
(attrib.), *Kitāb al-tabaṣṣur biʾl-tijāra*, Cairo 1966
(attrib.), *Kitāb al-tāj fī akhlāq al-mulūk*, ed. Aḥmad Zakī Pāshā, Cairo 1332/1914. Tr. C. Pellat, *Le livre de la couronne*, Paris 1944

al-Jahshiyārī, M. b. ʿAbdūs, *Kitāb al-wuzarāʾ waʾl-kuttāb*, ed. ʿAbd Allāh al-Ṣāwī, Cairo 1357/1938

al-Jarsīfī, *Risāla fīʾl-ḥisba*, in *Trois traités hispaniques de ḥisba*, ed. É. Lévi-Provençal, Paris 1955

al-Jīlī, Aḥmad b. Maḥmūd, *Minhāj al-vuzarā fīʾl-naṣīha*, Süleymaniye Kütüphanesi, ms. Aya Sofya 2907

Jones, A.H.M., *The Later Roman Empire, 284–602*, 2 vols., Oxford 1973.

Juvaynī, ʿAlāʾ al-Dīn ʿAṭā Malik, *Tārīkh-i jahān-gushā*, ed. M.M. Qazvīnī, 3 vols., Leiden and London 1912–37

Kaegi, W.E., 'New Perspectives on the Last Decades of the Byzantine Era', *Proceedings of the Symposium on Bilād al-Shām during the Byzantine Period*, eds. M. ʿA. Bakhīt and M. ʿAṣfūr, Amman 1986

Kangle, R.P., The Kauṭilīya Arthaśāstra, 3 vols., Bombay 1963

Karp, L.A., 'Sahl b. Hârûn: The Man and his Contribution to *ʾAdab*', unpublished Ph.D. thesis, Harvard University, 1992

Karpat, K., 'Some Historical and Methodological Considerations Concerning Social Stratification in the Middle East', *Commoners, Climbers and Notables. A Sampler of Studies on Social Ranking in the Middle East*, ed. C.A.O. van Nieuwenhuijze, Leiden 1977

al-Kāshī, ʿAbd al-ʿAzīz, *Rawḍat al-nāẓir wa nuzhat al-khāṭir*, Topkapı Sarayı Kütüphanesi, ms. 2452

Kāshifī, Ḥusayn Vāʿiẓ, *Akhlāq-i Muḥsinī*, Hertford 1850

al-Kashshī, M. b. ʿUmar, *Rijāl al-Kashshī*, ed. S.A. al-Ḥusaynī, Karbalāʾ n.d.

al-Kātib, Isḥāq b. Ibrāhīm, *al-Burhān fī wujūh al-bayān*, eds. A. Maṭlūb and Kh. al-Ḥadīthī, Baghdad 1387/1967

Kay Kāʾūs, ʿUnṣur al-Maʿālī b. Iskandar, *Qābūsnāmeh*, ed. Gh.Ḥ. Yūsufī, Tehran 1368

Kennedy, H., 'The Last Century of Byzantine Syria: A Reinterpretation', *Byzantinische Forschungen* 10, 1985

Kent, R.G., *Old Persian*, New Haven 1953

al-Khūʾī, Ḥasan, *Ghunyat al-kātib wa munyat al-ṭālib*, ed. A.S. Erzi, Ankara 1963

Khuri, F., 'Work in Islamic Thought', *al-Abhath* 21, 1968
al-Khwārazmī, *Kitāb mafātīḥ al-ʿulūm*, ed. G. van Vloten, Leiden 1895
Kimber, R.A., 'The Early Abbasid Vizierate', *JSS* 37, 1992
Kinberg, L., 'Compromise of Commerce. A Study of Early Traditions Concerning Poverty and Wealth', *Der Islam* 66, 1989
Kirmānī, Afḍal al-Dīn, *ʿIqd al-ʿulā lil-mawqif al-aʿlā*, Tehran 1311
Kirmānī, Nāṣir al-Dīn, *Nasāʾim al-asḥār min laṭāʾim al-akhbār*, ed. Jalāl al-Dīn Muḥaddith, Tehran 1338/1378q
Simṭ al-ʿulā lil-ḥaḍrat al-ʿulyā, Tehran 1328/1949
Kister, M.J., '"Do not assimilate yourselves . . ." *Lā tashabbahū*', *JSAI* 12, 1989
'Ḳays b. ʿĀṣim', *EI2*
'Land Property and jihād', *JESHO* 34, 1991
Kister, M.J. and M. Plessner, 'Notes on Caskel's Ǧamharat an-nasab', *Oriens* 25–26, 1976–7
Kohlberg, E., 'Āmedī, Abu'l-Fatḥ Nāṣeḥ al-Dīn', *Encyclopaedia Iranica*
Köpstein, H., 'Das 7. Jahrhundert (565–711) im Prozess der Herausbildung des Feudalismus in Byzanz', *Byzanz im 7. Jahrhundert. Untersuchungen zur Herausbildung des Feudalismus*, eds. F. Winkelmann, H. Köpstein, H. Ditten and I. Rochow, Berlin 1978
Krader, L., *Peoples of Central Asia*, The Hague 1971
Social Organization of the Mongol-Turkic Pastoral Nomads, The Hague 1963
Kraemer, J.L., *Humanism in the Renaissance of Islam. The Cultural Revival during the Būyid Age*, 2nd edition, Leiden and New York 1992
Kratchkovsky, I., 'Le *kitāb al-ādāb* d'Ibn al-Muʿtazz', *Le monde oriental* 16, 1924
Krenkow, F., 'al-Sakkākī', *EI1*
al-Kulīnī, *al-Kāfī*, 8 vols., Tehran 1377–81/1957–61
Kuthayyir, *Sharḥ dīwān Kuthayyir ʿAzza*, ed. H. Pérès, Paris-Algiers 1930
Lambton, A.K.S., *Continuity and Change in Medieval Persia*, Albany, New York 1988
'Islamic Mirrors for Princes', *Quaderno dell'Accademia Nazionale dei Lincei* 160, *La Persia nel medioevo*, Rome 1971
Islamic Society in Persia, London 1954
'Justice in the Medieval Persian Theory of Kingship', *SI* 17, 1962
'The Dilemma of Government in Islamic Persia: The *Siyāsat-Nāma* of Niẓām al-Mulk', *Iran* 22, 1984
'The Merchant in Medieval Islam', *A Locust's Leg. Studies in Honour of S.H. Taqizadeh*, ed. W. Henning, London 1962
Lapidus, I.M., *A History of Islamic Societies*, Cambridge 1988
'Muslim Cities and Islamic Societies', *Middle Eastern Cities*, ed. I.M. Lapidus, Berkeley and Los Angeles 1969
Muslim Cities in the Later Middle Ages, Cambridge, Massachusetts 1967
'The Arab Conquests and the Formation of Islamic Society', *Studies on the First Century of Islamic Society*, ed. G.H.A. Juynboll, Carbondale and Edwardsville 1982
'The Evolution of Muslim Urban Society', *Comparative Studies in Society and History* 15, 1973
Latham, J.D., 'Observations on the Text and Translation of al-Jarsifi's Treatise on "Hisba"', *JSS* 5, 1960

'The Beginnings of Arabic Prose Literature: The Epistolary Genre', *Arabic Literature to the End of the Umayyad Period*, eds. A.F.L. Beeston, T.M. Johnstone, R.B. Serjeant and G.R. Smith, Cambridge 1983

Lecomte, G., *Ibn Qutayba (mort en 276/889). L'homme, son oeuvre, ses idées*, Damascus 1965

Lévi-Provençal, É., *Séville musulmane au début du xiie siècle*, Paris 1947

'Un document sur la vie urbaine et les corps de métiers à Séville au début du XIIe siècle: le traité d'Ibn 'Abdūn', *JA* 224, 1934

Levy, R., *The Sociology of Islam*, London 1931–33; 2nd edn *The Social Structure of Islam*, Cambridge 1957

Lewis, B., 'An Epistle on Manual Crafts', *IC* 17, 1943

Islam from the Prophet Muhammad to the Capture of Constantinople, 2 vols., New York and Oxford 1987

The Origins of Ismā'īlism, Cambridge 1940

The Political Language of Islam, Chicago and London 1988

Linant de Bellefonds, Y., 'Kafā'a', *EI2*

Lindholm, C., 'Kinship Structure and Political Authority: The Middle East and Central Asia', *Comparative Studies in Society and History* 28, 1986

'Quandaries of Command in Egalitarian Societies: Examples from Swat and Morocco', *Comparing Muslim Societies. Knowledge and the State in a World Civilization*, ed. J.R. Cole, Ann Arbor 1992

Madelung, W., 'Al-Hamadani's Description of Northern Yemen in the Light of Chronicles of the 4th/10th and 5th/11th Centuries', *Religious and Ethnic Movements in Medieval Islam*, Hampshire 1992

'Ar-Rāġib al-Iṣfahānī und die Ethik al-Ġazālīs', *Islamwissenschaftliche Abhandlungen*, ed. R. Gramlich, Wiesbaden 1974

'Ḳarmaṭī', *EI2*

'Khurramiyya', *EI2*

Religious Trends in Early Islamic Iran, Albany, New York 1988

'Naṣīr ad-Dīn Ṭūsī's Ethics Between Philosophy, Shi'ism and Sufism', *Ethics in Islam*, ed. R.G. Hovannisian, Malibu, California, 1985

'The Assumption of the Title Shāhānshāh by the Būyids and "the Reign of the Daylam (*dawlat al-Daylam*)"', *JNES* 28, 1969

Malaṭyavī, Muḥammad b. Ghāzī, *Barīd al-sa'āda*, ed. M. Shīrvānī, Tehran 1351/1972

Mālik, *al-Muwaṭṭa'*, ed. M.F. 'Abd al-Bāqī, Cairo 1370/1951

al-Maqdisī, *Kitāb al-bad' wa'l-ta'rīkh*, 6 vols., Beirut n.d.

Marlow, L., 'Some Classical Muslim Views of the Indian Caste System', *Muslim World* 85, 1995

'Kings, Prophets and the *'Ulamā'* in Mediaeval Islamic Advice Literature', *SI* 81, 1995

Masse, H., 'Ibn al-Faḳīh', *EI2*

al-Mas'ūdī, 'Alī b. al-Ḥusayn, *Kitāb al-tanbīh wa'l-ishrāf*, ed. M.J. de Goeje, Leiden 1967

Murūj al-dhahab, 4 vols., Beirut 1404/1984

Maududi, S. Abul A'la, *Political Theory of Islam*, Lahore 1980

Witnesses unto Mankind. The Purpose and Duty of the Muslim Umma, Leicester 1986

al-Māwardī, Abū'l-Ḥasan 'Alī b. M., *Adab al-dunyā wa'l-dīn*, ed. M. Karīm Rājiḥ, Beirut 1401/1981

al-Aḥkām al-sulṭāniyya, Cairo 1960
al-Nukat wa'l-'uyūn, Tafsīr al-Māwardī, ed. al-Sayyid b. 'Abd al-Maqṣūd b. 'Abd al-Raḥīm, 6 vols., Beirut 1412/1992
Qawānīn al-wizāra wa siyāsat al-mulk, ed. R. al-Sayyid, Beirut 1979
Tashīl al-naẓar wa ta'jīl al-ẓafar fī akhlāq al-malik wa siyāsat al-mulk, ed. R. al-Sayyid, Beirut 1987
al-Mawṣilī, al-Mubārak b. Khalīl, *Adab al-siyāsa bi'l-'adl*, Köprülü Kütüphanesi, ms. 1200
al-Maydānī, *Majma' al-amthāl*, 2 vols., Beirut 1961–1962
McAuliffe, J.D., *Qur'ānic Christians. An Analysis of Classical and Modern Exegesis*, Cambridge 1991
Minorsky, V., 'The Older Preface to the *Shāh-nāma*', *Studi orientalistici in onore di G. Levi della Vida*, vol. 2, 1956
Minovi, M. (ed.), *Tansarnāmeh*, Tehran 1932. Tr. M. Boyce, *The Letter of Tansar*, Rome 1968
Minovi, M., 'Az khazā'in-i Turkīyeh', *Majalleh-yi Dānishkadeh-yi Adabīyāt* 4, 1335/1957
Minovi, M. and V. Minorsky, 'Naṣīr al-Dīn Ṭūsī on Finance', *BSOAS* 10, 1940
Miskawayh, A. b. M., *Tajārib al-umam*, 3 vols. Leiden and London 1909–17
Tahdhīb al-akhlāq, ed. C.K. Zurayk, Beirut 1966. Tr. C.K. Zurayk, *The Refinement of Character*, Beirut 1968
Molé, M., *Culte, mythe et cosmologie dans l'Iran ancien. Le problème zoroastrien et la tradition mazdéenne*, Paris 1963
Morony, M., 'Conquerors and Conquered: Iran', *Studies on the First Century of Islamic Society*, ed. G.H.A. Juynboll, Carbondale and Edwardsville 1982
Iraq after the Muslim Conquest, Princeton 1984
Mottahedeh, R.P., 'Attitudes Towards Absolutism', *Israel Oriental Studies* 10, 1980
Loyalty and Leadership in an Early Islamic Society, Princeton 1980
'The Shu'ûbîyah Controversy and the Social History of Early Islamic Iran', *IJMES* 7, 1976
Mourad, Y., *La physiognomie arabe et le Kitāb al-firāsa de Fakhr al-Dīn al-Rāzī*, Paris 1939
Mousnier, R., *Social Hierarchies*, New York 1973. Tr. P. Evans
al-Mubashshir b. Fātik, *Mukhtār al-ḥikam wa maḥāsin al-kalim*, ed. 'Abd al-Raḥmān Badawī, Madrid 1377/1958
Muḥammad b. Ibrāhīm, *Tārīkh-i Saljūqīyān-i Kirmān*, ed. M.Th. Houtsma, *Recueil de textes relatifs à l'histoire des Seljoucides*, vol. 1, *Histoire des Seljoucides du Kermân*, Leiden 1886
al-Muḥāsibī, al-Ḥārith b. Asad, *al-Makāsib*, ed. 'Abd al-Qādir Aḥmad 'Aṭā, Beirut 1407/1987
Muslim b. al-Ḥajjāj, *al-Ṣaḥīḥ*, 8 vols., Beirut n.d.
Mustawfī, Ḥamd Allāh, *Tārīkh-i guzīdeh*, London 1910–1913
al-Muttaqī al-Hindī, 'Alī b. 'Abd al-Malik, *Kanz al-'ummāl fī sunan al-aqwāl wa'l-af'āl*, 16 vols., Aleppo 1969–78
al-Nāhī, Ṣalāḥ al-Dīn, *al-Khawālid min ārā' al-Rāghib al-Iṣfahānī*, Amman and Beirut 1407/1987
al-Najāshī, *Kitāb al-rijāl*, Tehran n.d.
al-Nasā'ī, A. b. Shu'ayb, *Sunan*, ed. M. 'Alī Da''ās, 2 vols., Homs 1388/1968

Nāṣir-i Khusraw, *Safarnāmeh*, ed. M. Dabīr Siyāqī, Tehran 1354. Tr. C. Schefer, *Sefernameh. Relation du voyage de Nassiri Khosrau*, Amsterdam 1970
Niẓām al-Mulk, *Siyar al-mulūk* (*Siyāsatnāmeh*), ed. H.S.G. Darke, Tehran 1347. Tr. H.S.G. Darke, *The Book of Government or Rules for Kings*, London 1960
Nöldeke, Th., 'Geschichte des Artachšîr i Pâpakân', *Beiträge zur Kunde der indo-germanischen Sprachen* 4, 1878
al-Nuʿmān b. Muḥammad, al-Qāḍī, *Daʿā'im al-Islām*, Cairo 1383/1963
Patlagean, E., *Pauvreté économique et pauvreté sociale à Byzance, 4e–7e siècles*, Paris 1977
Pellat, C., 'al-Aḥnaf b. Ḳays', *EI2*
'Ǧāḥiẓiana, I: Le *kitāb al-tabaṣṣur bi-l-tiğāra* attribué à Ǧāḥiẓ', *Arabica* 1, 1954
'Ǧāḥiẓiana, II: Le dernier chapitre des *Avares* de Ǧāḥiẓ', *Arabica* 2, 1955
'Ǧāḥiẓiana III. Essai d'inventaire de l'oeuvre ğāḥiẓienne', *Arabica* 3, 1957
'Nouvel essai d'inventaire de l'oeuvre ğāḥiẓienne', *Arabica* 31, 1984
'Une charge contre les secrétaires d'état attribuée à Ǧāḥiẓ', *Hespéris* 48, 1956
'Un document important pour l'histoire politico-religieuse de l'Islam: La «Nâbita» de Djâhiz', *AIEO* 10, 1952
Perikhanian, A., 'Iranian Society and Law', *Cambridge History of Iran*, vol. 3 (2), ed. E. Yarshater, Cambridge 1983
Peters, F.E., *Aristotle and the Arabs, the Aristotelian Tradition in Islam*, New York 1968
Pines, S., 'Aristotle's *Politics* in Arabic Philosophy', *Israel Oriental Studies* 5, 1975
Pingree, D., *The Thousands of Abū Maʿshar*, London 1968
Plato, *The Laws*, tr. T.J. Saunders, Harmondsworth, 1970
The Republic, tr. M.D.P. Lee, Harmondsworth, 1955
Plessner, M., *Der Oikonomikos des Neupythagoräers Bryson*, Heidelberg 1928
'Hermes Trismegistus and Arab Science', *SI* 2, 1954
al-Qāḍī, W., 'An Early Fāṭimid Political Document', *SI* 48, 1978
'Early Islamic State Letters: The Question of Authenticity', *The Byzantine and Early Islamic Near East*, vol. 1, *Problems in the Literary Source Material*, eds. Averil Cameron and L.I. Conrad, Princeton 1992
'The Earliest "Nābita" and the Paradigmatic "Nawābit"', *SI* 78, 1993
al-Qālī, Abū ʿAlī, *Kitāb al-amālī*, 3 vols., Cairo 1344/1926
al-Rabīʿ b. Ḥabīb al-Farāhīdī, *al-Jāmiʿ al-ṣaḥīḥ*, Cairo 1970
al-Rāmhurmuzī, al-Ḥasan b. ʿAbd al-Raḥmān, *K. amthāl al-ḥadīth*, ed. Amatulkarim Qureshi, Hyderabad 1388/1968
Rashīd al-Dīn, *Mukātabāt-i Rashīd al-Dīn Faḍl Allāh*, ed. M. Shafīʿ, Lahore 1376/1947
Rawḍat al-nāẓir wa nuzhat al-khāṭir, Süleymaniye Kütüphanesi, ms. Fatih 5324
al-Rāzī, Abū'l-Futūḥ, *Tafsīr-i rawḥ al-jinān wa rūḥ al-janān*, ed. ʿAlī Akbar Ghaffārī, 13 vols., Tehran 1398h
al-Rāzī, Fakhr al-Dīn, *al-Tafsīr al-kabīr*, 32 vols., Cairo 1934–62
Jāmiʿ al-ʿulūm, ed. M.Ḥ. Tasbīḥī, Tehran 1346
al-Rāzī, Najm al-Dīn Dāya, *Mirṣād al-ʿibād min al-mabda' ilā'l-maʿād*, ed. Ḥ. al-Ḥusaynī al-Niʿmatullāhī, Tehran 1312. Tr. H. Algar, *The Path of God's Bondsmen from Origin to Return*, New York 1982
Rescher, O., 'Arabische Handschriften des Top Kapú Seraj', *RSO* 4, 1912
Excerpte und Übersetzungen aus den Schriften des Philologen und Dogmatikers Ǧâḥiẓ aus Baçra (150–250 H.), Erster Teil, Stuttgart 1931
'Über arabische Handschriften der Aja Sofia', *WZKM* 26, 1912

Richter, G., *Studien zur Geschichte der älteren arabischen Fürstenspiegel*, Leipzig 1932

Ritter, H., 'Ein arabisches Handbuch der Handelswissenschaft', *Der Islam* 7, 1917

'Studien zur Geschichte der islamischen Frömmigkeit', I, 'Ḥasan al-Baṣrī', *Der Islam* 21, 1933

Rodinson, M., 'Histoire économique et histoire des classes sociales dans le monde musulman', *Studies in the Economic History of the Middle East*, ed. M.A. Cook, Oxford 1970

Roques, R., *L'Univers dionysien: structure hiérarchique du monde selon le Pseudo-Denys*, Paris 1983

Rosenthal, E.I.J., *Political Thought in Medieval Islam*, Cambridge 1962

Rosenthal, F., 'Al-Mubashshir b. Fātik: Prolegomena to an Abortive Edition', *Oriens* 13, 1961

'From Arabic Books and Manuscripts, XVI: As-Sarakhsī (?) on the Appropriate Behavior for Kings', *JAOS* 115, 1995

'Ibn Abī Ṭāhir Ṭayfūr', *EI2*

Knowledge Triumphant, Leiden 1970

'On the Knowledge of Plato's Philosophy in the Islamic World', *IC* 14, 1940

'State and Religion According to Abū l-Ḥasan al-ʿĀmirī', *IQ* 3, 1956

The Muslim Concept of Freedom, Leiden 1960

Rosenthal, F. (tr.), *The Muqaddimah, An Introduction to History*, 3 vols., Princeton 1967

Rowson, E.K., 'al-ʿĀmirī', *EI2* (Suppl.)

'al-Rāghib al-Iṣfahānī', *EI2*

A Muslim Philosopher on the Soul and its Fate, New Haven 1988

Sadan, J., 'A "closed-circuit" saying on practical justice', *JSAI* 10, 1987

'Kings and Craftsmen. A Pattern of Contrasts', *SI* 56, 1982 and 62, 1985

Sadighi, Gh.H., *Les mouvements religieux iraniens au IIe et au IIIe siècle de l'hégire*, Paris 1938

al-Ṣadr, al-Sayyid Ḥasan, *Ta'sīs al-shīʿa*, Tehran n.d.

Ṣafā, Ẓabīḥ Allāh, *Hamāseh-sarāʾī dar Īrān*, Tehran 1363

al-Ṣafadī, Khalīl b. Aybak, *Kitāb al-wāfī bi'l-wafayāt*, Wiesbaden 1962–

Ṣafwat, A. Zakī, *Jamharat rasā'il al-ʿarab fī ʿuṣūr al-ʿarabiyya al-zāhira*, 4 vols., Cairo 1356/1937

Saḥnūn, Abū Saʿīd b. Saʿīd al-Tanūkhī, *al-Mudawwana al-kubrā*, 16 vols., Cairo 1323/1905

Ṣāʿid al-Andalusī, *Kitāb ṭabaqāt al-umam*, tr. R. Blachère, *Le livre des catégories des nations*, Paris 1935

Salem, E.A., *Political Theory and Institutions of the Khawārij*, Baltimore 1956

Salinger, G., 'A Muslim Mirror for Princes', *Muslim World* 46, 1956

Samarqandī, Niẓāmī ʿArūḍī, *Chahār maqāleh*, ed. M.M. b. ʿAbd al-Wahhāb, London 1910

Sanjana, D.D.P. (ed. and tr.), *The Kârnâmê î Artakhshîr î Pâpakân*, Bombay 1896

al-Sarakhsī, M. b. A., *Kitāb al-Mabsūṭ*, 30 vols., Cairo 1324–1331/1906–1913

al-Sayyid, R., 'al-Khilāfa wa'l-mulk: Dirāsa fī'l-ru'ya al-umawiyya lil-salṭa', *Proceedings of the Fourth International Conference on the History of Bilād al-Shām During the Umayyad Period*, ed. M.ʿA. Bakhīt, Amman 1989

al-Umma wa'l-jamāʿa wa'l-salṭa, Beirut 1404/1984

Mafāhīm al-jamāʿāt fī'l-Islām, Beirut 1984

Schoeler, G., 'Verfasser und Titel des dem Ǧāḥiẓ zugeschriebenen sog. *Kitāb at-Tāǧ*', *ZDMG* 130, 1980
Schönig, H., *Das Sendschreiben des ʿAbdalḥamīd b. Yaḥyā (gest. 132/750) an den Kronprinzen ʿAbdallāh b. Marwān II*, Stuttgart 1985
Schwartz, M., 'The Old Eastern Iranian World View According to the Avesta', *Cambridge History of Iran*, vol. 2, ed. I. Gershevitch, Cambridge 1985
Sellheim, R., 'Abū ʿAlī al-Qālī. Zum Problem mündlicher und schriftlicher Überlieferung am Beispiel von Sprichwörtersammlungen', *Studien zur Geschichte und Kultur des Vorderen Orients. Festschrift für Bertold Spuler zum 70sten Geburtstag*, eds. H.R. Roemer and A. Noth, Leiden 1981
Die klassisch-arabischen Sprichwörtersammlungen insbesondere die des Abū ʿUbaid, The Hague 1954
Serjeant, R.B., 'A Zaidī Manual of Ḥisbah of the Third Century', *RSO* 28, 1953
'Social Stratification in Arabia', *The Islamic City*, ed. R.B. Serjeant, Paris 1980
'South Arabia', *Commoners, Climbers and Notables. A Sampler of Studies on Social Ranking in the Middle East*, ed. C.A.O. van Nieuwenhuijze, Leiden 1977
'The Caliph ʿUmar's Letters to Abū Mūsā al-Ashʿarī and Muʿāwiya', *JSS* 29, 1984
Sezgin, F., *Geschichte des arabischen Schrifttums*, 9 vols., Leiden 1967–
al-Shāfiʿī, M. b. Idrīs, *Kitāb al-umm*, 8 vols., Cairo 1381/1961
Shaked, S., 'From Iran to Islam: Notes on Some Themes in Transmission', *JSAI* 4, 1984
'From Iran to Islam: On Some Symbols of Royalty', *JSAI* 7, 1986
Shahîd, I., 'Ghassānid and Umayyad Structures: A Case of *Byzance après Byzance*', *La Syrie de Byzance à l'Islam, VIIe–VIII siècles*, eds. P. Canivet and J.-P. Rey-Coquais, Damascus 1992
Shaki, M., 'Class System', iii, *Encyclopaedia Iranica*
'The Social Doctrine of Mazdak in the Light of Middle Persian Evidence', *Archív Orientální* 46, 1978
al-Shaʿrānī, ʿAbd al-Wahhāb b. A., *al-Mīzān al-kubrā*, 2 vols., Cairo 1940
Shatzmiller, M., 'Aspects of Women's Participation in the Economic Life of Later Medieval Islam: Occupations and Mentalities', *Arabica* 35, 1988
Labour in the Medieval Islamic World, Leiden 1994
al-Shaybānī, *Kitāb al-kasb*, ed. S. Zakkār, Damascus 1400/1980
al-Shayzarī, ʿAbd al-Raḥmān, *Nihāyat al-rutba fī ṭalab al-ḥisba*, ed. al-ʿArīnī, Cairo 1365/1946
Shīrāzī, Quṭb al-Dīn, *Durrat al-tāj*, ed. S.M. Mishkāt, 2 vols., Tehran 1317–1324/1938–1945
Sourdel, D., 'Barāmika', *EI2*
Le vizirat ʿabbāside de 749 à 939 (132 à 324 de l'hégire), Damascus 1959–1960
'Questions de cérémonial ʿabbaside', *REI* 28, 1960
Spuler, B., 'Die historische Literatur Persiens bis zum 13. Jahrhundert als Spiegel seiner geistigen Entwicklung', *Saeculum* 8, 1957
Iran in früh-islamischer Zeit, Wiesbaden 1952
'The Evolution of Persian Historiography', *Historians of the Middle East*, eds. B. Lewis and P.M. Holt, London 1962
Steinschneider, M., *Die hebräischen Übersetzungen des Mittelalters und die Juden als Dolmetscher*, Graz 1956

Rangstreit-Literatur. Ein Beitrag zur vergleichenden Literatur und Kulturgeschichte, Vienna 1908

'Über die arabischen Übersetzungen aus dem Griechischen', Erster Abschnitt, *Zentralblatt für Bibliothekswesen*, Beiheft 12, 1893

Stern, S.M., 'New Information about the Authors of the "Epistles of the Sincere Brethren"', *Islamic Studies* 3, 1964

'The Authorship of the Epistles of the Ikhwān-aṣ-Ṣafā', *IC* 20, 1946

Storey, C.A., *Persian Literature, A Bio-Bibliographical Survey*, London 1927–1936

Stroumsa, S., 'The Beginnings of the Muʿtazila Reconsidered', *JSAI* 13, 1990

al-Ṭabarānī, *al-Muʿjam al-ṣaghīr*, ed. ʿAbd al-Raḥman Muḥammad ʿUthmān, Cairo 1388/1968

al-Ṭabarī, Abū Jaʿfar. *Jāmiʿ al-bayān ʿan taʾwīl al-Qurʾān*, eds. M.M. Shākir and A.M. Shākir, 16 vols. Cairo 1373/1954–

Taʾrīkh al-rusul waʾl-mulūk, ed. M. Abūʾl-Faḍl Ibrāhīm, 11 vols., Cairo 1977

Tafazzoli, A., 'Āʾīnnāme', *Encyclopaedia Iranica*

'Observations sur le soi-disant Mazdak-Nāmag', *Acta Iranica* 23, 1984

al-Tawḥīdī, Abū Ḥayyān, *al-Baṣāʾir waʾl-dhakhāʾir*, ed. W. al-Qāḍī, 8 vols., Beirut 1408/1988

Kitāb al-imtāʿ waʾl-muʾānasa, eds. A. Amīn and A. al-Zayn, 3 vols., Beirut 1966 (reprint of Cairo edition, 1939)

al-Thaʿālibī, Abū Manṣūr, *Ghurar akhbār mulūk al-Furs*, ed. H. Zotenberg, Paris 1900

Laṭāʾif al-maʿārif, eds. Ibrāhīm al-Ibyārī and Ḥasan Kāmil al-Ṣayrafī, Cairo 1379/1960. Tr. C.E. Bosworth, *The Book of Curious and Entertaining Information*, Edinburgh 1968

al-Thaʿlabī, A. b. M., *ʿArāʾis al-majālis*, Cairo 1929

al-Tirmidhī, M. b. ʿĪsā, *al-Jāmiʿ al-ṣaḥīḥ*, ed. ʿAbd al-Raḥmān Muḥammad ʿUthmān, Medina n.d.

al-Tuḥfa al-bahiyya waʾl-ṭurfa al-shahriyya, Constantinople 1302

al-Ṭurṭūshī, Ibn Abī Randaqa, *Sirāj al-mulūk*, Cairo 1354/1935

Ṭūsī, Naṣīr al-Dīn, *Akhlāq-i Muḥtashamī*, Tehran 1339

Akhlāq-i Nāṣirī, ed. M. Minovi, Tehran 1356/1978. Tr. G.M. Wickens, *The Nasirean Ethics*, London 1964

Rawḍat al-taslīm, ed. W. Ivanow, Leiden 1950

al-Ṭūsī, M. b. al-Ḥasan Shaykh al-Ṭāʾifa, *Tafsīr al-tibyān*, ed. A.Ḥ.Q. al-ʿĀmilī, 10 vols., Najaf 1376–1383/1957–1963

Urmavī, Sirāj al-Dīn, *Laṭāʾif al-ḥikma*, ed. Gh.Ḥ. Yūsufī, Tehran 1351

Vadet, J.C., 'Le souvenir de l'ancienne Perse chez le philosophe Abū l-Ḥasan al-ʿĀmirī (m. 381 H.)', *Arabica* 11, 1964

van Ess, J., *Die Gedankenwelt des Ḥāriṯ al-Muḥāsibī*, Bonn 1961

Theologie und Gesellschaft, 6 vols., Berlin 1991–

Zwischen Ḥadīṯ und Theologie, Berlin 1975

van Gelder, G.J., 'The Conceit of Pen and Sword: On an Arabic Literary Debate', *JSS* 32, 1987

Vaṭvāṭ, Rashīd al-Dīn, *Maṭlūb kull ṭālib min kalām ʿAlī b. Abī Ṭālib*, ed. M.H.L. Fleischer, *Ali's hundert Sprüche*, Leipzig 1837

Maṭlūb kull ṭālib min kalām amīr al-muʾminīn ʿAlī b. Abī Ṭālib, ed. Jalāl al-Dīn Muḥaddith, Tehran 1342sh/1382q

von Grunebaum, G., *Medieval Islam, A Study in Cultural Orientation*, Chicago 1946

Wagner, E., 'Die arabische Rangstreitdichtung und ihre Einordnung in die allgemeine Literaturgeschichte', *Abhandlung der Akademie der Wissenschaft und der Literatur in Mainz* 8, 1962

Waldman, M.R., *Toward a Theory of Historical Narrative: A Case Study in Perso-Islamicate Historiography*, Columbus, Ohio 1980

al-Wāqidī, Muḥammad b. ʿUmar, *Kitāb al-maghāzī*, 3 vols., ed. M. Jones, London 1966

Wellhausen, J., *Die religiös-politischen Oppositionsparteien im alten Islam*, Berlin 1901

Werkmeister, W., *Quellenuntersuchungen zum Kitāb al-ʿIqd al-farīd des Andalusiers Ibn ʿAbdrabbih (246/860–328/940)*, Berlin 1983

Wickens, G.M., 'Al-Jarsīfī on the *ḥisba*', *IQ* 3, 1956

Widengren, G., 'The Sacral Kingship of Iran', *Studies in the History of Religions*, Supplements to *Numen*, vol. 4, *The Sacral Kingship, la regalità sacra*, Leiden 1959

Wilkinson, J.C., 'Ibāḍī Ḥadīth: An Essay on Normalization', *Der Islam* 62, 1985

Winkelmann, F., *Quellenstudien zur herrschenden Klasse von Byzanz im 8. und 9. Jahrhundert*, Berlin 1987

'Zum byzantinischen Staat', *Byzanz im 7. Jahrhundert. Untersuchungen zur Herausbildung des Feudalismus*, eds. F. Winkelmann, H. Köpstein, H. Ditten and I. Rochow, Berlin 1978

al-Yaʿqūbī, *Ta'rīkh al-Yaʿqūbī*, 2 vols., Beirut n.d.

Yāqūt, *Muʿjam al-udabā*, 20 vols., Cairo n.d.

Yarshater, E., 'Iranian National History', *Cambridge History of Iran*, vol. 3 (1), ed. E. Yarshater, Cambridge 1983

al-Yāzijī, Nāṣīf, *al-ʿArf al-ṭayyib fī sharḥ dīwān Abī'l-Ṭayyib*, 2 vols., Beirut 1384/1964

Zaehner, R.C., *The Dawn and Twilight of Zoroastrianism*, London 1961

al-Zamakhsharī, Maḥmūd b. ʿUmar, *al-Kashshāf ʿan ḥaqā'iq al-tanzīl wa ʿuyūn al-aqāwīl*, 4 vols., Cairo 1385/1966

al-Mustaqṣā fī amthāl al-ʿarab, 2 vols., Hyderabad 1381/1962

Zaydān, J., *Ta'rīkh ādāb al-lugha al-ʿarabiyya*, 4 vols., Cairo 1957

Ziadeh, F.J., 'Equality (*kafā'a*) in the Muslim Law of Marriage', *American Journal of Comparative Law* 6, 1957

Zimmermann, F., 'The Origins of the So-Called *Theology of Aristotle*', *Pseudo-Aristotle in the Middle Ages*, eds. J. Kraye, W.F. Ryan and C.B. Schmitt, London 1986

Index to Qur'ānic verses

2:247, 3
2:251, 4
3:195, 19
4:28, 146n12
4:59, 137
4:95, 3–4
5:48, 149, 151
6:124, 145
6:143, 134
6:165, 149, 151
8:28, 3n9
11:117–118, 146, 149–50, 151
13:4, 150, 151
16:71, 146n13
16:75, 3
17:21, 4, 35n132, 149, 151
17:84, 151, 152n44
18:47, 3, 113
22:5, 149n27
23:53, 150, 151, 152n44
23:55–56, 3n9
24:37, 154
25:20, 152n44
26:88–89, 3
26:215, 131
30:22, 149n27
32:18, 3
34:37, 3n9
39:6, 134
42:27, 153
43:32, 4, 148–9, 151, 152n44
49:13, 2–3, 3n6, 24, 28, 32, 94, 96–9, 105n45, 106, 175
63:9, 3n9
64:15, 3n9
66:6, 154
67:3, 148
68:14–15, 3n9
71:14, 37n137, 148, 151

General index

ʿAbd al-Ḥamīd al-Kātib, 14n3, 20, 39, 100, 119
ʿAbd al-Malik, 24n54, 33n120, 36n134, 118
Abū'l-ʿAtāhiya, 163
Abū Ghānim, 33
Abū Ḥanīfa, 32
Abū Sufyān b. Ḥarb, 35, 36n135
Abū ʿUbayd, al-Qāsim b. al-Sallām, 17, 18, 27
Abū Yūsuf, 31
accountants, 7, 57, 81, 82, 135, 161
al-Afwah al-Awdī, 60
agriculture, 7, 64, 86, 127, 142, 147, 158, 159, 160, 162, 163, *see also* cultivators
Aḥmad b. Ḥanbal, 31, 32, 165
al-Aḥnaf b. Qays, 38, 154n52
Alexander, 47, 75, 100
ʿAlī b. Abī Ṭālib, 5, 14, 15, 16, 28–30, 36n135, 87, 94, 114, 122–5, 128n61, 130, 139–41, 154, 163
al-ʿĀmirī, 27, 28n78, 50n45, 55, 58, 59, 60, 62, 84, 88–9
Anūshīrvān, 28n78, 73, 83–7
Ardashīr, 40n150, 60, 70n20, 73, 74, 75, 76, 83–7
Aristotle, 27, 28n78, 47, 48, 49, 50, 51, 52, 54, 58n89, 59, 60, 62, 75, 100, 127n57, 131, 176
artisans, 64, 70, 71, 72, 73, 75, 78, 79, 80, 81, 82, 83, 84, 84n88, 123, 124, 125, 126, 127, 131, 134, 135, 147, 154, 157, 166
al-ʿAskarī, Abū Hilāl, 18, 19, 20, 21, 22
audiences, 16, 34–6
Avesta, 69–70, 72, 88

Bābak, 95–6
Baḥr al-favā'id, 135–6
Balʿamī, 79, 80, 81, 82, 83
Banū Hāshim, 23–24, 102
Banū Umayya, 23, 24n54
Barmakids, 38, 104n41
Baṣra, 18, 34, 38, 112n79, 115n86
al-Bayḍāwī, 96, 97
Bayhaqī, Abū'l-Faḍl, 56
al-Bayhaqī, Ibrāhīm b. Muḥammad, 17n16, 109
beggars, 59, 127, 154
Bih'āfarīd, 95
al-Bīrūnī, 74, 84, 88
biṭāna (caliphal entourage), 119, *see also ṣaḥāba*
builders, building, 64, 82, 126, 159, 161, 163
Buzurgmihr, 109n68, 113n83

Christianity, 1, 6, 43, 44–5, 64
cultivators, 7, 40n150, 57, 70, 71, 72, 73, 75, 79, 80, 82, 83, 84, 85n90, 86, 87, 123, 124, 126, 127, 130, 131, 134, 135, 142, 147, *see also* agriculture
cuppers, 33, 152, 153, 155, 161, 162, 163, 165, 167

al-Dimashqī, Jaʿfar b. ʿAlī, 160–61, 164, 169

Egypt, 42, 43, 44, 45, 46, 48, 64, 65, 160, 167

al-Faḍl b. Yaḥyā al-Barmakī, 38
al-Fārābī, 49, 50–55, 56, 57, 60–62
al-Farazdaq, 19, 20n31
Firdawsī, 73, 80
fuqahā', see *ʿulamā'*

Gardīzī, 81
genealogical rivalry, 5, 22ff, 98, *see also nasab*
al-Ghazālī, 138, 148, 152–3, 154–5, 159, 164–5, 166

Ḥanafīs, 31, 33, 158, 163
Ḥanbalīs, 158
ḥasab (inherited merit), 5, 20, 24, 25, 29, 31, 32, 39, 62, 75, 98, 102, 103, 109, 110, 111, 119, 125, 131
al-Ḥasan al-Baṣrī, 122
Hāshimites, see Banū Hāshim
Hellenism, 44–5, 46, 47, 65
Hermes, 47–8

Hishām b. ʿAbd al-Malik, 38, 39, 100
ḥisba, 39n149, 166–8

Ibāḍīs, 33
Ibn ʿAbd Rabbihi, 17, 18n18
Ibn Abī Laylā, 31
Ibn Abīʾl-Rabīʿ, Shihāb al-Dīn, 134–5
Ibn al-Athīr, 79
Ibn Bābawayh, 33
Ibn Bājja, 52
Ibn al-Balkhī, 81–2, 83, 88
Ibn al-Dāya, Aḥmad b. Yūsuf, 63
Ibn al-Faqīh, 38
Ibn al-Ḥabbāriyya, 113
Ibn Ḥamdūn, 39
Ibn Isfandiyār, 74, 83
Ibn Kathīr, 98
Ibn Khaldūn, 171
Ibn al-Muqaffaʿ, 9, 66n1, 74, 75, 76–7, 94, 100–104
Ibn al-Nadīm, 73, 77
Ibn Qutayba, 17, 20, 27, 28, 85n92, 94, 98, 99, 107
Ibn al-Rūmī, 110–11
Ibn Rushd, 49
Ibn Sīnā, 52, 56
Ibn Taymiyya, 159
Ibn al-Ṭiqṭiqā, 171
Ibn al-Ukhuwwa, 167–8
Idrīs, 47–8, 113n83
Ikhwān al-Ṣafāʾ, 54, 59, 126–8, 144, 159, 160
Iran, 7, 9, 27, 40, 65, 66–90, 99, 104, 105, 107, 130, 131, 132, 133, 142, 175, 176
Iraq, 15, 18, 25, 30, 32, 34, 36, 46, 65, 67, 68, 77, 78, 99, 132, 142, 163, 175
al-Iṣfahānī, Abūʾl-Shaykh, 18, 21
Iṣfahānī, ʿAlī, 113
al-Iṣfahānī, Ḥamza, 73
al-Iṣfahānī, al-Rāghib, 19, 21, 108–109, 144, 145, 148–55, 159
Ismāʿīl b. Bulbul, 110, 170n83

Jāhiliyya, 26, 33, 98, 109
al-Jāḥiẓ, 18, 29, 39, 51n46, 64–5, 66, 77, 94, 105, 106n51, 107–108, 158, 159, 162, 164
al-Jahshiyārī, 80–81
Jamshīd, 48, 70, 78–83
al-Jarsīfī, 166–7

al-Kāshī, ʿAbd al-ʿAzīz, 141
Kavād, 68
Kay Kāʾūs, 132–3
Khālid al-Qasrī, 30, 38
Khālid b. Ṣafwān, 37, 38
al-Khallāl, Aḥmad, 158
Khārijites, 4, 14, 30, 32, 33n118, 34, 119, 163
al-Khūʾī, Ḥasan b. ʿAbd al-Muʾ min, 169–70
Khurāsān, 78, 95, 99, 101, 104
Khurramiyya, 96
Khwadāynāmag, 72, 78, 83, 85n90, 100n26
Kirmānī, Afḍal al-Dīn, 27, 28n78, 130–32
Kūfa, 14, 18, 33, 34, 37
al-Kulīnī, 33
Kuthayyir, 19

Lambton, A.K.S., 7
maḥāsin literature, 17
al-Mahdī, 101, 104
Malaṭyavī, Muḥammad b. Ghāzī, 139
Mālik b. Anas, 31, 32
Mālik al-Ashtar, 8n32, 30n98, 122, 124, 125, 128n61
al-Maʾ mūn, 30n103, 104, 105, 107n58, 158
al-Manṣūr, 28n78, 39n149, 101, 104
al-Manṣūr bi-llāh al-Qāsim b. ʿAlī al ʿIyānī, 125–6
marriage equality (*kafāʾa*), 2, 16, 19, 25n63, 30–34, 163, 164
marriage guardianship (*wilāya*), 31, 32
al-Masʿūdī, 74, 77, 87
mawālī, 15, 16, 25, 30, 32, 33, 36n134, 40, 96, 99, 101, 107, 111, 112n79, 115n86
al-Māwardī, 146–8, 158, 159
al-Maydānī, 19, 21
Mazdak, 68, 76n56, 96
merchants, 7, 8, 9, 26, 57, 64, 73, 75, 81, 84, 85n90, 105, 106n52, 112n77, 123, 124, 125, 126, 127, 128, 130, 131, 134, 135, 136, 147, 152, 154, 157, 160, 161, 166
Miskawayh, 73, 80–81, 85, 144
Mītham b. ʿAlī b. Mītham, 140
monotheism, 2
Muʿāwiya, 14, 15, 35, 37, 38, 40
al-Mubashshir b. Fātik, 63, 89
muḥtasib, see *ḥisba*
al-Muqannaʿ, 95, 96n8
muruwwa, 24, 28n78, 60, 76, 103n39, 113, 125, 131
al-Mutanabbī, 110, 131
Muʿtazila, 39, 106, 112n79

Nahj al-balāgha, 8n32, 30n98, 122–5
nasab (genealogy, lineage), 5, 15, 19, 22, 24, 25, 28, 30, 32, 35, 39, 75, 88, 96, 102, 107, 109, 110, 111, 115, 119, 131, 133, 135, 138, 140, 141, 164, *see also* genealogical rivalry
Neoplatonism, 45, 46, 50n43
Niẓām al-Mulk, 129–130, 132, 170
Niẓāmī Samarqandī, 81, 171
nobility–piety equation, 24, 25, 28, 98, 105, 109, 115, 139

pen, men of the, 7, 8, 82, 134, 137, 168–72
physicians, 7, 8, 57, 71, 73, 75, 81, 84n88, 136, 161, 162, 168, 170

Plato, 7n29, 48–9, 50, 51, 55–7, 58, 59, 62, 63, 89, 176

al-Qāḍī al-Nuʿmān, 122, 125
Qarmaṭīs, 6n26
al-Qāsim b. al-Ḥusayn al-Zaydī, 125
Quraysh, 23, 32, 35, 102, 107

al-Rabīʿ b. Ḥabīb al-Farāhīdī, 33
al-Rāzī, Abū' l-Futūḥ, 19
al-Rāzī, Fakhr al-Dīn, 144n5, 145, 159n20
al-Rāzī, Najm al-Dīn Dāya, 134, 143n2
Ṛg-Veda, 69, 70

sābiqa (Islamic priority), 14, 15, 36
ṣaḥāba, Companions of the Prophet, 14, 27; companions of the caliph, 101–103, *see also biṭāna*
Sālim Abū' l-ʿAlā', 100
Salmān al-Fārisī, 26n66, 30, 35, 109
al-Sarakhsī, 19, 22, 32
Ṣaʿṣaʿa b. Ṣūḥān, 20n36, 37n139, 38
al-Sayyid, R., 158
secretaries, the secretarial art, 7, 57, 72, 73, 75, 79, 81, 82, 83, 84, 85n90, 86, 87, 100, 103, 104, 105, 106, 119, 120, 123, 124, 125, 126, 129, 130, 131, 153, 159, 162, 163, 169, 172n96
servants, 79, 82, 84, 127, 135, 162
al-Shāfiʿī, 31
al-Shaybānī, 31, 158
al-Shayzarī, 167–8
Shīʿites, 14, 33
Shīrāzī, Quṭb al-Dīn, 159
shoemakers, 86–7
shuʿūbiyya, 17, 19, 25, 27, 28, 36, 98, 99, 102, 104–108, 109, 115
Shurayk, 95
Sufyān al-Thawrī, 32
sword, men of the, 7, 168–72
Syria, 42, 43, 44, 45, 46, 64, 65

al-Ṭabarī, Abū Jaʿfar, 73, 78–9, 80, 81, 84, 88, 96, 170n83
Ṭāhir b. al-Ḥusayn, 120–21, 122, 123
al-Thaʿālibī, 73, 81, 83, 87
tribalism, 2, 4–6
al-Ṭurṭūshī, Ibn Abī Randaqa, 28
Ṭūsī, Naṣīr al-Dīn, 1, 7–8, 52, 53–4, 55, 57n82, 58, 135, 144n5, 153, 158n12, 161, 174, 175, 176
al-Ṭūsī, Shaykh al-Ṭā'ifa, 98

ʿulamā' (religious scholars), 25, 79, 81, 82, 83, 87, 93, 96, 102, 103, 104, 115, 116, 118, 126, 131, 134, 135, 136, 137, 138, 139, 141, 143, 159, 169, 174
ʿUmar b. ʿAbd al-ʿAzīz, 38, 122
ʿUmar b. al-Khaṭṭāb, 14, 15, 24n55, 25n63, 30, 33, 34, 35, 36, 46, 94, 154, 168
Urmavī, Sirāj al-Dīn, 114, 137–8, 145
al-ʿUtbī, Abū'l-Ḥusayn, 170
ʿUthmān, 36n135, 37

varṇa, 70, 176–7
viziers, 38, 52, 110, 124n49, 129, 130, 147, 161, 169, 170–71

Wāṣil b. ʿAṭā', 30
wealth, 3, 25–6, 27, 29, 38, 39, 43, 45, 57, 59, 61, 84, 102, 103
  as a cause of social conflict, 62–4, 148ff as a criterion for marriage equality, 31, 32, 34
  its value compared with that of knowledge, 112–14
weavers, weaving, 33, 59, 152, 153, 155, 159, 160, 162, 163, 166, 167

Yaḥyā b. ʿAdī, 49
al-Yaʿqūbī, 21
Yūsuf Khāṣṣ Ḥājib, 133–4, 171

al-Zamakhsharī, 20
Zarādusht of Fasā, 67–8
Zayd b. ʿAlī, 33
Ziyād b. Abīhī (b. Abī Sufyān), 14n4, 35, 60
Zoroaster, 69, 70
al-Zuhrī, 36n134, 106

LaVergne, TN USA
20 August 2010

193983LV00004B/17/A

9 780521 894289